S0-AEJ-311

DEMOCRATIC DISTRIBUTIVE JUSTICE

By exploring the nature of economic justice and of democracy, Ross Zucker seeks to explain how democratic countries with market economies should deal with the problem of high levels of income inequality. Revising a basic assumption of social thought, Zucker suggests that people are more equal than political theorists usually suppose them to be – in regard to their attributes, wants, and economic contributions. Such equality morally warrants corresponding limits on income inequality, beyond the measures suggested by Rawls's theory of justice. The origin of equality lies in formative relations between persons, for example, those in the economy, and this book contends that the study of persons-in-relations can provide perspectives on equality that have been overlooked. Zucker also considers the manner in which the ethics of community bear on the just distribution of property. There is, he argues, a dimension of community in market economies that extends more widely and inheres more deeply than liberals, communitarians, Marxists, and social theorists recognize, and it provides further moral support for limiting income inequality.

Integrating this view of economic justice with democratic theory yields "democratic distributive justice," whose central proposition is that the preservation of a redistributory property right is among the chief ends of democratic government. While prevailing theory defines democracy in terms of the electoral mechanism, the author holds that the principles of just distribution form part of the very definition of democracy, which makes just distribution a requirement of democratic government. The problem of income inequality is thus an inherently interdisciplinary one, and grappling with it requires extensive use of political, economic, legal, and philosophical theory.

DEMOCRATIC DISTRIBUTIVE JUSTICE

ROSS ZUCKER

PUBLISHED BY THE PRESS SYNDICATE OF THE UNIVERSITY OF CAMBRIDGE
The Pitt Building, Trumpington Street, Cambridge, United Kingdom

CAMBRIDGE UNIVERSITY PRESS
The Edinburgh Building, Cambridge CB2 2RU, UK
40 West 20th Street, New York, NY 10011-4211, USA
10 Stamford Road, Oakleigh, VIC 3166, Australia
Ruiz de Alarcón 13, 28014 Madrid, Spain
Dock House, The Waterfront, Cape Town 8001, South Africa

http://www.cambridge.org

First published 2001

Printed in the United States of America

Typeface Sabon 10/12 pt. *System* QuarkXPress [CTK]

A catalog record for this book is available from the British Library.

Library of Congress Cataloging in Publication Data
Zucker, Ross, 1952–
Democratic distributive justice/Ross Zucker.
p. cm.
ISBN 0-521-79033-6
1. Democracy. 2. Distributive justice. 3. Income distribution. I. Title.
JC23.Z83 2000
330.1-dc21 00-023631

ISBN 0 521 79033 6 hardback

For Herbert Zucker

Contents

Acknowledgments *page* ix

1. Democracy and Economic Justice 1

Part I. Unequal Property and Individualism in Liberal Theory

2. The Underlying Logic of Liberal Property Theory 27
3. Unequal Property and Its Premise in Locke's Theory 33
4. Unequal Property and Individualism, Kant to Rawls 56

Part II. Egalitarian Property and Justice as Dueness

5. Whose Property Is It, Anyway? 85
6. The Social Nature of Economic Actors and Forms of Equal Dueness 108
7. Policy Reflections: The Effect of an Egalitarian Regime on Economic Growth 142

Part III. Egalitarian Property and the Ethics of Economic Community

8. Deriving Equality from Community 153

9. The Dimension of Community in Capital-Based Market Systems: Between Consumers and Producers 169

10. Endogenous Preferences and Economic Community 188

11. The Dimension of Community in Capital-Based Market Systems: Between Capital and Labor 220

12. The Right to an Equal Share of Part of National Income 246

Part IV. Democracy and Economic Justice

13. Democratic Distributive Justice 269

14. Democracy and Economic Rights 287

Conclusions 301

References 303

Index 319

Acknowledgments

The greatest intellectual debts are sometimes personal ones. Charles E. Lindblom aided my education in many crucial ways, such as giving needed support for this research, providing rigorous and eloquent critiques of several drafts, and removing or helping me to overcome various obstacles. I am extremely grateful to have had the opportunity to study political economy with this man, whose sophisticated knowledge taught me much, and whose exemplary human qualities taught me even more. My father, Herbert Zucker, enhanced the possiblity that this book would come into being by responding to numerous trial balloons during the formative stages of the work and preparing a commentary on a draft of the whole manuscript. The interest and involvement he took were sustaining, and it is to him that this book is dedicated.

One day many years ago, while attending a class on classical political economy taught by David P. Levine at Yale, some of the basic ideas of this book occurred to me quite suddenly, though it has taken much time to work them out. Moreover, Levine's writings contain insights into the social nature of the individual that I have found useful in developing a social theory of economic rights and of democracy.

When the manuscript was nearing its final stages, Robert Dahl examined it, gave me his well-considered judgment, and formulated a strategy of revision that was helpful in making final improvements. Carol C. Gould and Sidney Morgenbesser pressed me to elaborate the relationship between equality and community that I had sketched at a seminar, and on other occasions Gould made a variety of helpful suggestions and provided important forms of support for this project. Gary Mongiovi, coeditor of the *Review of Political Economy*, shared his considerable knowledge of economics with me in a detailed commentary on the manuscript. Claire Cook provided the benefit of her general editorial expertise to a project that fell outside her usual literary specialty. I am very grateful for her contribution. Valuable assistance was also rendered by Sandy Thatcher, Minae Mizumura, Ben Gregg, Jeffrey Gordon, and especially Elizabeth Mazzola, to whom I would like to express my deepest appreciation. At Cambridge University Press, the copyediting by Russell Hahn was very helpful, and I appreciate his thoroughness and keen eye. The manuscript was ably stewarded through the publication process by Lewis Bateman, political science editor, Camilla T. Knapp, production editor, and Alex Holzman, senior editor.

Consideration of my ideas at scholarly forums fostered development of the work, and I am obliged to colleagues for helpful suggestions on papers presented at the Twentieth World Congress of Philosophy (1998), the annual meetings of the American Political Science Association (1996, 1995, 1992, 1991), the Seventeenth World Congress of the International Association for Philosophy of Law and Social Philosophy (Bologna, 1995), the Eighth Malvern Political Economy Conference (U.K., 1994), the annual meetings of the Society for the Advancement of Socio-Economics (New York and Stockholm, 1993, 1991) and the Law and Society Association (Amsterdam, 1991), and the MIT faculty seminar on Global Transformations and Property Rights (1992). I also wish to express my appreciation to the University Seminars of Columbia University for financial assistance with the preparation of the manuscript for publication. The ideas presented have benefited from discussions in the University Seminar on the Political Economy of War and Peace.

Some of my ideas were first presented in journal articles. Chapters 5 and 6 modify and expand "Whose Property Is It, Anyway?," *Review of Political Economy,* vol. 7, no. 4 (October, 1995). Chapter 3 extends the analysis of "Unequal Property and Its Premise in Liberal Theory," which appeared in the *History of Philosophy Quarterly*, vol. 17, no. 1 (January 2000). Chapter 11 includes portions of "System-wide Community in Capital-based Market Systems," *Journal of Socio-Economics,* vol. 28, no. 5 (1999). Thanks are due the editors and publishers of these journals for permission to reprint material here.

Given the high caliber of assistance received, it is all too obvious that the remaining faults are entirely my own. Finally, Bess Zucker and Andrea, Jim, Ryan and Heather Wegner made the surrounding environment worthwhile, and to them go my heartfelt thanks.

New York City
April 2000

I

Democracy and Economic Justice

THE INTERSUBJECTIVE VIEW OF THE PERSON AND THE PRINCIPLE OF EQUALITY

Social aspects of the person should have a salience that they are not usually accorded in considerations of relative distribution. When their relation is adequately taken into account, economic justice can be seen to be different from that which is ordinarily posited. Conceptions of economic justice differ on the question of the relative distribution of income. But they do not sufficiently consider how some social aspects of the person might bear on the question. This book develops the view that these aspects of the person affect the degree of equality that is involved in the conception of economic justice.

A revised understanding of economic justice, derived from social premises, can then have implications for the nature of democracy. These implications are, however, often discounted in theories of democracy. For example, the "procedural" theory of democracy does not incorporate considerations of economic justice, because it views democracy and economic justice as separate concepts by defining democracy solely in terms of political equality. This book, by contrast, postulates an integral relation between democracy and economic justice that leads to the inclusion of principles of distributive justice within democratic rule. I develop a "substantive" theory, holding that the just distribution of economic resources is a defining characteristic of democratic rule. The theory cannot simply be synthesized with existing concepts of economic justice, because new principles for regulating the distribution of income and wealth are needed. These may be developed by revising the ethics of reward for economic contributions and the ethics of economic community.

Normative views of economic justice depend on theoretical analysis of economic society, since appropriate regulative principles for the economy emerge from the character of that society. How income should be distributed is partially a matter of who contributes (and to what extent) to the creation of economic value. Assessing contributions requires a theory of the determinants of economic value. Modern economics interprets contributions to value as the products of individual choices about how much or how hard to work, which career to undertake, and what qualifications or skills to acquire. In other words, it identifies contributions with individual differences in diligence, willingness to develop skills, and psychological attitudes toward risk taking. This approach justifies unequal remuneration and distribution of income.

But in my view, social influences on individuals play a more central role in actuality than they do in modern economic theory. They greatly affect the formation, character, and extent both of individuals' productive capacities and activities and of their other economic qualities and actions, such as consumer wants and purchases, that also help determine the value of goods and services. Social analysis reveals that economic agents subject to similar influences and conditions develop some of the same characteristics and undertake some of the same activities in producing or otherwise creating economic value. The argument that there are some equal attributes and actions and that they lead to equal contributions invites revision of conventional formulas of remuneration.[1] The long-standing tendency in modern economics to subordinate this consideration is comparable to leaving gravitation out of astrophysics.

In competitive markets, individuals receive incomes proportionate to the value of their productive contributions, according to conventional economists. Indeed, markets would not distort income distribution if forms of equal contributions were generally commodified and had prices attached to them, but this has not been the case. There are equal contributions in the economy that are like unpaid factors of creation of economic value. Economic agents are generally unaware of the uncommodified forms of equal contributions, so their moral reasoning usually stresses difference and what difference deserves: "If I work harder or better, why shouldn't I make more?"[2] But should not equal contributions neglected by the market be given their due?

Ethicists of contributions have proceeded largely in isolation from modern economic theory since 1870. They work mainly on the assump-

1. This proposition is not intended to deny that there are also unequal contributions that result from differential attributes and actions.
2. McClosky and Zaller 1984, pp. 120, 156.

tion of classical political economy that the value of commodities is created entirely by producers. But modern or neoclassical economics has shown that consumers help to determine value, and ethics therefore needs to give greater consideration to the role of consumers when assessing contributions. The ethics of contributions can also benefit from a reinfusion of certain older themes in economic theory. The individualistic theory of consumer satisfaction – the so-called "utility" theory – in modern economics should be replaced by earlier (classical and Marxian) ideas about the social composition of agency – altered, however, to apply to consumers as well as to producers.

Distributive rules and forms of property can also be developed within the ethics of economic community. Capitalist systems possess, not only an overt dimension of individualism, but also a less obvious one of community, that morally entails a different distributive rule than does the former dimension. Competing economic actors simultaneously stitch together something of a community by engaging in common actions for certain common ends. Each one does things for others that they would otherwise have to do for themselves – the very essence of common action. The capitalist economy thus is a peculiar mass race where each contestant carries – and is carried by – the members of the other competing teams part of the way to the finish line.[3]

I refer here to a dimension of *genuine* community in capital-based market systems, not just a fragment, semblance, or second cousin of community. For it extends more widely and inheres more deeply in the economy than in the small-scale communities or external communities posited by communitarians. Arguably, all economic agents have a common goal of preserving and expanding capital, because all the goods and services that they desire hinge on the ongoing circuit of money and commodities, that is, on the circuit of capital.

The common actions sustaining that circuit are generated by socially influenced but individually willed actions. An element of cooperation arises between firms because they have to adjust their production processes to what other firms provide and need. Though opposed in some ways, capital and labor also unite to produce and gain portions of social wealth. Mutual adjustment is required for joint production. Laborers and managers of capital acquire skills and pattern their work for the efficient production of goods and capital. Moreover, since profits depend on sales, production and consumption are interrelated as well.

3. To be sure, runners in the economic race reach different finish lines, but these are all variations on the same theme, rather than utterly different pursuits. The participants win different-sized pieces of the same prize.

While producers orient output toward the satisfaction of consumer wants, they also shape those wants by advertising their products and by other means.

Since capitalism is a society of mixed metaphors, with all its members in the same boat and yet pulling themselves up by their own bootstraps, principles of distribution should reflect both communal and individualistic aspects. Total social income should be distributed unequally to the extent that it is produced by distinct individual actions, and it should be distributed equally to the extent that it is created by the joint activity of people shaped by social conditions. Communitarianism can jeopardize property rights, but in my theory economic community proves compatible with the supreme ethical worth of individuals, and hence with their entitlement to rights. While liberal property rights derived from society as a plurality of distinct individuals sharply constrain redistribution, property rights based on a dimension of economic community come with strong redistributory strings attached.[4]

Absorbed into democracy through the ideal of rule for the people, these principles of distributive justice change the hue and cast of democracy as currently practiced.

DEMOCRACY AND REDISTRIBUTORY PROPERTY RIGHTS

The theory of justice and democracy that I propose introduces moral grounds for equalizing the distribution of a portion of total income and for forming a more egalitarian economic order than is available under current forms of capitalism. Although these considerations, if valid, warrant greater equality than do prevailing theories of economic justice and democracy, they do not support a strictly equal distribution of income. A different set of considerations justifies unequal accumulations of another portion of income.

The principle of equalizing a portion of income takes the form of a property right, an individual's right to own something. When redistribution has this form, titles to redistributed income are assigned to individuals rather than to the state. In this respect, they resemble traditional property rights, in contrast to later distributions undertaken by the liberal welfare state, where the reflux from progressive taxation or

4. Rawls's moral derivation of distributive rules from an assumed society of independent ("distinct") individuals precludes egalitarian distribution in most circumstances, since Rawls seems to believe that inequalities are just because they create incentives that increase social wealth, improving the lot of the worst off. See Rawls 1971, pp. 29, 151, 158.

inheritance taxes often goes to the state, not to the individual. Such titles may therefore be termed "redistributory property rights."

The individual's entitlement may also be considered a property right because it has the same moral underpinning as a traditional property right. In the prevailing theory, individuals are assigned property because they are ethically entitled to it. Similarly, in my analysis, individuals have a redistributory property right because of their moral worth. Since entitlement is determined on the basis of individual qualities, the redistributory property right cannot be assigned to social aggregates, such as firms, communities, or states. The proposal for this right is then distinguished from any strategies according communitarian rights to social aggregates.

A right to an equalized portion of income does not obstruct or deny the operation of markets. It affects part of the income devoted to consumption but does not govern the revenues reinvested in a firm for the purchase of plant and equipment. While it selectively controls the distribution of one part of income, it otherwise leaves the distribution of income and revenue to market forces.[5] Thus, in terms of professional economics, it does not impede the "law of value."

The idea that individuals have a right to equal shares of part of total social income is not reflected in the actual world of democracy, which at present does not recognize this right or put it into practice. To interpret this state of affairs one needs to distinguish between nominal and true democracies. Countries that are conventionally known as democracies may or may not possess the defining characteristics of democracy, and I refer to countries that do not possess these characteristics as "democracies." I omit the quotation marks for systems that have these defining features in some significant measure, even if the systems exist only in theory at this time. A theoretically derived system may qualify as a true democracy if it has the requisite characteristics even though it does not yet exist.

What is the significance of the fact that current "democracies" do not recognize a redistributory property right? Does it mean they are not truly democratic on this score? Or that they can be fully democratic without possessing such a right? Does it mean that they are democratic but unjust? Or finally, does it mean that they are both undemocratic and unjust in their failure to implement a redistributory property right?

Assuming that redistributory property is in principle a right, but not part of the democratic ideal, some might say its absence from current

5. On selective centralization of the distribution of income, see Dahl 1982, pp. 116–120.

"democracies," such as the United States, does not diminish their democratic standing. Because democratic rule does not require the majority to redistribute income if they do not want to, their disinclination to do so does not constitute a failure to achieve a democratic ideal. In this way of thinking, the redistributory right, though extrinsic to democratic ideals, may still have moral standing as part of economic justice. But even if it does, the demos is not obligated to institute it, according to some scholars, because economic justice is not morally superior to the principles of democracy; on the contrary, democracy is the highest court of moral appeal.

Other scholars who assume that the redistributory property right is ethically valid might hold that current "democracies" without this right, however democratic in principle, are not sufficiently just. In this view, the ideal of economic justice obligates people to implement the redistributory property right even though it is not part of democratic rule, because economic justice (subsuming the redistributory property right) is morally superior to democratic ideals.

Taking yet another position, I contend that current "democracies" that lack the redistributory property right do not qualify as true democracies along this dimension. But how can such a right be intrinsic to the idea of democracy? Democracy, it is often supposed, consists in majority rule, elections, and the rights involved in these processes, and the redistributory property right does not seem to fall into any of these categories. In my view, however, this right passes into democratic ideals over an internal bridge linking the concepts of democracy and economic justice. One of the main arguments of this book is that the democratic ideal of rule for the people morally requires the demos to maintain the principles of economic justice.

Part I examines the underlying assumptions – in particular the concept of autonomous persons – that justify unequal distributions of income and wealth in liberal theories of property. Parts II and III involve the development of alternative assumptions that justify a redistributory property right. Part II discusses property within the ethics of dueness for economic contributions, arguing that the notion of socially formed persons affects calculations of dueness in ways that lead to a more egalitarian form of property rights than is found in classical or welfare state liberalism. Part III focuses on property within another system of ethics, the ethics of economic community. The social theory concludes that capital-based market systems have a dimension of community, which supports a more equal distribution of income and wealth than does liberalism. Part IV integrates democracy and the redistributory property right.

DISTRIBUTIVE JUSTICE AND THE DEVELOPMENT OF POLITICAL AND ECONOMIC THOUGHT

Theories of property and distributive justice are only as strong as their premises about individuals and society allow them to be. Problems in the premises unfortunately impair the ethical constructs reasoned from them. As I have already noted, many theories use overly individualistic concepts of the person that emphasize internal origins and causes of personal attributes and ends. While some acknowledge the social formation of the individual, they usually formulate it unsystematically, supplying an inadequate foundation for theories of property, because they fail to recognize that agents in an economic system are likely to be affected by the system itself. Despite some controversy about the effect of individualistic and unsystematic social premises on distribution and property, the subject has not yet been sufficiently examined.

It does not help that some scholars prefer to deflect the issue. They argue that social, communitarian, and liberal theories have no irreconcilable differences. As they see it, individualistic and social theoretical premises about the person are morally neutral, and the debate over them is sterile and devoid of normative significance. Their reaction to controversy, then, is to blur differences, minimize the deficiencies in premises, and underestimate the possible ramifications of the debate. In contrast, I suggest a focus on premises, convinced that principles of distribution must derive from them.

Excessively individualistic and unsystematically social premises about the person, when used in justificatory arguments, warp principles of distribution by skewing them in an inegalitarian direction. While a weakly formulated social concept of the person may point toward an egalitarian distribution of income and property, it cannot ground this principle firmly enough to prevent backsliding. But if the social concept of the person is strengthened and the correct inferences are drawn from it, it can securely underpin the egalitarian principle.

In liberal theories of property and distributive justice, the failure to give centrality to the social formation of the person may have several explanations, including a propensity for individualistic approaches. John Rawls, for example, treats social influence only as a background or peripheral issue. He and others give heuristic rationalizations for extreme postulates of subjective individuality that disguise their lack of substance.[6] Neoclassical economists put forward a systematic account of

6. Rawls rationalizes the premise of the priority of choice to social influence on the ground that to do otherwise would bias the form of the community that would

relations between commodity exchangers and producers, but their account is strangely asocial. Instead of rigorously analyzing the social formation of economic actors, these theorists build a conception of the system either from given preferences or from an unsystematic account of the social determination of individuals.

Neoclassical and Rawlsian theories represent the culmination of liberal thinking about property and distribution. Though somewhat diverse, they have common structural features: (1) a combination of abstract equalities shared by persons, who all have free will, and concrete differences in their wants, wills, and preferences, (2) an abstract community living under the same rights and freedoms and a concrete multitude with disparate ends. Echoing a classical liberal thesis about society, Rawls holds that "the plurality of distinct persons with separate systems of ends is an essential feature of human societies,"[7] while Robert Nozick declares, "There is no social entity with a good. . . . There are only individual people, different individual people."[8] Foundational conceptions of society in liberalism usually lack concrete forms of commonalities and equalities among persons.[9]

In liberal theories, the dual premise of abstract equalities and concrete differences among persons gives rise to the familiar right to highly unequal amounts of income and wealth. The absence of concrete equalities among individuals' conceptions of the good led the classical liberal Immanuel Kant to conclude that there could be no common principle of distribution of economic resources, and thus no principle of equalization of economic resources. Using the premise of separateness and difference

be chosen, not realizing that the premised priority of choice itself skews the reasoning about community. See Rawls 1971, p. 264.

7. Ibid., p. 29.
8. Nozick 1974, pp. 32–33.
9. Rawls 1971, p. 29. There is some recognition of community in Rawls's theory, as when he says that society "is a cooperative venture for mutual advantage . . . typically marked by . . . an identity of interests" (p. 520). Moreover, he claims that his theory provides "a satisfactory framework for understanding the values of community" (p. 520). But Rawls does not concretely elaborate his conception of community, and the part that he does describe seems to be the opposite of a community. His method is to develop a conception of the good of community from the assumption of a "deep opposition of interests" (p. 521). But in this case his conception of community seems to be not, at base, a conception of community at all. It is hard to understand how one could deduce a conception of the good of community from a premise – the opposition of interests – that is antithetical to the stated purpose of the reasoning. It would be rather like deducing the moral implications of free will from the premise of instinctual behavior: completely inappropriate to the subject under consideration.

among individuals, Nozick develops a neoliberal justification for Kantian rights as "side constraints" demarcating inviolable moral spaces around individuals that can not be breached without their consent. Because redistributive policies cannot secure unanimous agreement, they are effectively prohibited by these prior rights.[10] Separate existence dissolves moral bonds among people, exempting individuals from any claims made by others to a share of their resources. In Nozick's words, "The moral side constraints upon what we may do reflect the fact of our separate existences . . . that no moral balancing act can take place among us."[11] The same standpoint infuses the anti-egalitarian rhetoric of neoliberal politicians, as in Margaret Thatcher's famous quip, "There is no such thing as society, there are individual men and women . . ."[12]

Liberal theories are not wholly invalid – members of civil society have concrete differences and the abstract common goal of freedom – but the theories may be seriously incomplete. For it is possible that the social world contains, not only liberal features, but also concretely equal characteristics and concrete common ends. If concrete unity and concrete equality do in fact exist, the way to uncover them would be to analyze their social formation. Then their distributive implications could be explored.

Hegel pioneered the analysis of systemic forms of social influence and disclosed some concrete forms of equalities and commonalities. Although others had studied social influence, he was unique in demonstrating that socially generated concrete equalities and commonalities are universal to the members of civil society, not characteristic only of subsets of the aggregate. He wrote,

> The particular person is essentially so related to other persons that each establishes himself and finds satisfaction by means of the others, and at the same time purely and simply by means of the form of universality.[13]

> A particular end . . . assumes the form of universality through this relation to other people and it is attained in the simultaneous attainment of the welfare of others.[14]

> The fertility of the soil varies, . . . one man is industrious, another indolent. But this . . . arbitrariness generates universal characteristics.[15]

10. Nozick 1974, pp. 30–33, 48–51, 149–160.
11. Ibid., p. 33.
12. Thatcher 1993, p. 626.
13. Hegel 1952, para. 182, pp. 122–123.
14. Ibid., add. 116 to para. 182, pp. 266–267.
15. Ibid., add. 120 to para. 189, pp. 268–269.

> The fact that I must direct my conduct by reference to others introduces here the form of universality. It is from others that I acquire the means of satisfaction and I must accordingly accept their views.[16]

The universality of concrete equalities and commonalities within civil society is important because it can yield general rules of distributive justice and property, not merely optional ethics for small groups.

Laying another foundation for the social theory of rights, Hegel reconciled the classical liberal antinomies of social determination and self-determination by showing that the fundamental social influences – produced by and for the essential constitutive relations of civil society – do not violate self-determination, despite their having a huge formative impact. In his analysis of self-seeking within an exchange system, for example, Hegel showed that individuals have to be socially conditioned in accordance with the requirements of mutual dependence in order for this system to exist, but that individuals thus determined can still realize their own ends. Moreover, although the multiplication of wants through exposure to the products of the division of labor constitutes a social determination of wants, it also expands the individual's range of choice and freedom. The reconciliation of social determination and self-determination was logically necessary to the theory of rights, for if social determination overrode self-determination, individuals would lack the quality that confers supreme ethical worth and entitles them to rights. Few theorists before or since Hegel rivaled his handling of this treacherous issue.

For a long period Hegel's thought was closed out of the "open society" (a society that officially tolerates freedom of thought) because his views allegedly have an affinity with the "closed society." Scholars in the 1970s and 1980s rediscovered it, creating a sort of Hegel renaissance.[17] Though he does indeed provide some grounds for a social theory of rights, his reasoning has serious limitations. Equalities and commonalities among economic agents are not sufficiently developed, concretized, and elaborated, since they are not formulated within a developed theory of the system of economic relations. Another problem is his failure to give serious attention to the natural moral implication of these concrete equalities and commonalities: that there should be an equal distribution of some property and income.[18]

16. Ibid., add. 123 to para. 192, p. 269.
17. For the view that Hegel's philosophy is a harbinger of totalitarianism, see Popper 1963. On Hegel's contribution to a social theory of rights, see Benhabib 1977. Pelczynski 1971 exemplifies the Hegel renaissance.
18. He was, of course, aware of this possible implication, but he dealt with it only cursorily.

A social theory of property rights considers the moral implications of its premises within the framework of an "entitlement logic." It reasons principles of just distribution and property from such ideals as freedom, equality, fairness, community, and dueness. To make the task manageable, I focus on two ideals: people should be rewarded for their economic contributions, and people are entitled to things on the basis of their membership in a community.

Contributions may not seem like a good basis on which to argue for egalitarianism, because ubiquitous differences in contributions frequently supply the argument against it. "The evident differences in capability between persons," writes Phelps Brown, "have always been seen to call for differences of treatment . . . To assign the same pay to workers of different ability seems as unnatural as to issue the same clothes to people of different size . . . The very idea of justice, as it appeared in the Greek principle of suiting rewards and penalties to people's actions, involved differentiation."[19] But if egalitarianism could be defended on grounds of contributions, the very vantage point from which it has been chiefly attacked, the case would be especially strong. The strategy would be to identify equal forms of contributions. Contributions are so widely presumed to differ, even by egalitarians, that the assumption is rarely scrutinized, and it deserves reconsideration. Focus on contributions is warranted, moreover, because they are a realistic moral consideration. The idea of giving people their due makes sense to ordinary people in everyday life, who commonly believe that compensation should be based on contributions.[20] "If I work harder or better than someone else, then I should make more," the majority of Americans would argue. Unless greater equality can be defended from the standpoint of contributions, it is unlikely to attain the moral appeal of differential pay.

To be precise, this argument rests not on "rewarding" people for their contributions, but on according them their "due." The change in termi-

19. Phelps Brown 1988, p. 246. Aaron Wildavsky more recently attacks egalitarianism from the contributions standpoint. He writes that egalitarian redistributive policies disparage accomplishment and penalize the deserving, a position that assumes that contributions are entirely differential, otherwise equalization would not disparage them but would honor them. "Equality of condition," he holds, "is the perfect reproach because it is always lacking in some respect. Americans may not succeed but if they do, things are set up so that they won't be able to enjoy it." And, "It is difficult to enjoy the fabled American trip from rags to riches when other people are busy making sure that your riches will turn to rags. This is the reverse Cinderella syndrome of sorts. It is a product of generalizing from Groucho's Law: Anything America can achieve isn't worth accomplishing." See Wildavsky 1991, from the back flap.
20. McClosky and Zaller 1984, pp. 84, 156.

nology reflects a different substantive emphasis emerging from the social theory of the ethics of remuneration. Whereas the conventional ethics of reward assigns reward for subjective qualities, the social theory of "dueness" rests on objective social qualities of persons that contribute to the creation of wealth and income.

The ethics of community, the other entitlement logic I employ, may also initially appear to be a weak basis for economic egalitarianism. One version of these ethics holds that there should be equal fulfillment of the ends of association, so that membership in a community would morally entail a principle of equal distribution of relevant resources. While contemporary liberal writers subscribe to this view for some social contexts, they doubt that it can be systematically applied to actual economies. Such an attempt would be unrealistic, they maintain, since capital-based markets are competitive, not communal, and thus not morally obligated to implement a communitywide principle of equal distribution.

Although liberals assert this proposition with the utmost certainty, it has a crucial defect that threatens to unravel the anti-egalitarian argument. Upon reexamination, capital-based market systems have a systemwide dimension of community, notwithstanding their equal and countervailing dimension of competition, and on this basis, they may incur an obligation to redistribute income.

The deficiencies in concreteness and economic understanding that I ascribed to Hegel's theory are not as pronounced in Marx's theory. Marx conceives of laborers and capitalists as socially constituted in concrete ways within a system of circulating capital that he explains in fairly systematic and sophisticated fashion. Arguing that social labor is the sole source of value and that capital adds no new value, he concludes that the means of production should be collectively owned by a workers' state. Subjected to sustained critique by neoclassical economic theorists from the 1870s onward, Marx's theory was all but left in shambles. But, although the good English and Austrian doctors Jevons, Edgeworth, Menger, Walras, and Bohm-Bawerk would have been content to let the patient expire under the surgeon's knife, it survived to become the most influential egalitarian theory of property in history, unduly affecting ownership forms in the Soviet Union, Eastern Europe, the People's Republic of China, Cuba, North Korea, and North Vietnam. Even now, when the collapse of the Soviet Union has left Marxian theory in grave doubt, it lives on because in some ways it has not been bettered by other theorists.

The neoclassical critique not only hobbled Marxism, but also made all schools of ethical theory seem unqualified to deal with the subject matter. The neoclassical principle that there can be "no quantitative interpersonal comparisons of utility" erected a high hurdle in the path of economic ethics. By contrast, Marx's approach clears the way for further consideration by satisfying several requirements for a social theory of rights. He employs a social concept of economic agents; concretely specifies their nature; systematically formulates social determination; elaborates it within a developed theory of economic relations; and recognizes the egalitarian moral implications of his social premises. His approach is, however, bedeviled by two fundamental problems that cannot be overcome except by restructuring the social theory of economic rights.

Social determination has such force and primacy in Marx's "holistic" social theory that it calls into question whether economic action can still be individually willed in any strong sense.[21] With the individual subordinated, the social whole gains moral priority, authorizing social ownership of the means of production and dispossessing the individual. In this way, Marx walks right into a trap that Hegel nicely avoided.

In its moral implications, the social formation of the individual moves more readily toward individual property than toward socialization of ownership in the hands of the state, as Hegel well knew; yet it also warrants more equal property than he supposed. Instead of vitiating free will, social formation can help develop free will by providing essential ingredients for the self. For example, an individual formed by and within a system of reciprocal recognition of rights and mutual dependence develops a dual will to contract, that is, a will to acquire property through surrendering property, rather than a unilateral will to appropriate, conquer, and seize the property of another. The individual determined in this way is better able to achieve his ends than one in a life-threatening state of nature, so socially formed persons are no less capable of self-determination than are the subjectively constituted persons of individualistic theories. Consequently, individuals, not the social organism, possess the supreme ethical worth that justifies an entitlement to property rights. At the same time, however, society's important role in shaping individuals forces a departure from the distributory rules that derive from individualistic views of their formation. Social influences

21. Gould characterizes as "holistic" socialist theories that "counterpose sociality and individuality" (Gould 1988, p. 7). She distinguishes prevalent socialist theories from Marx's theory, which she does not regard as holistic. Marx's theory may, however, also be considered holistic. Even though Marx sometimes unites sociality and individuality, the subordination of individual will to social determination is at the root of his socialization of ownership.

generate forms of equal contributions, common action, and common purposes that morally warrant some equalization of income and wealth. In sum, the persistence of self-determination amid social determination simultaneously precludes the socialization of ownership in the state and calls for some egalitarian redistribution.

Marx's ethics of distribution and ownership also suffer from problems in the theory of value underlying his conclusions. A theory of value explains how commodity prices are set. To determine appropriate remuneration, the ethics of reward usually presuppose a theory of value that identifies contributions. Believing that social labor is the sole origin and cause of the value of commodities, Marx reasons that workers are collectively entitled to the full value of the industrial product. Like other classical political economists, he presupposes that value is determined entirely on the production side, concepts of demand notwithstanding, and fails to recognize the substantial role played by relatively autonomous consumer preferences.[22] As neoclassical theorists have demonstrated, however, this approach is misguided. They dismantle Marx's theory of exploitation and socialized ownership by arguing that value is established, not only by labor, but also by consumer preferences, that is, by the product's "utility" for consumers.

While modern economics assimilates the neoclassical theory of value, neither it nor any other discipline dealing with the ethics of reward directly confronts the implications of consumer contributions. A theory of dueness, however, extends credit and recognition to all economic agents who contribute to value. In discussions of entitlement, "economic agents" usually means producers, but there is no reason not to include consumers under this rubric, for their value-creating actions fulfill the criterion of entitlement on a principle of dueness.

The proposed approach to the ethics of dueness involves (1) adopting Marx's emphasis on the social composition of economically creative attributes, albeit in a way commensurate with the supreme ethical worth of the individual, (2) rejecting his exclusive focus on productive factors, (3) adopting neoclassical theory's inclusion of consumers in the theory of value, (4) rejecting its overly individualistic formulation of consumer preferences, and (5) establishing the social formation and constitution of consumers' economically creative attributes and their indirect causes.

Responding to criticism of their individualistic approach, neoclassi-

22. The point holds despite his comments on the realization process, for consumer valuations within this process are merely channels through which deeper productive factors determine value. In classical political economy, demand can affect prices but not production values or production prices.

cists developed a theory of "endogenously formed preferences," that is, of preferences created by social influences, not originating within the subjective self. Yet this development did not overcome the limitations of their argument. While the ethics of dueness requires an account of the profound and systematic social influences that form the essential and determinate aspects of individuals, the theory of endogenous preferences looks instead at arbitrary and capricious social influences on their preferences, such as bandwagon effects or peer pressures. It cannot, therefore, provide an adequate theory of dueness.

Neoclassical theory argues that there cannot be a scientific egalitarian ethics – that is, an economic ethics founded on reason – though ethics can still exist as a matter of opinion and ideology. The conception of subjective preferences precludes any quantitative interpersonal comparisons of utility, because subjective preferences are irreducibly different. Equal distribution of income would be unlikely to bring equal satisfaction, and in the absence of a common standard of comparison there would be no way of knowing whether it did. Thus, egalitarian distribution cannot be logically justified on neoclassical assumptions. But a social theory that identifies concrete equalities in socially formed individuals can found egalitarian principles on reason.

The neoclassical theory of endogenous preferences cannot identify the sort of equalities needed for an egalitarian theory, because it does not look at influences that are necessary to the existence of the system. In contrast, social theory can find general equalities because it examines social influences that flow from the requisites of the system. The requirements of the system produce broad and deep influences affecting all alike.

An opposing position, one that is currently gaining prominence, regards the principle of equality as too abstract to be applied. This argument can have severe and damaging consequences, for it means that society cannot be guided by the ideal of equality. Exemplifying this opinion, Douglas Rae writes, "Equality is . . . the most abstract of notions, yet . . . the world [is] irremediably concrete and complex," so equality "cannot govern" the practices of the world.[23] But I would counter that the principle of equality is susceptible to concretion and thus capable of

23. Rae 1981, p. 150. Another variant of this view is developed by Sen, who holds that reality cannot be governed by a principle of equality except if it is accompanied by a principle of inequality, due to the diversity of individuals and the complexity of social reality. See Sen 1992, pp. xi, 19–20. Similarly, Johnston suggests that moral pluralism makes it impossible to "escape the possibility that a distribution . . . that looks egalitarian from one point of view will look inegalitarian from a different point of view." Thus he concludes that the probability

intersecting the reality needing regulation. While reality is indeed complex, it is not hopelessly complex: concrete equalities have an integrity rather than dissolving into infinitely many particulars. If by justice one means a sort of perfection in the basic structure of society, then equality will not provide justice. Perfection, however, is a fiction, while economic society is a human reality that can be redeemed. If the demos has the will to deal with problems of unregulated property, the principle of equality has the way to reduce injustice.

Communitarianism is another ethical view enjoying a considerable vogue, but it needs to be reformulated if it is to provide valid rules of distribution. As currently formulated, communitarianism would undermine the theory of property rights, including redistributory property rights. Michael Sandel, for example, privileges the social entity over the individual as a "subject" of entitlement, that is, as the being to which entitlements are ascribed. On this basis he calls for the "dispossession" of the individual in favor of a "wider subject of possession," which means that the community as a whole is assigned entitlements to all social resources. The concept of a "wider subject" derives from the assumption that the individual is indebted to the community for the formation of his or her personal identity.[24] The depth of that indebtedness implies that the individuals are "radically situated subjects" (persons abjectly dependent on society); otherwise membership would not exact such a heavy toll that it deprives them of their property. Because Sandel's notion of a wider subject of possession directly contravenes his other principle, that there should be no radically situated subjects, his communitarianism is founded on an unresolved antinomy.

The reasons given earlier for rejecting Marxian socialization apply equally to Sandel's position. Individuals should retain ownership of much of the property in society because they have supreme ethical worth, and they do not lose this worth simply by joining a community, nor even by being formed by a community, since the formation of persons within an ethical community generates self-determined individuals who are therefore worthy of rights. In this regard, the proposed ethics of economic community resembles, not communtarianism, but Hegel's theory of ethical community, which recognizes property.

Apart from this point of overlap, the ethics of economic community needs to stake out a new realm distinct from Hegelian ethical community. Hegel believes that property rules out an egalitarian regulation of

of finding the currency of egalitarian justice approaches that of finding the philosopher's stone. See Johnston 1995, p. 39.

24. Sandel 1982, pp. 142–146.

economic resources by government (while granting corporate subcommunities a limited right to alleviate the distress of people in great need, but not to equalize distribution). Although property rules out state ownership, it is, contrary to Hegel, fully compatible with redistribution to reduce inequality, so long as the redistribution goes back to individuals, rather than to the state. Meanwhile, the condition of community within civil society generates moral bases for justifying income redistribution. So an ethical community is one where the joint conditions of property and community prohibit state ownership and invoke redistribution.

Despite all the work being done on community, economic community is still not adequately understood. Analysts often think dichotomously about community and competition. A system is either communal or competitive; there is no matter of degree. This way of thinking frequently leads to the false conclusion that community cannot exist in capitalist economies. If we insist that a system cannot be called a community unless it is entirely communal, then capital-based market systems, because of their element of competition, cannot be deemed communities. But a capitalist economy is, I argue, only partially competitive, for it is also partially communal. It therefore lies somewhere on a continuum between absolute competition and pure community; rather than being either competitive or communal, it is both at once. Moreover, the dimension of community runs throughout the system; it is not merely a feature of a subcommunity within the whole.

Rules of distribution for an economic community must derive from a theory of economic community. The point is obvious, yet rarely treated. I know of no such theory in the existing literature.[25] Communitarianism concentrates on community within subsystems of the economy, such as the firm; investigates economic preconditions of political community; describes noneconomic communities, such as the polity, the tribe, and the religious group; and postulates a noneconomic supracommunity at the national level. But none of these constitutes systemwide community in the economy. Just as general rules of distributive justice cannot be based on equalities limited to subsets of the population, they cannot be derived from small-scale communities. Only a concept of systemwide economic community can generate rules of distributive justice applicable to all economic agents.

Theorists disagree about the implications of economic community for

25. Jonathan Boswell discusses systemwide economic community, but the conception that he works out is a community in the organizational superstructure of a quasi-corporatist structure added to the market, not a community amid market relations themselves. See Boswell 1990.

rules of distributive justice. Some think that economic community morally entails equal distribution, others that it entails unequal distribution, and still others that it calls for neither alternative. I defend the view that economic community morally entails equal distribution, because cooperation cannot be entirely resolved into separately identifiable actions but must at some point remain ineluctably cooperation, something in its own right. For to resolve it into purely individual actions would negate the premised quality of jointness and convert it conceptually into its opposite – an effect like resolving genius into a lot of stupid people, or perseverance into lackadaisical behavior. Since in assessing common action we cannot entirely separate out individual actions –even though only individuals can cooperate – there is no basis for distributing purely differential rates of pay. Equal distribution, therefore, should be proportionate to the extent of common action in the economy, with unequal distribution reserved for noncommunal actions.

Once we have derived rules of distribution for an economic community, the next step is to consider their possible application to real-world economies. Unless capital-based market systems possess a dimension of community, communally derived rules will not apply to them. The question, then, is: do capital-based markets have a systemwide dimension of community?

The dominant paradigm in economics, the neoclassical theory of general economic equilibrium, argues that such a community does not exist. Conceiving of the economy simply as an adjustment mechanism that responds to the imperatives of many exogenous causes is hardly consistent with viewing it as a community with common actions and common ends, for such a system is pressured toward many diverse external ends. One can conceive of community only within an economy that is defined quite differently. Toward this end I use a social theory of capital circulation. The unity of labor and producers and of production and consumption in the circulation process provides a logical foundation for a conception of community that involves common action undertaken for common ends by all agents along a dimension of economic life.

In developing a theory of competitive cum communal capitalism, it is important to reconsider assumptions about systems theory that are implicit in current theory of endogenous preference formation. Since this theory understands the economic system as an adjustment mechanism responding to external conditions, it is embedded in a theory of exogenously determined systems. In some respects, the theory of endogenous preferences has to be reconnected to a conception of the economy as self-ordering to some significant extent. This is a system that regulates, to a degree, its elements in ways that are necessary for its existence and development.[26] A system of socially determined individuals is not necessarily self-ordering, since arbitrary social disturbances can threaten it. For example, when the actual amount of labor demanded relative to its supply differs from the customary amount of labor demanded relative to its supply, the gap can set in motion forces that lead to deflation, economic crisis, or inflationary hysteria.[27] To the extent that social influence is bound up with a self-ordering system, however, social determinants are connected to and emerge from the requirements of the system and, as a result, help to create conditions that maintain and develop the system.

Why is this connection important for communal properties of the economy? By generating broad social influences that shape constituents in ways necessary for the system's survival, a partially self-ordering system generates commonalities among its members.[28] The social influences in a self-ordering economy induce consumers to fulfill the vital common purposes and requirements of the association. For example, the self-ordering system of capital circulation patterns consumer preferences in ways indispensable to the preservation and expansion of capital, a common end vital to the system.

For a dimension of community to exist in an economy, there must be some community between capital managers and labor. Here the proposition of economic community runs into opposition from Marxists, who regard capitalism essentially as a system of class division. But Marx's own work can be useful in developing the idea of community within capitalist economies. Labor in his theory is united with the means of production in a particular firm, whose production process has itself been differentiated within a system of production processes, thereby uniting the immediate process with the system to some extent. Labor within the

26. For more on systems theory, see von Bertalanffy 1968.
27. Iwai 1981, p. 121.
28. Alfred North Whitehead argued for the existence of a link between a self-ordering system and commonalities between constituents when he wrote: "A nexus enjoys 'social order' where (i) there is a common element of form illustrated in the definiteness of each of its included actual entities, and (ii) this common element of form arises in each member of the nexus by reason of the conditions imposed upon it by its prehensions of some other members of the nexus, and (iii) these prehensions impose that condition of reproduction by reason of their inclusion of positive feelings of that common form." See Whitehead 1960, pp. 50–51. Whereas the self-ordering system formulated by Whitehead imposes common properties on its members, a capital-based market system has a form of self-ordering that generates commonalities, but does necessarily impose them, since it can consist in socially self-determined individuals rather than externally ordered ones.

firm is thereby indirectly united with the system of production processes as well as with other laborers in the system. These connections can be interpreted as a dimension of common action for common ends – therefore, as a dimension of community.

Using Marx's theory to demonstrate a communal dimension of capitalism may seem inappropriate, in view of his emphasis on class opposition and conflict. Distributive injustices provide some support for his view. But in basing his judgment largely on one phase of capitalism, distribution, Marx goes too far when he condemns the capitalist economy as wholly competitive, for other phases of the circulation process are replete with common action for a common end. Moreover, recognition of a dimension of community in capitalism has radically different moral implications from those Marx would have inferred. To him it would have represented an attempt to legitimate exploitation, but it actually calls for an equal distribution of income proportionate to the extent of community.

THEORY AND THE PROBLEM OF INEQUALITY

The theory and philosophy of democracy and distributive justice are important because income inequality, a matter of central concern to this theory, has been a problem in "democratic" capitalist systems for many years, and in some countries it has worsened during the last two decades. The United States has operated with great disparities in income and wealth since the nineteenth century, and the level of inequality rose dramatically during the 1980s and 1990s. Indeed, in that period the gap between rich and poor was wider in the United States than in any large industrial nation.[29] But the country's strong economic performance by world standards blunted criticism of inequalities and lent support to the status quo. Income inequality also rose during this period in Japan, Australia, Britain, and in five continental European countries.[30] The allegedly more efficient U.S. brand of capitalism tempted Western European countries to adopt it, and emulation will likely breed more inequality. Now Eastern European countries in transition from "communism" to capitalism have embraced ideals of "free market" capitalism and noninterventionist democracy that involve considerable inequality in income distribution.

29. Keith Bradsher, *The New York Times*, October 27, 1995, section D, p. 2. Report on a study by Timothy M. Smeeding, Lee Rainwater, and Anthony B. Atkinson for the Organization for Economic Cooperation and Development. See also Miringhoff and Miringoff 1999, pp. 107–108.
30. Ibid.

Democratic theory and the theory of economic justice can have practical ramifications, because they help to determine whether inequalities are compatible with democracy and justice. Such theories therefore bear on whether the United States should conserve or progressively modify its political economy and on whether Western Europe, Eastern Europe, and the former members of the Soviet Union should follow or reject the American model – or to what degree they should do either of these things.

The recent widening of the income gap between rich and poor has attracted considerable attention from scholars seeking its causes and the extent of its consequences for health and well-being. Their findings have received a lot of publicity, and candidates and elected officials have debated the effects of tax and budget policy on relative distribution.[31] But the issue of democracy and distributive justice would not lose importance or relevance if the income gap temporarily stabilized or modestly lessened, for high levels of inequality are a long-standing problem, not an episodic one.

The income gap opened sharply between 1816 and 1856 and has lasted for most of the history of industrialized America. The free farmer society of America in 1800 probably had more equal distribution of pay and of key economic resources than we have today, but inequality increased precipitously during three later periods: 1816 to 1856, 1896 to 1914, and 1981 to the present.[32] Williamson and Lindert's careful study of nineteenth-century distribution found that "[i]n four short decades [after 1816], the American Northeast was transformed from the 'Jeffersonian ideal' to a society more typical of developing economies with very wide pay differentials and, presumably, marked inequality in the distribution of income."[33] Periods of growing disparities of income were interspersed with periods of (1) stability or modest leveling, from 1856 to 1896, (2) decline and sharp drop-off, from 1929 to 1945, and (3) mild decline or flatness, from 1945 to 1981, but these extended inter-

31. On the health consequences of socioeconomic inequality, see Miringoff and Miringoff 1999, pp. 108–109; Erica Goode, *The New York Times*, June 1, 1999, section F, pp. 1, 9; and Richard A. Shweder, *The New York Times*, March 9, 1997, section 4, p. 5. Between 1994 and 1999, there were 193 papers on the health consequences of socioeconomic status, twice the number published in the previous five years; see Goode 1999. On the political contestation, see Keith Bradsher, *The New York Times*, October 27, 1999, section D, p. 2. Among the myriad of studies published in the last decade on the causes of increased inequality, see Galbraith 1998.

32. Dahl 1971, pp. 53, 56, 72; Phelps Brown 1988, p. 322.

33. Williamson and Lindert 1980, pp. 131, 58.

ludes did not permanently check or reverse long-term tendencies toward high levels of inequality, which continue to this day.[34]

Over the past half-century, despite transfer payments made by the welfare state, percentage changes in distribution have been small (though not insignificant) and disparities therefore remain high. The poorest 20% of families received 4.5% of the total income in 1950 and 4.2% in 1997, while the top 5% received 17.3% in 1950 and 20.7% in 1997.[35] To bring out the human meaning of statistics on income distribution, the Dutch economist Jan Pen used the image of a parade in which the marchers, representing everyone in society, take their place in line according to their height, which is proportional to their income. Viewed in this way society would appear as a "parade of dwarfs (and a few giants)."[36]

Although a high level of income inequality has been an enduring feature of American political economy, the recent increase underscores the importance of analyzing its democratic character and ethical validity. Inequalities in 1999 were twice the size of those in 1977, measured by the ratio of the income of the top one percent to that of the bottom group.[37] In 1999, the top one percent, 2.7 million people, had as much after-tax income as 100 million people at the bottom of the income hierarchy.[38] In 1977, the top one percent received as much after-tax income as the bottom 49 million Americans. While some CEOs in the 1970s made 35 times the amount paid their lowest wage earners, by 1998 the average CEO made 415 times the amount paid the average manufacturing worker.[39]

During a period when the economic pie expanded considerably, 80% of American households, amounting to 217 million people, were left with a smaller proportion of total national after-tax income in 1999 than in 1977.[40] Four-fifths of the households received less than 50% of the pie in 1999, compared with 57% in 1977. The decline in the total

34. Phelps Brown 1988, p. 321; Wolf 1995, p. 28.
35. U.S. Bureau of the Census, *March Current Population Survey*, 1998, Table F-2.
36. Pen 1971, p. 48.
37. David Cay Johnston, "Gap between Rich and Poor Found Substantially Wider," *The New York Times*, September 5, 1999, p. 16. Report on the Center on Budget and Policy Priorities analysis of data from the Congressional Budget Office.
38. Ibid.
39. "CEO Pay in '98: Insanity Marches On," *Too Much*, vol. 5, no. 1 (Summer 1999), p. 3. Report of *Business Week* research, spring 1999.
40. Johnston, "Gap between Rich and Poor," p. 16.

after-tax income was 12% for the poorest fifth of households, 9.5% for the next lowest fifth, and 3.1% for the middle fifth. Analysis of data from the Congressional Budget Office by the Center on Budget and Policy Priorities indicates that in 1999 "the poor not only have a small slice of a big economic pie, but the pie is bigger [than it was in 1977] and their piece is even smaller."[41] Exacerbating the picture, the top one percent garnered more than 90% of the growth in after-tax income.[42]

Americans expect chief executives of major companies to become multimillionaires, but they might be surprised to learn that in 1998 five chief executives each made more than a quarter of a billion dollars, with stock options included in the pay package.[43] Specifically, they received $233 million, $326 million, $336 million, $476 million, and $495 million – more than $240,000 an hour. The extent of inequality can be grasped by juxtaposing this executive compensation with the average annual earnings of workers in the United States in 1998: $23,000.[44] In 1996, Lawrence Coss of Green Tree Financial "earned" $11,695 an

41. Ibid.
42. Ibid. In the view of some liberals and conservatives, inequalities of income are mollified by a high degree of social mobility (see Erikson and Goldthorpe 1993, p. 368). But some studies indicate that social mobility is declining in the United States and that rich and poor are not likely to trade places. If a child's father belongs to the lowest five percent in income, he or she stands only one chance in twenty of achieving the income level of the top twenty percent of families (Gary Solon, *American Economic Review*, cited by Sylvia Nasar, "Those Born Wealthy Stay So, Studies Say," *The New York Times*, May 18, 1992, section A, p. 1. See also Erikson and Goldthorpe 1993, pp. 366–367).
43. United for a Fair Economy, "CEO Pay in '98: Insanity Marches On," *Too Much*, vol 5, no. 1 (Summer 1999), p. 3. Report of the analysis of executive compensation by Craef Crystal, *USA Today*, April 7, 1999. See also Jennifer Reingold, "Executive Pay," *Business Week*, April 21, 1997, pp 58–68. It would take a million people earning a million dollars a year to equal the total wealth, one trillion dollars, of the world's 200 richest billionaires in 1999. On the last point, see United for a Fair Economy, "The Trillion-Dollar Gang," *Too Much*, vol. 5, no. 2 (Fall 1999), p. 1.
44. The figure is for production and nonsupervisory workers on private nonfarm payrolls. See *Employment and Earnings*, vol. 46, no. 9 (August 1999), p. 45. Typical earnings in various occupations include: cab driver ($13,000), gas station attendant ($10,000), doorman ($28,000), bus driver ($50,000), church pastor ($33,000), phone operator ($24,000), art museum waiter ($32,000), clothing saleswoman ($14,000), coffee shop waitress ($14,000), schoolteacher ($28,740), fruit cart attendant ($13,000), and firefighter ($47,800). These are 1996 annual wages, as reported by Richard Wilner, *The New York Post*, April 11, 1997, p. 7.

hour, even while asleep; in contrast, the average worker had to work for more than six months to accumulate that sum.[45] But the most extreme case is that of Bill Gates, whose holdings reached $100 billion in 1999. A person making the median income of $50,000 would have to work for two million years to amass that sum. Or two million Americans making the median income would take a year to do so.[46] As incomes reached stratospheric levels, so did consumption. The entire inventory of seventy toy Jaguar convertibles priced at $80,000 each sold out within hours after they appeared in Nieman Marcus's Christmas catalogue.[47] But benefits were not broad-based, and America, the world's richest country, sank to eighteenth in life expectancy.[48]

45. For Coss's salary, see Richard Wilner, "The Buck Stops Here," *The New York Post*, April 11, 1997, p. 7. Report of research by *Business Week*; see Reingold 1997, p. 58. The figure for workers' annual wages is for production and nonsupervisory workers on private nonfarm payrolls. See *Employment and Earnings*, vol. 46, no. 9 (August 1999), p. 45.
46. Verlyn Klinkenborg, *The New York Times*, Sept. 4, 1999, section A, p. 12.
47. Robert H. Frank, "Timmy's Range Rover," *The New York Times*, Dec. 22, 1998, p. 31.
48. For figures on life expectancy, see Paul Spector, "Failure, by the Numbers," *The New York Times,* September 24, 1994, Op Ed page. Report on the United Nations 1994 Human Development Report.

Part I

Unequal Property and Individualism in Liberal Theory

2

The Underlying Logic of Liberal Property Theory

Theories of property are concerned with the question, what entitles a person or other unit to property-objects? And to what does property, that is, the right, entitle him or her? The right of property could conceivably come in different forms: a right to highly unequal amounts of value (income and wealth), a right to relatively equal amounts of value, or a right to strictly equal amounts. It could, further, be a composite: a right to an equalized portion of one part of total social income and a right to unequal amounts of the rest of total income. Which form is rightful?

One can begin by examining liberal theories, the dominant approach to property in the West, and searching for their patterns of response to these questions. Liberal theories of property include the theories of Hobbes, Locke, Rousseau, Bentham, Austin, Hegel, Pound, Felix Cohen, the New Economic Analysis of Law, Keynes, Nozick, and Rawls, among others. Scholarly opinion divides on whether liberal theory tends to support a right to highly unequal amounts of property.[1] Some scholars hold that significant representatives of liberal theory do not support it. In my view, most of the important liberal theories may be considered inegalitarian in the sense that they posit a right to highly unequal amounts of income and wealth or subsume such a right under a broad concept of exclusive individual dominion. There are commentators who acknowledge this but nevertheless maintain that liberal theories are still

1. For the argument that Rawlsian liberalism entails sharp economic inequalities, see Barry 1973, p. 46; Shapiro 1986, p. 230; Rae 1975; Macpherson 1985, p. 12. For views stressing economic egalitarianism in one or more liberal theorists, see Cobban 1964, p. 131, passim; Schaar 1980, pp. 167, 171; Shapiro 1986, pp. 40, 70–73, 87–89; Dahl 1985, pp. 77–78; Quinn 1991, pp. 263–281.

egalitarian because they reach these unequal outcomes through arguments that treat people equally every step of the way.[2] But the tendentiousness with which liberal theories are found to posit rights to unequal property in Part I raises a question about their claims to treat people equally.

Studying the history of theories of property may provide valuable leads in the attempt to determine ethically valid forms of property. By identifying the major bases of the liberal right to highly unequal property, one can find the crucial considerations on which the validity of this "right" hinges, which can help establish a direction for reexamining its validity.

Scholars divide on what can be said to constitute the foundations for liberal conclusions about property and other matters. Some argue that they depend on individualism, while others offer a variety of other interpretations.[3] I defend the view that the entitlement to and relative distribution of property in liberal theories have been profoundly affected by individualism.

With regard to the moral source of entitlement, the person's entitlement to property in liberal theories largely flows from aspects of the person or personality. (The legal entitlement endowed by law is then usually derived from, secondary to, or executory to the fundamental moral entitlement in liberal theories.) The aspects of the person warranting entitlement to property in liberal theories reflect a certain model or conception of what people are like. The form of property – the right to unequal amounts of value – is also deduced and justified on the basis of such a model. I want to suggest that a model of what may be called the "subjective person" or "subjective personality" forms the conceptual mainspring of the person's entitlement and the basis of the form of property rights in liberal theories, namely, the right to highly unequal amounts of value. Although liberal theories do not use the terms "subjective person" or "subjective personality," these terms can denote the nature of the person in liberal theories. By "personality" in this context, I mean any or all aspects of the self, including attributes, faculties, mind,

2. Shapiro 1986.
3. Those who ascribe a highly individualistic concept of the person to liberal theory include Hegel 1952, p. 33; Macpherson 1962; Unger 1975, pp. 81–83; Sandel 1982, pp. 11–12, 53, 60–65; Winfield 1990, pp. 2–3, 19–24, 35, 99, 115–116; Benhabib 1977; Gould 1988, Chapters 1, 5, pp. 172–176. For the view that liberal theory is not excessively individualistic, or not as individualistic as has been alleged, and that it admits a social concept of the person, see Shapiro 1986, p. 121 n1; Ewald 1988, p. 682; Wallach 1987, p. 584; Kaufman 1999; Laursen 1989.

will, reason, satisfaction, choice, and preferences. The model of subjective personality consists in the view that the content of personality – will, aims, ends – is essentially derived from within the self rather than from external causes. The individual, in this conception, is highly independent in the midst of social relations, because his or her nature is ultimately formed autonomously rather than by social conditioning. A subjective person is one whose physical and intellectual nature is distinct from other persons rather than connected with them. This usage differs from the ordinary sense of the word "subjective," in which it refers to an arbitrary opinion rather than to an objective assessment.

The liberal model of the person stands in contrast to a conception of personality with an intersubjective inner structure formed through interaction with other persons. This conception entails a right to an equalization of a portion of income, whereas the conception of the person as a subjective being supports ownership of highly unequal amounts of income and wealth.

If subjective personality, that is, the independently formed and independently acting self, were widely known to be the basis of liberal property entitlement, there would not be much need for an exposition of this foundational conception – and similarly, if the "right" to unequal property value were well known to have a foundation in subjective personality. But on the contrary, there is a need for such analysis because liberal theories rarely, if ever, give subjective personality as the explicit ground for property or for a right to unequal property value.

Instead, the history of liberal property theory provides numerous other warrants for its conception of property. The person is entitled to property because property is necessary for personhood (Holland, Savigny). Or the person is entitled to things when they are part of him or her (Locke), or mixed with his or her labor (Locke), or connected with him or her (Kant). The person deserves property because he or she produced it (Locke, Lawrence Becker). The person is entitled to property because property is necessary for the security of his or her expectations of advantages or benefits from things (Bentham, Pound). Or the person is entitled to property because it is a necessary condition for utility maximization (Posner, the New Economic Analysis of Law, Lawrence Becker). Or the person is entitled to property because property is necessary for objective freedom of will in relation to things (Kant). And so on, almost endlessly.

To all appearances, then, liberal theories are irreducibly different in their bases for property entitlement. Yet underlying these seemingly disparate entitlement logics rests the hidden premise of subjective personality, as reexamination of the texts can show. The relationship between the premise of subjective personality and the right to highly unequal amounts of value (income and/or wealth) may constitute the fundamental logical structure of liberal property.

Interpretations of liberal theories as individualistic and inegalitarian have increasingly been met with careful and informed objections by revisionist critics. In view of the critiques, the thesis that liberal theories deduce unequal property from subjective personality cannot be reasserted without reexamination of classic texts and contemporary commentary. Some commentators claim to see strong communitarian, social theoretical, and egalitarian tendencies within the liberal tradition.[4] William Ewald holds that so-called liberal theories display more diversity and difference than commonality, and that they do not revolve around individualism: "Even if we restrict our attention to philosophers who can be fairly uncontroversially classified as 'liberal' – such as Kant, Bentham, Mill, von Humboldt, Green, Dewey, and Rawls – the amount of metaphysical, epistemological, psychological, and even political diversity is striking."[5] Shapiro also maintains that liberal theories cannot be characterized en masse by single-unit themes such as individualism.[6] While commentary such as Ewald's and Shapiro's brings out the rich, multifaceted nature of liberal theory, it also underestimates the importance of individualism and highly unequal property within liberal theories of property rights. Individualism, social theory, highly unequal property, and egalitarianism are not randomly distributed in liberal theories. The fundamental logic – a right to highly unequal amounts of value deduced from subjective personality – reappears with a frequency suggesting that it may be the essential structure of liberal theories of property, with some variation in the degree of extreme inequality posited.

What does subjective or intersubjective personality have to do with equality or inequality under property right? These assumptions about the person can affect rules of distribution, because they crucially affect how much the individual is responsible for the income and wealth he or she possesses, how much credit the individual can take in demanding differential economic reward, what is due the individual, and how much the individual is beholden to others as a member of an economic quasi-community, among other reasons.

Consider the entitlement logic whereby the person becomes entitled to things (including things of highly unequal value) by virtue of being "connected" to them. This major entitlement from seventeenth- and eighteenth-century liberal theory was central to the theories of Locke

4. Ryan 1993. 5. Ewald 1988, p. 682.
6. Shapiro 1986.

and Kant. In these theories, it is only because I am a subjective being, that is, an independent being, that when I am connected to something it is connected to me only. And it is only because it is connected solely to me that it is proper to me and to no one else. No matter how many things I have relative to what others have, they belong exclusively to me because, when connected to me, they are connected to me only. But there is a related matter that liberal theorists leave unexamined. If a thing pertains solely to me because I am an independent being, then by the same token if I were instead connected to others, then the object connected to me would be indirectly connected to others. They would therefore have a claim to a share in the value of the property object. Property would not then be a right to highly unequal value but a right to some equalization of property value. For these reasons, the liberal entitlement to exclusive individual ownership, and the entitlement to highly unequal property value, hinge on a premise of subjective personality. They do so no less crucially for the fact that neither Locke nor Kant said anything explicit about subjective personality, but only about connection to the person.

Many entitlement logics in liberal theories can be shown to work in opposing ways depending on whether one inserts a postulate of subjective or intersubjective personality into them. The former always logically produces a right to possess unequal amounts, while the latter always logically requires some equalization, no matter which entitlement logic one inserts them into.[7] Thus, most of the houses in the village of liberal theories of property would collapse if the subjective premise on which they rest is wrong.

SELECTION OF CASES

In order to support the proposed interpretation of how liberal property theories are constructed, a broad range of such theories must be considered. These theories can be classified into fifteen types:

I. A. Natural law theories
   B. Metaphysical theories
   C. Positivist theories
   D. Sociological theories

II. A. Natural need theories

7. Theories sometimes *attempt* to deduce a principle of equal distribution from premises of subjective personality (such as subjective utility), but the conclusion does not follow *logically* from the premise; see Chapter 5 of this volume, note 54.

B. Labor desert theories
C. Utilitarian theories
D. Personality theories

III. A. Social contract theories
B. Twentieth-century jurisprudence
C. Keynesian economic ethics
D. New Economic Analysis of Law
E. Neoclassical economic theory
F. Modern theory of justice
G. Contemporary "egalitarian liberalism"

Part I demonstrates the presence of the subjective personality/unequal property structure in representative examples from each type.

Hobbes, Locke, and Rousseau are taken as representatives of the natural law theories of property.[8] Kant and Hegel represent the metaphysical and idealist schools of liberal theories of property.[9] Pound represents the sociological school of theories of property.[10] Hobbes and Locke can do double duty as representatives of the natural need theories of property. Locke's theory also serves to represent the labor desert theories of property. Bentham and Austin represent utilitarian theories of property.[11] Kant and Hegel also serve well to represent the personality theories of property. Locke and Kant can serve yet again as representatives of the social contract theories of property. Pound can be taken as the founding member of twentieth-century sociological jurisprudence and of the theory of property associated with it. Felix Cohen represents the "relational" school of mid twentieth-century property theory.[12] Keynes's economic ethics may be taken as representative of the rules of distribution in modern liberal welfare state theories.[13] Demsetz can represent the theory of property in the New Economic Analysis of Law.[14] Several representative treatments of property in neoclassical economic theory are considered.[15] Rawls represents well theories of property within modern theories of justice.[16] And contemporary "egalitarian liberalism" can be represented by Dworkin.[17]

8. See Chapter 3 of this volume.
9. See Chapter 4 of this volume.
10. Ibid. 11. Ibid. 12. Ibid.
13. See Chapter 12 of this volume. 14. See Chapter 4 of this volume.
15. See Chapters 5 and 6 of this volume. For heuristic purposes a theory of property (of the ethics-of-reward-for-economic-contributions type) is formulated in the neoclassical style in Chapter 6, pp. 109-110.
16. See Chapter 4 of this volume.
17. See Chapter 13 of this volume.

3

Unequal Property and Its Premise in Locke's Theory

John Locke made two major contributions to the theory of property: a justification for assigning the right of property to individuals rather than to collectivities and a justfication for a principle of unequal distribution of economic resources, goods, and money. The repudiation of Soviet communism in the late twentieth century has rendered Locke's first justification less controversial because it has led to more general agreement on assigning property to individuals rather than to states. But the reduction in the threat of Soviet communism may make his second justification more controversial, because market societies may become secure enough to contemplate the great disparities of income and wealth that prominently mark their social landscapes.

Many opinion leaders will look to Locke's theory as an intellectual bulwark against an egalitarian distribution of economic resources, while others will abjure it for precisely that reason.[1] Therefore, Locke's theory will continue to be an important subject of study. Scholars disagree over what makes his theory the classical liberal theory of property, yet they agree that it conveys something essential about the liberal way of looking at property.[2] With some frequency scholars formerly viewed the theory as a justification of a right to unequal property based on individualistic assumptions, and many still do.[3] By now, however, leading Locke

1. The high regard that contemporary theorists have for the theory is indicated by the lengthy sections devoted to it in Munzer 1990 and Waldron 1988. Some have argued that the theory could have egalitarian implications for distribution, for example, on the basis of the second proviso. But as we shall see, it provides a weak limitation on the scope of inequalities in a monetary economy.
2. Schlatter 1951, p. 151, calls it "the standard text of liberalism and natural rights."
3. Since the 1960s the theory has been regarded in this way by left-leaning scholars (e.g. Macpherson 1962, pp. 214–215), by members of the critical legal stud-

specialists have overturned interpretations of Locke's theory as primarily individualistic and inegalitarian.[4] Yet I see a basis for reasserting the previous view that individualism is the root cause of distributive inegalitarianism in Locke's theory. Demonstrating this will entail reexamination of the text and of contemporary assessments of it, and some new argumentation.

According to Macpherson, Locke justifies class differentials in natural rights based on class differentials in rationality.[5] Revising this approach, one scholar disagrees with the view that Locke relied upon the differential rationality of the social classes, while he concurs that Locke maintains a right to unequal possessions. Shapiro maintains that Locke should be considered egalitarian in the sense that his argument treats men equally every step of the way.[6] To a considerable extent this revisionist view is correct: the main course of Locke's reasoning develops from a conception of persons as equals. However, I question the conclusion that Locke is egalitarian, because the revisionist criterion is not an adequate gauge of egalitarianism. A principle of extremely unequal distribution can be deduced from a conception of equal persons. This should alert us to the possibility that not all conceptions of the equality of persons are egalitarian. We therefore need an additional criterion for an egalitarian theory of property. An egalitarian theory, I suggest, is one that conceives concrete forms of equality among persons. By this I mean equalities regarding the specific content of the person, such as the content of his or her labor. Abstract equalities simply regard the fact that one has a will or a capacity to labor. Locke's justification for unequal property does not use a conception of concrete equalities among persons, and so his theory is not egalitarian by such a criterion.[7]

dies movement, including Roberto Unger, and by neo-Marxists. Before that, mainstream scholars and law professors at major universities also embraced the interpretation of Locke's theory as a justification of inequality based on individualistic assumptions, because they simply assumed that accumulations due to individual drive and initiative are virtuous. Donahue, a professor of property law at Harvard, stated: "the Western legal concept of property has always been associated with various forms of individualism" (Donahue 1980, pp. 58, 40). Simmons holds that Locke justifies inequality on the basis of the "voluntary" consent of "men" to the use of money (1992, pp. 303, 304). See also Donahue 1974, pp. 249, 253–254; Berry 1980, p. 90; Berolzheimer 1968, pp. 135–136; Singer 1997, pp. 14–15.

4. See Ashcraft 1987; Ewald 1988, p. 682, a critique of Unger 1975; and Shapiro 1986 with its critique of Macpherson 1962.
5. Macpherson 1962, pp. 232–238.
6. Shapiro 1986.
7. In characterizing Locke as inegalitarian, I am not, however, reasserting Mac-

Locke scholars of the 1940s and 1960s, such as Strauss and Macpherson, commonly portrayed him as a secular individualist, but the prevalent view today is that theological and natural law arguments dominate his reasoning about property, casting serious doubt on the earlier emphasis on the individualistic element in Locke scholarship.[8] The question of what premises ground Locke's right of unequal property needs to be reopened. Rights justified by theological and natural law arguments may not be as important, as realistic, or as genuinely theoretical as rights derived from natural rights arguments or convention-based arguments in the state of nature. In this case, the centrality of theological and natural law to his account may be subject to doubt. The law of reason, natural right, and conventional right are more compatible with the requirements of a theory of rights, and they supply some of the more important and realistic rights in Locke's account. Since these matters are founded on individualistic assumptions, individualism plays a central role in Locke's deduction of the right to unequal property.

THE GENERAL JUSTIFICATION OF PROPERTY

In the beginning, according to Locke, God gifted the world to mankind in common. Some interpreters suggest that individuals in this condition could use parcels of the world, but did not own them. The gift of common ownership, they say, only confers on each person a communitarian "use-right" to the commons, not a property right.[9] The difference is that a use-right is an inclusive right that assures access to the commons, whereas property confers exclusive individual dominion. If Locke's analysis were about justifying a use-right based on positive community, individualism would be much less central to the theory than has been supposed.

Such an interpretation, however, misconstrues Locke's main point.

pherson's differential rationality thesis. Locke's premise for unequal partage is not differential rationality but differential industriousness.

8. For the recent revisionist view that Locke presented a primarily theological argument, see Ashcraft 1987 and Dunn 1969, p. 222. Previously, Palmer and Colton had characterized Locke "as an almost entirely secular thinker," 1995 [1950], p. 312. Also at mid twentieth century, Strauss saw secular individualism as central to Locke's theory: "Locke's teaching on property, and therewith his whole political philosophy, are revolutionary not only with regard to the biblical tradition but also with regard to the philosophical tradition. Through the shift from natural duties or obligations to natural rights, the individual . . . had become the center of the moral world" (Strauss 1950, p. 248).
9. For example, Tully 1980, p. 130.

Locke's overriding purpose in the analysis of property is to show that a right of property, in the sense of exclusive individual dominion, can arise out of a condition of common ownership. He repeats the point four times, evidently not wanting to leave any confusion in the matter.[10] After mankind received the world in common, Locke thought that no one could use the world unless he had exclusive individual dominion. Property derives its very justification from the fact that it is a necessary condition for anyone to be able to use or derive benefit from the world:

> There must of necessity be a means to appropriate them some way or other before they can be of any use, or at all beneficial to any particular Man. The Fruit, or Venison, which nourishes the Wild Indian, who knows no inclosure, and is still a Tenant in common, must be his, and so his, i.e. a part of him, that another can no longer have any right to it, before it can do him any good for the support of his life.[11]

It is not that common ownership justifies an individual use-right, but that the necessity of property for use justifies property (in the sense of exclusive individual dominion). By implication, individualism supersedes considerations of positive community in the justification of external right, and in the substance of the right justified.

Locke's argument for property as a necessary condition for use is a "general rights justification" that justifies property by showing why this right is important.[12] Such moral reasoning is distinct from a "special rights justification" stating "why . . . an individual who does action A to a resource gets to be its owner."[13] Waldron maintains that Locke does not have a general rights justification of property, or at least not much of one.[14] Yet Locke's justification of property as a necessary condition for use is a significant general rights justification that creates a duty not to take away resources from someone who has rightfully obtained them.

The general justification for property has a highly individualistic structure that rests on the simple idea that men do not share stomachs. Men can use only things over which they have exclusive individual dominion because of the nature of man. They can satisfy their needs only through exclusive consumption because needs belong to entirely discrete persons, separate from others. In the wild Indian passage, Locke

10. See Locke 1963, para. 33, p. 333; para. 51, p. 344; para. 39, p. 338; para. 26, p. 328; para. 27, p. 329.
11. Locke 1963, para. 26, p. 328.
12. Waldron 1988 develops the distinction between general and special rights justifications.
13. Waldron 1988, p. 27.
14. Ibid., pp. 137, 251, 284.

carefully adds that items of use must be "so his" and "a part of him." Locke thus emphasizes that a man uses things by making them part of himself. The need to incorporate things makes property necessary only because they are being incorporated into independent beings. Thus, independence of the person lies at the basis of the necessity of property and, therefore, of Locke's general justification of property.

The primacy of the premise of independent persons in Locke's general justification of property should qualify revisionist claims about the centrality of theological and natural law considerations in his theory. Nor does Locke's general justification of property supply grounds for the revisionist view that his theory rests on an ensemble of different arguments. Rather, the individualistic nature of men's needs makes property necessary.[15] One scholar has suggested a "modified version" of Macpherson's possessive individualism thesis, in which individualism pertains "mainly to the substance of the rights," that is, what they are rights to.[16] The need to take satisfactions independently, however, means that individualism figures prominently in the purpose or reason for property as well.

Locke's general justification of property gives rise to a principle of unequal distribution of things. The inegalitarian implications spring from the nearly absolute form of exclusive individual dominion in which things must be "so his, i.e., a part of him that another can no longer have any right to it." The degree of exclusive individual dominion in Locke's theory leads some scholars to think it gives the owner full control over the product of his labor.[17] A nearly absolute form of dominion implies a justification for unequal amounts of property: a man can justly have "as much as he can make use of to any advantage of life before it spoils" (Locke 1963, p. 332). If property is justified because one cannot use anything without having exclusive individual dominion over it, then the justification authorizes unequal possessions, though not a totally unlimited right to inequality.

Since individualistic considerations underlie the general justification of exclusive individual dominion, they also underlie the justification for unequal property. For the former justification implies the latter justification. This concurs with Phelps Brown's view that a right to inequality is subsumed under Locke's belief in the sanctity of property, itself derived from the supreme value Locke places on the self and its independence. "The fact is," writes Phelps Brown, "that Locke sees property

15. Shapiro 1986, pp. 4–5.
16. Ibid., p. 144.
17. Donahue, Kauper, and Martin 1974, p. 249.

from the first as part of the fortress of the self, whose independence and liberty he affirms with apostolic fervour. He can no more allow private property to be invaded, than one man to be subordinated to another. . . . There is no room for egalitarianism here."[18]

Waldron's study of Locke sees a different basis for inequalities in theories of rights. He suggests that general rights justifications of property are "radical" in their implications for distribution, while special rights justifications are conservative or inegalitarian.[19] Locke's conservative position on distribution is largely due, according to Waldron, to his use of a special rights justification rather than to making any substantial use of a general rights justification. Waldron's interpretation overlooks the fact that Locke's general justification – that property is necessary for use – is neutral between egalitarian and inegalitarian distributions. The conservative implications of Locke's justification flow rather from the assumption that men do not share stomachs. An alternative assumption, interdependent needs or reciprocal need, inserted in Locke's general justification, would divert the reasoning toward a more egalitarian conclusion.[20]

THE SUBJECT OF ENTITLEMENT

Locke's theory of rights studies the kind of creature that can become entitled to rights. Leading Locke scholars interpret Locke as saying that men have rights, and are equally entitled to them, because God conferred qualities on them that inherently contain rights.[21] "[W]hat is absolutely crucial," writes Ashcraft, "to Locke's description of the state of nature is his characterization of human nature in terms of God's workmanship and purposes."[22] Theological argument undoubtedly plays a major role in the account of the subject of rights, but men's nature as self-determined beings also plays a major role. Rights to freedoms inhere in men because they have the equal capacity for self-determination. "Every man is born," Locke writes, "with . . . a Right of Freedom to his Person, which no other Man has a Power over" (Locke 1963, p. 441, para. 190). Although there is a transcendental determination of men's qualification for rights because God created man, there is also an internal qualification for rights within the nature of man,

18. Phelps Brown 1988, pp. 62–63.
19. Waldron 1988, p. 444.
20. See Chapters 6 and 12, this volume; and Zucker 1995, pp. 208–209.
21. For example, Waldron 1988, p. 142.
22. Ashcraft 1987, p. 104. See also Dunn 1969, pp. 106–107.

because men are self-determined. A man's nature as a self-determined creature is the proximate source of his status as a subject of right. If self-determinedness is the immediate qualification for being a subject of right, then divine creation is once removed as a condition for being a subject of right.[23] Since self-determination is the proximate qualification for a subject of rights, individualism is central to Locke's account of the subject of rights, and it does not figure only in the account of the substance of rights, contrary to the suppositions of some.

INDIVIDUALISM AND UNEQUAL PROPERTY – PREMONETARY NATURE

Although the general justification for property justifies the institution of property, it does not create distinct titles to particular parts of the commons. Locke next explains the logic of entitlement, that is, what a man must do to accrue such titles. Exegeses of the text by other scholars provide a good understanding of this part of the argument,[24] but I want to attend more closely to the working of individualistic assumptions in the creation of distinct titles.

Locke maintains that "Whatsoever he . . . removes . . . he hath mixed his Labour with, and joyned it to something that is his own . . . thereby makes it his Property" (Locke 1963, p. 329, para. 27). One should not mistake this logic of entitlement for a theory of reward for productive action or effort. The individual creates a property right by making things part of himself. When he mixes his labor with a thing, he joins it with something that is his own. A person's labor is part of himself. It is himself dynamically considered. So laboring on something makes it part of himself in action. When he makes something part of himself, he makes it "properly" his (Locke 1963, p. 329, para. 27).

Though scholars question the meaningfulness of the mixing metaphor,[25] one has to take it into account to understand Locke's treatment of property. It is clear why Locke, a very good logician, thinks that making something part of oneself creates a property. The word "proper" is, of course, the root of "property." So you can prove a property if you can prove something is proper to someone. Now, for a thing to be proper to someone means that it is part of him; "proper" means "property or quality of the thing itself, intrinsic, inherent."[26] Since "proper" is the

23. As indicated by Locke 1963, para. 32, p. 333.
24. See Munzer, Waldron, Shapiro, Becker, and others.
25. Nozick 1974, p. 160; Waldron 1988, pp. 185–186; Munzer 1990, p. 66.
26. *The Compact Edition of the Oxford English Dictionary*.

root of the word "property," and proper means part of, one can see why Locke supposed that one could deem things property that are part of a person. The notion of mixing is necessary to complete the incorporation logic of entitlement because it supplies an explanation of how external things could become part of oneself.

One can identify the structure of Locke's labor theory of appropriation by probing the premise or premises leading to the determination of men's distinct titles to things. On the surface of the account, mixing labor appears to create a distinct title. At base, however, it is the mixing of *independent* labor, the labor of a subjective being, discrete from others, that creates property. When labor is independent activity, a person who mixes his labor with something is making it part of himself and only of himself. This makes the thing his property alone. If a person's labor were instead interdependent and were mixed with others' labor, then she would pour in their labor as well when she mixed her (social) labor with a thing. These others would accrue an indirect title to a share of the thing, yielding a system of indirect entitlements. Since Locke stipulates property rather than indirect entitlements, he must be assuming independent, subjective labor, otherwise exclusive individual dominion would not be implied. Individualism is therefore critical in Locke's formulation of the right to property at a premonetary stage of nature.

Ewald challenges Unger's ascription of individualism to classical liberals. Unger defines individualism as a condition in which "[a] group is simply a collection of individuals . . . [T]he whole is just the sum of its parts."[27] Ewald contends that the imputed principle "is vague to the point of emptiness" and that there is "no justification for attributing it to any influential thinker who actually existed."[28] Yet we do find this individualism in Locke's premonetary state of nature. Creating distinct titles by independent labor and justifying dominion by the separateness of stomachs exemplify Unger's principle.

The acts of creating property in the state of nature go on in a context of natural law obligations. Men create rights of property while they carry out their natural law obligations to provide for their own subsistence. This does not, however, preclude the idea that labor is the proximate source of natural titles. Ashcraft overemphasizes natural law sources of property right when he writes, "It is not the individual's labour that gives him a 'right' to the property it produces. . . ."[29] For the text expressly and repeatedly states that it can: "Man . . . had still in

27. Unger 1975, p. 81.
28. Ewald 1988, p. 682.
29. Ashcraft 1987, p. 130.

himself the great foundation of property."[30] And, "*Labour . . . gave a Right of Property.*"[31] The creation of property by labor is all in the details, so to speak. It is in the fact that Locke invokes the idea of mixing as a way of making something proper to a person; that he invokes the idea of making something proper to a person as a way of making it his property; and that he has to presume independent labor in order for all of this to cohere in a right of exclusive individual dominion. So one cannot "clear away this underbrush" of individualism, as Ashcraft proposes to do, without clearing away the theory.[32]

Even if carrying out natural law were sufficient for creating rights, and labor played a diminutive role, individualistic assumptions would have to be embedded in the natural law formulation in order for the latter to create property. Fulfilling natural law obligations can only create exclusive dominion if men do not share stomachs and do not form a compound productive subject, performing naturally collective labor. Though "God commanded Man . . . to labor," such a command could create property only because labor is independent activity (Locke 1963, p. 333, para. 32). If labor were conjoint activity of several souls, then one would have common property, not exclusive individual dominion. The theology cannot get to exclusive individual dominion simply from divine commands to subservient persons, but has to assume the subjective nature of need and the independent nature of labor. This gives individualism a degree of importance that qualifies the theological emphasis of Ashcraft, Riley, and Tully.

UNEQUAL PROPERTY AND NATURAL LAW PROVISOS

Natural law, which of course is a matter of divine law, bounds property and inequality in Locke's account (Locke 1963, p. 335, para. 36). The law of nature limits each man to the enjoyment of what he can use without spoilage (Locke 1963, p. 332, para. 31). This assures the fulfillment of a second proviso, that he leave "enough, and as good" for the use of others (Locke 1963, p. 335, para. 36). Some scholars, such as Schlatter, hold that the natural law qualifications make Locke's theory egalitarian.[33] However, the account permits considerable inequalities of property even at the premonetary stage, because the proviso to leave "enough

30. Locke 1963, para. 44, pp. 340–341; see also para. 28, p. 330; para. 27, p. 329.
31. Ibid., para. 45, p. 341; emphasis in the original.
32. Ashcraft 1987, p. 127.
33. Schlatter 1951, p. 157; Lakoff 1964, p. 93. On Locke's juridical egalitarianism, see Dunn 1969, p. 112.

and as good" does not oblige men to bring about an equal distribution of property. Within the natural law boundaries, acts of labor can create unequal property and "different degrees of Industry were apt to give Men Possessions in different Proportions" (Locke 1963, p. 343, para. 48). These titles derive from the fact that some individuals mix their *independent, subjective* labor with more things and land than others do. Individualistic considerations are decisive in the creation of unequal titles.

Since the condition of distribution at the premonetary stage of nature is one of unequal property, we can infer that inegalitarian labor-based natural rights are most important in Locke's account, for they have outweighed the influence of egalitarian natural law provisos.

One should not, however, minimize the egalitarianism of the natural law provisos that assure equal availability of the major nonhuman factor of production, land, and to key consumption goods, fruit and animals. If premonetary property were as important as monetary property, and if natural law had as potent effects upon a monetary condition as on a premonetary one, then theological and natural law arguments would be central elements in Locke's discussion. Neither of these presumptions of revisionist Locke scholarship is warranted, however. Theological egalitarianism pales before individualistic inegalitarianism in Locke's monetary state of nature, because the right to monetary inequalities is more realistic and covers more of the wealth of society than does the bounded right to subsistence goods. The greater importance and realism of property in the monetary condition, and of individualistic considerations in it, give individualism greater overall importance in the theory.

DISTRIBUTIVE JUSTICE AT A MONETARY STAGE OF NATURE

At the monetary stage, common ownership of the world's resources and natural law limits on use do not assure a moderately equal distribution of property. The monetary state of nature is one of widening disparities. "And as different degrees of Industry were apt to give men Possessions in different Proportions, so," Locke writes, "this Invention of Money, gave them the opportunity to continue to enlarge them" (Locke 1963, para. 48, p. 343). Locke says that money arises from the "tacit and voluntary consent" to the use of money (Locke 1963, p. 344, para. 50). "Disproportionate and unequal possessions" arise, in turn, from the use of money. So inequalities are leveraged in through the tacit consent to the use of money. These inequalities do not violate anyone else's rights and are "fair" (Locke 1963, p. 342, para. 46; p. 344, para. 50). Locke does not, however, explicitly state how *particular* titles to money are created. Using inference from what he does say, it will be useful to reconstruct what he might have said about the process of forming particular titles to money.

To gain a title to money one exchanges, for money, property previously obtained by mixing one's labor with something. Because one obtains the money by exchanging something that had been part of oneself, the title to money is derived from a natural right and is not merely a convention-based right. Moreover, Locke assumes the equivalence of monetary and labor values: labor is the "measure" of value (Locke 1963, p. 344). Titles to unequal sums of money arise through a series of derivations from natural titles to labor-produced goods. A person acquires unequal titles to money by repeatedly exchanging the products of his labor for more and more money.

Let us consider the fundamental structure of Locke's – or a Lockean – account of unequal titles to money. When someone exchanges produced goods for money, the money is equivalent to something that had been part of him. Money that one acquires through exchange is proper to oneself because it is obtained with an object that one had mixed one's labor with. It can only have this quality because labor is independent activity. Locke's rudimentary notion of the social division of labor was never operational in his work, because he did not fully crystallize it in his mind, contrary to Ritchie.[34] If one substitutes an assumption that laboring capacities are socially produced or socially interdependent, different conclusions follow. A person who mixed his labor with something would mix in the labor of others, who would then accrue an indirect entitlement to a share of the produced good; he would not create exclusive individual dominion. For Locke to come to the contrasting conclusion – *exclusive* titles to unequal amounts of money – he must be proceeding from the sale of exclusive natural titles created by acts of *independent* labor repeated over and over until unequal monetary wealth is accumulated.

Locke's justification for highly unequal holdings on individualistic grounds becomes an implied moral basis for his prohibition of government redistribution of property and, by subsumption, of any public effort to increase equality of ownership. Although Locke sanctions government regulation of property, he rules out public control or redistribution of property for public purposes: "the Prince or Senate, however it may . . . make Laws for the regulating of *Property* between the Subjects one amongst the other, yet can never have a Power to take

34. See Locke 1963, para. 43, p. 340; Ritchie 1894, p. 269.

themselves the whole or any part of the Subjects *Property*, without their consent" (Locke 1963, p. 407, para. 139). The prohibition on redistributory policies delegitimates any governmental policies to increase the equality of property holdings. Egalitarian redistribution requires a public agency to extract property from its owners through taxation and to use it for a public purpose, that is, for the goal of creating a more equal society, which would abrogate the owner's right of private use. Because the right of private use stems from titles gained by repeated acts of independent labor, the Lockean prohibition on egalitarian redistribution stems from moral entitlements built on independent labor.

Critics who accuse Macpherson of "inflicting" individualism on Locke sometimes miss the relevant kind of individualism.[35] They demonstrate that Locke's account does not use the individualistic notion of the rationality of unlimited desire. The absence of this form of individualism does not, however, disprove that Locke's formulation is individualistic; for a different type of individualism – independent labor – is present, and it serves as the decisive foundation for unequal titles to money.

The natural law provisos, based on theological arguments, remain valid at the monetary stage of nature. The spoilage proviso and the divine injunction to leave as much and as good for others are not transcended (Locke 1963, p. 342, para. 46, contrary to Macpherson 1962, p. 204). These provisos do not, however, keep inequality in check at the monetary stage because the use of money satisfies the second proviso not by limiting inequality but by increasing the general wealth of society. Greater disparities now prevail, Locke clearly states. Without being transcended, the natural law provisos are nonetheless exerting less influence on relative inequality at the monetary stage of nature. All that the provisos require is the use of money to prevent spoilage and to prevent encroachments on others' possessions, both of which are compatible with rising inequalities (Locke 1963, p. 342, para. 45). So accumulating monetary inequalities fulfills the natural provisos without limiting the extent of inequality. Moreover, there is a new factor of production on the scene, money-capital, that the natural law provisos do not effectively control, which provides an additional source of unchecked inequalities.

Now that natural law boundaries provide no effective limit on inequalities of monetary wealth, theological considerations possess considerably less significance in the account. The account of monetary inequalities is perhaps the most realistic and relevant part of Locke's the-

35. Dunn 1969, p. 262.

ory of property, and the minimal role of theological considerations at this point means that they cannot be central parts of Locke's theory of property. The dominant quality of distribution at the monetary stage of nature – enlargement of inequalities – is explained and justified by an argument grounded on individualistic considerations, which then are the crucially important features of the theory. Revisionist Locke scholarship aiming to establish that his theory is characterized by an ensemble of different "isms" seems to be balanced and moderate in approach, but it evidently underestimates the significance of individualism.

INEGALITARIAN DISTRIBUTIVE JUSTICE

Macpherson thought that Locke was inegalitarian because his theory subjects people to differential treatment. Different classes gain differential natural rights in relation to their greater or lesser rationality.[36] More recent analysts suggest, however, that Locke justifies unequal property entirely in accordance with the assumption of equal rational potential. The revisionist view is correct, I believe, because the large amount of inference and synthesis Macpherson needed to discern differential rationality indicates that it could not be Locke's dominant thesis. Shapiro judges Locke's theory of property to be egalitarian in a sense: "Locke's arguments provided many of the ideas that would become central to legitimating capitalist economic practices, not by . . . claiming the lower classes were incapable of rational behavior, as Macpherson claimed, but by . . . doing this in universalist and egalitarian terms."[37] Moreover, "Since for Locke all civil rights arise from the institutions geared to the preservation of man's natural rights, this egalitarian view of the subject infuses his entire political theory."[38] However, whether Locke's property theory is egalitarian or not depends on the criterion for egalitarianism in a theory. Applying a principle of equal treatment is not enough to make a theory egalitarian. Such a principle will call for equal treatment only insofar as the theory recognizes equalities in the nature of persons. A theory that uses a principle of equal treatment but conceives of few equalities, and sees mainly differences, delivers mostly differential treatment.

An egalitarian theory of property or distribution identifies the *kind* or *degree* of equality in the nature of persons that invokes an equal distribution of some portion of income. While Locke saw equal rational fac-

36. Macpherson 1962, pp. 232–238.
37. Shapiro 1986, p. 80–81.
38. Ibid., p. 89.

ulties as the basis for an equal right to property, he also believed that another dimension of the person is mainly differential in its bearing on distribution. In "different degrees of industry" Locke saw a moral warrant for "Possessions in different proportions," with few bounds at the monetary stage (Locke 1963, p. 343, para. 48). Differential labor is even more important in justifying unequal titles than the consent to the use of money, which merely authorizes, but does not create, titles to unequal amounts of money. The latter are created through sale of titles to goods acquired through differential labor.

It is by contrast to Locke's account, not by his example, that one can see how to construct an egalitarian theory. One can distinguish an egalitarian theory from an inegalitarian theory by the abstractness or concreteness of the equalities that are ascribed to the nature of persons as a basis for moral deductions about relative distribution. An egalitarian theory would not just posit that all persons have the capacity to labor, which, taken alone, could justify highly unequal incomes from different degrees of diligence. It would additionally conceive of concrete equalities in the composition of individuals' labor, productive capacities, and other faculties that would morally entail a more equal distribution of some part of social income or wealth.

Locke's ascription of the faculty of labor to everyone identifies an abstract equality among people. But his simultaneous ascription of differences in industriousness overlooks concrete equalities in the composition of individuals' labor. The peculiar combination of abstract equalities and concrete differences in Locke's theory of the person lead him to justify an equal right to highly unequal property in a monetary condition, which is the hallmark of an inegalitarian theory. Although Locke's theory treats men equally as far as it goes, it treats a very incomplete person equally, compared to what egalitarian theory would require.

Locke's theory has another feature that disqualifies it from being an egalitarian theory. One of the philosophical grounds that can invoke a principle of equal distribution of a portion of income is membership in a community. When common activity and a unity of purpose make a certain end possible, there is a moral basis for equally distributing the fruits of community. Locke's account of the state of nature posits the independence of labor and the separateness of men's purposes rather than common action and common purpose. In fact, the major point of Locke's exercise is to show that independent action for separate purposes can overcome the distributional implications of common ownership of the world. In this respect, Locke's account lacks a necessary presupposition for invoking a principle of egalitarian distribution.

Considerations of community do figure in the background of the analysis. Locke scrutinizes different kinds of labor, such as unequal partage, and decides which of them is more beneficial from the standpoint of the common life of mankind, not just the individual life. From Ashcraft's point of view, considerations of common purpose dominate in Locke's analysis:

> [A]ll natural rights are, for Locke, traceable to some specific obligation laid upon individuals by the Law of Nature. In this instance, the obligation – and hence the basis for their rights claim – is to preserve themselves by providing for their subsistence. Even this phrasing is too individualistic, for a better statement of the natural law obligation would be that everyone has a duty to provide for the subsistence of everyone else.[39]

One can, however, infer that considerations of community do not predominate in Locke's analysis. If they were the predominant part of his account, the analysis would have posited a principle of equal distribution of a portion of income. Locke knew that membership in a community warrants sharing, as is evident in his position that the common ownership of the Earth morally requires equal access to natural resources (Locke 1963, p. 331). But Locke denies any really significant community of action or purpose in the state of nature. The absence of a principle of equal partage is symptomatic and indicative of this fact. Any such principle gets derailed by the assumption that rights of property are generated by independent labor rather than by common actions, and by the assumption that persons take their pleasures independently because they don't share stomachs.

The divine injunction that a man should help his brother under conditions of severe privation qualifies property, but only in the case of "extream want" (Locke 1963, p. 206, para. 42). It does not require transfers to reduce inequality in the case of more moderate wants. Theological communitarian restrictions on property are comparatively weak, since their distributional implications are outweighed by the inegalitarian implications of the individualistic justification of natural rights. Because Locke's account subordinates the elements of common life that morally invoke egalitarian principles of distribution, his theory cannot be adjudged egalitarian in matters of distributive justice.

THEORY, THEOLOGY, AND INDIVIDUALISM

Theological considerations doubtless have an important presence in Locke's discussion. But to what extent are they part of a contribution to the theory of property, strictly speaking? Ashcraft advances:

39. Ashcraft 1987, p. 127; see also p. 36.

> [t]he general point . . . that, instead of focusing upon the declarative, naturalistic language of rights, we [should] view Locke's discussion of property in terms of the intentional language of divinely instituted obligations . . . Lockean natural rights are always the active fulfillment of duties owed to God . . . [T]hese rights are never simply posited as logical inferences based upon any set of empirical observations concerning "the nature of man."[40]

Downgrading the primacy of individualism, Shapiro pronounces that the theological emphasis called for by the Dunn–Tully–Riley–Ashcraft view is now established, and he accepts it "as conclusive."[41]

However, a proponent of the theological interpretation makes a stunning concession that can unravel a large part of the revisionist project. Ashcraft observes that the use of money at a monetary stage of nature "has no direct authorization by natural law or a command of God."[42] Accumulated monetary inequalities acquire authorization instead from the tacit consent of men to the use of money. By implication, natural law and divine law have a much smaller role than do conventional or natural right at a monetary stage of nature. They are still there, but their effects on distribution are simply not as significant as they were at a premonetary stage of nature.

But the significance of Ashcraft's acknowledgement may go well beyond this. Titles to monetary inequalities have much greater theoretical validity than titles to the products of independent labor in a premonetary condition. Most real-world economies with which we are concerned, and with which Locke was concerned, are monetary economies. Most of the wealth in society is produced with a stock of money-capital or is exchanged for money. Under conditions of division of labor, most of the property possessed by a person will have been obtained through the use of money. This makes the titles to monetary inequalities far more realistic and more important than titles to the products of labor at a premonetary stage of nature. Since the natural law and divine injunctions do not particularly apply to the more valid and realistic form of property in Locke's account, they are distinctly less significant parts of his discussion, judged by the criterion of validity and realism.

Convention-based right and natural right have greater validity and application to real-world monetary economies and, in this sense, they form the major part of Locke's discussion. The consent-based justification of unequal amounts of money is grounded in subjective individual-

40. Ashcraft 1987, p. 135; see also pp. 126–127.
41. Shapiro 1986, pp. 108, 143–144.
42. Ashcraft 1987, p. 141.

ism. Consent is a condition in which the will of each person happens to agree with the will of all the rest. There is no social determination of will through social interaction or interdependence in Locke's account. Since the title to monetary wealth at a monetary stage of nature is perhaps the most important and realistic property right in Locke's entire discussion, and since it has an individualistic logical structure, individualism is a primary premise.

Ashcraft's acknowledgement that rights to monetary inequalities lack a theological basis does not lead him to moderate his stand on the centrality of theological considerations in Locke's account. Rights to monetary inequalities could not be as important as natural rights, he holds, because they are "nothing more than conventionally held rights," not natural rights.[43] They lack the absoluteness and unlimitedness of natural rights.[44]

Convention-based rights to monetary inequalities have, however, greater significance, absoluteness, unlimitedness, and naturalness than the revisionist view suggests. It can be difficult to draw a sharp line between a natural right to property and a convention-based right to monetary inequalities. Titles to money are suffused with natural rights claims because they derive from exchanges for natural rights–based properties, as shown previously. The money is equivalent to something that was part of himself, and the title to money is then equivalent to a natural right. Although we can not be certain that Locke thought this –because he did not explicitly discuss it – it would be consistent with his view on barter, where he says that labor-based titles are the basis for titles acquired through barter (Locke 1963, p. 343).

Titles to monetary inequalities gain a high ethical validation in another way, as well. Since the consent to money, which morally authorizes these inequalities, is given in the state of nature, they have a prepolitical ethical validity in Locke's account. Issuing from natural consent, rights to monetary inequalities have some of the absoluteness and unlimitedness possessed by natural rights. As products of natural consent, rights to monetary inequalities should not be abrogated or limited by legislative enactments, any more than a natural right could be. Their range of application is unlimited, as a natural right is, because their prepolitical ethical validity means that they should be respected by any actual civil government. As already noted, individualism is at the basis of the rights to monetary inequalities. The consent to money is voluntary, which is an

43. Ibid., p. 139.
44. Ibid.

individualistic basis for rights. As the basis for rights with considerable absoluteness and unlimitedness, individualism founds some of the most important rights in Locke's account.

A focus on Locke's theology of property would be warranted in a history of theologies of property, in an intellectual biography of a seventeenth-century mind, in a study of the development of the liberal ideology of rights, or in a study tracing Locke's influence on other liberal thinkers. In an account of Locke's contribution to the *theory* of property, strictly speaking, however, it may not form a large part. To suppose that it did would involve a misconstrual of the nature of the theory of rights. Such a theory has to assume, first, a subject of rights capable of exercising rights and, second, a subject with supreme ethical worth, otherwise he or she could become the property of another. These criteria, in turn, presuppose a self-determined subject, who, however, could be construed either as a socially or as a subjectively constituted agent, depending on whether self-determination is formed through a subjective or a social process. Rights are authorizations for certain kinds of exercise of free will, and they cannot be exercised unless the subject has the capacity for self-determination, which is, then, a necessary premise for the theory of rights.

In their natural law form, Locke's theological arguments for rights do not meet the foregoing requirements for a theory of rights. Locke's rights of property are created by human actions that are externally determined by God's command: "He that in obedience of this command of God, subdued, tilled and sowed any part of it [the earth], thereby annexed to it something that was his property . . ." (Locke 1963, p. 333, para. 35). The wants impelling men to labor are divine interpositions, and titles to property produced by labor represent the fulfillment of divine purpose. The divine injunctions are imperious forces that penetrate the individual ("God Commanded, and his Wants forced him to labour") and are not merely external restrictions on an inwardly free and self-choosing being as some have supposed of Locke's theory (Locke 1963, p. 334, para. 35; see also p. 324, para. 22). These features of Locke's theory are inconsistent with the self-determination required by the theory of rights. As Winfield writes, "Since His commands are laws of nature, they have a necessity quite unlike human laws on which justice must depend. If they are laws of nature in the sense of operative rules of necessity, there is no justice in conforming to them, since no choice is involved."[45] Since natural law arguments do not meet the requirements of the theory of rights, they should not be taken as the central part of Locke's contribution to

45. Winfield 1990, pp. 21–22.

the theory of property. Locke's treatments of natural rights and convention-based rights assume a self-determined subject, and they therefore satisfy the requirements of the theory of rights. Consequently, they comprise his contribution to the theory or property. Since the natural rights and convention-based accounts of rights are fundamentally individualistic, as we have seen, individualism is the major underpinning for Locke's contribution to the theory of property, strictly speaking.

Locke's entire discussion of natural law does not, however, have to be bracketed as nontheoretical, because natural law is also the law of reason in Locke's account (Locke 1963, p. 311, para. 6). The law of reason constitutes a theory of rights because it offers reasons for obeying natural laws rather than simply laying down divine commands. Because of its equivalence with the law of reason, natural law shares the individualism predominant in the law of reason, which assumes "independent" beings (Locke 1963, p. 311; p. 332, para. 31). The individualism of the law of reason gets carried into the law of nature to the extent that the latter law is equivalent to the former law.

LOCKE AND OTHER CLASSICAL LIBERALS

Scholars frequently maintain that Hobbes was more of a social theorist than Locke and that Rousseau's approach was both more social theoretical and more egalitarian. In his book *Montesquieu and Rousseau,* Durkheim depicted Rousseau as a founder of modern social theory. David P. Levine more recently has done for Hobbes what Durkheim did for Rousseau, bringing out Hobbes's important contribution to the theory of the social constitution of the self and of property.[46] Many scholars emphasize the strong egalitarian thrust in Rousseau, and thereby distinguish him from Locke. Thus Cobban writes: "his theory of property differs from Locke's in that it is modified by the ideal of equality."[47] If these interpretations are correct, then Locke's individualism and inegalitarianism are not typical, but a variant of a more diverse classical tradition. Using Locke to represent that tradition would then give a misleading impression of classical liberalism.

Commentators are correct that some liberals have a social concept of the person, but they often overlook the fact that such liberals frequently use that concept not in the analysis of property or of inequalities under property right, but in other parts of their formulations. Notwithstanding the views of Levine, Durkheim, and others, I believe that within

46. Levine 1978–1981, vol. 1, pp. 201, 34; Levine 1977, Chapter 1, pp. 3–31.
47. Cobban 1964, p. 132.

Hobbes's and Rousseau's theories of property, individualistic and inegalitarian elements are crucial to the principle of relative distribution of property. The individualistic features of Hobbes's and Rousseau's analyses account for the deduction of a property right subsuming a right to highly unequal amounts of income in both cases. Placing Locke in the context of the individualism and inegalitarianism of other classical liberals helps us to understand the truly classical nature of his thinking about property.

Hobbes contributed greatly to the development of a social theory of property through the idea that property is created by reciprocal recognition of right in acts of exchange and contract. Yet the social origin of property does not bear significantly on his account of distribution of property. Hobbes's conclusion that unequal amounts can be justly owned implicitly follows from two individualistic assumptions: one, that contracts are formed through the voluntary actions of independent individuals, and two, that value is produced by individual productive activities.

Hobbes's theory of property rights is a rudimentary form of Hegelian theory of the creation of property through relations of reciprocal recognition of right. Property is created in Hobbes's account through the renunciation of the natural right to everything. "And when a man has in either manner [renunciation or transfer] abandoned or granted away his right," writes Hobbes, "then he is said to be OBLIGED or BOUND not to hinder those to whom such right is granted or abandoned."[48] Renunciation of the natural right to everything is tantamount to creation of property through reciprocal recognition, though it grasps the latter merely in a negative and preliminary fashion. One might suppose that there is in this account a social theory of the right to own unequal amounts of value. But such an interpretation would be off the mark.

In trying to understand Hobbes's account, we must ask, why if property is created by joint action may there be a differential distribution of value among the members of the system of exchangers? One can, I think, infer that the jointness of action creating property drops out of Hobbes's mind. The individualistic elements latent in the account come to the fore, where they are the operative factors in determining his moral judgment about distribution. For, if the jointness of property-creating action were still influencing Hobbes's judgment, one would have expected that he would have considered the moral possibility of equal distribution of some wealth. Cognizance of common action would have invoked considerations of the principle of equal distribution. But Hobbes does not

48. Hobbes 1958, p. 111.

attend to such considerations. We know that Hobbes instead gave moral approbation to highly unequal accumulations. So what in Hobbes's account, except for the individualistic elements, could account for the moral affirmation of ownership of unequal amounts of wealth? The individualistic elements of voluntary agreement to the terms of exchange and individual production of objects are the factors that implicitly move Hobbes to accept unequal distribution. Hobbes justified unequal returns to members of corporations in proportion to the extent of individual participation: "every man may . . . participate of the gain according to the proportion of his adventure."[49] In his account, the priority of individual adventure to the fact of group action accounts for the legitimation of unequal distribution. Contrary to Ewald, then, Unger is to some extent right that in liberal property theory as represented by Hobbes, "[a] group is simply a collection of individuals . . . [T]he whole is just the sum of the parts."[50] The notion that a liberal theory may be "individualistic" in the sense defined by Unger is therefore not "empty";[51] it has a decisive impact on the morality of unequal distribution in Hobbes. The only modification that needs to be made with regard to Unger's view is that there is a genuinely social account of the creation of property in Hobbes, though not of the principle of just distribution of property.

When Hobbes formulates the provisions of property bearing upon distribution, he does not take into account the fact that property can be created only by reciprocal recognition. Distribution of wealth is determined by the terms of exchange to which voluntary exchangers agree.[52] In this way, the just distribution of income, for Hobbes, reduces to the distribution accepted by the choices of the agents involved. The property created by joint action of contract is not factored into the moral calculus of distribution. If one were to take into account the fact that property is created by joint action, then one would also consider the egalitarian moral implications for distribution that are attendant upon common action. In sum, Hobbes's theory of distribution of property exhibits as its fundamental structure, subjective personality cum unequal property – notwithstanding some exceptional contributions to social theory.

Considered from the standpoint of the theory of democracy and the theory of the state, Rousseau is certainly one of the greatest social liber-

49. Ibid., p. 186.
50. Unger 1975, p. 81.
51. Ewald 1988, p. 682.
52. Hobbes 1958, p. 79.

als. But in *The Social Contract* Rousseau conceives of property as a right of first occupancy, which is one of the most primitively individualistic notions of property ever propounded in the history of liberal thought.[53] The occupancy theory of property confers a right of exclusive individual dominion on the basis of the idea that two people cannot occupy the same space. Social production forms no part of the theoretical basis for entitlement and distribution in Rousseau's theory of property.[54] Basing property on first occupancy makes Rousseau no more a social theorist of property than William Blackstone was. Rousseau qualifies the right of first occupancy by the right of just possession, a seemingly more egalitarian principle that can limit certain economic inequalities arising on the basis of first occupancy. Yet this right is only invoked on an extraordinary basis, as a condition for precluding the extreme case of the Spanish king engrossing the whole "universe."[55] While ruling this out, just possession leaves extremely wide lattitude for unequal accumulations under property right.

However social and egalitarian Hobbes and Rousseau may be in their theories of the state and civil society, one cannot characterize these thinkers primarily as social egalitarians when it comes to property right. They hue closely to the individualistic inegalitarianism of the liberal vision of property in Locke, whose work on property typifies the classical approach to property.

CONCLUDING REMARKS

This chapter has rehabilitated, on some new grounds, the old proposition that individualism is a central part of Locke's theory of property, and especially of the distributional implications of the theory. It has cast doubt on revisionist interpretations of the theory either as predominantly theological or as an ensemble of different arguments.

The analysis has demonstrated that, in a premonetary stage of nature, Lockean titles to unequal possessions derive from the fact that some individuals mix their *autonomous* labor with more things and land than others do. In this respect, inegalitarian distributional implications of

53. Rousseau 1967, Chapter 10.
54. For a concurring view, see Winfield 1990, p. 23. Levine correctly notes a conception of social production in Rousseau, but I would emphasize that it is not particularly utilized by Rousseau in formulating his property theory; see Levine 1978–1981, vol. 1, p. 202.
55. Rousseau 1967, pp. 19–20, 21.

autonomous labor outweigh egalitarian distributional implications of theological premises. The analysis has also demonstrated that, at Locke's monetary stage of nature, individuals derive titles to unequal wealth through exchange for titles gained by mixing their autonomous labor with more or fewer things than others do. The fact that these titles are not significantly limited by natural law provisos limits the significance of theological considerations. It was shown that a major proponent of the theological emphasis in Locke scholarship has acknowledged that Lockean titles to monetary inequalities have no authorization in natural law or divine commands. Since individualistic considerations underlie these titles, and since titles to monetary inequalities are among the most important rights in Locke's theory, I conclude that individualistic considerations do play a central role in Locke's account. Though theological elements also play a role, they are not genuinely theoretical arguments, and thus they are not strictly speaking part of Locke's contribution to the theory of property. Moreover, the role of individualism is not limited to Locke's discussion of the substance of the right of property. It has wider significance, figuring prominently in Locke's accounts of the subject of right, the general justification of property, and the purpose of property as well. As such, individualism is not simply one of an ensemble of premises; it permeates the entire theory of property.

This analysis has challenged the revisionist view that Locke can be considered an egalitarian theorist in the matter of distribution. His argument does treat people equally, but the important point is that the equal treatment is not very thoroughgoing, judging from the standpoint of what an egalitarian theory would require. The reason for this is that Locke's theory does not conceive of the kinds of equalities in the nature of persons that morally entail more equal distribution of income and wealth. An egalitarian theory would involve conceiving of more concrete equalities in the composition of individual's economic capacities and attributes, and on this basis would invoke a more egalitarian distribution than Locke's theory requires.

Finally, this analysis has offered a different view of the sources of inequality in Locke's theory than that advanced by a recent study of the foundations of inequalities in theories of rights. The crucial determinant of Locke's inegalitarian position on distribution is not his use of a special rights justification of property rather than a general rights justification. Rather, it has to do with the personological assumption of individualism incorporated into both his special and his general rights justifications.

4

Unequal Property and Individualism, Kant to Rawls

Many late eighteenth- through twentieth-century liberal theorists are found to be social theorists, not just adherents of individualism, by commentators. If such an interpretation is intended to apply to liberal theories about the distribution of property, it would seem that commentators have not looked at the premises that guide those theories' conclusions about relative distribution.

KANT'S THEORY OF PROPERTY

For most seventeenth-century political theorists, the concept of the self-determined person, an individual largely formed independently of others, legitimates the "right" to unequal property distribution. Does this concept continue to dominate in the next important phase of liberal thought on property and distribution, the eighteenth- and early nineteenth-century metaphysical school of jurisprudence launched by Kant, particularly in *The Metaphysical Elements of Justice* (1797)? Or does it give way to a social concept of the person – that is, a concept of the person as self-determined only insofar as he or she is constituted by and within a system of individuals?

Private Right

The theory of property Kant wants to construct would explain how something can belong objectively, universally, and truly to "me," the subjective individual.[1] For Kant, something is not simply mine because I think it is, but also because other individuals choose the institution of

1. Kant 1887 [1796], p. 61.

property, which then reflects the free will of others. If they do choose it, then the external thing can be regarded as mine by the social order – that is, my ownership can gain social recognition.[2] Moreover, if the opinions of others are merely arbitrary and the institution of property is not compatible with their freedom, despite having been chosen by them, then the thing will not be truly my property because something can be mine at all times and circumstances only if my ownership is an ethically valid right, which requires that ownership be in accordance with the freedom of each and all.

The objectivity and universality Kant claims for his form of property may seem to be at odds with a subjective individualist theory, but the persons in his theory who reason about the right to property do not have the characteristics of socially constituted beings. Since Kant's concept of valid property depends on the premise of self-determined, autonomous persons, his theory is fundamentally a subjective individualist one.

Kant explains that the person gains rightful possession of things through a "connection" between him and his possessions: "Anything is '*mine*' by right, or is rightfully mine, when I am so connected with it, that if any other person should make use of it without my consent, he would do me a lesion or injury."[3] Whereas Locke conceives of a physical "mixing" between owners and possessions, Kant postulates a mental connection as the moral ground legitimating entitlement. For Kant, all possession is intellectual.

In Kant's theory it is not only connection that explains why something belongs to only one person, but also the premise underlying connection. The premise is a subjective person (a discrete being unconnected to other persons). We can infer this from Kant's discussion in which the lesion that would be caused someone by extracting his or her possessions provides the rationale for exclusive dominion. This consideration justifies exclusivity only because the injury to a person hurts that person alone, and the harm is limited to that person because the person is presumed to be autonomous. Something is connected exclusively to a person only because he or she is autonomous. By contrast, a person with an intersubjective inner structure would be intellectually connected to other persons, who would accrue indirect entitlements to the thing through their connection to the subject in question. Subjective personality is crucial to Kant's concept of exclusive individual dominion, because it accounts for the monological relation between person and thing. Hence it is also crucial to his authorization of unequal property on the basis of connection, for only a subjective person can have exclusive ownership

2. Ibid. 3. Ibid.

rights unencumbered by others' indirect entitlements. A person acquires *more* property than another person by connecting himself or herself to more things than another person does. But the act of connecting is not the only thing that explains rights to *unequal* property; the premise of subjective personality also explains them. It is the connecting of a *subjective personality* to more things that creates the exclusive title to unequal amounts of things and value. If the person were an intersubjective personality, intellectually linked to other personalities, then the unequal amounts of things that the person is connected to would be indirectly connected to those others, giving rise to indirect entitlements or common property.

Differences between Kant's and Locke's theories of property seem to suggest that liberalism is marked more by diversity than by commonality.[4] The two philosophers differ about the activity that creates titles (laboring versus willing), the logic of entitlement (mixing versus connecting), and the nature of the connection (physical versus intellectual). However, since profound similarities underlie their differences and lead to the same basic conclusions about property, commonality actually overwhelms diversity. Locke and Kant make remarkably similar assumptions about the owners of property, postulating, in particular, subjective persons. In Locke's theory, labor is just personality considered from a dynamic point of view – personality and will in action. One gains ownership of a thing by mixing one's labor with it, so that it becomes part of oneself, just as in Kant's theory one gains property by a thing's connection to oneself. One connection is to the person considered dynamically, the other to the person taken statically. But in both cases it is the connection to a subjective personality – the person in action or the self proper – that confers property or unequal property. Mixing and connecting are virtually interchangeable bases of entitlement. Locke's idea of things being "part of" one or "mixed with" one's labor has much in common with Kant's notion of "connection" to a person: "part of" means integral to, while "connect" means join or unite with. Most important, the shared premise of a subjective personality gives rise in both accounts to a high degree of exclusive individual dominion and titles to highly unequal amounts of things.

After formulating the logic of gaining titles to external possessions, Kant addresses the justification of property. In his view, to deny that anything could rightfully belong to a person contradicts the principle of right by conflicting with freedom of will. If property is disallowed, he argues, "freedom would so far be depriving itself of the use of its vol-

4. For example, Donahue, Kauper, and Martin 1974, p. 262.

untary activity, in thus putting *usable* objects out of all possible *use*."[5] Here, strictly speaking, freedom is construed as the use of *will*, not of objects, and the use of objects is involved only insofar as it is a use of will. Moreover, Kant's notion of the person's "use of . . . voluntary activity" with respect to things stresses the unconditioned quality of will and the absence of external agencies conditioning action.[6] The implication is that the will is fully formed prior to its relation to things and social conditions, that it is simply awaiting its own discretionary impulse to relate to them rather than being in some way constituted through relating to them. Property is thus held to be consistent with freedom and right because it is consistent with subjective will and subjective personality.

There must be not only property, according to Kant, but private property. Unless the common possession is broken into private possessions, things are "unappropriable" as objects of self-will.[7] The will of others must be "interdicted" and suspended with reference to one's things if possessions are to be subject solely to one's autonomous will.[8] For the will cannot be a will, a power of self-determination, unless it is free from external determinants. So far as the property of individuals is concerned, only private property that is unencumbered by indirect entitlements accords with Kant's notions of right and freedom, since these assume pure, subjective self-determination.

Public Right

Some recent scholars dispute the claim that Kant's principle of property distribution stems ultimately from individualistic premises. New analysis challenges both current communitarian commentators who impute a conception of "an antecedently individuated subject" to Kant's theory of justice"[9] and libertarians, from Humboldt to Hayek, who have allegedly "misappropriated" Kant's work as the moral foundation for a night watchman state permitting unlimited inequality in the distribution of property.[10] The traditional individualistic, inegalitarian image of Kant's theory is giving way to the view that Kant takes an intersubjectivist approach to the defense of a welfare state. Kaufman, for example, holds

5. Kant 1887 [1796], p. 62.
6. Ibid. 7. Ibid., p. 69.
8. Ibid. Kant writes, "by Right (*jure*) he resists every other person who would hinder him in the private use of it" with the aid of juridical means when public law exists.
9. See Kaufman 1999, p. 3.
10. See Kaufman 1999, p. 1 (on Hayek 1976, p. 43; and on Humboldt 1969 [1852]).

that Kant's theory of property and distributive justice is grounded not on individualistic premises but on intersubjective judgements: "Kantian political judgment . . . generates an account . . . grounded in the intersubjective judgments of members of the community (the *sensus communis*)."[11] Moreover, these judgments, scholars have recently maintained, are not inegalitarian but support redistributory measures, such as the welfare state's assistance to the poor.[12]

Although the new scholarship deserves credit for recognizing intersubjective judgments in Kant's theory of justice, these are not the *ground* on which he derives a principle of just distribution of property. Moreover, although intersubjective judgments play a role in Kant's apparent justification of the welfare state, his theory continues to authorize a highly unequal distribution of property on the basis of individualistic premises. Intersubjective judgments do not decisively determine the principle of just distribution of property; they could support either a highly unequal or a relatively equal distribution, depending on other considerations. The intersubjective judgments are merely mediating factors; individuals participating in these judgments reason about individualistic considerations and factors, and it is these factors that point their reasoning toward support of highly unequal distribution. Kant's account of intersubjective judgments pushes the highly individualistic factors into remote parts of his argument, but from this vantage point they ultimately determine his principle of unequal distribution of property.

According to Kant, property can exist only through the united will of all individuals in a civil society.[13] It is merely provisional in the state of nature, for when another person denies one's claim to ownership, possession is insecure.[14] Guaranteed possession depends, then, upon "a collective, universal (common) . . . Will."[15]

The general will is not only a necessary condition for property but also the agency that selects the principle of distribution, for notions of right and justice must reflect a general consensus, in Kant's view.[16] Selection, however, does not mean that the principle is founded on inter-

11. Kaufman 1999, p. 3.
12. Ibid., pp. 1–35.
13. Kant 1965, p. 65. In preparing this account of Kant's derivation of just distribution I found Kaufman's exegesis illuminating, for he brings out some elements of the *Rechtslehre* that were previously not well understood (Kaufman 1999, pp. 135–156). However, I come to a different assessment of the balance of intersubjective judgment and individual choice in Kant's account.
14. Kant 1965 [1797], pp. 64, 65.
15. Ibid., p. 65. 16. Ibid., p. 78.

subjective judgment. It depends, rather, on the kinds of considerations – social and individual – that guide the general will's reasoning about just distribution.

In setting the rules of property, the general will is not licensed to do just as it pleases but is obligated to conform to ideals of justice, that is, to shape the rules in order to bring about a rightful condition of civil society. In itself, that constraint leaves the general will leeway to ground the rules on either intersubjective or individualistic premises, depending on whether Kant construes a just society as founded on independently formed agencies or on socially constituted agencies.

The sovereign in Kant's analysis is the "person" of the general will. He, she, or it (in the case where sovereignty is vested in the legislature) carries the authority of supreme proprietor (of the land).[17] In deriving this authority, Kant reasons that the rules of distribution cannot be established by the unilateral will of one person, because a single will lacks the moral authority to bind everyone else. Only rules determined by a general will have that power. To design and carry them out, the sovereign needs to have supreme proprietorship. In this capacity, he, she, or it represents "the necessary unification of the private property of all the people under a public general possessor."[18]

This authority should not be confused with collective ownership in the usual sense of the term. As the common general possessor, the sovereign "possesses nothing," and so he (or she or it) does not have license to do as he (or she or it) pleases with property. Supreme proprietorship is, rather, the authority to distribute property: "All land belongs to the people . . . not collectively but . . . distributively."[19] The sovereign apportions property to each citizen according to a principle of division, not of aggregation from the individual to the whole.

Kant thinks that a just division of property strives toward social transformation.[20] The sovereign should not assume the justice of existing property holdings, but should distribute property to bring about a rightful condition of society. This transformation, of course, requires some criterion for determining the rightness of one distribution over another. The basis for judgment must be derived, not from given attributes peculiar to individuals at a particular time and place, but from the essential quality of all persons, their humanity – that is, their power of self-determination, their "independence from the constraint of another's will."[21] This quality gives every citizen an innate right to freedom,

17. Ibid., p. 90. 18. Ibid. 19. Ibid.
20. As Kaufman points out; see Kaufman 1999, p. 144–145.
21. Kant 1965 [1797], pp. 43–44.

and this equal right, in turn, makes citizens equal members of a just society.

Citizens' equal entitlement to freedom implies that the rightful condition of society is one in which individuals have an equal opportunity to achieve their self-defined purposes, but this condition does not morally require equal outcomes for all.[22] Though obligated to avoid creating unequal access to opportunity, the sovereign may authorize an extremely unequal distribution.

Since the right to equal opportunity is indicated by the right of citizens to define and seek their own ends, the sovereign should allow unequal distributions to arise from different choices of occupation. As Kaufman acknowledges, "The choices made by individuals determine the actual pattern of distribution of resources."[23] If choice is the basis of Kant's principle of just distribution, then it cannot be true that Kant grounds redistribution on intersubjective judgment, for this formulation is indistinguishable from Nozick's maxim: "From each as they choose, to each as they are chosen," which is the quintessential individualistic inegalitarian standpoint.[24] Although the members of Kant's society collectively favor rightful property distribution, they recognize that this distribution, because of their separate and different purposes, need not be equal. Thus Kant's principle of distribution of property rests on individualistic assumptions rather than on intersubjective judgments.

Kaufman interprets the foundations differently, and he suggests that Kant's justification for highly unequal property distribution arises not from individualistic premises but from a holistic argument. The transformation of holdings proceeds, Kaufman suggests, in accordance with a "notion of society as a self-organized entity" that represents "individual members of society . . . as parts which are reciprocally cause and effect of the whole."[25] But Kant is assuming that individuals set their own distinctive ends and pursue them at their own initiative – not a particularly holistic assumption. And so it is individualistic factors that underlie Kant's view that unequal distribution is the just principle of distribution of property.

Kant does not believe in, nor does he contemplate, the kind of foundations that would support a social theory of distribution of property. He does not take into account that the members of the economy may have overarching common ends, a possibility that could have different

22. Kaufman 1999, p. 147.
23. Ibid., p. 151.
24. Nozick 1974, p. 160; emphasis removed.
25. Kaufman 1999, pp. 147, 146.

moral implications. If individuals will the same economic end (capital or wealth) and pursue it through some common action (a partially cooperative system of capital-based economic relations), then respecting and protecting their self-defined ends would entail some equalization of outcomes. Kant fails to consider this hypothesis because he does not believe that the requisite commonality can exist. "Men have different views on the empirical end of happiness," he writes, "so that as far as happiness is concerned, their will cannot be brought under any common principle."[26] Although he sees society in part as a self-organized entity, he does not discern any processes of reciprocal causation that could give rise to shared economic ends warranting some equality of outcomes.

PROPERTY IN UTILITARIAN JURISPRUDENCE

Bentham justifies property in terms of individual utility and a social principle of general utility. His analysis begins with the famous pronouncement that property is socially determined. The shape of property and the security of property, he says, are entirely the work of law.[27] Possession, "which, in the natural state, was an almost invisible thread, in the social state becomes a cable."[28] On the basis of this statement, many commentators reject the ascription of individualism to liberal theories of law. But denials of individualism in Bentham reveal a superficial understanding of what a social theory of law entails. The portion of the "cable" of individualism that runs through his work is made of steel, not of rope.

In shaping property, there is no hint that the Benthamite legislator sees knowledge about the social composition of the individual as something important to take into account. The term "social" in Bentham's analysis refers to property secured through a social agency (law), not to the social constitution of the person. Social determination is an external restriction on individuals already formed. It prevents them from attacking and destroying their fellows, but it does not contribute to their inner makeup as persons.

Bentham sees property as justified because it enables a person to expect to be able to use a thing for his or her own advantage or enjoyment. "The idea of property," he writes, "consists in an established expectation; in the persuasion of being able to draw such or such an advantage from the thing possessed. . . . I cannot count upon the enjoy-

26. Kant 1970, pp. 73–74.
27. Bentham 1871, pp. 109–110.
28. Ibid., p. 113.

ment of that which I regard as mine except through the promise of the law which guarantees it to me."[29] Justified as a condition for an "expectation" of enjoyment, property should be instituted and shaped to enhance this state of mind. It should be protected so that owners can advance their self-interest through independent activities that create things of subjective value.

In a philosophy whose first principle is utility, to define property as "an established expectation of advantage" implies an expectation of a favorable utility position, itself defined as a purely subjective evaluation. The rationale and justification for property refer, then, to the individual independent of any specified external determinant. In other words, property is justified because it is a necessary condition for autonomous activity for self-gain.

Given the subjective nature of property – the way it is used, the interest and purpose that it serves – individuals have a right to accumulate it in highly unequal amounts. Accumulation is one of the subjective uses of property. It is to an individual's advantage; it is the result of his or her activity; it pertains to his or her own enjoyment. Equalized distribution, which extracts things from their owners, should not be promoted, for it violates the expectation of gaining personal advantage and enjoyment from a thing.

In discussing property Bentham scarcely invokes the term utility, but the principle infuses his whole account. General utility is his sole ground for bestowing approbation on an institution.[30] Alternative grounds are held to be reducible to utility.[31] As already noted, property, for Bentham, secures the "expectation" of "enjoyment" from the use of a thing. Considered with respect to general utility, property is justified because it secures the aggregate of individual expectations and enjoyments. But the general utility of property simply reduces to the sum of its individual utilities, because the community is just the sum of individual interests: "The interest of the community is," Bentham writes, "one of the most general expressions that can occur in the phraseology of morals . . . when it has a meaning, it is this. The community is a fictitious *body*, composed of the individual persons who are considered as constituting as it were its *members*. The interest of the community then is, what? – the sum of the interests of the several members who compose it."[32] The

29. Ibid., p. 112.
30. Whether utility is actually the "sole ground of approbation we ever bestow" is a question set aside as speculative (Bentham 1970, p. 28).
31. Bentham 1871, p. 1.
32. Bentham 1970, p. 12; emphasis added.

social interest that property serves consists not in a sum of the interests of socially constituted persons but in the sum of subjectively formed utilities. Thus justification of property on the basis of general utility is deduced by aggregation from its contribution to subjective individual utilities.

Some scholars hold that utilitarian theories of property can be constructed on stronger social foundations, such as socially formed preferences.[33] But it would clearly be a mistake to impute such a notion to Bentham in his theory of property. If social influences on preferences figure significantly in his justification of property and distribution, why would he not list them among the considerations shaping his view of property? In fact, he explicitly denies such influences, lest anyone misapprehend the individual interest as objective and social rather than subjective.[34]

Liberal theories of property frequently invoke social interests, social grounds, and social principles to justify either property or restrictions on its use. But in so doing, as this analysis of Bentham indicates, they are often referring only to the totality of subjectively formed interests, not postulating the social constitution of individual interests.

The next major figure in utilitarian jurisprudence, John Austin, conceives of property in this way: "Taken with its strict sense it denotes a right – indefinite in point of disposition – and unlimited in point of duration – over a determinable thing." And,

> I mean by *property* . . . any right which gives the entitled party an indefinite power or liberty of using or disposing of the subject: or (in other words) which gives to the entitled party such a power or liberty of using or disposing of the subject as is not capable of exact circumscription; and is merely limited generally by the rights of all other persons, and by the duties (relative or absolute) incumbent on himself.[35]

Austin views the state and property law as necessary conditions for freedom of use. His concept of property begins, as Bentham's does, with a seemingly massive social determination of the individual, but it actually involves extreme postulates of subjective individuality. In authorizing indefinite use, the state presumes that individuals have an inner capacity for unlimited use, that they are autonomous agents or, to use a Lockean term, "self-proprietors" of their own faculties. Their power to use things originates within themselves, independent of others. The purposes to which property may be put are entirely subjective, incapable of

33. See Munzer 1990, pp. 219–224.
34. Bentham 1871, p. 18; see also Austin 1869, vol. 1, p. 162.
35. Austin 1869, vol. 2, pp. 817–818, 822.

exact circumscription. Accordingly, individuals must be granted extremely wide latitude in the disposition of things, and unequal accumulations are permissible because they are part of the right to unlimited use.

This argument assumes autonomous persons, for social determination of individual ends might produce a common end that *is* capable of exact circumscription. If the individual's freedom of use were social, and if people had to participate in some common action to make or use things, then others might be indirectly entitled to a share of what each individual accrues.

HEGEL'S THEORY OF PROPERTY

Hegel's "social" theory of property seems an improbable place to find unequal distribution of property justified by an argument founded upon subjective personality, but this liberal strand of reasoning has remarkable reach. Although Hegel formulated a theory of rights within the overall context of a great social theory of the person,[36] his social theory has less bearing on property right than one might suppose. Property right is largely deduced from residual individualistic premises. Contemporary scholars rightly regard Hegel as the founder of modern social theory, but law professors have traditionally remarked, also with good reason, that his property right is based on the pure subjectivity of abstract personality, rather than on socially constituted persons.[37]

Hegel regards conditions as rights if they are necessary for the existence of free will. Since he views property as essential to the objective freedom of the person, not to the existence of socially constituted persons, his reasoning does not qualify as social theoretical. "The rationale for property," he writes, "is to be found not in the satisfaction of needs but in the supersession of the pure subjectivity of personality."[38] For this reason, generations of law professors have seen Hegel's treatment – together with Blackstone's – as the exemplar of property as a dyadic relation between person and thing.[39]

The relation between Hegel's theory of property and his social theory is episodic, not dialectical. In reasoning about unequal distribution under property right, he occasionally incorporates significant social premises, but these are both preceded *and followed* by a dominating

36. Hegel 1952.
37. Cohen 1954, pp. 361–363.
38. Hegel 1952, add. to para. 41, pp. 235–236.
39. F. Cohen 1954, pp. 361–363.

combination of residual and explicit individualism. Property, for Hegel, is created through reciprocal recognition of rights between contracting parties. "Contract," he writes, "presupposes that the parties entering it recognize each other as persons and as property owners. . . . Contract brings into existence the property."[40] The notion of property created through mutual recognition is a revolutionary advance toward specifying property as a social condition, in contrast to Locke's theory, where property results from independent acts of appropriation and labor.[41] Yet the infusion of social theory is followed by a highly individualistic declaration that social considerations are irrelevant to relative distribution under property right: "If at this stage we may speak of more persons than one, although no such distinction has been made, then we may say that in respect of their personality persons are equal. But this is an empty tautology, for the person, as something abstract, has not yet been particularized or established as distinct in some specific way." And, "'Equality' is the abstract identity of the Understanding; reflective thought and all kinds of mediocrity stumble on it at once when they are confronted by the relation of unity to a difference. At this point, equality could only be the equality of abstract persons as such, and therefore the whole field of possession, this terrain of inequality, falls outside it."[42] Persons accrue rights, not because of what each wills, but because each has a will. The question of how much property a person can have is not even appropriate here, for as Hegel reminds us, the abstract personality and its contentless will have no relation to socially formed ends and aims. Undifferentiated by contrastive social relations, abstract personalities are identical, but this contentless equality of persons is not concrete enough to call for any equalization of possessions (things or money).

Although the analysis of property in abstract right militates against equality of resources and possessions, Hegel scholars have commented that in Hegel's theory "the property rights of individuals are always subject to higher classes of rights."[43] If the higher classes of rights include redistributory rights, then the Hegelian system could have significant egalitarian features. Some commentators understand Hegel to say that concrete needy individuals in civil society can morally entail redistributive entitlements, even though abstract personalities in the sphere of

40. Hegel 1952, para. 71, pp. 57–58.
41. Hobbes had a negative and implicit understanding of this 150 years earlier, but Hegel was the first to formulate it in a fully explicit and positive way.
42. Hegel 1952, para. 49, p. 44.
43. Donahue, Kauper, and Martin 1974, p. 264.

abstract right cannot do so. To some degree Hegel is open to this interpretation,[44] but he also contradicts it. Hegel uses the analysis of abstract right as an argument against equality with regard to resources and possessions. And to some degree, the analysis of abstract right precludes subsequent equalizations. Since one becomes entitled to property on the basis of abstract personality, not on the basis of needy individuality, the theory of abstract right forecloses, to a significant degree, the issue of entitlement; property, therefore, cannot be easily limited by later restrictions on unequal accumulations. As Hegel writes,

> Of course men are equal, but only qua persons, that is, with respect only to the source from which possession springs; the inference from this is that everyone must have property. . . . But this equality is something apart from the fixing of relative amounts, from the question of how much I own. From this point of view it is false to maintain that justice requires everyone's property to be equal, since it requires only that everyone shall own property.[45]

But since property rights are partially subject to higher classes of rights, one might argue that substantial redistribution could be authorized by Hegel's theory. This should not, however, obscure the fact that Hegel's analysis of civil society reinforces rather than undercuts the inequality that he previously found to be compatible with abstract right. Beyond the property right based on abstract personality, Hegel indicates, in both implicit and explicit ways, that concrete differences and concrete equalities in civil society can affect distributive justice.[46] The differentiation of mind through social relations warrants an unequal distribution of income. "The demand sometimes made for an equal division of land, and other available resources too," Hegel writes, "is an intellectualism all the more empty in that at the heart of particular differences there lies . . . the whole compass of mind, endlessly particularized and differentiated, and the rationality of mind developed into an organism."[47] Later in the analysis Hegel repeats that the conditions of civil society justify the inequalities that were earlier found to be compatible with abstract right. In his words,

> Men are made unequal by nature, where inequality is in its element, and in civil society the right of particularity is so far from annulling this natural inequality that it produces it out of mind and raises it to an inequality of skill and

44. In view of Hegel 1952, para. 217, p. 139.
45. Hegel 1952, add. 29 to para. 49, p. 237.
46. That concrete equalities among persons can affect distributive justice is *implied* by Hegel 1952, para. 49, p. 44. That concrete differences among persons can affect distributive justice is *explicitly* argued by Hegel.
47. Hegel 1952, para. 49, p. 44.

resources, and even to one of moral and intellectual attainment. To oppose to this right a demand for equality is a folly . . .[48]

This reasoning may suggest to some a sharp divergence from the individualism of traditional liberal theory. And to some it may warrant a new classification: social inegalitarian liberal. While such a classification may seem appropriate, it overemphasizes the role of social elements in Hegel's theory. Hegel seems to realize that socially formed concrete equalities between persons would morally entail some equalization of possessions,[49] and he does find socially formed "universals" among economic actors in civil society, not only differences between them.[50] But he does not bring these concrete equalities to bear on his reasoning about rules of relative distribution or property, where they might have justified a correlative equalization of resources. The omission or exclusion of this line of thought implies a recursion to the mean: subjective inegalitarian liberalism.

Hegel's deduction of a principle of unequal possessions from concrete social differences qualifies the thesis that liberal property theories can be characterized as individualistic inegalitarian. But his failure to endorse a principle of equalizing part of national income reflects residual individualistic inegalitarian ways of thinking. Hegel's property theory, therefore, suggests a hybrid category of individualistic cum social theoretical inegalitarianism.

PROPERTY IN EARLY TWENTIETH-CENTURY JURISPRUDENCE

One might expect the concept of the person in early twentieth-century property theory to be more social than the subjective personality postulated by Kant over a hundred years earlier. Kant's formulation was exceptionally pure. By the 1900s, presumably, liberals would have added Hegelian social philosophy and arrived at a more balanced view. To see whether this is so, let us consider Thomas Holland's *Elements of Jurisprudence*, a not-very-great work of theory that can, however, serve as a time capsule of liberal jurisprudence from the turn of the century.[51] The striking fact is that Holland's analysis has to be classified with the purest subjective personality theories of property.

Holland justifies property as an institution necessary for achieving a

48. Ibid., remark to par. 200, p. 130.
49. Ibid., para. 49, p. 44.
50. Ibid., para. 182, pp. 122–123; para. 185, p. 123; para. 194, p. 128; add. 116 to para. 182, p. 267; add. 123 to para. 192, p. 269; add. 120 to para. 189, p. 268.
51. Holland 1928, p. 207.

certain purpose: preventing one person from injuring another person to obtain his or her possessions.[52] This rationale simply reiterates Savigny's argument for property. In this argument, there is no property in the sense of a person's interest in a substance distinct from personality, but only property in the sense of an individual's interest in protecting personality from harm. Property, in this view, is not a distinct right, but rather is derived from a primary right of personhood. Someone injured by the forcible extraction of a possession is dealt a blow as an independent being formed prior to its relations to things. Holland is not speaking of a blow to an objective personality or to a socially constituted personality, one formatively related to things and other persons. His rationale for property is extreme in its assumptions of subjective personality, involving only the subjective personality's interest in itself, and not extending to the personality's interest in a substance distinct *from* itself.

Echoing earlier personality theorists, Holland views property as "an exten[sion]" of "personality" "over a wide circle of matter."[53] External things are subjectified and possess almost no independent reality. As the person absorbs things into the self, he or she has few substantive relations to other persons. Property is the subjection of things to a subjective personality that is formed prior to, or independent of, its relations to other persons. Property law provides external security for the personality's unlimited extension over the world of things, but social conditions and intersubjective features are not essential to, or constitutive of, personality, and therefore are not taken into account in the shaping of property right.

In Holland's theory, property subsumes the right of individuals to own highly unequal amounts. To redistribute property would limit individual personality by restricting its extension over the world of things. Since the realization of personality does not depend on other persons, there is no ground for limiting ownership for the sake of others, except to preserve their correlative right. No social basis exists for limiting inequalities by relative distribution.

PROPERTY AND "SOCIOLOGICAL" JURISPRUDENCE IN THE FIRST HALF OF THE TWENTIETH CENTURY

Roscoe Pound's five-volume treatise *Jurisprudence*, along with his other works, assures him "a pre-eminent place among the world's legal scholars, educators and philosophers" in the first half of the twentieth cen-

52. Ibid. 53. Ibid., p. 193.

tury.[54] For "65 years [Pound] . . . threatened to make American jurisprudence a one-man show,"[55] and he continues to be considered one of the foremost figures in "sociological jurisprudence."[56]

Nevertheless, while Pound raises questions about methodological individualism, it is precisely this approach that his concept of property represents. He justifies property not only as a necessary means of securing the individual "what he discovers and reduces to his power" and "what he creates by his own labor,"[57] but also as a condition for a particular subjective state of mind (the individual must be able "to control . . ."). The rationale for property has a subjective goal, to fulfill purposes beneficial to the individual. It is necessary to secure independent forms of use and creation, that is, for subjective acts of appropriation ("what he discovers and reduces to his power") and for the possession of subjectively created objects ("what he creates by his own labor").[58]

The underlying premises of subjectivism justify a right to highly unequal amounts of property. Given the assumption of independent labor, the individual can accumulate whatever amounts of property he can discover and reduce to his own power or create by his own labor. Things in his possession cannot be redistributed, because that would violate the purpose of property, to serve subjective goals.

Pound's logic closely resembles Bentham's. Where Bentham refers to the expectation of "advantage," Pound discusses control for one's own "benefit." Where Bentham refers to the security of expectations, Pound says the person must be able to control. Where Bentham says the individual alone draws the advantage from things, Pound holds that the individual "creates by his own labor." Thus one of the most advanced "sociological" theories of property in the first half of the twentieth century echoes the individualistic inegalitarian themes of Benthamite jurisprudence.

PROPERTY IN HOHFELDIAN JURISPRUDENCE

Arguing that every entitlement involves a correlative duty and a correlative exposure, Hohfeld redefines property in terms of "jural rela-

54. Evaluation by the publisher, West Publishing, Introduction to Pound, *Jurisprudence*, p. iii. One can, of course, expect an author's own publisher to be favorably disposed to him, but this view is shared by many other legal scholars.
55. Llewellyn 1962, p. 497.
56. According to a contemporary survey of his work; see McLean 1992.
57. Pound 1959, vol. III, p. 106.
58. Ibid., pp. 105–106.

tions."[59] Thus his jurisprudence seems to challenge the ascription of individualistic inegalitarianism to liberal theories. But in determining whether a theory of property is genuinely social, a critical issue is whether it takes into account the social formation of the individual or assumes a subjectively formed individual. Since Hohfeld says practically nothing about the composition of the individual, it is rather astonishing that his jurisprudence is widely considered to be a social theory.

When Hohfeld introduces the interpersonal notion of jural relations into mainstream property theory, he does not reformulate the liberal concept of the subjective person that prevails in jurisprudence of his day. Presumably, therefore, he assumes that individualism is a serviceable foundation. Moreover, some textual evidence also indicates that his social relations are between subjectively constituted individuals. In delineating person A's "legal interest" or "property," Hohfeld reiterates the traditional view of individual aims as mere matters of subjective discretion: "A has an indefinite number of privileges of doing on or to the land what he pleases . . ."[60]

Why is the constitution of the person critical in determining whether a theory qualifies as a social theory? A philosophy in which interpersonal connections do not affect the participants' nature, but merely form a superstructure on a substratum of individualism, is not basically social. Hohfeld's jurisprudence leaves the fundamental structure of liberal individualistic inegalitarianism intact and entails no changes in relative distribution under property right.

"RELATIONAL" PROPERTY IN MID-TWENTIETH-CENTURY AMERICAN JURISPRUDENCE

Karl Llewellyn, Robert Hale, Felix Cohen, and Leon Green are sometimes thought to have opened a new chapter in the history of American jurisprudence, in part because of their increased technical and conceptual sophistication but also because of their more explicit and thorough attention to social factors. By virtue of this emphasis, they have become known as the "relational" school. Viewed in light of these theorists, the subjective individualism of Pound might seem uncharacteristic of American jurisprudence in the first half of the twentieth century. Nevertheless, a reexamination of this school, as represented by F. Cohen, suggests that individualistic premises and inegalitarian conclusions are perpetuated in the relational period of American property theory.

59. Hohfeld 1923.
60. Hohfeld 1923, p. 96.

In his "Dialogue on Private Property" and in other works, Cohen develops a conception of "property as social relations."[61] He wants, first, to eradicate the nominalist view of property as merely a "collection of letters" and to establish a view of property as a real existent. Such a revision alters neither the traditional liberal assumptions of subjective individualism nor the entailment of unequal property. It maintains rather than shifts the paradigm. In a second refinement, Cohen recognizes such intangible possessions as the copyright to a song, a future interest, or a patent on a chemical process – intellectual assets excluded from the definition of property as an external object. His subtle reasoning about the *object* of property also leaves intact fundamental liberal beliefs about the *subject* of property and about this subjectively constituted person's moral implications for unequal property.

F. Cohen seeks, third, to refute the seminaturalism of Hegel's and Blackstone's view of property as a dyadic relation of person to thing. In redefining "property as social relations," however, he argues in generalities, as a typical passage shows: "property . . . always does involve relations between people. . . . I suggest we consider this as [a] tentative conclusion with respect to the nature of property. Property . . . is basically a set of relations among men."[62] In this formulation, the relations could be either those between subjectively constituted persons or those through which persons are constituted. Here again there is no substantive supersession of subjective individualism. If Cohen subscribed to a concept of social self-determined persons, he could be expected to state it.

Apparently sensing that the abstraction "property as social relations" cries out for to be made concrete, F. Cohen adds a fourth element, property as the security of reward for planned production.[63] This proposition seemingly makes property social because production implies a social origin for things, but it does not specify the form of production. Is it production by independent laborers or by a capital-based division of labor united by exchange relations? Are individual productive capacities created socially or subjectively? Without posing these questions or answering them in a certain way, Cohen neither establishes a social concept of property nor supersedes Locke's independent labor theory of property. Moreover, without indicating the form of production, one cannot assess its social implications for relative distribution.

In a fifth contribution to relational theory, F. Cohen abandons the

61. F. Cohen 1954; and his introduction to Cohen and Cohen 1951.
62. F. Cohen 1954, p. 363.
63. Ibid., pp. 363, 368.

absolute exclusivity of Blackstone's version of property and stresses that individual domain is subject to numerous social limitations.[64] Yet since he does not tell us what they are, we do not know how significant they are. Earlier liberal theorists who modified Blackstone's absolute dominion coupled their reservations with assumptions of subjective individualism entailing a high degree of exclusivity and a right to highly unequal accumulations. So Cohen's position does not in itself establish a departure from the traditional logic of subjective individualism and inequality.

While Cohen qualifies exclusivity, it remains a dominant feature of his own concept of property, as can be seen from Cohen's widely cited definition:

> That is property to which the following label can be attached:
>
> To the world: Keep off X unless you have my permission, which I may grant or withhold.
>
> Signed: Private Citizen
> Endorsed: The State[65]

Exclusivity becomes the primary characteristic of property when individual action is understood as autonomous effort for self-defined interests, and this is clearly how Cohen understands it.[66] His emphasis on exclusivity is inconsistent with a major redistributory provision involving a strongly inclusive element of property.

Cohen's sixth point is that objects need not have economic value in order to be property.[67] This observation disconnects the theory of property from the theory of economic value. And, accordingly, it disconnects the theory of property from the concept of the social constitution of the individual, for the study of economic value encompasses the determination of value by individuals formed by and within the system of capital-based economic relations.

Cohen, seventh, modifies the traditional liberal notion of the exclusivity of property by adding an inclusionary element of sharing. "Private property is a relationship among human beings such that the so-called owner can exclude others from certain activities *or permit others* to engage in those activities . . ." And, "The essential factor that we are reaching for here *is the power to exclude*, whether that power is exclusive *or shared with others*."[68] The notion that individuals "can impose

64. See Blackstone 1979 [1766], vol. 2, section 2; Cohen 1954, pp. 370, 362.
65. F. Cohen 1954, p. 374.
66. Ibid., pp. 278–279.
67. Ibid., pp. 363–369.
68. Ibid., p. 370.

or withdraw" exclusions affecting "the rest of society" assumes that social relations are discretionary rather than necessary to the constitution of the individual.[69] The individual is primary and substantive, and society is secondary. Given this individualistic foundation, sharing falls under the right of exclusion, and it does not become a rule of distributive justice. Ultimately, property right appears as a matter of private freedom, not of public freedom, common action, or common ends. "Private property . . . presupposes a realm of private freedom," Cohen holds. "Without freedom to bar one man from a certain activity and to allow another man a certain activity we have no property. If all activities were permitted or prohibited by general laws there would be no private property."[70] As a largely private freedom, the entitlement to property seems to authorize accumulations of highly unequal amounts of income and wealth.

If the "relational" theory of property represented by Cohen's treatment is a social theory, then it has major gaps as a social theory. The essence of traditional property theory – highly unequal property based on subjective individualism – remains embedded in his subtle, lawyerly refinements of the liberal paradigm.

PROPERTY AND THE NEW ECONOMIC ANALYSIS OF LAW

The New Economic Analysis of Law, led by scholars such as Coase, Demsetz, and Posner, forms a dynamic center of contemporary legal thought. Whether the premise of subjective personality and the conclusion of unequal property are present within its analysis bears on whether these premises continue to play a part in current liberalism, as they have in past liberalism.

Contemporary theorists of law and economics justify property as a condition necessary for the maximization of utility or efficiency.[71] Property enables individuals to economize in the use of resources, to internalize externalities, and to make trades for more desirable market-bundles. In the New Economic Analysis of Law such considerations can sanction highly unequal distributions, because "any change in allocation or distribution which does not move things toward the economic ideal is unjustified."[72] Utility maximizing can, for example, generate inequal-

69. Ibid., pp. 278–279.

70. Ibid., p. 373.

71. Demsetz 1967, pp. 541–613; Posner 1972; R. Coase 1960, pp. 1–44. For an analysis of the foregoing theorists, see Becker 1977, pp. 57–74.

72. Ibid., p. 73.

ity through "harming a competitor by producing superior products."[73] Thus the right to highly unequal amounts is implicit in the individual's wide latitude in pursuing utility, a subjective dimension of the person.

PROPERTY IN THE CONTEMPORARY LIBERAL THEORY OF JUSTICE

Contemporary commentators contest the thesis that liberal theory is built on an individualistic foundation supporting an inegalitarian property structure. They contend that the concept of socially constituted individuals has become a commonplace of contemporary liberal thought and, further, that some liberal theories of justice are economically egalitarian.[74] These arguments, however, often exemplify the saying, *plus ça change, plus c'est la même chose.*

In examining contemporary liberal theories, we can at this point focus on John Rawls, leaving the discussion of Dworkin's liberal theory for Chapter 13. Rawls clearly seems to be a social theorist when he writes, "It is a feature of human sociability that we are by ourselves but parts of what we might be,"[75] and some of his statements resound with egalitarian sentiments: "The social order can be justified to everyone, and in particular to those who are least favored; and in this sense it is egalitarian."[76] Like most contemporary liberal theories of justice, Rawls's theory admixes social considerations with individualism, inegalitarianism with egalitarianism; but the individualism and the inegalitarianism dominate the distribution of property. Although he acknowledges social attributes of the self, his basic postulate is that the self and choice prevail over social influences.[77] Rawls is quite explicit about this priority: "The essential idea," he writes, "is that we want to account for social values, . . . community, and associative activities, by a conception of justice that in its theoretical basis is individualistic."[78]

The key principle in Rawls's theory of distributive justice is the difference principle, which holds that social and economic goods are to be

73. Demsetz 1967, p. 347.
74. See Gutman 1985, p. 320; Flathman 1987, pp. 111–222; Ryan 1993; Shapiro 1986, p. 320. Wallach 1987, p. 584, ascribes a social concept of the person to Dworkin's work, and Quinn 1991, pp. 263–281, sees the latter as egalitarian. Dworkin might be thought to have a social concept of the person on the basis of Dworkin 1981, pp. 302, 288.
75. Rawls 1971, p. 529.
76. Ibid., p. 103.
77. Sandel 1982.
78. Rawls 1971, pp. 264, 520.

distributed equally unless an unequal distribution would improve the position of the worst off. In deducing this principle, subjective individualism is demonstrably the operative ontological assumption; the social concept of the person – that "we are ourselves but part of what we might be"[79] – is not actually employed in the reasoning leading to the difference principle. The difference principle is chosen by rationally self-interested agents who "do not take an interest in one another's interests" and who are solely "concern[ed] to further their own interests."[80] Rawls explicitly rejects principles of justice that require identification with others, because "this identification is difficult to achieve" and these principles consequently fail to meet a major criterion of his contractarian doctrine: stable acceptance by the people.[81] By contrast, one of the "main grounds" for the difference principle is that acceptance of it follows from the psychological law that people are rationally self-interested: "[w]e can explain acceptance of the social system and the principles it satisfies by the psychological law that people tend to love, cherish, and support whatever affirms their own good."[82] A discussion of social union occurs some 359 pages after the deduction of the difference principle, and so, strictly speaking, it falls outside Rawls's distribution theory.[83] While "mutually disinterested" persons may demand insurance for themselves against the exigency of winding up among the worst off, they never have to contemplate the personal ramifications of having *others* fare much worse than they do. Shaving away considerations that might move a person toward egalitarian principles of distribution, Rawls's argument moves from an assumption of subjective personality (the "mutually disinterested" person) to a difference principle that has elements of equality but that, I argue, ultimately allows extreme inequalities of income.

> Now this general conception [the difference principle] imposes no constraints on what sorts of inequalities are allowed . . .[84]

> [O]nce a suitable minimum is provided by transfers, it may be perfectly fair that the rest of total income be settled by the price system . . .[85]

> What . . . can possibly justify . . . inequality in life prospects? . . . [T]he greater expectations allowed to entrepreneurs encourages [sic] them to do things which

79. Ibid., p. 529.
80. Ibid., p. 151, 11.
81. Ibid., p. 177.
82. Ibid. 83. Ibid., pp. 150–160.
84. Ibid., p. 151.
85. Ibid., p. 277.

raise the long-term prospects of laboring class. Their better prospects act as incentives so that the economic process is more efficient . . .[86]

Some scholars might, nevertheless, challenge the ascription of inegalitarianism to Rawls's difference principle, since it holds that "social and economic inequalities are to be arranged so that they are . . . to the greatest benefit of the least advantaged."[87] In the accompanying sample table of allocations (Table 4.1), however, the difference principle's selection of allocation B over allocation A, which marginally improves the holdings of the bottom group, seriously worsens the relative resources of the middle social strata, which constitute nearly 90 percent of the community.[88]

An isolated example, however, cannot prove that the difference principle is determinately inegalitarian. Against any such interpretation, some might argue that Rawls endorses unequal distribution only in circumstances where equal distribution would damage incentives, thus decreasing economic efficiency and total social production. But this argument, I think, underestimates the scope of Rawls's approval of inegalitarian distribution. His account implicitly or explicitly assumes differential incentives both in the absence and in the presence of fair equalities of opportunity – in short, in a wide enough range of circumstances for a high degree of inequality to be generally tolerated.

Rawls contends that income inequalities tend to occur only when fair equality of opportunity is not in evidence, and that when it is in evidence "the relative difference in earnings between the more favored and the

Table 4.1. *The difference principle and inequality*

Group ranked by possession of economic resources	Allocations of economic resources	
	A	B
Top .5%	30	50
Upper-mid 45%	30	20
Lower-mid 44.5%	30	19
Bottom 10%	10	11

86. Ibid., p. 78.
87. See DiQuattro 1983; Rawls 1971, p. 83.
88. See Rae 1975.

lowest income class tends to close."[89] I would argue, however, that sharp inequalities are consistent with the difference principle in both circumstances. In the first case, Rawls justifies differential incentives on the basis that they are necessary to elicit adequate productive activity that will redound to the benefit of the worst off.[90] But whereas fair equality of opportunity, as Rawls reasonably suggests, reduces income inequality, it does not eliminate extreme inequalities. Equal training generates more equal productive capacities among workers and, correspondingly, more equal remunerations. But market rewards to productive agents depend not only on training and education but also on the demand for what is produced. Differences in demand for different capacities can generate highly unequal incomes – say, a $4 million annual salary and a $30,000 one. Such an inequality will be deemed legitimate under the difference principle if it increases the amount going to the worst off.

THE MODEL OF LIBERAL PROPERTY

From this analysis of the development of traditional liberal theory one can produce a model of its fundamental structure. (Later chapters deal with contemporary social liberal theories). The underlying assumption of subjective personality profoundly affects all of the four major elements of a property theory:

1. the nature of the subject entitled to property,
2. the objects to which the subjects are entitled,
3. the scope or latitude of the subject's control over the disposition of property-objects, and
4. the entitlement to equal or unequal value and control accumulated through the use of property.

First, where some quality or faculty of a person – wants, will, capacity for choice, autonomy, utility, preference, labor – is basic to the reasoning for property right, property belongs to the individual, but more particularly to the subjective individual. In this context, property is usually considered largely private. The relative amount that can be accumulated is unrestricted by the claims of others. The subjectively determined individual, implicitly conceived in a very special way but officially regarded in a general and unspecific way, tends to be seen as the principal subject of property, in contrast to the community, the state, the cor-

89. Rawls 1971, p. 307.
90. See ibid., p. 306.

poration, or the intersubjectively formed individual, whose relations to things involve the claims of others. Whereas the social entities are subjects of property in secondary and derivative or problematic personified senses, the intersubjective person is the subject of property in hardly any sense that affects the scope or shape of the property right.

Second, when the faculties, attributes, and purposes of the subjective individual are thought to confer a supreme ethical entitlement to things, the category of objects that private individuals can own is correspondingly broad. In liberal theory this superior entitlement is indicated by the right of private individuals to own corporations, preempting any competing claims to ownership of corporations by members of the organizations.

Third, where persons are understood as ultimately self-determined by their inner faculties and powers, freedom is understood as the absence of outside interference with subjective tendencies. Consequently, the property right accords individuals extremely wide latitude in using and disposing of their possessions. Assuming that the individual will is subjective, no arbitrary external limit can be legitimately placed upon it, save that it respect the equally unlimited wills of others. The scope of property right is therefore, in the terminology of liberal jurisprudence, "indefinite in point of user." Or at least it is nearly indefinite, for although it is subject to jural relations, it is not constrained by any entitlement or principle superior to subjective individuality. The owner's use of a thing is unrestricted provided that it does not prevent other individuals from using their own things.

Fourth, where subjective persons use property to acquire more valuable property, or to obtain greater control over things, they are viewed as having a right to these gains. Property right permits an unequal accumulation precisely because the increment arises from using one's holdings for subjectively constituted acts of will or from applying one's subjectively conceived efforts – in other words, from attempting to realize one's own subjective will. This will, being entitled to unlimited use of possessions, is entitled to property of unequal value, because it is seen as the source of that value. Will and other subjective attributes of personality are posited without addressing either the formation of these qualities or any purpose beyond the locus of the self.

CONCLUSION

In liberal property theories and especially in the treatment of distribution within these theories, individuals are ethically worthy of entitlement to property, including highly unequal accumulations, because they are self-determined beings pursuing self-goals. Beneath this official or explicit rationale lie heavy presumptions about what constitutes the self. It is assumed to be a structure composed solely of autonomous qualities devoid of social influences. The goal of self-seeking is understood to be a subjective state of mind. The ascription of property to persons and the principle of highly unequal distribution in liberal theory ultimately stand or fall on the premise of subjective personality and its interests.

This general argument may initially seem implausible. It may be difficult to believe that a variety of theorists, with divergent approaches, from Hobbes to Rawls, share a fundamental assumption that logically determines the liberal principle of distribution of property. But in some cases this common basis was rather easy to demonstrate because of similar language, and in other cases it became evident through analysis of implicit logic.

Once recognized, the logical substructure linking all traditional liberal property theories should become the primary focus in assessing their validity. Their basic conclusions can be reaffirmed if the long-assumed pure subjectivity of personality is at last demonstrated. If, however, theoretical analysis reveals an intersubjective inner structure of personality formed by and within the socioeconomic system, the liberal principle of distribution of property is cast in serious doubt.

Part II

Egalitarian Property and Justice as Dueness

5

Whose Property Is It, Anyway?

Ethics of dueness for economic contributions usually neglect some forms of economic contributions and they, therefore, need to be reformulated. When the range of relevant contributions is taken into account, the ethics of dueness lead to a principle of egalitarian distribution of a part of national income. Reformulating these ethics also involves reconceiving property, for property is, among other things, an ethic of dueness for economic contributions.

Analysts often assume that economic contributions consist in a contribution to the production of a product. Yet the wealth of a nation does not derive only from being produced. Individuals also generate wealth in the course of their participation in – and contribution to – the ongoing circulation of commodities. The self-seeking individual, furthermore, contributes to wealth through his or her acts of consumption and exchange as part of a system of interdependence in the satisfaction of needs. Produced commodities will not have value – will not form particles of wealth – unless they are wanted or needed. If being wanted or needed is an essential component of a thing's economic value, then people may be due the value created by this contribution, and not only the value created by their productive actions.

When consumption-side contributions are incorporated into the logic of dueness, it is necessary to adjust the way they are formulated. The full source of the consumption-side contributions cannot be captured without paying attention to the process of social formation of consumption-side activities. The social formation of consumptive attributes, such as wants and needs, is part of the determination of economic value by wants and needs, and in this sense makes an indirect contribution to economic value. The major contemporary schools of economic thought do not provide an adequate guide to formulating the social formation of consumer attributes and acts. Microeconomic theory conceives of the consumer in terms of preferential agency, leading such theory to understate social determinants of consumer aims. Marxist analysis is known for its social account of economic life but reduces economic contributions to productive contributions. The present approach, which takes into account social formation, may be denoted a "theory of needy individuals," as distinct from the subjective theory of consumer behavior in neoclassical economics. While contemporary analyses of needs often reduce them to the requirements for survival, the theory of needs does not necessarily consider people solely with respect to subsistence needs. People may also be considered, as this analysis does, in terms of their need for items of wealth, not only for the necessaries of survival.

Reorienting the study of contributions can have synergistic effects on the theory of property rights. If consumer attributes and activities – and not only production activities – are economically creative and a source of value, then people may be due for them as well, not only for productive activities. The individual's economically creative attributes and activities may be the result of a social process of formation, which becomes a source of contributions and a determinant of the distribution of contributions. Patterns of dueness will, therefore, be affected by taking into account the social formation of consumer attributes and activities. Shifting from agents of subjective choice to the standpoint of socially self-determined needs can compel a revision in prevailing formulas of dueness. In particular, it can entail a principle of egalitarian distribution of a portion of total income.

The essential elements of the theory of dueness are these. First, "dueness" is an element of economic justice that can provide an ethical basis for the conferral of title to property. A person can justly claim entitlement to things that are "due" him or her (Chaper 5, pp. 91–95). Second, the kind of activities for which a person is "due" a benefit are economic contributions, with the degree of dueness corresponding to the amount of a person's economic contributions (pp. 91–94, 96). Third, economic contributions are found to consist in contributions to the creation of value (considered in the sense of exchange value), not only in acts of production taken independently of the creation of exchange value. Dueness should, therefore, be assessed in terms of contributions to value, in the sense of exchange value, not only in terms of productive activities per se (pp. 96–97). Fourth, consumer attributes and activities can contribute to the creation of value; consumer activities should, therefore, be categorized as economic contributions. As such, the value created by them should be distributed to them under the ethics of dueness for economic contributions (pp. 98–105). Fifth, the neoclassical way of understanding the consumer does not adequately grasp the nature of consumers' contributions to value on the consumption side. The basic contributions to economic value by needy individuals consist not only in individualistic agents maximizing subjective preferences, but also in activities flowing from socially self-determined attributes (Chapter 6, pp. 109–124). Consumers adopt their own attributes, but their attributes are also constituted through formative interactions with other members of the system of economic relations. The social influences should be counted in calculations of dueness, for indirect sources of value are still economic contributions so long as they come from within the economic system (pp. 110–111).

Sixth, responsibility for these indirect economic contributions spreads to all members of the economic system, because all the members have such influence upon the consumer. The social influence upon the consumer is systemic, coming from all individuals in their capacity as system members, rather than emanating from just a subset of individuals within a subsystem (pp. 111–124). Seventh, the spread of responsibility socially, to all members, brings about a vast social dispersion of dueness, and a corresponding entailment of an equalization of a portion of income (pp. 113–124). Eighth, the principle of equalization of a portion of income is morally supported by the fact that individuals have, in some ways, a roughly equal amount of formative influence on one another's economic contributions (pp. 114–124). In some ways, needy individuals make relatively equal contributions to value, and they are equally due for these contributions (pp. 114–124). Ninth, differences in intensity of consumer preferences pale before the profound infinitude of wants common to all persons' socially self-determined wants. The latter kind of wants, not only subjective preferences, are among the fundamental determinants of value. People, therefore, make some equal contributions to value. Tenth, these steps imply a right to an equalization of some income, inasmuch as property is based on dueness for contributions. Eleventh, the theory of property based on dueness can provide a large and meaningful part of a theory of property rights, but not a complete theory of property. Twelfth, there are not only equalities but also differences in the amounts of contributions that needy individuals make to the creation of economic value, and so the theory of dueness does not call for strict equalization of income. The analysis of the contributions of needy individuals forms only part of the theory of dueness, and a full theory would also take into account productive contributions. Productive contributions are a mixture of equal and unequal contributions, which is another reason why the principle of dueness does not take the form of a strictly equal distribution of income.

Crucial to this approach to property is the contention that certain assumptions about the person can affect the relative amount of property to which he or she is entitled. My thesis about property reflects the view that the concept of the person, when validly formulated, logically entails greater equality of amounts than prevailing theories recognize. It is generally assumed that there is an *equal right* to property; but the question of whether there is also a right to an equalization of a portion of income remains unanswered.

Concepts of the person have implications for relative entitlements when these concepts are incorporated into arguments of a certain kind. The arguments in question deal with the grounds on which a person can be entitled to property, and are thus known as "entitlement logics." The conclusions flowing from such arguments – egalitarian or inegalitarian – vary with the particular concept of the person assumed by the argument.

The present study explores the effect of such premises on the outcome of an "entitlement logic" in which the person is held "due" for a benefit in proportion to his or her economic contribution. Justice as dueness may be an unfamiliar basis for property. The intended kind of theory may be roughly indicated by reference to the familiar class of "desert" theories that seek to define property by determining how much each person "deserves." The "dueness" theory of property also bears some resemblance to a category of economic ethics known as "the ethics of reward for economic contributions." The terminological departure from these alternatives is motivated by two main theoretical differences. Theories that prescribe remuneration to people for what they "deserve," or that "reward" people for some action, very often have a highly subjectivist tone. Rewarding people for "effort" or "ambition" is associated with recognizing the self-reliance of individuals, and thus it seems to place value on the kind of attributes that originate in the autonomous material of the self. A distinguishing feature of the "dueness" theory, by contrast, is that it develops reasons for redistributing income for certain intersubjective aspects of the person, that is, for particular aspects of personality that develop through formative relations to other persons. Moreover, desert theories and ethics of reward are so much concerned with rewarding people for contributions to the production of a product that we cannot retain that terminology. For the dueness theory holds that a broader range of factors than merely productive factors make important economic contributions, and that these additional factors must also be taken into account when according remuneration.

The frequency (though not the uniformity) with which liberal theories of property and relative distribution allow sharp economic inequalities of income should, I think, be a matter of concern. The notion of a right to inequality seems to strain the very notion of a right, to the point of sounding oxymoronic.[1] We should be careful before endowing severe inequalities with the protected status of a right. Moreover, since liberal justifications of unequal amounts of income and wealth have an extremely important logical origin in a premise of subjective personality, this foundation urgently needs to be reexamined.

The contemporary period is witnessing the development of more social and egalitarian theories by Unger, Gould, and Munzer. Unger sketches a "prospective" theory of needs that, he speculates, may have redistributive implications.[2] Gould justifies egalitarian distribution of health care, education and training, and basic goods on the basis of her persuasive "social ontology." This approach, however, leaves a lot of room for highly unequal distribution of much of the commodity wealth on the consumption side of the economy.[3] Munzer develops a multi-principled justification for a moderately egalitarian view of property. His approach gathers strength for its conclusion by drawing on many different entitlement logics that provide overlapping layers of support. The "revised labor theory of property" presumes, however, that the analysis of economically creative activities can be limited to productive activities.[4] Such a methodology may neglect indirect entitlements from other kinds of economic contributions. In view of the pervasiveness of inegalitarianism in liberal theories, the insufficiency of the egalitarianism in contemporary social theories, and the problematic egalitarianism of contemporary hybrid theories, a reconsideration of the possibility of an egalitarian theory of property is certainly in order.

THE LOGICAL STRUCTURE OF THE CONTRIBUTOR'S SOCIAL PERSONALITY

Changing the premise of subjective personality can reduce the inequality in relative income that a person can be entitled to under property right. Persons who are socially self-determined morally entail some significant equalization of income and wealth when this social premise is incorporated into widely respected entitlement logics. Scholars of property rights have not sufficiently understood how this entailment arises.

1. This observation is due to Benjamin Gregg. For an opposing view, that all rights are rights to inequality, see Marx 1959, p. 119.
2. Unger 1975, pp. 271–272.
3. See Gould 1988, Chapter 5.
4. See Munzer 1990 and compare statements on the back cover with p. 192; and see the following discussion.

Marx made headway on the justification of equalization using social premises about labor, but his materialistic conception of persons as natural beings undermined the social concept of the person that creates equalizing entailments. Marx emphasized social labor as a productive factor and depreciated the role of social consumers in creating value. During the process of "realization" of production values that he formulated, consumer valuations of the product are a by-product of production determinants of value, so they have little independent effect on the creation of value. Since the consumer is attenuated as a source of value, the sociality of the consumer cannot be a significant source of value in Marx's analysis. In consequence, it cannot have any moral entailment with respect to the distribution of value; it calls for neither equalization nor differential distribution.

The particular form of social self-determination used in the theory of property should, in my view, be drawn from contemporary social theory, especially from neo-Hegelian social theory. It can share some features with contemporary communitarian theory. The concept may initially be formulated in terms of an elementary "vision" of the individual's relationship to society – a vision that can reduce a complicated theoretical elaboration to bare essentials. After that, it can be differentiated from contemporary communitarian approaches. First, the notion of social self-determination explodes the traditional dichotomy between self-determination and social determination.[5] Instead of emphasizing one of these poles, it conceives of the person as self-determined only insofar as he or she is also socially determined. This means something more than just that the consumer enters into instrumental relations with others for the sake of pursuing given ends. The needy individual is more deeply intersubjective in the sense that his or her inner nature and ends are constituted through formative relations to others. Contemporary communitarian theories already grasp general and political forms of social determination, but the conception needs to be developed differently in a theory of dueness for economic contributions.[6] Such a theory needs to take into account certain attributes of economic actors – particularly attributes that make economic contributions – and their social self-determination by and within the system of capital-based economic relations.

In a logic of dueness for economic contributions, social self-determination has egalitarian implications because it affects how much is due

5. See Benhabib 1977; Levine 1978–1981; Winfield 1990. For the first formulation of this concept, see Hegel 1952.
6. On the lack of a communitarian theory of property, see Derber 1993, pp. 53–78.

the individual. That is, it can affect how much credit the individual can take in demanding differential reward. At the same time, it can increase the degree to which other members of the system can claim credit for some of the consequences of her economically valuable activities.

PROPERTY AND JUSTICE AS DUENESS

The theory of property that I will develop is a value theory of property and a theory of property as dueness. The former is a theory in which entitlement is linked to the theory of value of commodities. It is an idea that "he" who is the source of the value of commodities should get it. The value theory of entitlement is based on a notion of justice as dueness or desert. This is the idea that each individual should get his or her due. Property as dueness is an important part of a complete theory of property, but not the whole of the matter. Property also needs to be shaped by the other central elements of justice, which according to Mill include freedom, moral right, the performance of promises, and fairness.[7] Munzer's multiprincipled theory of property shows that entitlements can be derived from the contribution principle and from other considerations.[8] Though a multiprincipled account is ultimately needed, I shall not attempt a complete theory. Grand synthesis seems premature because existing analysis of dueness is faulty and it needs reexamination in its own right. A focus on dueness is not, however, a narrow approach; indeed, it is one that comprehends a venerable line of development in property theories, including Locke, Marx, Mill, Tully, Munzer, Shapiro, elements of Hayek, and many others.

The notion of justice as dueness, one of the most ancient notions of justice in jurisprudence, goes back at least as far as Justinian's *Institutes*, which held that justice is "the constant perpetual will of giving everyone his due."[9] J. S. Mill eloquently expressed the same view in modern times, saying "it is universally considered just that each person should obtain that . . . which he *deserves*."[10] "Dueness" or "desert" continues to have wide appeal to contemporary thinkers on the just distribution of economic resources, such as Marxists, social critics, market enthusiasts,

7. Mill 1962, pp. 298–301.
8. Munzer 1990.
9. Justinian quoted in Barry 1989, p. 149. Indeed, a full account of the origins of the notion of dueness could trace it back even further to traditional notions in pre-Platonic Greek society, not simply to Justinian and late Rome. For favorable assessments of the notion of justice as dueness, see Sher 1987; Becker 1977, pp. 49–52. For a critical analysis of it, see Rawls 1971, pp. 103, 310–314.
10. Mill 1962, p. 299.

ethicists of marginal productivity, Munzer in his revised labor theory of property, Shapiro in his neo-workmanship ideal, Gauthier in his notion of proportionate entitlement to a cooperative surplus, and many others.[11]

Dueness for economic contributions has certain limits as an ethic of distribution that prevent it from providing a complete basis for distribution. The dueness principle might leave some disabled or infirm people partly out of account. Better protection for such people might be secured, according to critics of dueness for economic contributions, by a set of minimal entitlements derived from the person's basic humanity. Yet the incompleteness of the dueness principle does not mean that it should be dispensed with altogether. Its ethical importance arises after the most minimal entitlements have been provided under a principle of basic humanity. For at that point, the person's abstract moral worth or intrinsic humanity affords little guidance in distributing the rest of the income and wealth. As Dahl writes, "Standing alone . . . the Idea of Intrinsic Equality [or equal moral worth] is not robust enough to justify much in the way of conclusions . . . [W]hatever limits it may set on inequalities are extremely broad."[12] In contrast to considerations of elementary humanity, the principle of dueness can indicate ethical directions for distributing income above a minimal floor.

Claims to title based on contributions may appear weak, as justice claims, in the sense that they seem to appeal only to instrumental values. But the principle of dueness or of contributions can also have strong appeal from the standpoint of basic humanity. The dueness principle connects economic action (the creation wealth) to the purpose of economic action (the acquisition and enjoyment of wealth), thereby helping to assure the integrity of purposive activity. It can also contribute to the person's freedom of will – a fundamental attribute of his or her humanity. For redistributing income to individuals for participating in the creation of wealth can be viewed simply as the fulfillment of the will of the persons involved. Since they want to receive remuneration proportionate to their contributions, they could realize this objective by receiving an equal share of a portion of national income, if they had made some equal contributions.

The "precept of contribution" is not "satisfactory," according to Rawls, because the fairness of rewards depends on the justice of the basic structure of the economic system.[13] Rawls's low appraisal of it,

11. See Okun 1975, p. 41; Munzer 1990; Becker 1977; Gauthier 1986.
12. Dahl 1989, p. 87.
13. Rawls 1971, p. 308. Apart from this particular Rawlian reservation about the contributions precept, I largely agree with Cohen that Rawls's reservations

however, is mistaken about the precept's role in his own theory, where the contribution idea plays a greater part than acknowledged. The difference principle, for Rawls the more fundamental principle, permits the better off to keep the fruits of their activity so long as the worst off benefit from this arrangement. The better off are, implicitly, being accorded title to larger shares *because they created these shares, else their possession of such shares would be a kind of theft*. In this way, the principle of contributions plays a great, though neglected, role even within the workings of Rawls's difference principle. Though the contributions principle has an implicit basis in Rawls's account, Rawls applies it inadequately. The account of earnings by the better off underestimates, in my view, the contribution by indirect contributions, that is, by the impact that each person has on the formation of other persons' economically creative capacities and attributes, and the contribution made by cooperation considered as an irreducible factor of production and economic creation (see Chapter 6, pp. 112–124, and Chapter 8, pp. 161–164).

The notion of an "ethics" of remuneration for economic contributions has come under some additional fire, but the criticisms are limited and surmountable. Hayek and Okun contend that market remuneration for economic contributions is not a matter of "moral desert" or "merit." For them, morality pertains to psychological or subjective dimensions of achievement, such as "pain and effort" or "the state of mind and feelings."[14] But it should be underscored that Hayek and Okun nevertheless endorse market remuneration for economic contributions in accordance with the benefit to society as measured by the market. Hayek and Okun prefer to call such endorsement a "value judgment" rather than a "moral judgment."[15] Since this endorsement is, however, a principle of remuneration for economic contributions, it is also a species of dueness theory, not a fundamentally opposed approach. Moreover, the implicit logic of their analyses is that productive activity *should* be remunerated in this way because it is valuable to do so. As a prescription for economic distribution, Hayek's and Okun's value judgment verges on a moral judgment, for an ought judgment is an essential element of a moral judgment.

Dueness for economic contributions may be brought more emphati-

about the precept are not thoroughgoing. Cohen points up that Rawls merely holds that it is difficult to tease out the deserving from the undeserving, and that Rawls does not deny that some economically creative activities can form a basis for deserving reward, if they can be identified. See G. A. Cohen 1993, p. 14.

14. Hayek 1960, pp. 94–95; Okun 1975.
15. Hayek 1960, pp. 98, 94–97; Okun 1975.

cally within the rubric of ethics, not only of "value judgment." Intuitively, it can be just as moral to labor fruitfully but effortlessly toward the benefit of one's fellow men and women as it is to labor fruitlessly but strenuously in the production of something no one wants, and in most cases a good deal more moral. Notwithstanding Hayek's intimations to the contrary, he himself makes a similar moral judgment when he uses "success" as a ground of *justificatory* argument.[16] Moreover, giving people their due – or rewarding them according to social valuation of the benefit – falls within the province of ethics defined as the universal principles that reconcile the will of each and all in civil society.[17] For this criterion of distribution is a kind of reconciliation of the interests of each (in receiving their "due" for contributions) with the social interest (in valued or needed objects).

This analysis converges with some elements of Hayek's and Okun's analysis while diverging from others. In sum, the position that I have developed on the ethics of remuneration has three major components:

1. Individuals should be given their due – or rewarded for economic contributions – when these contributions are socially valued.
2. The foregoing proposition accords with Hayek and Okun in that they endorse this kind of distribution to the individual (a) except that they decline to call it moral; (b) whereas the present analysis ascribes a moral element to such contributions, not just a "value."
3. In accord with Hayek and Okun, the standpoint of the present analysis is that subjective merit considered by itself (that is, considered apart from contributions to economic value) has no ethically valid claim to economic remuneration.

Another criticism of entitlements for economic contributions is that property is only a "limited and conditional" part of social justice. Shapiro says "we should not expect too much" from property, implying that the concept has little internal content of its own.[18] But this view derives property from and subordinates it to a politics of "democratic justice," which I think underestimates the integrity of the concept of

16. Hayek 1960, pp. 97, 85.
17. For this concept of ethics, see Hegel 1952, pp. 75–105, 155.
18. Shapiro 1991, pp. 48, 63–66.

property.[19] To be sure, a complete theory of property must take into account all of the abstract ideals of justice, and also must balance each right with the system of rights. But property has a certain relative autonomy from other concrete spheres of justice because it regards a particular fundamental freedom of will of equal importance: the freedom of will in relation to and over external things. To define and derive this freedom primarily from other supposedly "just" claims would warp it or violate it – just as defining democratic freedoms through property claims would distort them by authorizing the purchase of votes. Primary emphasis, therefore, must be on the internal logic of the concept, rather than on its derivation, epiphenomenally, from other external claims like "democratic justice."

PROPERTY AS A REDISTRIBUTIVE RULE

Principles of distribution of property can be derived from within the analysis of property and are part of property right, rather than forming a separate branch of distributive justice apart from property. The analysis of property, that is, of what is "mine" and "thine," subsumes redistributive rules, because what belongs to me may currently lie in the hands of another, while what is "thine" may currently be in my possession. The contrary has frequently been assumed, as in the famous saying, "possession is nine-tenths of the law," which makes property a barrier to redistribution. But what is "mine" depends on moral principles, such as the principle of giving each person his or her due, which can involve redistribution. Economic value created by person 1 may, through the vagaries of the market, wind up in the hands of person 2, 3, or 4, though these people are less responsible for its creation than is person 1. In this case, to give person 1 his or her due, property has to be redistributory. When and if market distributions do not reflect patterns of dueness, the law must redistribute to bring market distribution in line with property right.

19. This order may appear to be reversed in Shapiro's concept of the democratic process as a "subordinate foundational good." The concept seemingly makes the sphere of property superordinate to the democratic process. But I do not think this concept provides a secure place for property within a democratic order. When democracy is understood as a subordinate foundational good, the democratic process is the only foundational moral commitment. This denies property the status of a foundational commitment or of a right, thereby eroding property's autonomy vis-à-vis claims coming from democratic politics. See Shapiro 1994, pp. 124–151.

What is "his" or "hers" – the essential element in entitlement – is, then, a redistributive question. Claims to an equalized portion of income can have high moral value and moral status because they are matters of property and entitlement, not just optional redistributive rules, when they are shaped in accord with considerations of "mine" and "thine" based on the pattern of actual dueness. The principles of distribution of income have as much moral value and standing as property right, because they are aspects of property.

PROPERTY AND THE THEORY OF ECONOMIC VALUE

The notion of property as dueness does not by itself specify a particular distribution of commodities and money as just. One still needs a theory in order to determine what is due a person.[20] Most of the things that are due persons are related to their *economic* contributions, since this is how most objects of property are created in a capital-based economy.

Theorists divide on what constitutes an economic contribution or economically creative activity. On the one hand, "production theories of property," as we may call them, assert that production is the essence of economically creative activity, and therefore that production should be rewarded. Reward, in this view, should be proportionate to productive contributions or subjective effort. Examples of the production approach include aspects of the theories of Locke and Marx, Shapiro's reconstructed "workmanship ideal," Becker's theory, and Munzer's "revised labor theory of property."[21] On the other hand, there are "value theories of property" that hold that the creation of economic value is the essence of economically creative action, and therefore that human contributions to the value of commodities should be remunerated. By "value," I mean relative price, command over other commodities, or components of the wealth of a nation. In a property theory based on value-contributions, the theory of the value of commodities becomes the main instrument for determining dueness for a benefit. The value theory determines the individual's contributions to the value of commodities and, therefore, also determines what is due him or her. Examples of value theories of property include aspects of the theories of Locke, Marx, Hayek, and Levine. But a fine line cannot always be drawn between value theories of property and production theories of property, and thus some theorists are counted twice.

Production theorists of property think that production is the essence

20. Barry 1989, p. 149.
21. Locke 1963, paras. 42, 43, 40; Marx 1959, pp. 117–118, passim.

of economically creative activity because production takes unwrought materials in nature and shapes them in conformity with human purposes. These theorists, morever, think that production gives things "value," but in the sense of "use," not of exchange-value, and thus they are not value theories of property as I define the term. A recent rehabilitator of Locke's "workmanship ideal" holds that "making" is the creative, purposive activity and that it is craftsmanship that merits entitlement, irrespective of value in exchange. "The ideal," says Shapiro, "rests on the moral thesis that the legitimate basis of entitlement lies in productive action."[22] Some variants of the labor theory of property hold that the subjective experience of effort – the Smithian "toil and trouble" – is the morally worthy feeling meriting entitlement.[23] Attainment of exchange-value is not essential to the production theorists' idea of economically creative activity because it is distinct from the activity of making a product and from the subjective effort or satisfaction entailed in production. And owing to its separation from production, the generation of exchange value does not carry the moral appeal legitimizing entitlement. For this reason Shapiro argues that the labor theory of value has moral significance only because it contains the idea of production, not because it involves exchange value.[24]

Production theories of property are increasingly prevalent, but there are significant problems in the way that they understand the nature of economically creative activity. These problems then impair their grasp of the moral basis for entitlement from economic contributions. Smith points out that after "the division of labor has been once thoroughly established," each man supplies only a "small part" of his wants through his own production, and must instead derive "the far greater part of them" from other persons.[25] Under these conditions, the individual does not acquire needed goods by production for self-consumption, but by production for others as a means of gaining exchange-value. With the exchange-value obtained, he is then able to acquire needed or wanted items. In an exchange system, individual action that fashions an object without value neither enables the producer to satisfy his economic needs, nor relates to the needs of other members of the system of needy individuals. Effort and production without production of value are not economically creative and a source of wealth, but wasteful and nearly pointless from an economic point of view. Subjective effort (Shapiro)

22. Shapiro 1991, p. 53; see also Tully 1980.
23. See Okun 1975, p. 44.
24. Shapiro 1991, pp. 52–53, 54.
25. Smith 1937, p. 22.

and production of a product per se (Munzer) should not, therefore, be conceived of as economically creative activity, and cannot be considered the source of the moral appeal legitimating entitlement.

The concept of economically creative activity must reflect the fact that production is not simply the means to the satisfaction of needs but the means to the satisfaction of needs *through a system of exchange*. The product must have value, in the sense of exchange-value, in order to have any economic worth to anyone. The "real worth" of an object to its producer, according to Smith, is its "value" ("command over other commodities"), not its use.[26] As Becker argues, "Labor alone – labor that neither adds nor diminishes value – does not deserve anything."[27] But both Becker and Munzer conceive value as something that "adds value" to the lives of others or is "needed and wanted."[28] That is, they conceive it as something that adds to pleasure or satisfaction, not as something that needs to create exchange value in order to be truly productive.[29] However, this view fails to recognize that, if something is wanted but is not an object of effective demand, and no one is willing to pay for it, then it has no economic worth.

Since activity that produces value – or otherwise creates it – is the sine qua non of economically creative activity, only this kind of activity can supply the moral appeal legitimating entitlement, and should shape entitlement. Production theories of property like the workmanship ideal, resting on the "idea of making something that one can subsequently call one's own,"[30] presuppose a rudimentary economic condition of "self-subsistent" production, to use Hegel's term.

ENTITLEMENT AND EXTRA-PRODUCTION SOURCES OF VALUE

It should be clear that the dueness theory of property needs a theory of value. The nature of value is, however, a controversial topic in economic theory, and several rival approaches have been developed. Since the dueness theory of property has to select a value theory, it must determine which kind of value theory is valid or appropriate.

Most modern and contemporary theorizing about the ethics of reward for economic contributions has not given sufficient attention to

26. Ibid., Chapter 5.
27. Becker 1977, p. 52.
28. Ibid.; Munzer 1990, p. 258 n2.
29. Becker 1977, p. 51; Munzer 1990, pp. 258 n2, 280.
30. Shapiro 1991, p. 59.

differences between theories of value. It has, moreover, tended to neglect developments in theories of value that have occurred since 1870 and it has, therefore, fallen out of step with developments in economic theory. Curiously, modern and contemporary theorizing about the ethics of contributions tends to assume the classical theory of value, one that views productive factors, such as labor and capital, as the major causes of economic value. In this respect, modern and contemporary ethics of reward are not modern. The modern, or neoclassical, form of economic theory has compellingly demonstrated that factors on the consumption side of the economy contribute heavily to the determination of relative prices. As a result, these determinants may be part of the process of creation of the value of commodities.[31] How should these consumption-side contributions be treated in an ethics of reward for economic contributions? Most modern and contemporary theorizing about the ethics of reward passes over this question because it assumes the classical theory of value and, therefore, continues to assign title primarily for productive contributions, while according individuals' consumption attributes at best a secondary role. But ethics of contributions founded on the classical theory of value are weakly founded, because this theory is inconsistent with a major proposition of modern economics, that consumers contribute to the determination of value. This is not to say that neoclassical economists believe that consumer contributions merit entitlements. Yet the central importance of consumer contributions in modern economics suggests that the ethics of contributions can no longer ignore them. Indeed, the possibility needs to be considered that the ethics of dueness should be revamped to bring them in line with the fact of consumer contributions.

The particular manner in which consumer contributions should be taken into account, and the question of what their nature is, may not have been adequately conceptualized by neoclassical economists, whose concepts may require revision. In taking consumers into account, there need not be any presumption that neoclassical economics adequately conceptualizes consumer contributions. The neoclassical school may, for example, neglect the sociality of consumer attributes; but its contention that consumers play a significant role in determing economic value has been established.

31. Other analysts may differ with the neoclassical conceptualization of consumption-side determinants in terms of utilities or preferences. Some call for an alternative formulation of consumer attributes in terms of socially self-determined wants. But this in no way denies that such attributes, in some form, must be included in the theory of value.

The first theory of economic value that I will be concerned with here is the labor theory of value, formulated by classical political economy and by Marx.[32] This theory holds that labor is the origin and cause of the value of commodities. The individual is consequently entitled, in one thread of Marx's thinking, to be remunerated according to the contribution of his labor to the value of commodities.[33] But the labor theory of value is beset by serious problems. It is inconsistent with cases where there is more than one nonproduced factor of production, joint production, alternative production processes, heterogeneous labor, substitution between goods due to price changes, and cases where surplus value is nonzero.[34] Even more important, Marx's labor theory of value gives inadequate recognition to the role of consumption-side factors in the determination of value. The first recognition that "the theory of consumption" is the "foundation of political economy" was made by "neoclassical" theory.[35] Value, W. Stanley Jevons argued, "depends entirely upon utility."[36] Against "opinions" that "made labour . . . the origin of value," neoclassical theory treats consumer preferences as one of the categories of ultimate determinants of the relative value of commodities.[37] Some importance had earlier been ascribed to demand, but classical political economy did not accord it a role in determining production prices and production values.

The utility theory of value was importantly revised in the general equilibrium theory of prices.[38] This systematic theory of price determination united the consumption and production sides of the economy, with utility standing as the origin and cause of value.[39] The approach gave a more valid account of relative prices, and became established as the standard theory of value in modern economics.

In two major regards theories recognizing a role for the consumption side in the determination of value have not been parlayed into a new ethics of reward for economic contributions. Neoclassical economists have not established such an ethic. Early neoclassical theorists attempted to formulate one in the form of an ethics of the marginal productivity

32. See Smith 1937, p. 30.
33. Marx 1959, pp. 117–118.
34. See Morishima 1973, pp. 181–196, 42; Samuelson 1957, p. 888; Samuelson 1971, pp. 404–405.
35. See Jevons 1871, p. 46.
36. Ibid., p. 2. See also Walras 1954, pp. 201–207, and especially p. 398, para. 344.
37. Jevons 1871, p. 2. Scarcity is another ultimate determinant of value in the neoclassical system.
38. Walras 1954; Debreu 1959.
39. Walras 1954, pp. 201–207, 398, 344.

theory of distribution.[40] But later neoclassical economists found serious mistakes in this theory of distribution.[41] Hicks pointed out that the marginal productivity of labor does not determine the wage, but only the demand for labor.[42] Modern neoclassical theory is also not notable for the formulation of an ethics of distribution, because subjective utility theory is incompatible with such an ethics. Individual utilities are unique and nonquantitative, which led neoclassical theorists to conclude that there could be "no interpersonal comparisons of utility," and the impossibility of these comparisons was thought to mean that no "scientific" judgments of the ethics of relative distribution are possible.[43]

Social theories of the economy – theories that employ concepts of the social formation of economic actors – have not solved the dueness theory of property, because they, like neoclassical theory, have not incorporated consumption into the ethics of dueness for economic contributions. A significant alternative to neoclassical theory, Levine's social theory of the economic system, employs a social theory of consumption in the theory of the value of commodities. Levine formulates socially self-determined needs in place of the neoclassical theory of preference, and has them playing the role of determinants of value. But Levine does not utilize such a social theory of value in formulating a new ethics of dueness for economic contributions.[44]

Contemporary theories of property take utility into account in distributive justice, but not in an ethics of reward or dueness for economic contributions. Hayekian "value judgments" about distribution fail to give utility an adequate role in the contribution logic of entitlement. Nor do either contemporary theories of property or Hayekian value judgments take into account a social theory of consumption in their ethics of reward or dueness for economic contributions. Each in his own way, Becker, Munzer, Hayek, and Okun shape and defend property as an institution that maximizes utility or efficiency, usually with inegalitarian consequences but sometimes in accord with "moderate egalitarianism."[45] In Hayek's and Okun's work, the principle of utility affects the amounts that producers are entitled to, that is, it determines the amount of the reward to *productive* activities. But these four theorists

40. See Clark 1902.
41. Hicks 1963; Hayek 1960, pp. 87–100. See also Samuelson's comment to J. B. Clark's son in Samuelson 1971, p. 423.
42. Hicks 1963 [1932].
43. See Sen 1979, p. 537–558.
44. See, for example, Levine 1991, pp. 19, 7.
45. Munzer 1990, p. 213.

do not treat the contributions of consumers as factors that can entitle them to value created.

Though the subjective utility theory may be a defective formulation of the consumer, neoclassical economics makes a major contribution to economic theory when it recognizes the role of consumers in the determination of value. This facet of neoclassical analysis can indicate areas where the theory of property stands in need of revision, if it is to be brought into accord with the state of economic science. As I have already shown, the dueness theory of property requires a theory of value in order to make judgments of dueness, and the contribution of consumers to value recognized by neoclassical theorists can alter the form of the theory of value that should be incorporated into this theory of property. If the dueness theory of property hinges on a theory of value of commodities, then it must take into account the role of consumers in the determination of value. Consumers' contributions to the determination of value can entitle them to a portion of the value created. A theory that divides up rewards in accord with economic contributions must register any human source of economic creation. An activity can qualify as an economically creative action if it contributes to the creation of the value of commodities. Consumer activities qualify as economically creative activities because consumer activities contribute to the determination of value and, therefore, satisfy the foregoing criteria of economically creative action.[46] For all of these reasons, consumer activities inexorably accrue titles, on a principle that each individual should get his or her due. Individuals *as consumers* are due value (income) by virtue of the fact that their consumption activities contribute to the determination of the value of commodities. When one shifts from a production theory of value to a theory of value that acknowledges a role for consumers, one cannot all of a sudden leave the theory of value out of the theory of entitlement. The theory of value does not lose its importance vis-à-vis the theory of entitlement when it addresses the role of consumer contributions. The notion of dueness retains application. For it is still compelling that value should accrue to those to whom it is due, regardless of whether it is due because of productive factors or because of con-

46. Support for the view that consumers make contributions to the creation of value may also be found in Keynes's formulation of the multiplier mechanism. In his analysis, augmentation of the aggregate level of demand leads to the growth of the capital wealth of the nation. See Keynes 1964, pp. 113–134. The multiplier mechanism is, however, a macroeconomic formulation that does not disaggregate consumption. The ethics of contributions, by contrast, proceeds through reference to microeconomic theory, because these ethics deal with relative contributions by individual agents.

sumption-side factors. Therefore, a dueness theory of distribution cannot exclude entitlements for consumer determinations of value without denying its own abstract ideal of justice: the principle of "giving each person his or her due."

Although entitlement for consumer contributions is a novel idea, there are some partial precedents for it. In his *General Theory*, Keynes proposed a set of redistributory death taxes that he justified on ground of the communal character of consumer contributions to the wealth of the nation.[47] In the neoclassical theory of externalities, nonmarket interdependencies between consumers and consumers or between producers and consumers are thought to warrant compensatory action. This theory deals with external economies and external diseconomies, where consumers can affect each others' satisfaction levels: "External effects," writes Scitovsky, "exist whenever the shape or positions of a man's indifference curve depends on the consumption of other men."[48] When the domain variables of a consumer's utility function are positively or negatively effected by another consumer or producer, neoclassical theory may support remedial policies, such as taxes (unilateral or bilateral), in order to improve efficiency.[49] The notion that interdependencies between utility functions can entitle consumers to remedial and compensatory policies constitutes a precedent for entitling them to benefits proportionate to their economic contributions.

As the dueness theory of property brings consumer contributions into the calculations of dueness, it does not necessarily have to use a standard neoclassical utility or preference theory of the consumer. It may use whatever theory of the consumer is valid and appropriate. The following analysis suggests that the neoclassical theory of consumer preferences is not, in fact, the most valid or suitable one for the theory of dueness. Instead, my analysis incorporates a social theory of the consumer with socially self-determined attributes (wants and needs) and behaviors.

Hayek's critique of the ethics of reward for contributions can be helpful in defending the notion that consumers are due for their contributions to value, though he did not himself propose such a view. The form of his argument is as follows. He suggests that only contributions to value should be rewarded, not subjective efforts to make something that

47. Keynes 1964, pp. 372–377. In 1999, the Japanese government distributed $6 billion in coupons to consumers under a plan to stimulate the economy by encouraging shopping. See Sheryl WuDunn, *The New York Times*, March 14, p. 6.

48. Scitovsky 1954, p. 143.

fails to sell. An implication of this argument (one not considered by Hayek) is that consumer contributions can entitle them to correlative value because such contributions create value even though they have no subjective merit.

Smith held that "toil and trouble" is the source of value. Hayek refutes this view by arguing that "subjective effort . . . may be . . . a complete failure" to achieve "a valuable result." Therefore, "what determines our responsibility [to remunerate others]," he appropriately concludes, "is the advantage" they provide us through creation of value, "not their merit in providing it."[50] So it cannot be "the producers' sense of subjective satisfaction from the productive endeavor" that merits entitlement, contrary to Shapiro's position.[51] Only contributions to the value of commodities warrant remuneration.

Once one appreciates that subjective effort and other qualities of subjective merit are irrelevant to entitlement (insofar as they do not create value), it is easier to see that consumption-side activities can be entitling. Consumption attributes are left with the same entitling quality that activities that are productive of value have: they give rise to genuinely creative activities in an economic sense – they contribute to the value of commodities. And so consumptive attributes fulfill the criterion for entitlement as much as productive activities do.

Elements drawn from Hayek's own argument compel a revision of his view of appropriate remuneration. Hayek assumes that only producers should be remunerated for economic contributions. In determining how they should be remunerated, he correctly says, "we do not wish people to earn a maximum of merit but to achieve a maximum of usefulness at a minimum of pain and . . . merit."[52] But if producers should be remunerated on the basis of usefulness, not merit, then it is only a small step to the recognition that people can earn titles for seeking want satisfaction, not only for productive activities. For this want seeking may be the most useful thing they do for the creation of economic value, even if their preferences are not particularly meritorious.

Although Hayek does not remunerate consumption-side activities, he implicitly gives a reason why we can consider consumers due for the value that is due to them. Hayek says that productive activity is not desirable unless valued by others.[53] Value, as such reasoning reveals, has a double source: it is created through the production of a valued object

50. Hayek 1960, pp. 94–95, 97.
51. Shapiro 1991, p. 59.
52. Hayek 1960, p. 96.
53. Ibid., pp. 87–100.

and through the consumer's valuation of the product. Now, if productive activities should be remunerated because they contribute to value, then consumption-side activities should get corresponding amounts of value, since they too contribute to the value of commodities. Thus, although accrual of title for consumption-side contributions seems surprising at first, it is simply an outgrowth of tendencies already present within existing theories of property.

No contemporary theory of property (of the ethics-of-contributions type) considers consumer contributions to value (exchange-value) as a ground of entitlement. Different perspectives on the consumer – the subjective utility theory of value and the social theory of consumer needs – do not lead theorists of property to different standpoints on this matter. Neoclassical theorists of property, using the subjective utility theory, do not treat consumer contributions as entitling; nor do social theorists of property, using a social theory of the determination of consumer needs. All modern theories of property based on dueness fail to incorporate an important basis of entitlement. This failure seriously distorts patterns of entitlement, if I am correct that consumer activities are contributions to value that warrant entitlements to value.

As neoclassical theories began to include consumption in theories of value, egalitarian theories of property fell into sharp decline.[54] Hayek held that the inclusion of utility in the ethics of dueness would lead to

54. It should be noted that there have been theorists who sought to defend egalitarianism on the basis of subjectivist foundations and premises. Cases in point include Cannan (as cited by Robbins 1984, pp. 136–137), Dalton 1920, Wicksell, and Munzer 1990, pp. 212–213. But my proposition that subjective utility theory *logically* implies inequality does not deny, nor is it refuted by, the fact that history has produced some attempts to formulate a subjectivist egalitarianism. The real question is whether those attempts have any hope of working well, and I suggest that they do not, because a consistent subjectivist cum egalitarian theory is not *logically* possible.

Dalton's approach is one of the bases for the view that a theory of subjective utility could lead to an egalitarian theory. Dalton's view, as summarized by Sen (1992, pp. 95–96), is that "social welfare was taken to be the sum total of individual utilities, and each individual utility was taken to be a function of the income of that individual. The same utility function was taken to apply to all individuals, and this fact, along with diminishing marginal utility from income, ensured that for any given total income . . . an equal distribution would maximize social welfare." But this presumption of a single utility function common to all is in fact an heroic assumption characteristic of the extreme measures that subjectivist egalitarians have employed in order to prop up their position. The ad hoc assumption of a single shared utility function gives rise to inconsistencies with central tenets of subjective utility theory. It is inconsistent with the premise that individuals are fundamentally independent choice agents. Such indepen-

the affirmation of inequality. In Hayek's view, shifting *from* reward proportional to "recognizable merit" *to* reward proportional to the benefit for others undermines egalitarian demands and "is bound to produce inequality," of a "desirable" sort.[55] Marx's theory of exploitation hinged on the labor theory of value. When neoclassical theorists showed that value was not simply produced, but was also determined on the consumption side, they refuted Marx's theory of value and the theory of exploitation based upon it. If utility, not labor, is the origin and cause of value, neoclassical theorists argued, then labor could not be viewed as exploited.

While theories of value acknowledging consumption's role have historically been used to refute egalitarian theories, they do not *necessarily* justify inegalitarian forms of property and distribution. The critical factor yielding inegalitarian forms of property has been the individualistic manner in which individual wants are usually incorporated into consumption-inclusive theories of value.[56] Substituting socially constituted wants and needs into the theory of value can lead to the formulation of more egalitarian entitlements.

dence necessarily gives rise to different preferences, as each individual's psychology becomes a unique principle of causality in the matter of preferences. Without Dalton's dubious assumption of a single shared utility function, an equal distribution of income would not maximize utility. Egalitarianism consequently lacks a sound foundation in Wicksellian subjectivist ethics and, I believe, in other subjectivist ethics.

55. Hayek 1960, pp. 93, 94, 85.
56. This contention, that consumption-inclusive theories of value have tended to neglect social formation of consumer aims and ends, might be challenged on the following grounds. In seeming contradiction to my claim that neoclassical theory neglects social factors, an anonymous reviewer suggests that marginal productivity theory takes into account social conditions and their contributions when it assesses remuneration. In the neoclassical formulation, w = (p)(MPl), the wage is determined not simply by productivity but also by the demand for the product. The demand for the product might be construed as a social determinant, because it reflects aggregate conditions, not just the preference of one person. And this social condition, the anonymous reviewer contends, constitutes a social determination of relative rewards. Wages in different countries, the reviewer points out in a country comparison, vary with differences in consumer preferences as between these countries, thereby incorporating "social" influences. However, I do not believe that the direction of this critique truly shows that marginal productivity theory takes adequate account of social factors in determining rewards. The social influences noted by marginal productivity theory only constitute a social valuation in the sense of an aggregation of demands ultimately derived from individual utility functions. Individual preferences, in the country comparison, are left with no theoretical account being offered of

their social formation. The formulation of demand does not state any social determination of preferences. Within the ethics of distribution, though, it is important to theorize the social formation of economic contributions – to give an account and not only to take account – because we must identify the causal sequence of contributions if we are to remunerate them appropriately. Marginal productivity ethics of distribution simply do not provide anything remotely resembling this.

6

The Social Nature of Economic Actors and Forms of Equal Dueness

> The correct regulative principle for anything depends on the nature of that thing.
>
> John Rawls

Consumer contributions should be taken into account by the ethics of dueness because, as the preceding chapter showed, they are factors in the creation of value and, as such, they can generate corresponding entitlements to value. When these factors are taken into account, how do they affect the principle of distribution of property? Do consumers make highly unequal or relatively equal contributions to the creation of the value of commodities? Or are they simultaneously equal in some respects and different in others? If individual consumers make entirely equal economic contributions, the ethics of dueness yields a principle of equal distribution of income. If consumers make highly unequal economic contributions, then such ethics require a principle of highly unequal distribution of income. But it is conceivable, furthermore, that each consumer makes some equal contributions and some unequal ones, on the basis of which he or she accures a compound right to an equal distribution of a portion of total social income and an unequal distribution of the rest.

Taking consumption-side contributions into account does not produce a complete ethics of dueness, only a theory of dueness for consumption contributions. A full ethics of dueness would combine this with producer contributions. At the present stage of developing the ethics of dueness, it is particularly important to incorporate the consumption side. Economists since the 1870s have known that consumers contribute to creating the value of commodities, yet this fact has not been adequately addressed by the ethics of dueness, which is still dominated by the obsolete assumption that only productive agents create value. Because the validity of the ethics of dueness hinges on incorporating consumer contributions, it is worthwhile to grapple with them.

Consideration of the ethics of dueness for consumer contributions may begin within neoclassical economic theory, because that theory pioneered the consumer's role in determining value. But since neoclassical economics does not remunerate consumer contributions, there is, strictly speaking, no neoclassical ethics of reward for consumer contributions. It would, however, be interesting to construct one, in order to see how calculations of consumer dueness would be affected be the neoclassical theory of value. As a first step, one has to import into the neoclassical schema the proposition that contributions warrant entitlements. Then the affect of neoclassical theory of value upon entitlements can be considered. The result is not a pure neoclassical ethics of dueness, for there cannot be such a thing; but the construct could be viewed as an ethics in the neoclassical style.

The overall objective of this exercise in not to develop a neoclassical theory of consumer dueness for value contributions. Rather, the neoclassical construct will be used in a comparison with an alternative theory of dueness to be developed in this chapter. The "reconstructed version" of the neoclassical ethics of dueness focuses upon the contributions to value made by consumers' subjective preferences. I then formulate a different theory incorporating a conception of the consumer as having socially self-determined wants. The validity of the alternative approaches to dueness can then be evaluated.

In standard neoclassical theory, the consumer's preference is self-determined, and is a *postulate*.[1] The premise can be *interpreted* as subjective or social, but "the interpretations are detachable" from the postulate.[2] For this reason, and also because a preference postulated prior to the deduction of the system cannot be causally determined by the self-same system, the preference is subjective vis-à-vis the system. Now, justice as dueness asserts that the person has a right to whatever value is created by her. *Since the individual's preferences are self-determined, and since her preferences contribute to the determination of value (and in this sense to the creation of value), the remuneration is due her and her alone for this contribution.* The individualistic view of preference in neoclassical economics can give rise to highly unequal entitlements. Differences between individuals' utility-maximizing behavior generate

1. Hicks 1946, pp. 17, 55; Koopmans 1957, p. 132.
2. Koopmans 1957, p. 133.

different amounts of value, and these differences in contributions to value confer highly unequal entitlements. Thus the neoclassical theory of the consumer and of value leads logically to an inegalitarian ethics of dueness for economic contributions.

My agreement with neoclassical theory extends only to the point of acknowledging the role of consumer attributes in the determination of value, not to the further point of interpreting consumer attributes in terms of utility or preferences. The individual's consumption attributes can be better described in terms of wants that the individual shapes in accord with, and that are shaped by, the system of economic relations. Such a conception has various advantages, including the fact that it is logically consistent with other essential attributes of an economic system: mutual dependence, self-renewing economy, and ongoing circulation of commodities and money.[3] For these reasons, the social self-determination of wants should be included in the theory of value that the dueness theory employs.

Suppose, then, in sharp contrast to the neoclassical construct, that individual wants (and not just marginal rates of substitution) are formed through constitutive interactions with the other members of the system of commodity owners and exchangers.[4] Through their involvement in the formation of his wants, they are partly accountable for his contribution to the determination of the value of commodities, and hence for his contribution to the creation of value. This goes beyond conventional ideas of cooperation within a division of labor. Other persons not only make a contribution of their own to the product, but also play a role in the individual's own contribution.

But can these indirect social contributions gain a share of entitlements? It has already been shown that any human contribution, whether coming from the production side or the consumption side, can gain a share of entitlement for the value created thereby. The same basic arguments apply to the question of whether indirect social contributions can gain indirect titles to the value accruing to an individual. For example, on a logic of dueness for economic contributions it is compelling that any human contribution to economic value is due a benefit for value contributed. Therefore, since other persons contribute to the formation

3. For a discussion of how socially self-determined wants contribute to the circulation of commodities and money, see Chapter 10, this volume.

4. This position agrees with Heilbroner and Milberg's call for a vision of economics that replaces the "monadic individual" of neoclassical theory with the "irreducible sociality of the concept." The present analysis concretizes that vision with respect to the formulation of the economically creative activities of agents. See Heilbroner and Milberg 1995, p. 84.

of person A's wants, they should have a share of the entitlement to the value determined (hence created) by her wants.

The intuitive idea behind indirect entitlements for social contributions to the individual's economic capacities has been grasped by Shapiro: "Because human productive capacities are themselves partly produced by human work, it seems arbitrary to treat a given producing agent as the 'final' owner of his productive capacities to begin with."[5] Shapiro, however, ultimately desists from using it because he considers the pattern of influence indecipherable. But major elements of the pattern of influence are, I think, definable, so indirect entitlements for indirect contributions remains a meaningful idea and a practicable entitlement.

Another limitation in Shapiro's treatment of indirect entitlements for social contributions to economic value stems from his implicit assumption of a classical view of the economy. As a result of the assumption of production dominance, he recognizes only indirect entitlements for the economic value created by socially formed productive capacities, and he does not take into account the fact that consumers also contribute to the creation of economic value. But since consumer attributes are socially formed, there can also be indirect entitlements to economic value generated by them. If it is morally arbitrary to treat the producer as the "final" owner of his productive capacities, since they are socially formed, then it is no less arbitrary to treat the consuming agent as the "final" owner of her economically creative consumption attributes, if consumption-side activities are economically creative. Analysts who have acknowledged indirect entitlements for indirect contributions have recognized indirect contributions only to individuals' productive capacities, not to their consumptive attributes. But an analyst who accepts the first is logically obliged to accept the second, once it has been shown that consumer attributes can make contributions to the creation of value and that these attributes are socially formed.

In exploring the social self-determination of wants, two considerations are paramount. First, it is important to look for social determinants within the economy. The economy, more than any other sphere of social life, is directed toward the creation of wealth. It generates especially powerful influences upon the formation of individuals' value-generating attributes and capacities, giving the economic sphere special relevance to the dueness theory of property. Second, it is important to search out *systemic* social determination. This sort of determination is fundamental and generic, rather than arbitrary and transitory. Socio-

5. Shapiro 1991, p. 57.

economic determinants of a systemic kind are also important because of their long-neglected egalitarian implications.

PROPERTY AND SYSTEMIC SOCIAL SELF-DETERMINATION

The social self-determination of individual wants and aims – and their role in determining value – can be specified and logically developed by a sequence of models: (1) a system of mutual dependence, (2) a self-renewing economic system, and (3) a process of ongoing circulation of commodities and money.

Analysis of consumer contributions may begin with an initial assumption of equal incomes and equal wealth convertible to private consumption. If the analysis began with a condition of unequal incomes, rich people's wants would have greater capacity to affect the value of commodities. Since the rich would appear to contribute more, they would also deserve more. Unequal initial endowments and incomes therefore bias the account of entitlement. To avoid such bias, this analysis assumes an initial condition of equality of income and wealth.

System of Mutual Dependence and Equalizing Entitlements

Under conditions of division of labor, the individual must enter into the exchange system in order to satisfy the greater part of his economic needs.[6] He not only must satisfy his own needs but, as a means thereto, he must also provide means (i.e., commodities) to the satisfaction of the needs of others. This instrumental interdependence between needs that are given prior to the system constitutes the standard understanding of interdependence in neoclassical theory and in much of political analysis. But in order adequately to grasp mutual dependence, the interdependent formation of needs is also important to note. In order to be able to provide others with means to the satisfaction of their needs, the individual has to constitute herself – has to become the kind of person – who will be able to contribute means to the satisfaction of their needs. This is no native capacity, nor is it derived entirely from the subjective material of the self. It comes from a long personal history of taking into account the needs of others and fashioning her labor so that she will be able to make means to the satisfaction of their needs. In addition, to attain satisfaction from other persons' commodities, the person must constitute her-

6. The logic of social self-determination within a condition of mutual dependence is well developed by Levine 1978, vol. 1, 29–67. The first explicit theoretical analysis of it is Hegel 1952, pp. 124–127.

self and her needs in such a manner that she can be satisfied by what other persons can provide. Nor is this a native capacity or a subjectively derived one. Her needs develop in a process that involves relating to other persons and being influenced by what needs they will recognize. So there develops a universal element in self-seeking where the very content of self-seeking is shaped in accord with the ends of others.

When the intersubjective formation of wants is recognized, it becomes clear that the value of commodities cannot be determined by utility or subjective preference, as value's sole origin and cause. Rather, value is determined by individuals whose needs are socially self-determined by and within a system of mutual dependence. The interdependent formation of wants is not merely bilateral, but multilateral, extending throughout the system of mutually dependent individuals. When person 1 shapes his self-seeking so that he will be able to contribute means to the satisfaction of the needs of person 2, he is indirectly affected by the fact that person 2 has shaped his needs in accord with the fact that he needs those commodities in order to sell them to person 3, or in order to make other things that he plans to sell to person 3, and so on without end. Each person shapes, and is shaped by, other persons and, indeed, by the system of interacting needy individuals.

Since other persons play a role in the formation of this person's wants, they are partly entitled to the value generated by his wants. Indeed, these indirect entitlements are spread throughout the members of the system, because each person's wants – and the value determined thereby – are systemically socially self-determined rather than just bilaterally determined. With everybody involved in everyone else's economic contributions, each person acquires a right to a share of the income that accrues to the other persons. The right is, more precisely, a right to an equalized portion of some of the total income in the system. It is not a right to strict equality of all income, because, despite the form of equal contribution mentioned, there are a variety of other kinds of contributions with respect to which people are not equal, and do not deserve equal remunerations. Some people work harder or better than others, yielding differential amounts of value that warrant different pay.

The individual is not merely beholden to his family, his school, or certain advertisers. If each person's wants, attributes, and capacities were determined simply by a subset of other persons, such as parents or the Sunday school teacher, this would entail highly unequal remunerations. The small group in question would be due a benefit for its contribution to her economically creative qualities and the value created by those qualities. Other groups, less closely related to her contributions, would rightly receive a smaller share of the benefits. But each agent who helps form other persons' wants – and the value determined by these wants – does so as a member of the system, and is equal as a member of the system. No person is more or less responsible than any other for the formation of individual 1's wants – and for the effect of his wants on the determination of value. Because formative contributions come from persons who are *equally* members of the system, and because an irreducibly systemic process means that *all* exchangers make such contributions, the indirect entitlements are claims to relatively equal amounts of income. Since systemic effects are pervasive effects, everyone, not just a subset of persons, gains indirect entitlements, which clearly is more egalitarian than if just a subset of persons gained indirect entitlements.

Systemic interdependence in the formation of economic attributes means a vast dispersion of accountability for each person's value contributions, which in turn implies a vast dispersion and equalization of entitlements. Social self-determination of economic capacities and attributes does not warrant absolutely equal distribution of income, for value is also generated by subjective preferences, which justifies unequal distribution of a proportionate amount of income. But entitlements generated by socially self-determined capacities and attributes would certainly call for more equal amounts of value than unregulated market distribution.

Two major objections can be made to the foregoing argument, objections that might lead one to doubt the capacity of the contributions principle to serve as a moral ground for egalitarian distribution of property. The first objection is that consumers' purchasing activities do not have an equal influence upon the prices of commodities, or so one might argue. For one thing, people's preferences have different degrees of causal influence on the prices of commodities. Consumers have different intensities of preferences for various commodities, and divergent intensities translate into differential purchasing activities, with differing impacts on prices. Another source of unequal influence upon prices, hence a second objection to the present theory, could derive from the fact that the ability of persons to affect prices of commodities will depend upon the initial distribution of income and wealth. Different persons receive different endowments of wealth, and on this basis each person is given a different capacity to affect prices. A wealthy person has more resources with which to affect the value of commodities than does a poor person, seemingly rendering the wealthy person a greater contributor to the value of commodities.

Neither of these objections, in my view, can disprove the proposition that there are some categories of equal contributions by consumers to value. To begin with the second one, this objection points to a need to reiterate an assumption of the present argument, namely that the current economic period began with an equal division of income and wealth. In this model there cannot be unequal contributions from wealthy and poor people simply on the basis of their preexisting resources, because *ex hypothesi* there do not exist any rich or poor people. That leaves the first question: should we suppose that people's contributions differ due to different intensities of preference carrying different causal influence upon the prices of commodities?

The differences in intensities of preference are matters of subjective preferences. Equalities in consumers' influence upon the creation of economic value stem from socially formed attributes of consumers. Neoclassical economic theory assumes that subjective preferences are the sole fundamental determinants of economic value on the consumption side of the economy, and it therefore assumes that consumer contributions are entirely differential. But, contrary to neoclassical theory, the existence of subjective preferences does not preclude the existence of socially formed consumer attributes. Indeed, the latter category of consumer attributes are among the fundamental determinants of economic value on the consumption side of the economy. Therefore, they can be a focus, though not the only focus, in considerations of the relative value that is due individuals because of their consumption-side contributions.[7]

To fully appreciate the significance of social needs as determinants of value, we must know something more about the nature of value and of the system that gives rise to it. In studying the wealth of nations, economics is not simply seeking to explain how society or nature provides human beings with fixed means to the satisfaction of given subsistence needs. It is instead concerned with substances and processes that put society on a footing for the multiplication and expansion of means to the satisfaction of needs far beyond mere natural subsistence or simple reproduction. Indeed, the object of economic science is the satisfaction of needs capable of increase almost without definable limit. In a society capable of this, that which has (economic) value is not simply a means to the satisfaction of a given particular natural need. It must fulfill the condition of being a means to the fulfillment of needs that have undergone a quantitative and qualitative multiplication.[8]

Accordingly, (economic) value has two important qualities that con-

7. That is, socially self-determined wants and needs as described in this book, not necessarily as posited in another theory.
8. On the notion of a quantitative and qualitative multiplication of needs see Hegel 1952, pp. 126–128. The latter is a multiplication of the kinds of needs, whereas the former is a multiplication of the number of needs.

tribute to its emergence as a distinct social substance. Value is something that is multiple, and it is something that can be expanded. One way of assessing the value-contributions made by socially self-determined needs is to consider their contribution to the existence of value as an expandable and multipliable substance.[9]

Some intervening conditions need to be taken into account, because value, as I have defined it, depends on the existence of a certain kind of system of mutual dependence. So the issue becomes: what is the importance of social needs in the determination of the condition of mutual dependence, a condition that is itself necessary to the existence of (economic) value?

Mutual dependence is clearly a necessary condition for the existence of value. Division of labor, which is essential for the multiplication of society's productive powers, cannot develop adequately without the unification of labors through a system of exchange, which is a system of mutual dependence. Since mutual dependence is necessary for division of labor, and since the latter is necessary to multiply society's productive powers, mutual dependence is essential to the existence of value.

Where direct appropriation rather than contractual interdependence is the usual mode of acquisition of goods, individuals can be reduced to relying upon the naturally occurring surplus of fruits, nuts, and game. Such a surplus is not "value," properly speaking, that is, an expandable and multipliable substance, but rather a fixed and limited natural product.

Whatever accounts for mutual dependence and the multipliable aspect of value is, therefore, a necessary condition for the existence of value. Social self-determination of needs is among the key conditions for the existence of a system of mutual dependence, and therefore for the existence of value. The social structuring of self-seeking, such that each exchanger seeks his own ends by contributing means to the realization of the ends of others, makes a condition of mutual dependence possible. It does so by reconciling the free self-seeking of each person with the self-seeking of all the rest. Through its contribution to mutual dependence, social self-determination of needs contributes to the possibility of a vast multiplication of goods and commodities and of an ongoing expansion of the surplus. In this sense it contributes crucially to the emergence of value, properly speaking. By contrast, a neoclassical preference-satisfaction maximizer does not construe his wants in these

9. In evaluating the relative importance of subjective preference and social need, I have benefited from David Levine's work on the theory of value (Levine 1977, pp. 16–31).

ways,[10] and so such a notion of self-seeking cannot fulfill the conditions for mutual dependence, nor then for value.

Mutual dependence per se is not sufficient for the existence of value; a particular form of it is necessary. If it took the form of a mutual dependence among human beings with fixed and limited needs, then people would be motivated to trade or barter only for given particular use-values. Mutual dependence can contribute to the existence of value only if it consists of individuals subject to a quantitative multiplication of needs. The multiplication of needs, through a process of social self-determination of needs, provides the motivational spur for the multiplication of commodities and the expansion of value. Innumerable kinds and quantities of needs are excited by exposure to the vast multiplication of goods produced by the division of labor. Value, as something not limited to given particular use-values, can exist only if it stands in relation to expanding and multiplying needs. Therefore value is ultimately determined by the social self-determination of needs.

Neoclassical preference refers to person 1's desire for good X over good Y. Preferring good X to good Y does not, however, explain why a person wants more than a selection of subsistence objects, and indeed conflates the choice of subsistence objects with the choice of goods generally. Neoclassical thought, however, recognizes the limits of its concept of preference, for it finds it necessary to introduce a postulate that "consumers prefer more rather than less." But the postulate is unaccounted for, not deduced from any prior course of reasoning.

Social self-determination of needs supplies the missing point of argument, and as such it is a fundamental determinant of the existence of value. Therefore, socially self-determined wants and needs and their contribution to value form an appropriate focus for the ethics of dueness for economic contributions.

With respect to the social self-determination of wants, every person is approximately equal in the sense that their needs are all subject to a quantitative and qualitative multiplication. Virtually no member of a capital-based economic system is content with the biological minimum. With each person's needs subject to a quantitative and qualitative multiplication, each person is in this sense equally responsible for the existence of value as a distinct social substance. Differences in intensity of preference pale before this profound infinitude of wants, the sine qua non of (economic) value. Corresponding to the way in which individuals are equally responsible for the existence of value, they are equally due for the value that is generated by this kind of quality. They are not

10. See note 14.

entitled to strict equalization of total income, because in addition to the equalities in their contributions to value there are also differences, such as in the amount and kind of their productive activities.

There is a further objection to this argument that needs to be addressed. Even if it were true that needs are socially self-determined, this would not automatically imply that people contribute equally to the value of commodities. For one might still argue that some people have greater influence than others in the social formation of the content and direction of consumers' wants and needs, as these affect market prices. Opinion leaders, cultural figures, advertisers, and celebrities such as Michael Jackson and Brooke Shields arguably shape more consumers' preferences than the ordinary person does, and this might give such notables disproportionate responsibility for consumers' contribution to value, thereby skewing calculations of dueness far from equality.

But while advertisers and newsmakers in some ways shape consumer wants more than ordinary citizens do, the character of these effects does not entitle them to greater remuneration. When an advertiser influences a consumer's preference, the choice to purchase is still very much the consumer's own. Her purchase of the company's good is essentially a matter of preference and, as such, an optional matter of discretion. For her action she bears ultimate responsibility, not the advertiser. To be sure, heavy-handed advertising may somewhat distort the integrity of consumers, but it does not undermine their fundamental freedom of choice in any ultimate way. By contrast, without social self-determination of self-seeking by and within a system of mutual dependence, the person's freedom is severely attenuated, and in some cases could be all but destroyed. Individuals, not seeking the fulfillment of their needs through reciprocal relations of exchange, could then descend into direct appropriation, and thereafter into a Hobbesian war of all against all.

The essential difference between these two kinds of social determination of wants is that the advertiser–consumer example does not present a case of mutual necessities. The relation between them ultimately breaks up into subjective decisions that eradicate the kind of indirect responsibilities that might give rise to indirect entitlements. By contrast, the structuring of each person's self-seeking such that she seeks her own ends in accordance with the ends of others is essential to her own freedom and self-realization, as it is to theirs. It is a mutual necessity for which all bear equal responsibility, since mutual dependence is not possible on a systemic scale unless people generally abide by it.

Individuals qua members of the system of mutual dependence exert relatively equal influence on one another to fulfill the requirements for mutual dependence. Each does this by insisting on receiving consideration in return for benefits proffered, as well as in other ways. But the individual qua advertiser cannot claim a greater responsibility for the formation of the consumer's wants than an ordinary exchanger can, and so, the advertiser does not deserve a greater entitlement than the ordinary exchanger gets.

How much greater equality will the redistributory property right produce compared to what we now have? At present we have welfare entitlements that give the poor a claim to an economic minimum or floor. In this way welfare programs place some limit on the extremes of income inequality. But the right to an equal share of a portion of national income is not fulfilled simply by narrowing extremes. It will result in greater equality than welfare does, because it subjects a substantial part of all of the consumable income in the nation to a principle of strict equalization. This still leaves a question, however, of how much equality will be effected by the right if people assent to it. The right will institute tendencies toward a moderately egalitarian order, not just toward a reduction in extremes. It will do so because the forms of equal contributions to value are at least as important in creating value as the unequal contributions to value are. In view of the equal importance of the equal contributions and the unequal contributions, it may turn out that the right requires an equalization of fifty percent of the consumable income of the nation. But further analysis will be required before a precise quantitative determination can be provided.

Self-Renewing Economy and Equalizing Entitlements

An intuitive grasp of a more systematic form of social self-determination of needs and value can be attained by formulating a simple model of self-renewing economy. "The system . . . in a self-replacing state," Sraffa writes, is a genuinely circular process, unlike the neoclassical idea of a one-way avenue from production to consumption.[11] Consumption sets up the conditions for production in the next period rather than being the end point of the economic process. However, Sraffa provides a technological explanation of the reproduction of the system in terms of the "values [that] spring from the methods of production."[12] But this leaves a lacuna, which the present account addresses, in its analysis of the needs of the human participants who give life to the process, and without whom system renewal would grind to a halt. Sraffa's framework may then be put to a different purpose than he intended: the explanation of the formation of needs implicit in the self-replacing system, and

11. Sraffa 1960, p. 3. 12. Ibid.

the explanation of how relative prices (value) spring from needs thus formed. The analysis in this section does not attempt to overcome the limitations in Sraffa's formal analysis, which gives too much importance to the production side, yet it can serve a heuristic purpose. For it can be used to show that the social determination of individual needs is a massive abstraction from any determinacy of the individual in terms of purely natural or subjective attributes.

Suppose the economy consists of two producers, who are also consumers of each other's products. With 280 quarters of wheat and 12 tons of iron, individual A, the wheat producer, can produce 400 quarters of wheat, while individual B can produce 20 tons of iron with 120 quarters of wheat and 8 tons of iron.

$$\begin{aligned} 280 \text{ qr. wh.} + 12 \text{ t. ir.} &\rightarrow 400 \text{ qr. wh.} \\ 120 \text{ qr. wh.} + 8 \text{ t. ir.} &\rightarrow 20 \text{ t. ir.} \end{aligned}$$

After production has taken place, individual A needs 12 tons of iron in order to re-produce 400 quarters of wheat and thereby to sustain himself in the next period. He needs to exchange 120 quarters of wheat for 12 tons of individual B's iron. Individual A's fulfillment of this need also contributes to the satisfaction of individual B's need, but beyond that it also restores his own original set of commodities, individual B's original set of commodities, and, indeed, restores the original distribution of commodities of the whole two-person system. It is a need that is not only shaped to satisfy himself, but is shaped in accord with, and itself has an implied goal of, the renewal of the economic system as a whole. Individual A's interest in forming this kind of need is *socially* self-determined in the sense that his own need can only be fulfilled by shaping it in accord with the need of individual B and by meeting the replacement requirements for the renewal of the system of individuals.

The self-renewing system that shapes needs in this way and that is shaped by them may be expressed as follows:

$$\begin{aligned} P_aA_a + P_bB_a &= P_aA \\ P_aA_b + P_bB_b &= P_bB \end{aligned}$$

The unknowns P_a and P_b are respectively the values of the commodities a and b. Individual A's total production of wheat is A; individual B's total production of wheat is B; A_a is the wheat used in wheat production; B_a is the iron used in wheat production; A_b is the wheat used in iron production; B_b is the iron used in iron production. The solution values of the equation system are the unique set of exchange-values that restore the original distribution: P_b = 10 qr. wh. / 1 t. ir., P_a = 10 qr. wh. /10 qr. wh. Exchange-values that restore the original distribution of inputs, reflect – are determined by – needs that are shaped in accord with the requirements for the renewal of the economic system. These exchange-values, determined by socially self-determined needs, make it possible for individual B to give up precisely B_a and get A_b – in which event she will have been restored to the original position; and simultaneously the determination enables individual A to give up precisely A_b and get B_a – thereby restoring his original distribution.

Where the individual's needs are formed by and within the self-renewing economic system, the members of the system are fundamentally involved in each individual's contribution to the determination of the value of commodities. Since the members of the system help shape the needs of each individual, and since they thereby contribute to the exchange-values influenced by her needs, each of them are due a benefit for their indirect contributions. That is, indirect contributions gain indirect entitlements. The fact that, in a self-renewing system, one's needs are shaped by the members of the system as a whole, and not just by a subset of people, affects the proportions of property to which the participants are entitled. The determination of a set of exchange-values that restores the initial distribution of inputs for the economy as a whole is the result of a systemic determination of needs by the members of the self-renewing economy as a whole. Subsystemic influences would not determine a set of exchange-values that would restore the system as a whole. Where the formation of each individual's needs – and their contribution to value – depend upon the members of the system as a whole, all the other persons in the system have a right to a portion of the value that accrues to her. Property is thereby established as a right to a significant degree of equalization of value. The person is not simply partially beholden to a subset of others.

Circulation of Commodities and Equalizing Entitlements

Although the model of a self-renewing economy can provide insight into social self-determination of needs, it lacks the element of luxury consumption and overemphasizes technological determination of exchange-values. An account of the process of ongoing circulation of commodities can overcome both of these problems, and so is important in the further exposition of socially self-determined wants, value, and entitlement.

In order for the members of a system of commodity exchangers to be sustained, there must be an ongoing circulation of commodities. Ongoing circulation of commodities means the individual acquisition of commodities must not be dead-end consumption; it must eventually lead to another acquisition of commodities, and so on without end. The individual's acquisition of commodities must provide a basis for another exchange, and yet another one after that, ad infinitum. For without a follow-up exchange, the individual cannot be sustained over time. Through this process, value is sustained, and in this sense created. "The sale of commodity one (C_1) is the means to the acquisition of money (M) which is the means to the acquisition of commodity two (C_2). This act constitutes . . . no terminus for the movement but . . . the subsistence of value through the circuit," as the economic theorist David P. Levine points out.[13]

The neoclassical concept of the consumer as a maximizer of subjective preferences cannot fulfill the requirements for ongoing commodity circulation, and so inadequately comprehends the nature of the consumer. Such requirements can be met only by a person pursuing a socially self-determined goal of ongoing circulation, whether intentionally or not. The individual is not able to continue to participate in exchange relations – and the circulation will not continue – unless she manages to have some money at hand. But the notion of a maximizer of subjective preference does not give us any reason to think that she will consume in a way that will enable her to continue to sell her labor. She may very well consume in a way that undermines her capacity to make money, and this can happen even if she satisfies the budget constraint. She could consume in a way that erodes the skills or educational characteristics needed in order to sell one's labor. A case in point would be getting resoundingly drunk before a job interview. Thus the neoclassical idea of a subjective preference maximizer fails to fulfill the condition that the consumer will have money at hand, and therefore fails to satisfy a necessary condition for an ongoing circulation of commodities. A consumer who engaged in intertemporal utility maximization would also be unsuited to the task of fulfilling this condition.[14]

13. Levine 1978–1981, vol. 1, p. 117. See Levine for more on the individual within a process of ongoing circulation of commodities and money.
14. From a neoclassical perspective, an intertemporal subjective utility maximizer would pay adequate attention to the problem of having sufficient money in later periods. But it would not be consistent with the nature of such a consumer to do so. The condition that one pursue one's preferences in a manner consistent with the condition of having money at hand later would remove certain goods or consumptions from his purview, for which preferences are already built into his nature. So he could not accept the restriction. The neoclassical intertemporal maximizer, like the static maximizer, has a preference ordering ranging over all possible consumptions. But there is a wide range of conceivable consump-

The likelihood that a person will shape his consumption in accord with the condition for selling his labor and obtaining money is greatly increased if he has a goal of the ongoing circulation of money, and not only a goal of satisfying subjective preference. Contrary to the neoclassical view that preference maximization is the individual's sole goal, Adam Smith asserted that all individuals have a goal of having money at hand.[15] The goal of having money at hand has no meaning or purpose in itself, but derives significance from the fact that it is necessary for the circulation to continue. Therefore, the goal of having money at hand is, inferably, a tacit acceptance of the system goal of ongoing circulation of commodities and money. The individual has this goal through the effect of a social self-determination rather than through a subjective self-determination. Because individuals subsist within a system of commodity circulation, no one will give the individual anything economically valuable without receiving valuable consideration in exchange. The individual assimilates a goal of ongoing circulation because he must do so

tions that are ruled out by the condition that one pursue one's needs in a manner consistent with the requirements for the ongoing circulation of commodities. More specifically, a person who was not well tutored in the social requirements of modern economic life could have a dispreference for wearing the sort of clothes mandated by employers in a certain profession. He might stubbornly refuse to eat his meals at times when others are expected to do so. Maybe he is indisposed to rest at conventionally designated sleeping hours, leaving him unable to work when work is available. All of these are kinds of consumption.

That the individual eats at the accepted times, sleeps at the appointed times, forms needs that others can recognize and provide for, dresses himself according to socially accepted styles – are all things that we take for granted. But these are the acts of a person who conducts himself with reference to others, not the acts of a subjective utility maximizer, who in the matter of preferences is a law unto himself. Said acts represent a kind of self-seeking with an intersubjective inner structure, in which self-seeking has been shaped such that it proceeds by contributing means to the ends of others. This person's end, unlike the utility maximizer's, is not just to acquire property. He has a dual will: to acquire property by means of surrendering property to another. In the course of life, such a person absorbs modes of self-seeking that are consistent with the requirements of the system of individuals.

A socially self-determined person, who conducts himself with reference to others, is therefore the kind of person who can accept the limitation on consumption patterns that is necessary in order to assure that he will have sufficient money in later periods. The subjective utility maximizer is too solipsistic to accept this limit. The condition of having money at hand flows from a logic of mutual dependence rather than from the logic of subjective utility maximization.

15. Smith 1937, p. 22.

in order to subsist within a social process dependent upon ongoing circulation of commodities.

Self-seeking in accord with the goal of ongoing circulation is one of the individual's most important contributions to the subsistence of value through the circuit, and in this sense to the creation of value. Patterns of accountability for this kind of self-seeking therefore relate directly to the problem of determining individuals' dueness for value contributions, that is, for determining the amount of value that should be distributed to them because its creation is due to them.

The fact that the individual has a goal of ongoing circulation of commodities is partly due to every other member of the process. As determinants of her having this goal, they are also a fundamental source of her contribution to the value of commodities, for her actions in accord with this goal contribute to the subsistence, and therefore to the creation, of value. These other persons, therefore, have an indirect entitlement to a share of the value that accrues to her in the course of her socially self-determined self-seeking. This makes property a right to some significant equalization of value. In what way do they all contribute to the fact that she has and pursues a goal of having money at hand and a goal of ongoing circulation? When the individual approaches the world of commodity exchange with the intent of acquiring a desired good, no one will give it to her without receiving another good or money in return, because each knows that he can't survive and flourish in a process of ongoing commodity circulation unless he makes this stipulation. And this is an exceptionally strong inducement to the consumer to have a goal of having money at hand – the prime condition for the ongoing circulation of commodities and money. The contribution that each other commodity exchanger makes toward her having this goal is an equal one. The fact that a wealthier person declines to turn over goods without consideration is no more nor less responsible for her assimilation of said goal than the fact that a poorer person makes a similar stipulation for entering into exchange with her. It is clear, then, that everyone else has a relatively equal responsibility for the fact that the individual has a goal of the ongoing circulation of commodities and money. The people who exercise this indirect influence have an indirect entitlement to equal shares of a part of the value that accrues to the subject in the course of her market activities, specifically, the part of the value due to their indirect influence.

SOCIAL CONTRIBUTIONS AND FEASIBLE ACCOUNTING

Contrary to a widely held view, the social formation of economically creative attributes can lead to a coherent pattern of entitlements. More specifically, it leads to an entitlement to equal shares of one part of national income and wealth and unequal shares of a second portion of the national income that is assigned to consumption. According to Shapiro, the pattern of social formation of productive capacities is "exceedingly complex, arguably impossible" to trace, and gives rise to "a tangled and indecipherable web of overdetermined entitlements."[16] Munzer, similarly, says in his critique of Gauthier's notion of proportionate entitlements to the cooperative surplus that "one can rarely say *how* much" each contributed or deserved.[17] This appears to create a quandary for the present analysis by implying that socially formed consumptive attributes and related entitlements may also be unintelligible.

Although the task of identifying the social formation of consumption-side attributes is complex, complexity does not require that we throw up our hands. The informational requirements posed by Shapiro and Munzer are unnecessarily high. In these scholars' view it is necessary to conduct a holistic analysis that would trace the formative process within every social sphere bearing on productive capacities, ranging from Sunday school and parental influences to the economy and the state, and various "extra-social" sources.[18] Shapiro's methodology is at the same time highly individualistic, virtually entailing an economic biography in his example of the "the conventional wife's" productive capacities.

But between the holistic analysis and the overly individualistic level resides a systematic level of analysis that *is* feasible. This approach reduces the informational requirements while affording a sufficient account of the causal sequence. The systematic approach does not take account of all social spheres but justifies a focus on only one: the economy, the sphere with the greatest bearing on economic capacities and attributes.

In explaining the attributes of economic agents we are only beholden to fulfill the requirements of economic science for the account of any economic phenomenon, such as the prices and quantities of goods. Economics only gives an account of influences from within the economic system. When economic theory looks for "a definite causal relation

16. Shapiro 1991, pp. 57–58.
17. Munzer 1990, p. 273. See also Okun 1975, p. 46; Dahl 1982, pp. 182–85.
18. Shapiro 1991, p. 58; Munzer 1990, p. 273.

between two phenomena," it considers its task to be "accomplished" when it has traced the pattern of causation through all the economic variables, stopping at the "noneconomic" cause, rather than exploring the "noneconomic problem."[19] Theorists of general economic equilibrium, for instance, usually give an account of the formation of prices by and within the economic system, but do not consider themselves obliged to explain exogenous factors, such as the neurophysiology of preferences or the physical origins of natural resources. The proposed "systematic" account of the individual's consumption attributes generally accords with the methodology of economic science, since it provides an account of such attributes' economic causes rather than of their noneconomic causes.

Standard economic analysis probably errs in supposing that consumptive attributes are noneconomic, but it seems correct in positing that only economic causes of economic phenomena need a causal accounting. More than any other sphere of social life, the economy is directed toward the creation of social wealth. In driving toward that end, it generates exceptionally powerful influences upon the factors affecting the creation of wealth. It exerts enormous impact upon the individual's consumption attributes and productive attributes, profoundly shaping and molding them for the task of determining and creating value. As Smith points out, "the difference between a philosopher and a common street porter is not upon many occasions as much the cause, as the effect of the division of labor."[20] Various other social spheres also contribute in a diffuse way. But none rivals the economy's influence in shaping individual attributes and capacities specifically toward the generation of wealth. The educational sphere may, as Shapiro notes, affect a person's productive capacities, but this sphere's proximate aim is to develop knowledge, not wealth. Noneconomic social agencies should not, therefore, be considered "responsible" for creating wealth or wealth-creating capacities; they constitute only preconditions.

SOCIAL PERSONALITY AND TENETS OF THE THEORY OF RIGHTS

Rawlsian liberals often presuppose a conception of subjective personality even when they acknowledge that the person has a social nature. They posit subjective personality because they think that it must be pre-

19. Schumpeter 1951, p. 5; Koopmans 1957, p. 132; Robbins 1984, p. 86.
20. Smith 1937, p. 15.

supposed for the sake of the logical requirements of the theory of justice and right. It is indeed correct to suppose that freedom and individuality are necessary to the conceptualization of the moral subject, and in this way to the theory of justice and right.[21] But rather more questionable is the assumption that subjective personality is necessary to freedom and individuality.[22] Rawlsian liberals also postulate subjective personality (the "priority of the self") in order to elude the problem of ethical relativism. Positing particular social attributes of the self is thought to entail buying into the given social system that instilled those qualities, making justice relative to a particular social order.

But a substantial body of social theory strongly suggests that social determination does not necessarily violate free will or homogenize individuals.[23] When social determination is understood in terms of constitutive influences, in place of the old idea of it as a coercive force, it is necessary *to* free will and individual differentiation. As Adam Smith's analysis implies, individuality – the difference, say, between a street porter and a philosopher – is the effect rather than the cause of the division of labor and the concomitant differentiation of occupations.[24] Because a social concept of the person can provide a concept of a free individual, it is capable of satisfying the logical requirements for a concept of the moral subject and therefore also for a theory of rights.

Moreover, we can avoid the problem of ethical relativism attendant on the concept of social personality by positing only those social attributes that are logically necessary for the existence of *any* capital-based economic system. Social attributes that are indispensable to any such system would not be relativistic or particularistic, at least within the compass of capital-based economic systems. Global applicability of the theory would, then, only be limited by the utopian supersession of scarcity by unforeseeable means and by residual pockets of precapitalist society.

But it might be argued that the concept of social self-determination, though consistent with the theory of rights, is not necessary to it. T. H. Green argues that a person can be a self-determining and self-realizing moral subject without being socially determined.[25] However, in a theory

21. See Rawls 1971, pp. 264, 520, 560.
22. When Rawls posits that the self must be prior to social influences if it is to be free, he is implicitly opposing social determination to free will. See Rawls 1971, p. 560.
23. The *locus classicus* for this view is Hegel's *Philosophy of Right*. See also the neo-Hegelians Levine, Benhabib, and Winfield.
24. See the analysis of Smith in Levine 1977, Chapter 2.
25. Green 1967, pp. 9, 20–21; 1969, Book II, Chapter 1.

of property based on reward for economic contributions, it is important to focus on individuals within the sphere of economic relations. And, in a capital-based economic system, economic actors cannot generally be self-realizing unless they are shaped by – and shape themselves in accord with – several system requirements, including the requirements for the self-renewal of the economic system and the ongoing circulation of commodities and money.

CURRENT CONTRIBUTIONS VERSUS PREEXISTING INEQUALITIES

An approach to distributive justice emphasizing ongoing economic contributions tends to abstract from historically generated inequalities. Such a theory, it might be objected, bypasses other, more important sources of inequality that are germane to distributive justice. "Differential *initial* wealth," not the exploitation of ongoing labor contributions, Roemer argues, is "the central injustice of a capitalist system by virtue of the unequal opportunities that it creates."[26] Past accumulations, on this view, are more important sources of inequality than ongoing contributions, because they enable the rich to parlay their resources into greater current contributions than other citizens can. But worthwhile heuristic reasons exist for taking the contributions approach, which can even shed light on the ethical validity (or lack of validity) of preexisting inequalities.

The abstraction from historically accumulated inequalities has enabled us to glimpse the contours of some relatively equal contributions and entitlements that would otherwise be obscured by the towering peaks and abysmal canyons of preexisting inequalities. Far from presuming the justice of preexisting inequalities, however, this study puts preexisting inequalities in serious ethical jeopardy by showing that some forms of contributions are equal and that their corresponding entitlements are also equal, thereby calling in question the concentration of ownership of preexisting economic resources. Judging from the character of ongoing contributions, it does not appear that holders of great accumulations are really due them in the first place. This theory of dueness for economic contributions will provide cold comfort to defenders of preexisting inequalities. Even if an entrepreneur's accumulation of wealth could be justified as proportionate to his or her large previous contributions, this person's progeny could hardly sustain a claim that the wealth was due him or her.

26. Roemer 1988, p. 89.

Some analysts hold that preexisting inequalities of wealth are more important sources of current inequalities of income (due to current contributions) because they think economic "differentials will not be large" once the preexisting inequalities are eradicated.[27] While wealth differentials are clearly more unequal than income differentials, narrowing the former will not evidently eliminate the latter.[28] A comprehensive survey of the formation of distributions finds that "the occupational pay structure . . . has been mainly shaped by supply and demand," not by preexisting inequalities.[29] "Inequalities of wealth," Phelps Brown writes, "contribute only a small part of the inequality of incomes as a whole. If they were wholly removed, that inequality would not be much reduced. In the United Kingdom in 1977, rent, dividends and net interest amounted to little more than 6 percent of all personal income . . ."[30] In the United States in 1995, Hacker reports, "Even in the $100,000 to $200,000 bracket, almost 80 percent of all income is derived from employment" rather than from investments.[31] And 70 percent of the income of the best-off one percent of the population comes from employment rather than investments.[32] Much higher percentages of the income of those less well off comes from employment. So income has to be a major concern of distributive justice, which should not be occupied just with the distribution of wealth.

Studies that attribute "overwhelming" force to preexisting inequalities in determining the pattern of distributions are sometimes based on questionable accounting practices that amplify the importance of such factors. One study categorizes salaries and other rewards to directors and senior managers as income to capital rather than income to employment.[33] Senior managers are undoubtedly powerful, but one

27. Walzer 1983, p. 117. See also Rawls 1971, p. 307. In a similar vein, Roemer sees the problem of inequality primarily in terms of endowments and access to the means of production, rather than in terms of exploitation or unequal remuneration of current contributions; see Roemer 1988, p. 89, on "Exploitation Deemphasized."
28. For the view that supply and demand form a major determinant of current inequalities, and for a comprehensive study of the literature, see Phelps Brown 1988, pp. 349–52. Levy 1987, p. 121, similarly emphasizes the pushes and pulls of the labor market. Westergaard and Resler 1975, p. 52, cogently argue that "the first – and the overwhelmingly important –" force determining the pattern of distribution is the "private ownership of capital."
29. Phelps Brown 1988, p. 400.
30. Ibid., p. 343.
31. Hacker 1997, p. 85.
32. Ibid., p. 85.
33. Westergaard and Resler 1975, pp. 52–53.

should not underestimate the competitiveness of the labor market at the cupola of a society that, rightly or wrongly, regards executives as decisive to the success of corporations. Recognizing that senior executives' salaries are, to some significant extent, incomes to employment (whether excessive or appropriate) rather than incomes to property increases the relative importance of the former as a source of current inequalities.

To gain a sense of the inequalities stemming from ongoing contributions, as distinct from preexisting inequalities, consider differences in salary in the United States during the early 1990s between a tenured professor of economics ($50,000) and a medical specialist such as a radiologist ($230,000 or more for a surgical speciality);[34] between a university librarian with a Ph.D. ($30,000) and an entry-level attorney at a major firm ($85,000+); between a sports star (as much as $4 million) and a member of the farm team ($25,000); between an off-Broadway actor ($30,000) and a movie star (several million dollars); and between a director of a camp for hyperactive children ($65,000) and a Hollywood movie director ($2 million). Moreover, two entrepreneurs who possess equal capital resources can easily incur substantially different fortunes depending on the public's like or dislike of his or her brand of "pet rock."

These large differentials cannot be accounted for in terms of preexisting inequalities or initial capital endowments. They are primarily based on current capabilities. And "whether a given capability is great or small – indeed, whether it is a capability at all – depends on the demand for it," not just on preexisting inequalities, according to Phelps Brown.[35] Moreover, with regard to access to means of production, it may be noted that Bill Gates started out with little capital endowment and not especially great access to the means of production, yet his worth in 2000 is between $50 and $100 billion. These examples, and countless others that could be adduced, indicate a large domain of income differentials, continuously regenerating and highly unequal. Such a condition offends the ethics of dueness for economic contributions as understood by the present analysis.

34. Hilts 1993, p. 9.
35. Phelps Brown 1988, p. 409. By this I do not mean to assume, without qualification, Phelps Brown's theory of demand. His view of demand can be presumed to follow that of neoclassical theory, in which demand is derived from subjective preference, whereas I would derive it from the endogenous formation of preferences; see Chapter 10, this volume.

AN EGALITARIAN ORDER: CHARACTERISTICS AND PROSPECTS

At this stage in the evolution of social values, a great barrier to redistributory policy resides in commonplace ways of thinking about income. The idea of a right to an equalization of *a portion of* income can help overcome this barrier. People often think that they have an exclusive entitlement to all that comes to them in the course of market activity. The reactive position, along standard socialist lines, is that our income is entirely social and belongs to the state. In the suggested alternative, the individual has an exclusive title to part of his or her income, but another part should go in the direction of egalitarian redistribution. This position overcomes conventional alternatives, accommodating principles of both equality and difference.

Welfare state theorists troubled by great disparities of income and wealth also try to balance principles of equality and inequality accordingly. John Rawls's theory sanctions inequalities of income and wealth insofar as they improve the (absolute) position of the worst off. Keynesian economic ethics call for the reduction of disparities of wealth associated with rentier capitalism, but do not reduce the inequalities of income arising within the microeconomy. The Keynesian state eliminates inequalities due to the high cost of capital by providing capital more cheaply to prospective entrepreneurs, but permits differential incentives to inspire efficient allocation of productive resources.[36]

Yet the liberal welfare state approach to balancing equality and inequality ultimately permits extreme inequalities of income. Rawls acknowledges that "the most extreme disparities in wealth and income are allowed [by the difference principle] provided that the expectations of the least fortunate are raised in the slightest degree," but he discounts extreme inequality as an "abstract possibilit[y]" prevented by the operation of "the principles of equal liberty and open positions."[37] However, a system significantly oriented toward the worst off, and equipped with affirmative action to open positions, can heighten income inequalities. This is not merely a remote theoretical possibility but an existing fact.[38] Despite social spending on welfare reaching hundreds of billions of dol

36. Keynes 1964, Chapter 24.
37. Rawls 1971, pp. 157–158.
38. While Reagan himself was minimally concerned about the worst off, the system in place was, and welfare spending during his administration increased considerably.

lars in the 1980s in the United States, the top one percent of families increased their share of the growth of national income to sixty percent after taxes.[39]

The right to an equalized portion of income more evenly balances principles of equality and inequality. Rawls's difference principle regulates the absolute position of one category of citizens, the worst off, not the relative position of other strata. Most liberal theories of the welfare state resemble his theory in the sense that they focus on the worst off or the impoverished. They are particularistic on the subject of entitlement, handing out entitlements to the impoverished, the elderly, the infirm, and the unemployed. By contrast, every economic actor is a subject of the right to an equalized portion of income: it is a universal entitlement rather than a particularistic one. Thus, it does not regulate only the position of the worst off but also the relative position of other strata. Empirical evidence suggests that the redistributory measures of the American welfare state reduce the height of the income hierarchy somewhat but not a lot.[40] In this sense, this state institutes a principle of partial equalization. The right to an equalization of a portion of income distributes income more equally in the sense that the portion of income subject to redistribution is allocated by strict equality. (This right is also a form of partial equalization, because not all income is subject to its provisions.)

In the proposed right, the object of the right is more general than welfare state entitlements. A right to an equalized portion of income allocates money, a universal means to the acquisition of commodities. The object of the right is not limited, as welfare state entitlements frequently are, to specific categories of goods, such as public housing, food stamps, farm price supports, social security, and special aid programs.

Relative to liberal principles of the welfare state, then, the right to an equalized portion of income generalizes the subject of entitlement, generalizes the object of entitlement, and subjects a larger portion of income to a principle of strictly equal distribution. At the same time, it preserves a balance between equality and difference. The right of individuals to accumulate income for particular ends is not abridged. With respect to the second portion of income, the individual is unfettered and may accumulate as much as he or she wants relative to other citizens.

Current distrust of government programs makes the idea of a major new redistributory program seem politically irrelevant. But it is not unimaginable that the right to an equalized portion of income could be

39. Danziger, Sandefur, and Weinberg 1994, p. 9; Burtless 1994, p. 52; Nasar 1992.
40. Phelps Brown 1988, p. 341.

realized in the long run. We often forget that the existence of democracy in the United States is the product of a massive historical change from feudalism to independent proprietorship and capitalism. Democracy's current form is also the result of major transformations within U.S. democracy itself during the twentieth century, changes that have brought it from a fairly small state with minimal administrative capabilities to a regulatory welfare state. Given the magnitude of previous changes in distributory and redistributory institutions, it is not impossible that there will be further development of redistributory capabilities; indeed, it is more unlikely that they will not occur.

With a 40 percent inheritance tax on bequests over $600,000 and a 38 percent tax on capital gains, the United States, like other welfare states, already engages in a considerable amount of redistribution, but people do not experience the extent of it, because these taxes are statist, going into the coffers of the state for various "public" purposes, rather than flowing back to individuals. The proposed redistribution, by contrast, takes the form of a property right. As such, it has to be returned to individuals within civil society, and so it may be more acceptable to individuals than statist forms of inheritance and capital gains taxes. Except for this point of difference, the basic purpose of inheritance taxes – to break up massive concentrations of wealth[41] – is not very different from that of the right to an equalization of part of national income, which could then be a progression from the former, a coming phase of the unfolding logic of equality predicted by Tocqueville: "The gradual progress of equality is something fated. The main features of this progress are the following: it is universal and permanent, . . . and every event and every man helps it along. Is it wise to suppose that a movement which has been so long in train could be halted by one generation?"[42]

The problem that the proposed right will face is not political irrelevance but the fact that it can take a terribly long time for a meaningful idea to take hold (even assuming that it is an ethically valid right). Other democratic ideals met this difficulty during the course of their gradual realization. Prior to 1789, large-scale democracy was itself a political improbability. It had been tried only in small republics or city-states, and political philosophers thought it impossible on a large scale.[43] But democracy grew and grew, at least in part because it was a meaningful idea. The right to an equalized portion of income could also

41. Eisenstein 1956 cited in Caron et al. 1998, p. 2.
42. Tocqueville 1969, p. 12, cited by Rae 1981, p. 1.
43. Mansfield 1989, p. xix; Dahl 1973, pp. 4, 6; Rousseau 1967.

have practical force, if it too is a meaningful idea; but like other ideals of democracy, it would take a long time for it to be absorbed by the people.[44]

EQUALITY OF CAPABILITIES, NEEDS, OR INCOMES?

Theories of justice select one or more qualities, actions, or ends that, they reason, have high ethical worth or importance relative to other such things. Some stress the ethical worth of capabilities, others utilities, still others needs, free will, economic contributions, or membership in a community. Once the critically important qualities or actions are determined, the theory then sets out the conditions that these qualities entail or entitle the person to. It may also formulate principles of distribution regarding the means of realizing or satisfying them. The theory of justice may be described as a theory about what should be valued, coupled with a theory about the principles of distribution of valued things.

The theory of justice as dueness values contributions to the creation of economic value, and it holds that, for these contributions, people are due proportionate benefits in value terms, by which I mean money. Amartya Sen regards capabilities as critically important to human living – more important than utilities, primary goods, or income and wealth. Society and policy have the task of "achieving certain basic functionings and acquiring the corresponding capabilities."[45] Capabilities are the abilities to do certain things or, in Sen's thinking, to achieve certain functionings, such as "the ability to meet one's nutritional requirements, the wherewithal to be clothed and sheltered, the power to participate in the social life of the community."[46] According to the "basic needs" approach, certain needs are crucial to human life, and justice requires that everyone have essential goods.

A theory that attaches primary importance to a quality, such as free will, generally asserts a principle of equality with respect to it, such as that everyone should have equal freedom of will. Sen, who sees capabilities as crucial to human living, advances a principle of equality of capabilities. Needs theorists, who think everyone has a common set of basic

44. This is not to say that ideas alone could produce a new democratic age of distributive justice, but they do play a significant role in political development. Although Tocqueville thought democracy in the United States was underpinned by the extraordinary equality of condition that he found in the 1830s, he also maintained that democracy could not be explained without taking into account beliefs about equality. See Tocqueville 1945, vol. 1, Chapter 17.
45. Sen 1992, p. 109.
46. Ibid, p. 367.

needs, call for equal satisfaction of needs. Utilitarianism, which conceives of people chiefly as utility maximizers, gives "the same importance to the utilities of all people in the objective function," as Sen points out.[47] On the basis of equal forms of dueness, the proposed theory of justice as dueness posits a principle of equal distribution of part of national income.

To achieve one type of equality, one has to triage other types of equality, Rae maintains.[48] Similarly, Sen's view that every theory of justice has a basal equality coupled with a secondary inequality paradoxically converts arguments for equality into arguments against other sorts of equality.[49] "Any time you insist upon equality of capability," he writes, "there will be an inequality of income";[50] for bringing a slow learner up to a brighter person's level entails more tutoring, which requires extra money. The basic needs approach can justify inequalities of income for the sake of equal satisfaction of needs. A person with a high metabolic rate, for example, may need more income than another person would to satisfy his or her nutritional needs.

While Rae and Sen deserve credit for pointing out some trade-offs between equalities, their analyses create the false impression that equalities are mutually exclusive and therefore are self-nullifying. It has not been established, in my view, that all equalities conflict nor, in particular, that equality of incomes and capabilities pervasively conflict; thus, while there may be occasional conflicts between them, the extent of conflict may be much less than suggested. In a developed capital-based economy, the variations in metabolic rates to which Sen refers would not entail serious inequalities of income to bring people up to equal capability.[51] Extreme inequalities of wealth and income have historically been one of the greatest causes of inequalities in capabilities. Indeed, they have been so closely associated in some societies that the members of the upper class became known as the "aristocracy." Studies of educational attainments frequently show a strong dependence on socioeconomic background; as one such study reports, "the number of years of schooling is strongly associated with parental socioeconomic status."[52] For example, analysis of data collected by the U.S. Census Current Population Survey in 1962 indicates that a child whose parents are in the ninetieth percentile in socioeconomic status (defined in terms of income,

47. Ibid., p. 14.
48. Rae 1981, p. 151; Sen 1992.
49. Ibid., pp. 12–23.
50. Ibid., p. 58. 51. Ibid., p. 33.
52. Bowles and Gintis 1976, p. 30.

occupation, and educational level) can expect on average to have five more years of schooling than a child with a background in the tenth percentile.[53] The relationship between educational attainment and socioeconomic background cannot be explained away by the greater intellectual ability of those from higher socioeconomic backgrounds. Prospects for educational attainment are strongly dependent on socioeconomic background even for people who have similar childhood IQs.[54] In the United States, SAT scores are an important qualifying or disqualifying factor for admission to top colleges. Wealthy parents of children in New York's exclusive private schools seek out expensive tutoring for their children that can cost $400 an hour and can raise scores on "aptitude" tests by hundreds of points.[55] Since economic inequality has been a major factor in generating unequal capabilities, it can be expected that a significant increase in income equality would probably reduce capability inequality rather than increase it.

If economic resources were equalized across the board, then people who seek capabilities that require more expensive training and facilities would have less potential to develop them, generating capability inequalities between, say, physicists and English professors. The redistributory property right does not, however, generate this kind of capability inequality. Resources for educational development should be regulated by a separate principle of distribution of educational resources. The redistributory property right is a principle of partial equalization of income for purposes of consumption and, as such, it cannot regulate – nor disallow – unequal expenditures by educational institutions for equal development of different capabilities. In sum, the view that income inequality entails a basal inequality of capability arises, not from an actual inverse relationship between equal income and equal capability, but from conflating distinct domains of distributive justice.

It is important to explain why incomes should be one of the currencies of economic justice and why the focus of the principle of economic equality should be placed on incomes rather than on capabilities. Let us concentrate on economic capabilities, that is, the skills needed to perform a job, for the sake of brevity and because they are some of the most important to people, judging from the fact that people spend more of their waking hours performing them relative to other capabilities. Sen misconceives the purpose of capabilities, and he misorders them when he arranges them as morally prior to equality of incomes. The purpose of economic capabilities is not to achieve "certain functionings" but to

53. Ibid. 54. Ibid.
55. Tony Schwartz, *The New York Times*, January 10, 1999, pp. 30–51.

generate an income or to create wealth. Economic capabilities, such as the skills involved in operating complicated and dangerous machinery, are valuable to a person insofar as they enable him or her to create wealth or to obtain an income. He will not be pleased with the capabilities acquired through professional training if his job leaves him hungry and poor. Thus, income is clearly more important to people than economic capabilities, and it is absurd to say that equality of income should be subordinated to the goal of equality of capabilities.

Yet it would be an overstatement to suggest that economic capabilities are wholly without inherent value, since many people enjoy their jobs. But vast numbers of people would quit their jobs or drastically change them if income could be obtained in some other way, so economic capabilities could not have the primacy Sen accords them in the panoply of human values. Since capabilities significantly derive their value from their contribution to income and wealth, the principle of equality of capabilities cannot be used to justify inequality of income.

In making capabilities the primary focus of economic justice, Sen passes over a key proposition of neoclassical economic theory – that labor is a negative utility. While neoclassical theory may exaggerate the negative utility of labor, the idea of labor as a negative utility nevertheless grasps an important truth – that labor can be, and often is in many ways, an unpleasant way of obtaining an income. By positing capabilities as the object of economic justice, Sen distorts the very meaning of capabilities, treating them as ends and ignoring their essential character as means. Since economic capabilities are in reality means of obtaining income, incomes rather than capabilities should be the major currency of economic justice, and incomes should not be unequally distributed for the sake of equality of capability.

Although current needs-based theories of justice are problematic, justice as dueness might not conflict with a well-formulated needs-based theory of justice in regard to principles of distribution. It may be possible to synthesize the two types of theories under a more general theory of justice. But as currently formulated, needs-based theories of justice misconceive the nature of needs, and they unduly confine the scope of egalitarian justice.

The basic needs approach identifies requirements for human living, such as subsistence, shelter, health care, and so on. Contrary to this approach, however, needs are not limited to a fixed and given set of substances; they can be more accurately characterized in terms of a quantitative and qualitative multiplication in a capital-based economy. Even with regard to food, people have preferences regarding a vast number of different kinds of foods, cuts of meat, recipes, and cuisines. The elements of preference and will infusing need make it difficult to distinguish needs from the other kinds of things people want. One person's self-esteem may rest on having a library that covers the walls of his dwelling. Another's mode of living hinges on possessing a fine musical instrument. Still another person cannot feel good about himself unless he has a high-performance automobile, while another person's mode of life crucially involves a large-screen television and a home theater system. There are two implications. First, to conceive of needs in terms of a set of basic human needs is to take a reductive view of consumers. Second, because different things are imperatives to different persons, it may be impossible to establish the general hierarchy of needs on which needs-based principles of distribution depend.

A second problem with existing theories based on needs is that the principle of equal satisfaction of needs provides a guide to the distribution of only a fraction of national income, the part going to the acquisition of basic necessities. A vast portion of national income unrelated to basic necessities is not regulated by the principle of equal satisfaction of needs and is therefore morally indeterminate in needs theory. Since a very large portion of national income is left unregulated, needs-based principles of distribution can be highly inegalitarian. After equal satisfaction of needs is achieved through redistribution of basic income, the theory is fully consistent with extremely unequal distribution of the rest of national income.

Justice as dueness provides a more comprehensive rule of distribution. It regulates not only the distribution of the part of national income going to basic necessities, but also the distribution of all of the rest of the national income allocated for consumption. Justice as dueness is also more egalitarian than the basic needs approach. It calls not only for egalitarian distribution of the part of national income going toward basic necessities, but also for equal distribution of a large part of the rest of the consumable national income. Since expenditures on non-necessities are an increasingly large part of consumption as societies develop and grow richer, justice as dueness will become even more egalitarian relative to needs-based principles as time goes on.

The theory of justice as dueness overlaps the needs-based theory of justice because it views needs as contributory to the creation of income and wealth and compensates individuals for them. Needy individuals obtain income, however, not because of their neediness per se, but because of their role in another ground of entitlement – their contribution to the creation of economic value. Justice as dueness is therefore distinct from the ethics of need, but it is not opposed to the principles entailed by a well-formulated ethics of need. They both imply a right to equalization of part of national income and a right to unequal distribution of another part. A well-formulated theory of needs would recognize that each person has a need for wealth, not just for subsistence. It would also recognize that the common need for wealth subsumes wide differentiation with regard to the kinds of needs people wish to satisfy. On these bases, a well-formulated ethics of need would conclude upon a principle of equal distribution of part of income (related to the common need for wealth) and unequal distribution of another part of income (related to the differentiated needs for different kinds of substances and services). This compound principle of distribution mirrors that of justice as dueness, which holds that economic value results from the common need for wealth and differentiated needs for different kinds of things (on the consumption side) and from common and differentiated forms of labor (on the production side).[56]

SCOPE AND LIMITS OF THE PRINCIPLE OF EQUAL SHARES OF PART OF NATIONAL INCOME

The fact that principles of distributive justice do not hold across different domains of civil society suggests to some scholars that general principles of distributive justice are not possible.[57] Limited to the domain of consumption expenditures, the principle of income equalization seemingly fails to qualify as a general principle, since it does not regulate expenditures on formal education for developing different capabilities. Assigning a principle to a particular domain does not, however, preclude it from being a general principle. A principle can qualify as a categorical principle even when it is unable to displace judgments in other domains, so long as it displaces other considerations in its own domain. The principle of equal distribution of a portion of national income can be a general principle of justice because it is categorical within its domain, the domain of consumption, despite being displaced by other considerations in the domain of expenditures on formal education for different capabilities. The fact that the principle of equal income shares cannot prohibit unequal expenditures on formal education simply means that it has boundaries and that beyond these boundaries certain inequalities of economic resources are permissible. Considerations of appropriate domain define the scope within which the principle is meaningful; they do not

56. On the last-mentioned point, see Zucker 1990.

57. Due to multiple domains of justice and other considerations, Shapiro argues that there are no foundational general principles of distributive justice except the commitment to democracy. See Shapiro 1991, 1994.

qualify its applicability within its own domain, where the principle remains categorical. As Fried writes, "A categorical norm displaces other judgments in its domain, so that other values and ends may not be urged as reasons for violating the norm."[58] Thus this principle is general, but its scope does not stretch to absurd applications offensive to our sense of justice. While general, it obtains only insofar as it is meaningful to assert it, and after that point it simply does not apply. "In every case," Fried suggests, "the norm has boundaries and what lies outside these boundaries is not forbidden at all . . . Murder is wrong but killing in self-defense is not. The absoluteness of the norm is preserved in these cases but only by virtue of a process which defines its boundaries."[59]

Boundaries on the general principle of equal shares of a portion of income decouple it from the rules governing formal educational expenditures for developing different capabilities. So partial equalization of expenditures of income on consumption is not coupled with a basal inequality of capabilities.

CONCLUSIONS

Part II formulates an egalitarian theory of property based on an ethic of dueness for economic contributions. It demonstrates a principle of egalitarian distribution by revising basic notions of economic contributions. According to the ethics of dueness for economic contributions, property should go to individuals in proportion to their economic contributions. Economic contributions are those activities that contribute to the value of commodities, not just those activities that produce a product. Consumers, and not just producers, contribute to the creation of value, and these consumers can be due a benefit for these economic contributions. But the concept of consumer contributions needs to be recast, for consumer contributions do not consist in neoclassical, individualistic actors maximizing subjective preferences. Instead, consumers' economic contributions come from socially conditioned attributes, but still involve the individual's own mind and will. The fact that the individual's economic contribution has a social character means that responsibility for it is spread throughout economic society broadly, affecting calculations of dueness. Other members' indirect contributions are relatively equal in degree of responsibility for the social formation of some of the con-

58. Fried 1978, p. 12; emphasis added.
59. Ibid., p. 10.

sumer's economic contributions. The dispersion and equalization of responsibility for the creation of economic contributions entails a correlative equalization of some claims to value, on a principle of dueness for economic contributions. This implies a property right to egalitarian distribution of part of national income.

7

Policy Reflections: The Effect of an Egalitarian Regime on Economic Growth

INFERENCES FROM COMPARATIVE DATA

While a more egalitarian distribution may be just, implementing it would be imprudent if redistribution resulted in reduced savings and economic growth. A major axiom of modern economics holds that income inequality is positively related to savings, investment, and economic growth.[1] More equal distribution of income, the axiom cautions, would dampen savings, and it would, therefore, be unwise to undertake. But comparative analysis raises some doubts about the conventional axiom, for it shows that income equality is not necessarily related negatively to savings and growth. Prudence does not counsel against justice in income distribution.

In the conventional reasoning, the upper strata save a higher proportion of their income than do the lower income strata, because ample income leaves more left over for saving after consumption needs have been met. For this reason, it is held that an inegalitarian regime can generate more savings than can an egalitarian regime. By building greater national savings, an inegalitarian regime can surpass the productive capacity of an egalitarian system and it can, therefore, generate more national wealth. So everybody is better off than the members of an egalitarian system. The lower strata of an egalitarian society would receive a higher proportion of the national income than they would in an inegalitarian regime, the argument goes, but their absolute income would be lower.

An egalitarian regime could conceivably affect two types of savings,

1. See the discussion by Lodge 1987, pp. 12, 16.

Table 7.1. *Savings and income inequality in the United States and Japan, 1960s*

	Gross savings as a ratio of GNP 1960s	Inequality of income (post-tax), Gini coefficient
United States	19.7	39.0 (1966)
Japan	34.5	31.6 (1969)

Source: International comparisons of Gini coefficients by Sawyer 1976; gross savings as a ratio of GNP 1960s from OECD national accounts.

personal and corporate. Yet the redistributory property right does not regulate the proportions in which national income gets divided between investment in economic enterprises and in consumption, and it therefore does not obstruct capital formation by firms.[2] The more substantial concern is how it would affect personal savings.

Comparative analysis of the Japanese and American economies contradicts the conventional hypothesis on savings and income distribution. The Japanese economy achieved considerably higher savings with less income inequality than did the U.S. during the 1960s (see Table 7.1).

The 1970s repeat this pattern. While the poorest fifth of Japanese families received 7.9% of national income, there were savings of 30% of GNP and a growth of total output of 10.5% (1960–1973) and 3.8% (1973–1981).[3] By comparison, the bottom quintile in the United States received only 4.5% of national income; total savings were 20% of GNP; and the growth in total output was 4.2% (1960–1973) and 2.3% (1973–1981).[4] With about half as much income inequality, Japan achieved nearly twice the growth and fifty percent more savings during the 1970s. The comparative experience of these two countries in the

2. It only determines that the portion of national income going to personal consumption, whatever it may be be, will be subject to partial equalization. An egalitarian society needs to make a public decision about the relative amounts to be devoted to investment and consumption. On that decision hinges whether saving will be decreased, increased, or kept at current levels.
3. Source of distribution data: Sawyer 1976. Source of growth data: columns 1–4: International Monetary Fund, *International Financial Statistics* (various issues). Data for 1981 partly estimated by the American Enterprise Institute.
4. Data on savings from Reading 1992, p. 41.

1980s further negates the axiom that income equality and savings are negatively related.[5]

Faced with contrary evidence, modern economists try to shore up the conventional axiom by averring that the Japanese model rests on unique cultural traditions that are not replicable in the West. But Japan cannot be dismissed as a cultural exception, because some Western countries also deviate from the axiom. Between 1980 and 1987, Sweden maintained somewhat higher savings than the United States despite having substantially lower income inequality (see Table 7.2). Norway's performance on growth and income inequality closely resembles Japan's. Between 1980 and 1987, when Norway and Japan had savings rates of 28.53% and 31.10% respectively, the poorest tenth of Norwegians had 55.3% of the median income (1986), as compared to 49.5% in Japan (1985).

In 1986 the richest tenth of Americans received 206.1% of the median income, while Norway's top decile received only 163% of the median income. With substantially lower inequality, Norway defied the conventional axiom by achieving a high rate of savings, 28.53% of GNP, as compared to only 16.6% for the United States between 1980 and 1987. In fact, most OECD countries (Austria, Australia, Canada, France, Germany, Italy, Luxembourg, Norway, Sweden, Switzerland, United Kingdom, Finland, The Netherlands, New Zealand, and Ireland) broke the rule by attaining higher savings rates with lower income inequality than the United States displayed for the period 1980–87.[6]

At first glance, the Italian case, with high rates of both savings and inequality, supports the academic axiom, but on closer inspection it raises questions about the dependence of savings on high levels of income to the rich. Italy's savings rates are high by world standards because of strong motivation to save, not only by the rich but also by the other economic strata, as Jappelli and Pagano note: "The median saving rate is 0.28, the median wealth-income ratio is 3.48, and even the lowest quartile features high saving rates and wealth-income ratios."[7] High savings rates in Italy stem partially from factors widely diffused throughout the populace, such as the general indisposition toward the use of credit, and not just from the motivation of the rich.

5. A person in the ninetieth percentile of the income hierarchy received 188.2% of the median income in Japan (1989) but 206.1% of the median income in the United States (Atkinson, Rainwater, and Smeeding 1995, pp. 40, 70). With much greater income equality, Japan had total savings of 33.3% of GNP (1988) as compared to 15.1% for the United States (1986) (Reading 1992, p. 40).
6. Atkinson, Rainwater, and Smeeding 1995, p. 40.
7. Jappelli and Pagano 1994, p. 261.

Table 7.2. *Savings and inequality in OECD countries*

Country	Year	Income inequality Gini coefficient	National savings, 1980–7 (percent GNP)
Finland	1987	20.7	24.39
Sweden	1987	22.0	17.3
Norway	1986	23.4	28.53
Belgium	1988	23.5	15.91
Luxembourg	1985	23.8	42.67
Germany	1984	25.0	21.82
The Netherlands	1987	26.8	21.91
Canada	1987	28.9	20.71
Australia	1985	29.5	19.58
France	1984	29.6	20.11
United Kingdom	1986	30.4	17.53
Italy	1986	31.0	22.36
Switzerland	1982	32.3	27.70
Ireland	1987	33.0	18.13
United States	1986	34.1	16.60
Japan	1987	33.82	33.3 (1988)

Source: Gini measures for OECD countries, except Japan, from Atkinson, Rainwater, and Smeeding 1995, p. 46. Data on gross savings rates are from OECD national accounts. The Gini coefficient for Japan is from Tachi 1993, p. 127. Japanese savings are from Reading 1992, p. 40.

Although comparative analysis of income distribution and savings in OECD countries and Japan hints at the possibility that an egalitarian regime could be viable in developed countries, how would it fare in developing countries? Cross-national data from ten developing countries indicates that there is not a relationship between income distribution and the standard of living in the developing world (see Table 7.3).[8] Savings rates in countries with more equal incomes are almost the same as those in countries with less equal distribution, if one excludes Indonesia from the sample.[9]

In Korea, Indonesia, Hong Kong, and Thailand, countries with more equal incomes (the poorest 20% of individuals get 18% of the amount received by the richest 10% of individuals), gross savings are almost the same as in Malaysia, Turkey, and the Philippines, countries with less

8. Collins 1991, pp. 352–355.
9. "There is . . . little support," Collins reports, "for the view that saving is related to income distribution." See ibid., p. 355.

Table 7.3. *Income inequality, savings, and growth in ten developing countries*

	Income inequality	Gross savings (percent of GNP)	Real growth (percent)	Real per capita income
More equal countries	18.4	18.6	8.1	$1,684
More equal, excluding Indonesia	18.1	20.7	8.8	2,077
Less equal countries	10.3	20.1	5.5	1,667

Source: Collins 1991, p. 354.
Note: The measure of income inequality is the share of income that the poorest 20 percent of the population receive relative to the share received by the richest 10 percent. More equal countries include: Korea, Indonesia, Hong Kong, and Thailand. The less equal countries are Malaysia, Turkey, and the Philippines. The data are for the period 1980–1984.

equal incomes, where the poorest 20% of individuals receive only 10% of the incomes received by the richest individuals. If there is no relation between income distribution and savings in developing countries, as the data suggests, then an egalitarian regime might not have a very substantial impact on growth — positive or negative. However, if we include Indonesia in the sample, a positive relation obtains between income equality and growth, suggesting that an egalitarian regime might promote growth. It is also important to note that no relationship exists between income equality and standard of living in this sample of ten developing countries. Table 7.3 indicates that the developing countries with more equal income distributions have approximately the same per capita income as those with less equal incomes. The data do not justify concerns that an egalitarian regime would impair the standard of living.

ALTERNATIVE WAYS OF SPURRING GROWTH

Even if there were a positive relationship between inequality and savings, it would not be imperative for a country to maintain a high rate of inequality if that relationship were not crucial to generate savings. And it would not be crucial if there were other ways of spurring growth. In fact, numerous factors besides income distribution do enter into the determination of a nation's performance in savings. The existence of alternative paths or conditions for savings and growth means that income inequality may not be vital to economic growth and that adequate rates of growth can be maintained by other policies.

Various government policies may significantly affect saving. The Japanese government has relied on tax policy to effect a high rate of savings.[10] It has also done so by keeping public spending low by international standards.[11] A government can encourage savings through a general consumption tax or value added tax. Japan did not have this kind of tax until 1989, but it did levy a similar duty, a tax on conspicuous consumption that applies to specific goods deemed luxuries. The government also encouraged personal saving by keeping capital gains taxes low, and in that way it helped to supply industry with an inexpensive means of finance.

The Japanese government also encouraged corporate saving through tax policy. Levying high taxes on dividend income prompted companies to reinvest more of their earnings, which spurred growth and rewarded investors by the growth. Governmental and corporate decisions about productivity and growth can also have a positive effect on saving. Measures designed to keep productivity high helped Japan to attain high rates of investment. The high returns made possible by high rates of productivity drew a large part of the GNP to investment rather than consumption. The Italian case, which displays some of the highest savings rates in the world, shows another way in which savings can be generated: by limiting access to credit so that individuals have to self-finance large-scale purchases through savings rather than by borrowing.[12]

Since saving depends on many different conditions, a country wishing to stimulate saving is presented with numerous options that reduce the importance of high income inequality. The latter is simply not a necessary condition for saving, and a country need not rely on it to generate savings. Moreover, the interest of justice in equitable incomes counsels against the use of high inequality as a stimulus, because this violates the right to an equalization of part of national income. It would be ethically preferable – and quite possible – to use several alternative means, such as a general consumption tax, a tax on specific luxury goods, and social training in the norms of savings.

10. See Prestowitz 1989, p. 253.
11. Reading 1992, pp. 2–42.
12. Italians are motivated to save by the desire to acquire a house. People tend to finance the acquisition through self-financing rather than borrowing partly because of limits on credit.

EGALITARIANISM, INTERPERSONAL EFFECTS, AND THE MOTIVATION TO SAVE

Besides empirical problems with the conventional axiom, there are also theoretical issues about its validity. The conventional argument for this axiom holds that distributing a larger share of national income to the lower strata would decrease total savings because individuals in them are less motivated to save – since consumption needs are harder to cover with smaller incomes. The validity of this argument rests on the assumption that lower-strata consumption needs would remain relatively constant under an egalitarian regime, rather than becoming narrower. But the interpersonal dynamics of an egalitarian society could create tendencies toward narrowing the scope of the lower strata's consumption needs. And more money (from redistributive tax policies) and fewer needs to attend to would generate a tendency among the lower strata to save a higher proportion of their income.

The consumption behavior of the higher strata affects the scope of consumption needs of the lower strata by influencing the standard of consumption that is then emulated by the lower strata. During the industrial revolution in England, the working class followed the upper-class habit of tea drinking, and they spent a substantial portion of their income on tea, even when their incomes dropped below subsistence. Similarly, lavish spending by the rich in the contemporary era creates what Robert H. Frank calls a "luxury fever."[13] "The more your neighbor spends, the more you have to spend just to keep even. 'The . . . spending by people at the top of the scale sets a standard that affects everyone below.'"[14] By expanding the scope of the consumption needs of lower strata, high expenditures on consumption by the upper strata have a tendency to stunt the savings rates of the lower strata. The struggle to meet the upper strata's standard of consumption makes it more difficult for the lower strata to save.

Redistributory taxation upon the upper strata can reduce their (relative) income, and it can, therefore, reduce their expenditures on consumption. By restraining upper-class expenditures, such taxation can weaken the force of emulation, indirectly narrowing the scope of the consumption needs of the lower strata. With fewer consumption needs, the lower strata will be in a better position to save. "If everyone spent less on luxury goods," Frank holds, "there'd be . . . more savings for

13. Frank 1999.
14. Robert Frank, author of *Luxury Fever*, quoted by Tierney 1998.

capital investments that would make society richer in the long run."[15] Since redistributory taxation generates tendencies to reduce the lower strata's consumption needs, while giving them more money to spend on consumption, it would have some tendency to increase savings by the lower strata.

15. Ibid.

Part III

Egalitarian Property and the Ethics of Economic Community

8

Deriving Equality from Community

The ethics of economic community entitle members to equal portions of a part of national income. The argument from community in Part III supplements the derivation of the same redistributory property right in Chapters 5 and 6, where it is derived from the ethics of dueness for economic contributions. The ethics of economic community show that membership in an economic community entitles individuals to a right to equal portions of a part of national income because they are members of a community, whereas the ethics of dueness derive this right from a class of equal economic contributions. By supplementing the derivation provided by the ethics of contributions, the ethics of economic community provide additional ethical validation for the redistributory property right.

A principle of equal distribution is morally warranted by membership in a community, to the extent that the society consists in a community (see Chapter 8). This principle can be applied to the real world because, underlying the moral derivation of equality from community, there exists an actual dimension of community that runs throughout capital-based market systems (see Chapters 9–11). While community does not characterize every aspect of economic life – many activities are not communal but competitive and relatively independent – it is not limited to the subsystemic level, but exists systemwide. The dimension of community obtains between producers and consumers (see Chapters 9 and 10) and, moveover, between laborers and capital owners and capital managers (see Chapter 11).

The extent of this community justifies the equal distribution of proportionate income in capital-based market systems (see Chapter 12). Because the community found in these systems is greater in degree and kind than traditional liberal theories of property recognize, it entails an equalization of some economic resources rather than merely equal rights of property. It also exceeds the degree and kind of community recognized by modern welfare state theories, and so it morally requires greater equalization than they do. Beyond welfare state measures such as employment insurance, welfare, and social security, it extends to equal shares of a portion of total income.

The term "ethics of community" is included in this book advisedly. Since commonalities between individuals can be the basis for a principle of just distribution of property, the term's use is warranted. But in communitarian theory, it denotes an ethics where the community is the subject of rights. Taken in that sense, the present analysis is not an ethics of community, but an ethics of individual rights. Individuals are the subject of rights, because people remain individually willed despite being socially influenced.

COMMUNITY AND THE PRINCIPLE OF DISTRIBUTION

Suppose that a capital-based market system is not only competitive but also communal. It would then be important to know what kind of ethics should regulate distribution in the system. Does one set of rules apply to the economy to the degree that it is a community, but a quite different set insofar as it is an aggregate of independent actors? My thesis in this chapter is that membership in a community does entail a special rule of distribution. The conventional assumption that capital-based market systems are not communities does not make this a moot point, for as I attempt to show in Chapters 9–12, they do possess a dimension of community.

Historically, theorists are not completely agreed about the principles of distribution for regulating a community in an economy or elsewhere. Some, such as Charles Taylor, think that community morally entails equal distribution of relevant resources.[1] Others, like Michael Sandel, think it can sanction unequal distribution if inequality advances communal purposes.[2] Still others, such as Jeremy Waldron, find community morally neutral in regard to distribution. I agree with the first approach, with a qualification. While community entails a principle of equal distribution, a capital-based market system should not be regulated solely by this principle. Such a system is a mixture of community and relatively independent action that entails a corresponding hybrid of principles

1. However, he expresses this view with much ambivalence. Taylor 1985, pp. 289–317.
2. This can be inferred from analysis of Sandel 1982.

of equal and unequal distribution, not a pure principle of equalization.

The principle of equal distribution is not fully defined until one specifies the type of goods distributed by it. Does the principle of equal distribution regard welfare, goods, income, wealth, opportunities, or freedoms?[3] The question "equality of what?," which we began to consider in Chapter 6, will be further examined in Chapter 12. It is important to reexamine the prior question, "why equality?," dealing with the justification of equality. There is a crisis of confidence in the value of equality due to the poor performance of communist economies relative to capitalist ones. We also have had a long-standing gap in our commitment to equality: the principle of equality is still lightly held in economic life. Commitment to equality is not as strong as it might be, partially because equality's moral foundations in a condition of community remain obscure and need to be made more distinct and definite. If community's powerful egalitarian implications can be brought out, the value and validity of equality can be strengthened.

INDIVIDUALISTIC ETHICS OR ETHICS OF COMMUNITY?

An individualistic ethics starts from the assumption that individuals are primarily independent agents and reasons the principles of justice in accordance with this assumption.[4] It deduces principles demanded by justice as a matter of society's basic structure as a plurality of individuals.[5] The ethics of community, by contrast, proceeds from the assumption that individuals in society are members of a community, and it reasons the principles of justice in accordance with this assumption. That is, it deduces principles demanded by justice as a matter of society's basic structure as a community.

The form of ethics appropriate to a given association depends on the nature of individuals and of their relations. Rawls thinks that an individualistic ethics is appropriate because, in his view, the primary characteristics of individuals are distinctness and separateness.[6] They are

3. Scholars focusing on the "equality of what?" include Sen 1992, Cohen 1993, and Rae 1981, among others.
4. Rawls 1971, pp. 264–265, 29, 150–151.
5. Rawls 1971, p. 29.
6. Rawls defends an individualistic ethics on the ground that the theory of justice should not prejudge that community is good, nor affirm in advance that any given community is more just than another. To avoid prejudgment, Rawls begins from the assumption of independent individuals who have not been conditioned by the influence of any particular community: "the essential idea is that we want to account for the social values, for the intrinsic good of institutional, commu-

individuated prior to society: their faculty of choice is causally independent of that of other persons. People form associations through choices undetermined by association. Social theorists and communtarians, on the other hand, maintain that an ethics of community is appropriate because they consider relatedness and commonality to be the elemental conditions of the person, whose primary characteristics – including needs, will, and capacity for self-determination – are socially constituted within a community.[7] On the assumption that the social theorists and communitarians are right to some degree about this in regard to economic society, the economy should be governed in part by an ethics of community.

THE ESSENTIAL DERIVATION

Within the history of thought, the dominant position opposes an equal distribution of income and wealth. Most theorists oppose this distribution because economic conditions do not warrant it, since the economy is not a community. More often than one would expect, however, the dominant camp supports some reasoning that could ultimately be used to defend equal distribution of income. For example, this camp acknowledges that a principle of equal distribution is warranted where community exists. That acknowledgement can help defend equal distribution of economic resources if the economy proves to have a dimension of community. By demonstrating that theorists from various schools of thought accept the derivation of equality from community, one can adduce strong support for part of the argument for an equal distribution of income, and some additional argumentation can carry us the rest of the way.

As a moral rule, the principle of equality holds that relevant resources

nity, and associative activities, *by a conception of justice that in its theoretical basis is individualistic*"(Rawls 1971, pp. 264–265, emphasis added).

One cannot quarrel with Rawls's concern about not prejudging the just economy's form. But the proposition that individuals are independent and distinct is as much an assumption as is the assumption that society is a community. Rawls's selection of an individualistic ethics involves a built-in ontological bias. One can only avoid prejudging ontologies by not presupposing any given ontology. One instead has to make the study of ontology the main order of business from the start. For this reason, this study does not proceed through a postulational methodology in the matter of ontological propositions. Instead, it *inquires* into the nature and origins of individuals within the system of capital- based market relations.

7. Taylor 1985; Gould 1988.

should be distributed equally among entitled agents. Membership in a community can provide a moral foundation for this principle, because membership intuitively warrants sharing. Kant wrote one of the most profound statements of this derivation: "In all social contracts, we find a union of many individuals for some common end which they all ought to share. But a union as an end in itself in which they all *ought to share*."[8] Moreover, "The members of a civil society . . . united for the purpose of legislation . . . are entitled to demand to be treated by all other citizens with natural freedom and equality."[9] Membership in a community warrants equal distribution of (relevant) things because individuals who form a union for the sake of some end held in common ought to share in the attainment of that end. If common activity and a unity of purpose make a certain end possible, there is a moral basis for equal distribution of the fruits of this activity. There cannot be a differential distribution of the ends as would arise from independent action for separate ends. The content of the equal distribution – that is, which things are equally distributed – is determined when the aims of association are given.

More recently, Charles Taylor has derived equality from community in another notable way. The formation of a community for the advancement of some end held in common, he writes, calls for equal fulfillment of the ends of association. He elaborates this view in relation to a Lockean community: "The aim of association is to preserve property, which of course includes life, liberty and estate. But if all enter into society freely, then all should benefit from the association. This is the basis for a principle of equal fulfillment, that is, that society's aims should be equally fulfilled for each of its members . . ."[10] People who associate in a community to further their security deserve equal fulfillment of this end through equal rights of property. Human beings in nature are not joined together for the sake of their security, and they are, therefore, not obliged to protect each other equally.

Taylor goes on to suggest how certain kinds of common ends may justify a principle of equal distribution of income. The equal right to property correlates with the common goal of security, and is justified by it. But, as Taylor suggests, the scope of common goals may be broader than

8. Kant 1970, p. 73.
9. Kant 1887, pp. 167–168; see also Kant 1965.
10. Taylor 1985, p. 293. Here Taylor is explaining how a principle of equal fulfillment would arise in context of a Lockean community. Taylor is not an adherent of the Lockean view of community. He subscribes to a conception of community as a site of common deliberation rather than to a community of Lockean ends (e.g., security).

the pursuit of security. Consumption, production, and acquisition of goods is another common goal of association. Appropriate to this common goal, and justified by it, he suggests, is the principle of equal distribution of income. "[B]ecause of a common good which in fact is sustained by the common life of our society," Taylor suggests, "we ought to accept certain principles of distribution which take account of the real balance of mutual indebtedness relative to this good. For instance, that we owe each other . . . equal distribution . . . because in fact we are involved in a society of mutual respect, or common deliberation, and this is the condition for all of us realizing together an important human potential."[11]

English liberalism provided some early derivations of equality from community. Locke's phrase "sharing all in one Community of Nature" deeply apprehends the derivation of equality from community, albeit without systematic argument.[12] In the treatment of property, Locke discloses a profound connection between membership in a community and the entitlement to equal amounts of property. Nature "belong'd equally" to all men because "it was common."[13] Moreover, the natural law proviso, that there should be equal access to natural resources, is derived from a premise of common ownership. Men in the state of nature should leave "enough, and as good" for all the rest because the earth is owned in common.[14] The community of society provides a moral foundation for further equalities not provided by natural community. Benefits of commonwealth should be "mutual," Locke reasons, because they ultimately derive from the agreement to establish civil government, that is, from a unified state of society rather than a condition of isolated individuals.[15]

Welfare state liberalism in some ways diminished reliance on the derivation of equality from community as it fashioned a public philosophy from more individualistic premises.[16] It also had bursts of insight, however, into communal derivation of equality. Arthur Okun saw this derivation when he considered that joint productive activities should be rewarded differently than independent labor. Given their joint activity,

11. Taylor 1992, p. 298.
12. Locke 1963. 13. Ibid., p. 331.
14. Ibid., para 30, p. 331; para. 31, p. 332.
15. Ibid., para. 123, p. 395.
16. As Michael Sandel characterizes the development of modern liberalism, a voluntaristic conception of freedom and neutrality between subjective conceptions of the good became more important than the common good in formulating the public philosophy of the welfare state. See Sandel 1996, pp. 262–315.

productive agents should receive equal shares, like members of a World Series team. "Production," he writes,

> comes out of a complex, interdependent system and may not be neatly attributable to individual contributors. Henry Ford's mass-produced automobile was a great success in a country with a high average income, three thousand miles of unimpeded driving, an alert and ambitious work force, and a government that could protect travelers . . . In that sense, most production processes involve "joint inputs" like the two-handled saw. That aspect is recognized in a few private arrangements, which reward teams rather than individuals. The same world series *shares* are given to Johnny Bench and the bench-warming third-string catcher.[17]

To another welfare state liberal, Robert Reich, community in the political system provides a moral basis for reducing inequality of wealth that arises from individualistic pursuits in the economy. "Our civil culture [as distinct from our business culture] embodies a vision of community, premised on citizenship. Its concern with democratic participation and sharing of wealth stems from a conviction that such commitments enrich life and affirm the interdependency of individual lives."[18]

Although welfare state liberals, like Okun, know community morally entails equal shares, they do not advocate equal distribution. In their view, the prospect of differential rewards elicits greater work effort, and since they value productivity more than community, they endorse unequal distribution. Communitarians place greater moral weight on the equalities derived from membership, because for them community is a primary structure of society meriting foundational moral commitment. Sandel, for example, derives a principle of sharing from the condition that individual identities are communally formed, and he accords this principle centrality in his ethical system: "what at first appear as 'my' assets are more properly described as common assets in some sense; since others made me . . . it seems appropriate to regard them . . . as participants in 'my' achievements and common beneficiaries of the rewards they bring."[19] Moreover, "I must share 'my' assets with 'society . . . ' because this particular society has made me what I am . . ."[20]

Social theory is in some respects an ideological alternative to liberalism and communitarianism, but it joins these rivals in deriving a principle of equality from community. Social theory assigns entitlement to the

17. Okun 1975, p. 46.
18. Reich 1984, p. 4.
19. Sandel 1982, p. 145.
20. Ibid. See also Mansbridge 1980, p. 9.

individual, whereas communitarianism ascribes it to the community; yet both engage in a communal derivation of ethics that generates principles of equal distribution. Social theorist Carol Gould derives an equal right to participate in controlling economic enterprises from a condition of common activity for common purposes.

> Clearly, since the form of . . . common activity differs from individual activity, in which one makes decisions about one's own actions independently of others, the nature of decision-making in common activity must also differ. It cannot simply be the aggregate of individuals' decisions about their own separate actions. Rather, as joint activity defined by common purposes, it requires a form of participation in the common decisions which bind all members of the group. Thus, its appropriate form is codetermination or shared decision-making among equals. The general conclusion of this argument . . . is therefore that all individuals who are engaged in a common activity have an equal right to participate in the decisions concerning it.[21]

Gould's derivation is couched with respect to political control of enterprises rather than of economic resources, but one could readily derive a right to equal economic resources using analogous reasoning about common activity and purposes.

As this brief history shows, the derivation of equality from community receives support from political theorists at various stages of the history of thought and across ideological divides.

Egalitarian ethics of community have not, however, become established in economic ethics, which are still dominated by individualistic inegalitarianism. Theorists who derive equality from community in some matters and contexts usually do not endorse it with regard to income and wealth in the economy. Locke justifies equal access to natural resources on communal bases, but he defends unequal monetary incomes from individualistic premises.[22] Kant derives equal rights from the common will to live under conditions of right, but he holds that there should not be an equal distribution of economic resources because individuals differ about the ends of happiness.[23] Taylor thinks membership in a community justifies equal fulfillment of the ends of association, but he opposes the application of this principle in actual circumstances. Communal ethics are inapplicable, he believes, to modern industrial systems because, despite the fact of economic interdependence, individuals are steeped in individualistic traditions and view themselves as independent actors. Moreover, Taylor (ambivalently) recognizes a "contribu-

21. Gould 1988, p. 85.
22. See Chapter 3, this volume.
23. Kant 1970, p. 73.

tions precept" that assigns differential reward for different contributions.[24] Gould supports equal control of common productive activity, but she rejects equal distribution of income on the ground that self-development requires differentiated conditions.[25]

Clearly much remains to be done before a principle of equal distribution of a portion of income can be established. Yet the gathering of arguments and authorities for the general derivation of equality from community forms a foundation for the development of the principle of equal distribution of income. The moral grounds for this principle can be further developed by demonstrating that capital-based market systems have a dimension of community, and that this sort of community entails an equal distribution of a portion of income (see Chapters 8–12).

IRREDUCIBLE COOPERATION

Reviewing the preceding derivations leaves a nagging question. Why does community entail a principle of equality? If one person works harder or better, that is, participates more effectively, in public functions, shouldn't he or she receive more of the benefits of association?

Economists' views of distributive rules are influenced by the marginal productivity ethics of distribution. Although the marginal productivity theory of distribution is not, strictly speaking, a normative theory but a positive theory, an informal tradition exists where neoclassical economists pronounce that it is equitable to distribute pay proportionate to marginal products.[26] In other words, the ethics of marginal productivity has strong moral appeal to some neoclassical economists, but they do not put it forward as a rigorous theory. Modern economists know that processes of producing wealth involve cooperation and division of labor, not independent producers; and they consequently recognize that individuals are entitled to a share of the cooperative surplus, not to the entire product of the productive activity. But the marginal productivity theory of distribution leads economists to deny that individuals should receive equal shares, on the ground that different marginal products warrant different amounts of remuneration.

Marginal productivity is "the schedule of the increments in total 'product' obtainable through application of additional units of the 'factor'."[27]

24. Taylor 1985, pp. 306–307, 314.
25. Gould 1988, p. 161.
26. See Okun 1975, p. 48, notwithstanding p. 47; Zamagni 1987, p. 471; Weiss 1969, p. 69.
27. Machlup 1963, p. 191.

$$MP_l = \delta Q/\delta L = f_l$$

Each individual in a cooperative production process should receive a wage (rent) equal to the marginal product of his or her labor (land or capital). More skilled and diligent labor yields higher marginal products and, therefore, deserves higher wages, which a standard neoclassical text regards as efficient and ethical: "application of a . . . general rule, such as that of [marginal] productivity satisfies two fundamental principles: the principle of efficiency and the principle of equity (given that it is ethically legitimate that each benefits in accordance with his contribution)."[28]

The ethics of marginal productivity factor the total product into individual contributions to the product. A certain change in output, say q_1, is due to an extra unit of individual 1's labor. Another quantity change in output, say q_2, is associated with an incremental increase in individual 2's labor. Still a third change in output, say q_3, results from the application of another unit of individual 3's labor. When the marginal product of every worker and every other factor input is factored out, all of the contributions to production will have been reduced to individual laborers, capital, and land. The ethics of marginal productivity do not credit any of the output to cooperative activity per se. This is strange, for although the product could not be produced without common activity, cooperation is not counted among the factors contributing to production. When cooperation is uncredited as a productive factor, as it is in neoclassical economics, the individual is not remunerated in her capacity as a cooperative agent, but only as an individual agent.

Thus, the neoclassical view that cooperation does not warrant equal shares arises from the neglect of cooperation as a factor of production. When one takes cooperation into account, a moral basis emerges for equal shares of part of total social income. Given that cooperation is itself a factor of production, productive activity can be only partially factored into differential individual contributions meriting differential reward. Individuals who are equally members of a cooperative activity deserve equal pay for their cooperative contribution.

Different positions on equal or unequal remuneration assume different conceptions of cooperative action. Unequal reward assumes that cooperation is reducible to separate individual contributions. John Bates Clark wrote, "It was the claim advanced by Mr. Henry George, that wages are fixed by the product which a man can create by tilling rentless land, that just led me to seek a method by which the product of

28. Zamagni 1987, p. 1; original emphasis removed.

labor everywhere may be disentangled from the product of *cooperating* agents and *separately* identified . . ."[29]

In contrast to this view, cooperation is an elemental, irreducible part of economic activity. It needs to be underscored that, in a cooperative process, the marginal product of a factor is not the marginal product of that factor alone, but one that assumes a given level of operation of other factors.

$$\Delta q/\Delta x_1 = [f(x_1 + \Delta x_1, x_2) - f(x_1, x_2)] / \Delta x_1$$

Consequently, to assign the individual full credit for *his* marginal product exaggerates the individual's contribution and underestimates the contribution of cooperation as a distinct factor. Other workers do get compensated for their own marginal products in neoclassical ethics, but not for their contributions to *his* marginal product. Although neoclassical economics recognizes that individuals can have external effects on others that deserve payment for creating positive economies, it does not recognize that cooperation itself is a contribution to others' productivity and therefore that it deserves remuneration.

The system of capital-based economic relations is, in a sense, a single production process interrelated by a system of exchanges. The work that goes into the production of a manufacture is divided into a great number of branches. Of this number, the single plant or company is not an independent entity but a part of a societal production process. The labor of the individual within a system of division of labor does not constitute labor, but only a part of labor. The parts of labor unified by a system of exchange constitute the productive force of society. Cooperation is an irreducible element of the generation of wealth because the unity of the parts, not the parts taken separately, produces wealth.

The validity of principles of differential reward for cooperative activities hinges on the possibility of separately identifying individual's productive services. To reward one person differently than another, one needs to identify their distinct parts in production. But the converse of marginal productivity ethics holds to the degree that cooperation is not reducible to separately identifiable contributions. If, and insofar as, actions are genuinely common, there is no conceptual basis for analytically separating out individual contributions and, therefore, no ground for discriminating rates of pay. Since cooperation is irreducible, and since the economy has an element of community (see Chapters 9–12), one cannot find a principle of differential reward with respect to such

29. Clark 1902, p. vii, as cited by Ferguson 1972, pp. 393–394.

activity. This is the essential argument for equal shares from community membership. Corresponding to the dimension of common action in production, the cooperative surplus should be divided equally among individual productive agents. Equalization of total income is not, however, required, because productive activity is not entirely cooperative.

The problem with the ethics of marginal productivity is not that it treats the individual as an isolated producer, and to suggest that it does so, would be to set up a straw man. The view that individuals' contributions can be separately identified does not presume that they produce alone, but that their *part* in cooperative activity can be separately identified, as the mathematical formulation of marginal productivity makes clear. However, although neoclassical economists believe that their approach treats cooperation in terms of its constituent parts, it really treats cooperation in terms of its opposite – separate activities –because it does not recognize that cooperation is a distinct factor of production. After resolving cooperation into its opposite, it then rewards individuals for something other than cooperating, namely for their separate activities. But common action cannot be resolved into separate activities, any more than skill or effort can be resolved into incapacity or laziness. To reduce common action to separate activities would be to negate the premised quality of jointness, because separate activity is the opposite of common action. Common activity is a productive factor of monumental importance to output and, as such, it should be compensated in its own right. But cooperative activity, unlike skill and diligence, cannot be differentially remunerated. For while people can be analytically separated in terms of skill or diligence, they cannot be analytically separated in terms of cooperation, because that would treat common action as its opposite. In common actions, individuals are equally parts of the action and should receive equal compensation.

OBJECTIONS RECONSIDERED

To some theorists, community does not specially imply or morally require either equal distribution or unequal distribution.[30] Members may have the moral latitude to define rules as they choose and different associations may have different distributive principles. Take the case of a group that meets for a poker game. Alhough the game is played by a

30. Jeremy Waldron, for example, holds that community does not have any egalitarian moral implications. The example of a poker game was suggested by him in order to show this. His comments in this regard were made as a discussant on the panel Social Theories of Rights, APSA annual meeting, Chicago, 1995.

community rather than by isolated individuals, it does not morally entail an equal distribution of winnings. The common end of association – the fun of the game – entails the risk of losing.

A poker game is, however, a fictive and unnecessary community joined at one's discretion. Only for this reason may it distribute resources unequally in accordance with morally arbitrary rules of the game. But when reality intrudes, and real modes of economic acquisition replace the fictive mode, the common fun fades. Faces harden, and desperation may set in. Who can call it "community" when the windfall gain of one person can spell ruin for everyone else around the table? The dependence for life, freedom, and well-being of each on all the rest calls for recognition of common activity for a common purpose, together with the egalitarian moral implications of this kind of activity and purpose. Equality cannot be set aside for the fun of it, because no one participates in necessary community for the fun of it. It cannot be displaced for morally arbitrary reasons, because people participate in order to partake in the things necessary to their lives, freedom, and well-being.

THE DERIVATION IN ORDINARY DISCOURSE

Equality's moral foundation in community is keenly understood in ordinary moral discourse. It is generally recognized, for example, that survivors in a lifeboat should ration scarce resources equally among themselves. This rule of conduct reflects the common moral judgment that people should share in the resources affecting their common fate. The lifeboat and rationing have become the metaphor of community and its rule of distribution. People express a parallel between the desperate situation on the lifeboat and their own daily lives when they say "we're all in the same boat." The shared nature of their ultimate condition is invoked to justify shared sacrifice, rationing, or equal treatment. During the massive budget deficits of the late 1980s, people gave increasing acceptance to federal belt-tightening measures for dealing with their common plight when they recognized that sacrifices would be borne equally.

People engaged in a common endeavor often say "all for one and one for all," which grasps the intimate connection between common endeavor and egalitarian distribution. The underlying reason for this is that a number of individuals could not be *for* each one unless shares were allocated equally. Just as appeals to community justify equal shares in ordinary discourse, the absence of community is often invoked to justify unequal distribution. Where it is "every man for himself," the conditions of living justify unequal resources.

As the sense of community takes root in the political thinking and consciousness of a nation's citizens and officials, there can be a strong attendant commitment to equality. Communitarianism is a dimension of Japanese political economy, and it has spawned a major movement toward economic equality. This is not, however, to say that the country is entirely communitarian or egalitarian, for a current of authoritarianism also runs through the national psyche. Communitarianism and egalitarianism have not always characterized Japanese political economy, and they are, therefore, not entirely the result of unique cultural traditions and homogeneity. They have instead developed over time, partially through deliberate state policy.[31]

During the 1950s and 1960s, there was a series of divisive and violent strikes in Japan, culminating in the Mitsui Mine strike. The government cultivated a form of economic communitarianism by sponsoring the so-called Productivity Center, in which government, business, labor, and academia all participated, and further by touting economic growth as a matter of national economic security. The Productivity Center germinated the idea that shared sacrifice should lead to an eventual sharing in the economic growth made possible by it, an idea that came to be embraced by society more widely.[32] In exchange for a governmental commitment to equality, Japanese trade unions accepted a "rationalization" of wages for the sake of the national interest in economic growth. The sense of common purpose and common endeavor gave rise to a feeling that the "gains and losses of economic change" should be "shared in such a way that no group feels a disproportionate burden and that none experiences a disproportionate windfall."[33] The high value of equality, based on a sense of economic community, is partly responsible for the fact that "Japanese wages rose faster than those of any major industrial country. [B]y the 1970s, Japan had achieved a greater equality of income distribution than any other industrialized economy."[34] The fact of economic community was seen as justifying significant equality of results.

31. For a thorough account of the uses of policy to promote equality, see Milly 1999.
32. See the accounts by Oppenheim 1992, p. 28; and by Vogel in Lodge 1987, p. 165.
33. Reich 1984.
34. Oppenheim 1992, p. 28.

DERIVING EQUALITY ETYMOLOGICALLY FROM COMMUNITY

Some insight into the moral implications of membership in a community can be gained from the etymology of the word "participate," which is an affine of membership. In common usage, the word means to be a part of some activity. Yet the etymology reveals that it means to be a part of and to take, that is, it is linked to a rule of allocation. According to the *Shorter Oxford English Dictionary*, the verb "participate" comes from *parti*, meaning part or portion of a whole, and *cip*, which is the weak form of *cap*, the stem of *capere* – to take.[35] To participate, then, means to take something of what you are part of, to partake. You get to take something from the whole because of your condition, the condition of being part of a whole. As an example of this meaning, the dictionary cites the 1881 statement: "Sharing in whatever surplus profits are realized by the more efficient labour which participation calls forth." Also notable, the participial adjective "participate," now rare, came from the Latin *participatus*, meaning made to share. Furthermore, "particable," a word with the same root as the word "participate," namely *participer*, means capable of being participated or shared. The etymological meaning of "participate" is a powerful intuition about distribution embedded in a word.

SOME AGREEMENT ABOUT THE ETHICS OF COMMUNITY

As noted above, most theorists who acknowledge community's moral entailment of equal distribution do not support a principle of equal distribution of income. They oppose it because they reject the premise that economic community exists, not because they reject the derivation of the principle of equality from that premise. The fact that the derivation of the principle of equal distribution is subject to less controversy provides a kind of support for the derivation itself, and indicates that it is relatively secure, however precarious theorists may find the premise to be.

When Kant rejects the principle of equal distribution of goods because he thinks men "differ in the empirical ends of happiness,"[36] he is not rejecting the view that economic community would entail equal distribution if it existed; he is rejecting the premise that economic community exists. His statement clearly implies that he would support an equal distribution of goods if men had common ends of happiness.

35. Third edition, 1967, p. 1438.
36. Kant 1970, p. 73.

When Locke justifies unequal accumulations of monetary wealth because they are ultimately derived from autonomous labor, he does not doubt that equal distribution of monetary wealth would be warranted if it had been created by common action; he doubts only the premise that productive action is common action. Hegel favors an unequal distribution of economic resources because economic agents are essentially characterized by their "particularity" of skill and other qualities rather than by universal attributes.[37] This argument implies that Hegel affirms that an equal distribution would be morally entailed if the individual's characteristics corresponded more closely to the universal.[38] It is the existence of the concrete universal that Hegel is challenging here (surprisingly enough), not the idea that the concrete universal would morally entail a principle of equality.

Because theorists as diverse as Locke, Kant, and Hegel believe economic community would morally entail a principle of equal distribution if economic community existed, the derivation seems relatively sound and secure. It is the premise of economic community that has been problematic historically from the point of view of major political theorists. Demonstrating that such community exists is the major task at this stage of development of the ethics of community. This chapter has shown that, once the premise of economic community has been secured, there is no major objection to deriving from that assumption a principle of equal distribution of a portion of relevant resources.

37. Hegel 1952, remark to para. 200, p. 130.
38. Ibid.

9

The Dimension of Community in Capital-Based Market Systems: Between Consumers and Producers

Modern luxury is systematical.[1]

Sir James Steuart

Capital is not simply one element of . . . economic relations, it is the . . . unity of the economic process.[2]

David P. Levine

To the extent that an economy is a community, I have argued, it should be regulated by a principle of equal distribution (see Chapter 8). Whether this morally derived principle applies to real-world economies thus depends on their degree of community. The search for community can be limited to capital-based market systems, since they are the only kind of economy that can satisfy the dual conditions of economic justice: wealth and freedom.[3]

1. Steuart 1966 [1767], vol. 1, p. 281.
2. Levine 1978–1981, vol. 1, p. 152.
3. Community in communist command systems is not a foundation for a system of distributive justice, because it is fundamentally incompatible with justice. Communist systems, defined in terms of systems of state planning, are inefficient, and they constrict the production of wealth. By sharply limiting wealth, they abrogate justice because justice has an interest in wealth, since wealth is a necessary condition for freedom.

   In saying that distributive justice focuses on capital-based markets, I do not mean that the status quo satisfies the requirements of distributive justice. Rather, the just economy will be a refinement of capital-based market systems, not of some other type of system. Reforms should preserve the framework of capital and markets. Only reforms within this framework can provide valid ethical alternatives to current economies. A discovery of community within capital-based market systems could induce such reform. It would morally entail changes

To demonstrate a dimension of community in the economy, one has to show that the participants share certain attributes, actions, and ends. For this to be true, different categories of economic agents – consumers, producers, laborers, capital owners, and managers – would all have to have some fundamental attributes in common, and they would all have to be engaged in common action toward a common end. One would also have to account for the formation of these characteristics; otherwise, community would be indeterminate.

COMMUNITY AND THE CIRCULATION OF CAPITAL

Analysis of systemwide community in the economy may begin with the relation between producers and consumers, leaving labor and capital for a later chapter.

Neoclassical economic theory does not characterize the relationship between consumers and producers as communal in any degree. It divides the economy into consumption and production sectors and portrays agents within them in terms of opposing and conflicting interests: "[E]ach sector operates from quite different sets of goals or motivations just as each serves a different function in the economy."[4] Seeking to maximize profits, producers want to get high prices for their products. Consumers, who want to maximize their own satisfaction, instead "desire to give up as little money as possible for each unit purchased."[5] Economic life is a zero-sum condition: when prices decrease, the consumer's lot improves, and the producer's lot worsens. Opposing interests mean conflict: "With demanders competing freely among themselves to buy goods cheaply and suppliers competing among themselves to sell goods dearly, the market conflict is on," write Haveman and Knopf.[6]

Profit maximization is not, however, just an alternative goal to preference maximization. Consumers would have to perform this activity themselves if producers did not do it. So they induce producers to become profit maximizers by making profit maximizers better off than profit minimizers. The lure of greater returns from consumers engenders the goal of profit maximization in producers. It is not an autonomously formed goal in the mind of independent producers, but rather is the result of consumers bending producer actions to consumer desires.

in relative distribution within a framework of capital and markets. Alternative systems, such as socialist command systems or natural economies, violate the basic conditions of freedom or wealth or both.

4. Haveman and Knopf 1966, p. 34.

5. Ibid., p. 40. 6. Ibid., p. 41.

Producers freely accept action directives from consumers because they can become better off that way. Since producer activities are made to serve consumer goals through inducements offered by consumers, profit maximization forms a common activity with preference maximization, not simply an alternative to it.

On the basis of a concept of economic life as the allocation of resources between alternative ends, neoclassical economics is not likely to perceive community within the economy. A more promising place to look for it is in the process of circulation of capital.

The Circuit of Capital

We may begin with a capital owner (or manager) – let us say, a woman – holding a bag of money. Rather than hoard the money (M), she exchanges it for commodities in the form of labor and means of production (C). The transaction may be denoted M–C. The capital owner does not hoard the commodities, nor does she use them to produce goods for her own or her workers' consumption. Instead, she combines them as productive capital for the manufacture of commodities (C′) that can be sold for money (M′), that is, for as much money as, or more than, the cost of producing them. The sale returns the capital owner to the starting point at which we first observed her. Yet the process is not over. Once again, instead of holding on to the money, she uses it to buy labor and means of production. When viewed together, these steps form a connected process that may be designated . . . M–C–P–C′–M′. . . , a circulation process that repeats again and again.[7]

The capital owner's various actions do not have different purposes. By looking at the first and last phases, M–M′, one can see that they all share a single underlying goal: to acquire more economic value. As Marx writes, "the circuit made by money-capital is . . . the . . . typical form in which the circuit of industrial capital appears, the capital whose aim and compelling motive – the expansion of value – is thus conspicuously revealed (buying to sell dearer)."[8]

Taken together, these actions constitute an expansion of value. Abstracted from the circuit, they have no economic purpose at all. Purchasing C – labor and means of production – does not achieve an end in itself, because the capital owner does not purchase or consume her own product. Production simply provides commodities that can be sold

7. My analysis of the circulation of capital is indebted to Levine's account (Levine 1978).

8. Marx 1967b, p. 59.

to generate capital for more production. The acquisition of money is not a final goal, but just a means of renewing the circuit. Each of the capital owner's actions supplies the next with the requisites to fulfill its function in this continuing process. Working together, they form one composite action or single connected sequence of actions that ultimately returns the capital owner to her starting point and leads to multiple repetitions of the pattern. Production, then, is not simply production, but an essential part of a larger circulatory system.

The various actions of the capital owner constitute a circuit because they move a common substance – capital – through a series of metamorphoses. When the capital owner begins by exchanging money (M) for commodities consisting of labor and production equipment (C), she converts one form of capital into another, for C is no less a manifestation of capital than is M. Both play a role in preserving and expanding value. In a second action, the capital owner converts commodity capital into the productive phase of capital (P), which also has the potential of preserving and expanding value. In a third move, the capital owner converts capital in the form of saleable commodities (C′) into money capital (M′).

The producer enacts the circuit because it enables her to engage in repeated production, and repeated production enables her to continue to expand value. Why is circulation necessary for production and accumulation? The reflux of M′, after an initial advance of money capital, enables the producer to buy more means of production and thus to produce on a larger scale. Someone who produces outside of a circulation process, making things only for his own consumption, may perpetuate himself, but he cannot repeat or expand the production of capital.

This discussion implicitly defines capital as all elements of the circuit of commodities and money taken together – a sharp contrast to the standard view of capital. Conventionally, capital is either capital goods in production or an investment fund for buying plant and equipment. Here, though, the essential feature of capital is its potential for preserving and expanding wealth, which is not limited to capital goods or an investment fund. It resides in all forms of capital: the money advanced toward the means of production, labor and the means of production themselves, the production process in which they are combined, the commodity products, and the money returned through the sale of those commodity products. The potential for preserving and expanding capital exists in none of these individually, but in the circuit that connects them. As Levine writes,

> The capital is the totality of the sequence, and not any of its particular elements taken in isolation. Capital is money, it is labor power, and it is means of pro-

duction. Capital is the commodity products and the money which their sale provides. And capital is none of these. It is the process of movement within which each of the moments is constituted not as an isolated entity, but as a phase in the process of the whole. . . . Each element is, therefore, a particular form adopted by a single principle, capital; the movement as a whole is composed of a sequence of transformations. Capital is the principle which remains the same within the totality of the movement. It is the substance which establishes the unity of the process as a single connected movement.[9]

Consumers, Producers, and the Circulation Process

Consumer purchases help owners and managers to complete the circuit of their capital. By bringing owners back to their original position of holding money, consumers enable them to undertake another round of producing and selling commodities for money. While consumers do not purchase goods from an altruistic desire to aid producers, they need producers to continue producing, and producers cannot do so without receiving money for their products. Because consumer payment is a necessary link that completes the producer's capital circuit, the two constitute a common action.

In making purchases, the consumer may not intend to cooperate with the producer in a common action, but intention is not a precondition for its being common action. The purchase and transfer of goods form a common action (circulation of capital) without being combined through intention. The conjunction of purchase and sale is not a matter of mere habit or of an accidental convergence of individuals with separate purposes. It reflects centuries of accumulated experience with the circulation of capital, and societal acceptance of the practice represents a tacit recognition that payment for produced goods is a necessary condition for reproduction and expansion of capital. Moreover, the exchange cannot be written off as reflecting ideological hegemony or domination, because the circulation of capital is necessary even in a socialist market system.

Since consumption requires payment, it is essential to the renewal of production; and though consumers may not need a particular product or its producer to continue, they do need production in general to continue. To this extent they share an interest with producers, but the interests of the two groups do not correspond completely. Consumers show divergent needs by avoiding particular producers.

Because consumers make independent decisions about the kinds and

9. Levine 1978–1981, vol. 1, p. 249.

quantities of goods they buy – decisions that may injure the rejected producers – consumer "behavior" is not ordinarily understood as action taken in common with producers. But *some* independence does not prove that there is *no* commonality. In paying for products, consumers are carrying out a phase of the circulation of capital and therefore, to some degree, are acting in concert with producers. Since the different functions of the two groups are both involved in the same activity, they cannot be viewed as entirely separate activities for "alternative" ends.

A corresponding communal element inheres in the producer's relation to the consumer, but economists generally do not note it, because they think producers are simply out for a profit. Economists are partly right: the profit motive sets producers apart somewhat from consumers, leading them to make independent decisions about what to produce, which combination of factor inputs to choose, how much to produce, and at what price. Even these considerations, however, involve a *dimension* of common action with consumers. Since the production of useful or desirable things is generally part of the profit-making effort, the production process includes activities designed to give consumers what they want. The overlapping, interconnection, and interpenetration of want-fulfilling and profit-maximizing endeavors qualify them as common action.

Common action involves person A doing part of what person B has to do to achieve her own ends, while person B performs part of what person A has to do to achieve his own ends. When production provides consumers with useful objects, it does something that they would otherwise have to do themselves to achieve their ends. The profit-seeking production of desired objects and the satisfaction-seeking consumer's payment of money for them therefore form a quintessential common action.

In offering to pay for his bread, the consumer induces a considerable number of producers to utilize their resources as if they were his own. The baker, the miller, the farmer, the producer of ovens, of trucks, of millstones and grinders, and the operators of these tools all get assimilated into the task of provisioning the consumer's needs, forming a sort of common action. Cooperation results from consumers' molding of producers. "Everyone," writes Lowe,

> expects to receive the bulk of his provision from the combined production activities of many others. The resources on which he depends thus extend to resources . . . which those others dispose. Therefore, with the . . . division and cooperation of labor, every member's task of provisioning shifts . . . to 'molding men,' namely, to inducing fellow members to engage in such technical manipulations as serve as his own ends as well as theirs . . . [T]he *social patterns* of economic activity . . . make it possible for each economic actor to dispose of the

> resources of others as if these resources were his own . . . [I]n adopting such a behavioral pattern my proximate intent is the *psychological manipulation* of others, by bending their actions to my desires as my action is bent to theirs.[10]

Because the consumer makes it worth his while, the producer freely consents to the desired pattern of behavior; so there is a mutual bending of actions to each other's pursuits and desires, which is common action and therefore economic community, although Lowe does not call it such.

Some features of production cannot be accounted for without recognizing the common element. In pursuing profits by producing what consumers want, producers are not acting out of a subjectively defined self-interest. If they were, they would be seeking payments without going to the trouble of producing useful items for consumers. But we know that producers do go to this trouble, which means that their self-seeking is intersubjectively defined to take into account the interest of consumers. This connection between productive activity and consumer satisfaction forms a sort of common action. But ascribing common action to producers and consumers does not presume that the parties are altruistically motivated. They act together to promote each other's ends, but neither relinquishes self-interest for the sake of the other. Their coaction qualifies as common action, though self-interested, because each performs for the other a part of what the other would otherwise have to do for herself.

Each producer only supplies a subset of consumers, which seemingly implies that he is not part of a systemwide community of consumption. But provisioning the wants of the whole community is not required in order to be a communal producer. The individual producer who makes items for part of the market is interdependent with producers who produce for the rest of the market. Therefore, producer behavior forms in the aggregate a social production process that supplies broad coverage of consumer wants, so individual producer behavior serves a systemwide communal purpose.

The neoclassical conception of exchange as a mode of coordinating goods and preferences does not grasp the common element in it. When

10. Lowe 1965, p. 22. Lowe's recognition of social influence comes at the expense of a loss of individual freedom, because social influence takes the form of psychological manipulation. But the reciprocal influence of consumers and producers upon each other is better understood as a necessary condition for freedom, not as a manipulation. The conditions that each places upon the others is not incompatible with the freedom of the others, it is a necessary condition for that freedom. Producers would not continue to attain their ends, profits, if they did not accept the condition, imposed by consumers, that they produce useful objects.

the owner of goods exchanges them for money to buy consumption goods, the transaction leads to the conclusion of economic activity, not to its continuation. Thus abstracted from the ongoing circulation of commodities, exchange is removed from the context that could reveal common action. Exchange appears to form the sequence C_1–M–C_2, with consumption as the final phase of economic activity. This conception gets matters wrong, because individuals do not usually sell commodities (C_1) with a view to consuming commodities (C_2). Instead, they sell them to acquire money for more production, an act that makes consumption and exchange part of the circuit. Because producers insist on remuneration as a condition for delivering goods, consumers have to pay money as a precondition for consumption. Accordingly, the consumer's payment of money is not so much part of the unfolding logic of preference as it is part of the circulation process, an action consumers undertake in concert with producers.

What makes consumption part of the circulation of capital (and therefore part of common action), and not merely an isolated act, is that consumption takes the form of a sequence of consumptions.[11] Consumers' recurrent and multiple wants require a sequence of consumptions. The need for a car, for example, leads to needs for gasoline, a mechanic, a car wash, spare parts, a map, and insurance. Moreover, after the consumer fulfills these needs, there is a resurgence of needs leading to the subsequent and recurrent production of gasoline, spare parts, and repair services, thus renewing the circuit of producers' capital. In other words, these multiple, sequential, recurrent, and expanding characteristics make consumption and production form the common action of creating and acquiring capital.

Capital as a Common End

The preservation of producers' capital is vitally important to consumers, whether they know it or not. Consumers require producers who have a sort of wealth that can produce means of satisfying multiple, sequential, recurrent, and expanding wants. Capital has this potential because it can recurrently and multiplicatively generate commodities, and therefore consumers have an interest in its preservation. Producers obviously share this interest, since they acquire wealth through the preservation and expansion of capital.

Although one would think a common interest of this importance

11. Levine 1978, p. 139.

could not be overlooked, traditional economists not only fail to note it but even praise the market precisely for its noncommunal character. The market enables consumers with alternative goals to avoid producers who make undesirable "goods" or who use inefficient methods to manufacture commodities that could be made at a lower cost. The virtue of the market, from a neoclassical standpoint, consists in the ability of preference-maximizing consumers to damage unsatisfactory producers by doing business elsewhere. Microeconomic analysis also neglects consumers' and producers' commonality of interest in the preservation and expansion of capital when it posits a separating hyperplane radically distinguishing utility-maximizing from profit-maximizing decisions.[12]

The competitive theme involving alternative goals is part of the market story, but taken alone it obscures other aspects of consumers' relation to capital and thus to the productive ends of society. While producers pursue profit as their direct goal, consumers also have a strong interest in the preservation and expansion of capital, because capital is the means to the satisfaction of their needs. The preservation and expansion of capital is a common end of consumers and producers, one to which they both contribute in different ways. While producers want to get high prices for their products, and consumers want to "give up as little money as possible for each unit purchased,"[13] consumers stand to gain if producers succeed in expanding capital. There is no other economic goal that consumers would have producers pursue, for if producers lacked the necessary capital to provide what consumers want, consumers would have to provide for themselves, which they could not do well without fulfilling the requirements for capital.

Consumers can obtain ample and diverse goods only by buying commodity products. Other forms of production, such as natural production, self-subsistent production, and bureaucratic socialism, cannot achieve this quantity, diversity, and "fit" with consumer wants. In seeking commodity products, consumers are seeking a type of capital, for commodity products are just capital in commodity form. Producers, meanwhile, want to produce commodity capital desired by consumers because they want to acquire more money capital by selling commodity capital. Consumers and producers, therefore, both seek the same substance, capital (in different forms), which indicates a commonality in their ends.

Pursuit of a common end leads consumers and producers into the

12. On the separating hyperplane, see Koopmans 1957, pp. 17, 21, 29.
13. Haveman and Knopf 1966, p. 40.

common action of circulating capital. By paying for capital's products, the consumer provides the producer with money capital to finance the production of more commodities.

When consumers pay money for goods, thereby aiding producers in the preservation and expansion of capital, their actions indicate tacit acceptance of the producers' goal. Neoclassical theorists know that consumers, in buying goods subject to their budget constraints, help producers make a profit. Yet these economists do not infer common action from this practice. But one may ask, why – apart from the laws of property and contract – do consumers let themselves be constrained by producer interests? What is the economic rationale? It must be that producer goals also serve consumer goals. To the degree that this is true, the preservation of capital is the common end of both groups.

Though Marx and Levine do not posit common action in capitalist economies, their theories of circulation form a basis for doing so. While characterizing capitalism as essentially a system of class division, they nonetheless formulate "the unity of the process of production and circulation,"[14] a notion that can be used to conceptualize a dimension of economic community. If they are right about this unity, then the opposition of interests cannot be thoroughgoing. Common action has to be a dimension of economic activity. The lack of complete commonality, it is worth underscoring, does not mean that common action does not exist at all; a dimension of systemwide common action can still be present.

Though the Marx–Levine concept of circulation can provide a foundation for conceiving of community, their account has some problematic elements. The movement of commodities and money, in their view, "transfers" value between phases of the circuit. This formulation involves the metaphysical idea that the value of labor and the means of production are somehow embodied in the commodity product.[15] The notion of economic community could be undermined if it were based on this version of circulation. The metaphysical element can be removed, however, without losing the unity of circulation essential to economic community. Each phase of the circuit can be reconceived as a necessary and precipitating condition for the subsequent condition. The acquisition of money capital is a necessary condition for productive capital, which is a necessary condition for commodity capital, and so on. The circuit formed in this way, with each phase partially derived from preceding conditions, can provide a basis for conceiving of common action without involving metaphysical value transfers.

14. Marx 1967a, p. 100.

15. Marx 1967b, Chapter 1 and p. 352; Levine 1978–1981, vol. 1, Chapter 8.

Community and Interrelated Circuits of Capital

This analysis has focused on the relationship between the consumer and the circuit of individual capital. To demonstrate systemwide economic community, however, the analysis must be expanded to include the consumer's relations to the system of interconnected circuits of individual capitals. Each consumer interrelates not only with the firms from which he purchases, but also with the system of circulation, because the capitals of these firms are directly or indirectly related to those of other firms.

When producer 1 sells commodity products to producer 2, he obviously does so to get money in return, but his interest in the transaction can be broader than that. He has an indirect interest in having the exchange benefit producer 2 as well. If it does not help producer 2 to preserve and expand his capital, he may lose some ability to participate in the circulation system, so that in the future producer 1 cannot get the exchange value that he needs from producer 2. As Scitovsky writes, "the entrepreneur needs command over the products of other firms . . . In a real sense, therefore, the firm's capital consists of other firms' products."[16] Similarly, producer 2 has an interest in providing products that benefit his buyer, producer 3, and producer 3 has an interest in satisfying producer 4. A prevalent pattern of nonmutual exchange would force most producers to drop out of the system, causing it to break down. Therefore, to an extent, it is in each producer's interest to have the capital of other producers preserved. Indeed, each has an interest in having the system of producers realize capital. While neoclassical economics is correct in characterizing producer interactions as competitive, it would be a serious error to deny that they also have a dimension of common interest.

Producer 1's sale of commodities is producer 2's purchase of commodities. The realization of the circuit of producer 1's money capital presupposes the realization of producer 2's circuit of commodity capital. Producer 1 cannot undergo a circulation process unless producer 2 does so as well, so M_1–C–M_2' presupposes C_2–M–C_2. Similarly, producer 2's subsequent sale of commodity products to producer 3 helps further producer 2's circulation of capital. As Marx writes, "It is only because the farmer has sold his wheat that the weaver is enabled to sell his linen, only because the weaver has sold his linen that our Hotspur is enabled to sell his Bible, and only because the latter has sold the water

16. Scitovsky 1952, p. 216.

of everlasting life that the distiller is enabled to sell his *eau-de-vie*."[17] The interdependence of producers is systematic rather than merely bilateral. Exchange links each individual capital directly or indirectly with every other individual capital. As Nai-Pew Ong holds, "The movement of each individual capital is . . . at one and the same time both its individual movement and the 'integrating link in the movement of total capital.'"[18] Marx also stresses the general interdependence of producers: "the circuits of the individual capitals intertwine, presuppose and necessitate one another, and form, precisely in this interlacing, the movement of total social capital."[19] "The circuit made possible by one commodity in the course of its metamorphoses is," he holds, "inextricably entwined with the circuits of other commodities. This whole process constitutes the circulation of commodities."[20] The systemic interdependence of individual circuits implies a correspondingly systemic scope of common action within the economy. Since each individual circuit involves the conjoint activity of a system of other individual circuits, individual producers have an interest not only in the circulation of their own capital but also in the circulation of capital as a whole.

Consumers, too, have an interest in this larger goal. Because individual circuits of capital are interlocked, the consumer who buys a product from one firm participates in and depends on not only that firm's circulation of capital but also the general circulation process presupposed by the individual circuit. In other words, the consumer's purchase is part of a systemwide common action.

ECONOMIC COMMUNITY AND SELF-ORGANIZING ECONOMY

Whether the economy has a dimension of community depends on whether its members are endogenously or exogenously influenced – that is, whether they are socially self-determined by and within the system of economic relations or conditioned by outside agencies, causes, or forces. An economy unavoidably contains a measure of both modes of determination, but one or the other can have primacy – with important consequences for the existence of a community.

17. Marx 1967a, p. 112.
18. Statement by Nai-Pew Ong 1979, p. 216, containing a quotation from Marx 1956, p. 392.
19. Marx 1967b, pp. 353–354.
20. Marx 1977, p. 207. Or see Marx 1967a, p. 112, for a slightly different translation.

Suppose, on the one hand, that a capital-based market system hinges on a certain set of behaviors without which it simply cannot function. Because these behaviors are required for the survival of the system, they are not entirely subjective, but instead are bound up with the objective laws of wealth creation. People who benefit from the system and want it to continue must conduct themselves in accordance with these requirements, and in doing so they are in a sense influenced by a set of common causes, just as a religious group following the same scriptures is shaped by a set of common influences. When these individuals generate influences that induce others to comply with the requirements of the system, these others too are conditioned by a set of common causes, one that orients economic actors toward maintaining the system. Thus the system directs individual conduct toward common ends, and in generating common ends, endogenous determination generates community within the economy.

Now suppose, on the other hand, that the economy is mainly governed by outside influences. In that case, the individuals it comprises have many disparate ends arising from many external causes, rather than common ends. Antithetical to the idea of community, neoclassical economic theory defines the economic system as wholly a mechanism of adjustment to exogenous change.[21] "[It] consists," Samuelson writes,

> of a designated set of unknowns [for price and quantity] which are constrained as a condition of equilibrium to satisfy an equal number of consistent and independent equations . . . These are implicitly assumed to hold within a certain environment and as of certain data. Some parts of these data are introduced as explicit parameters; and, as a result of our equilibrium conditions, our unknown variables may be expressed in function of these parameters."[22]

The solution obtained for unknowns that fulfill the equilibrium conditions "indicates possible and necessary responses in our variables to changes in data."[23] In relation to the exogenous determinants, "the term causation is admissible. . . . [I]t may be said that changes in these *cause* changes in the variables of our system."[24]

Neoclassical economics declares that one model's exogenous factors are another's endogenous variables, but the rule is not regulative. In practice, neoclassical theory tends to treat tastes, technology, and

21. Adherents to this view include the original neoclassical theorists Jevons, Menger, Edgeworth, and Walras; the later "new welfare economists" such as Samuelson and Bator; and the general equilibrium theorists Arrow, Debreu, and Koopmans, among many others.

22. Samuelson 1948, p. 19.

23. Ibid., p. 12. 24. Ibid., p. 9.

resources as exogenously given and to attribute price and quality variables to changes in these external conditions.[25] Consumer preferences originate outside the domain of economic analysis, and they are "independent of the choices of other decision makers" rather than formed in relation to them.[26] Their causes are psychological, physiological, or cultural rather than economic, writes Lord Robbins.[27]

Exogenous influences are many and "impossible to list," according to neoclassical theorists.[28] Determination of individuals by many different external causes implies that they have disparate interests, not common interests, since each exogenous determinant belongs to an external system with its own distinctive imperatives. These direct individual behavior toward multiple, potentially conflicting ends: (1) natural needs direct behavior toward the ends of the biological system, (2) subjective preferences toward the ends of the system of individual psychology, and (3) resource endowments toward the ends of the natural system. Thus the effort to adjust to exogenous determinants does not incline individuals to act together toward a common end. Individual differences in ends reach an extreme of noncomparability in the neoclassical principle of "no interpersonal comparisons of utility," derived from the assumption of utter psychological uniqueness.

While neoclassical theorists recognize that the general cultural environment influences an economy, they do not ascribe common attributes, preferences, or aims to its agents.[29] Koopmans says that the cultural interpretation is "detachable" from the postulate on consumers (that they have complete, convex, representable preferences) and is therefore informal and dispensable.[30] Moreover, cultural influences somehow get resolved into unique and noncomparable preferences, which preclude common ends. There is reference to peer-group pressures, which conceivably could shape preferences in similar ways, but since different peer groups have different preferences there is no systemwide economic community.[31]

25. Ibid., pp. 8, 19, 22, 91; Silberberg 1978, pp. 217–218. Forms of endogenous formation of preferences are recognized in some nonstandard neoclassical models. Their implications, unfavorable and favorable, for economic community are considered later. On resource endowments, see Arrow and Hahn 1971, p. 75.
26. Koopmans 1957, pp. 44, 41.
27. See Robbins 1984 [1932], p. 86. On exogenous determination of the production side of the economy, see Debreu 1959, p. 37.
28. Nicholson 1985, p. 82.
29. Ibid., p. 79.
30. Koopmans 1957, pp. 132, 44.
31. Nicholson 1985, p. 79.

Compared to the externally determined system defined by neoclassicists, an economy can be more self-determined. Such a system contains most of the conditions necessary for its existence. It creates many of those conditions itself, so it is not as abjectly and comprehensively dependent on outside conditions as is an externally determined system. Since one requirement is that the actions and ends of its participants accord with the vital purpose of association – the generation of wealth – a self-organizing economy shapes the preferences of agents in ways that promote this purpose. To the degree that it comprises common actions and common ends, the self-determining economy is a community.

The notion of preferences formed to meet the purpose of association is alien to neoclassical theorists. Although they now acknowledge the endogenous formation of preferences, they deny any implication of common action, common ends, or community. Their position on endogenous preferences remains part of the theory of economic mechanism adjusting to exogenous changes, which splinters individuals' ends. By contrast, the view of endogenous preferences advanced here is part of a theory of self-determined systems. When formulated as part of the theory of self-determined systems, the theory of endogenous preferences implies economic community.

The nature of the production process indicates that the economy is more a self-determined system than an exogenously determined one. Modern production is a social process in which society contributes more than nature does to the production of wealth. Because social production internalizes many conditions for preserving and expanding wealth, it provides compelling evidence that the economy is in some ways self-determining. Instead of relying on nature for the means of satisfying wants and needs, societies often devise their own means. They do not simply transform natural resources into final goods, they also produce inputs to the production process, as Piero Sraffa emphasizes in *Production of Commodities by Means of Commodities*.[32] Social production creates "*un milieu interieur*" (as the physiologist Claude Bernard said of homeostasis), and it does not simply adjust in a neoclassical manner to the environment.[33]

In a well-expounded conception of a self-determining system, David Levine characterizes the circulation of capital as a self-organizing process. In his view, consumption, and not just production, is ordered in accordance with the requirements for preserving and expanding capital.

32. Sraffa 1960.

33. For a discussion of Claude Bernard, see Miller 1978, p. 135.

> For the circuit to exist it is necessary that the movement [of commodities] within it be continuous, that each particular exchange lead itself into a connected series of exchanges. . . . It is . . . required that there exist, within the circulation of commodities and money, an inner force by which the flux, in its entirety, is governed. It is this force which orders the circuit in such a way as to sustain the system in its entirety and thereby make possible the continuous movement which is its sole mode of existence. This inner force is also a principle of self-organization. . . . The comprehension of the inner law of the total movement requires that each exchange be subordinated to a principle and that the circuit as a whole be, in this way subject to an ordering. . . . [T]he principle . . . is that of the self-organization of the commodity circuit, the object of which is nothing more or less than its own maintenance and continuation. The determination of the circuit according to its continuation is the only basis on which the system of exchanges can be constituted as viable. Any other basis for the determination of the circuit must necessarily make the latter contingent upon extrinsic relations over which it exerts no force. This would necessarily make the circuit itself the accidental result of capricious conditions and would exclude any systematic conception.[34]

The goal of generating wealth consists in generating capital, for capital is what wealth is,[35] and the only way a society can adequately generate capital is to circulate it. Thus a wealth-oriented society conditions individuals to act in ways that, taken together, circulate capital. When economic activities are arranged to promote one overarching end, we may speak of a self-organizing process. The self-organizing capital circuit arranges individual actions to form an interdependent whole aimed at the preservation and expansion of capital.

Just as production is socially determined to meet the requirements for generating wealth, so too is consumption. Since multiple wants on the part of the consumer are needed to continue the circuit of capital by providing a market for products, a wealth-oriented system secures this condition by increasing consumer wants. The endogenous formation of preferences on the part of a self-determining system creates preferences that serve the vital purpose of association. By shaping preferences in

34. Levine 1978–1981, vol. 1, pp. 115–116. Levine does not discuss economic community in *Economic Theory*, vol. 1, nor does he subscribe to such a view of the economy, but his formulation has ramifications for community. His formulation is particularly fascinating because it shows how preferential choices can be subsumed under the principle of self-organization of the capital circuit. Levine thinks that the economy is riven by the opposed interests of labor and capital, which leads away from the idea of community. Yet relations between labor and capital can still constitute common action, however exploitative these relations may be. Even when benefits are unjustly distributed, production is the conjoint action of labor and capital services, and as such constitutes common action.
35. See Levine 1978–1991, vol. 1; Levine 1977.

ways that promote the preservation and expansion of capital, an economy builds this end into the natural tendencies of consumers, orienting them toward the same goal that capital owners seek and thereby composing a dimension of community.

In a self-ordering system, capital is not simply a means of satisfying preferences, as it is in customary economic thinking. When preferences are formed in the interests of preserving and expanding capital, capital has a certain precedence as an end, since it shapes preferences instead of merely adjusting to them. As the principle of self-organization of the market, capital subsumes individual preferences under a more general principle, and this umbrella constitutes a dimension of community between producers and consumers. It functions as a means determinant of ends, eliminating the condition of *purely* disparate and different individual preferences posited by neoclassical theory.

Often a religious society, such as a society of monks or nuns, is called a religious "order" because it has a rule of life that unites the constituents as a cohesive community. One may analogously speak of an "economic order." The economy has a rule of life – preserving and expanding capital – whose observance makes economic actors members of a community.

While self-organization is an important dimension of the economy, the system is not entirely self-determining. The influences that generate community do not pervade all dimensions of economic behavior. The economy is also subject to natural shocks to the resource base; and changes in consumer preferences and technical knowledge can have disequilibrating effects as well. Overlaid by external agencies and causes, the economy is affected by the multiple ends involved in their tendencies. As a result, the participants are not simply and solely oriented toward the vital purpose of the economic association, and the association is not a community on all dimensions.

Elements of this view accord with Adolph Lowe's argument that individuals' economic actions have a certain consistency; that their consistency stems from social patterning of behavior rather than from autonomous decision making; and that the social patterning proceeds from the requirements of the system. "*Patterns of behavior*," he writes, "[are] . . . created and maintained that make the actions of each one compatible with those of all the others, and also with the attainment of the final goals of all."[36] The condition of compatibility between individual self-seeking and the attainment of the ends of others is not achieved by accidental coincidence between autonomously self-deter-

36. Lowe 1965, p. 20.

mined actions. Rather, social patterning shapes individual behaviors so that individuals' aims are consistent or are directed toward a common end. Lowe argues, "Patterned behavior differs from random behavior in that each individual act, and any sequence of such acts, is consistent with the same purpose," which he describes as maximum aggregate output.[37]

Lowe's identification of a final common end implies the existence of economic community, though he does not draw the implication. Moreover, his view, that the patterning of behavior toward a shared end stems from influences generated in line with the requirements of the system, supports the idea of economic community, again without explicitly asserting that it does. Yet these requirements are not concretely defined as the requirements of capital, and in this respect his analysis is too abstract and unspecific to ground a conception of economic community.[38]

CONCLUSION

Consumers and producers have different particular ends in the sense that consumer 1 does not want good X produced by producer 2 and seeks instead good Y produced by producer 3. Therefore capital-based

37. Ibid., pp. 20–21. The orientation of individual self-seeking toward an end shared by all is due to "a structural change in the provisioning process that makes the consistency conditions more stringent. The object is now society at large or rather . . . the aggregate of its members. This makes it possible to reconcile the claims of individuals in a socially approved state of satisfaction of all. The content of the collective basket of goods thus established can be described as the *final macro-goal* to the attainment of which the activities of the members are devoted . . . [M]aximum aggregate output . . . must be postulated as the *productive optimum*, to be obtained through specific resource combinations."
38. Ibid., p. 26. We also see in Lowe's analysis elements of the process of general conditioning of economic actors toward a collective goal, which can advance the idea of economic community. The members of the economy receive action directives through interaction with other members of the system, leading them toward consistent and shared final ends. These directives stem from the requirements of the system of provisioning on which all individuals depend. Agents freely comply with these directives because they depend on the aggregate order for satisfaction of their wants. Lowe 1965, pp. 26–27, writes: "In searching for forces which *create* suitable action directives we cannot fall back on instinctual drives . . . The answer lies in the highly complex processes of interaction through which social consensus in general is generated . . . [T]he success of [these social processes] depends on the extent to which the large majority in a given society identify, consciously or unconsciously, with the requirements of an ongoing process of provisioning."

market systems cannot be *comprehensive* communities. Yet there is a community *overarching* the pursuit of different particular ends, because (1) it is in consumer 1's interest that every producer try to preserve his or her own capital, and (2) it is in the interest of producers' capital in general that consumers pay money for goods. Since consumer payments help preserve the capital of the system of producers, and since the system of producers helps consumers generally, there is a *dimension* of community.

Relatively independent actions and ends are subsumed under more general common actions and ends: the ongoing process of circulation of capital. The existence of an overarching community depends on the penetration of relatively distinct individual ends by general common ends. Although consumer 1 purchases producer 1's good Y rather than producer 2's good X, the common end of the preservation of producers' capital glimmers through because of the fact that he always pays money for goods received, which is a general need of all producers, not just of producer 1.

Although community is not comprehensive, it is not limited to subsystems (like the firm's relation to a target market) but extends systemwide, because consumer payments to particular firms are necessary for production in general, and because production of useful items is necessary for consumption in general.

10

Endogenous Preferences and Economic Community

> With the many fine recipes . . . in the . . . peanut publications, it is easy to find one that will please. . . . With these few suggestions, it is hoped the billion pound peanut crop will be utilized.[1]
>
> George Washington Carver, *The Peanut Journal*

In theory, the endogenous formation of preferences by and within the system of economic relations helps to form a dimension of community in the economy because it orients consumer behavior toward a vital purpose of association – the preservation and expansion of capital.[2] The question now is whether this logic has a real-world counterpart in the causal processes of actual capital-based market systems. If we can identify the actual processes of endogenous formation of preferences, then the logic of the previous chapter suggests that it would imply the existence of a dimension of community in the economy. This chapter undertakes an extended analysis of endogenous formation of preferences and elaborates the concrete workings of the process in order to demonstrate the presence of community in capital-based market systems.

1. George Washington Carver, letter to the editor of *The Peanut Journal,* December 15, 1931, cited in Kremer 1987, pp. 118–119.
2. Although the term "endogenous formation of preferences" connotes the internal formation of preferences within the individual, its meaning is different in economics and political science. In these disciplines it means social formation of preferences. As I use the term, it signifies a particular type of social formation where preferences are formed by and within a system of individuals. This definition does not preclude that inner influences may play a role in the formation of preferences, but it defines the locus of possible influences more broadly than that.

ENDOGENOUS PREFERENCES, THE SYSTEM OF COMMODITY PRODUCTION AND EXCHANGE, AND ECONOMIC COMMUNITY

Consumer wants are endogenously formed partly because producers cannot create wealth without using methods that must create wants in order to work. Commodity production is the essential method of producing wealth. It, alone among production processes, can multiply production processes and multiply products necessary for the production and acquisition of wealth. The purpose of commodity production – to satisfy multiple, virtually unlimited wants – drives production to levels productive of wealth. Commodity production is production for a mass market comprised of people with needs having a certain generality, objectiveness, and universality. Given this market, commodity production can employ techniques of production and forms of labor that stamp out the same product continuously. It, unlike an alternative form of production, artisan production, uses machine production, assembly line production, and factory production to make uniform products that can be turned out over and over again. An artisan who designs something with the unique tastes of a particular patron in mind may make only one-of-a-kind objects. With its unique capacity for multifold repetition of production processes, commodity production holds the key to the creation of wealth.

Because creating wealth involves multiplying products and multiplying production processes, producers incur dependence on consumers with multiple, virtually unlimited, needs. The producer's recourse to endogenous formation of consumer preferences is rooted in this dependence. Producers cannot sell enough products to create wealth if consumers do not have multiple wants. Thus, producers have a strong reason for generating wants: it helps them to secure a precondition for commodity production and the acquisition of wealth. In this way, the endogenous formation of preferences becomes a necessary and integral part of a system of wealth, not merely a dispensable adjunct. As Russell Lynes wrote at midcentury:

> The making of tastes . . . is, in fact a major industry. . . . In the last century and a quarter the purveying of tastes has become a big business, employing hundreds of thousands of people . . . If the taste industry were to go out of business we would have a major depression. . . . This is not, however, a catastrophe we are likely to encounter, because the taste industry has gradually become essential to . . . capitalism.[3]

3. Lynes 1949, p. 4.

The endogenous formation of preferences is not simply a form of production determination of wants. For, although producers influence (multiply) preferences, they are led to do so by the conditions of commodity exchange. The producer's goal, to acquire more money, extends into a sphere beyond production, and so it can only be realized by satisfying the requirements of commodity exchange. To get more money, the producer has to produce objects capable of attracting buyers. The mediation of production by exchange means that the social conditioning of preferences does not reflect the imperatives of production as much as it does the requirements for the circulation of commodities and money. Producers who have to satisfy the requirements of commodity exchange have a strong interest in multiplying the kinds and number of consumer wants. The process of endogenous formation of preferences should, therefore, be understood as coextensive with the conditions of commodity production cum exchange rather than with production alone. It is a process in which the influence of producers upon consumer preferences is a reflection of the fact that production has a determination within commodity exchange.

If the social conditioning of preferences were simply a production determination, exclusively reflecting the imperatives of production, there would be no genuine community within the economy. Consumers would be unfree subordinates of the production process. And, if there were a community, it would be a narrow one, restricted to the sphere of production. But because "the conditions necessary for . . . production . . . are no[t] given immediately in the production process,"[4] community extends to the system of commodity producers and exchangers. Wealth created by this process does not represent the limited purpose of producers alone, but the social purpose of the system of commodity producers and exchangers: wealth. Thus the social determination of consumer preferences orients them toward the vital purpose of association, not just toward producer goals, thereby creating a community of ends among producers and consumers. In sum, since endogenous formation of preferences is coextensive with the system of commodity production *and* exchange, community has the broad scope of this system as well.

THE DEVELOPMENT OF ENDOGENOUS FORMATION OF PREFERENCES

At the beginning of the new economic order in seventeenth- and eighteenth-century England and France, economists and political thinkers

4. Levine 1978–1981, vol. 1, p. 243.

took note of the evidence of endogenous formation of preferences. Precursors of Adam Smith, such as Sir James Steuart, witnessed the creation of new and different needs in towns where capitalist production and exchange had taken root. They particularly noted that needs in the towns were multiplied, whereas they were fixed and limited in the country, where "natural production" prevailed. There was under way, not only a refinement of tastes regarding food and necessaries, but also a multiplication of wants beyond the needs "for our being well fed, well clothed, and well defended."[5] To political and economic analysts of the time, the cause was clear. Steuart wrote that "riches inspire a taste for luxury."[6] The multiplication of wants was caused by the system of wealth. "Luxury is the child of wealth," as he poetically put it.[7] Wealth, in turn, was created by individuals "who apply themselves to industry" in the towns, rather than to agriculture.[8] The multiplied wants, then, result from industry.

These new causes and effects were so important that economists of the day saw the social stimulation of preferences as a defining feature of the new economic order. Standard neoclassical theory would later turn this great insight inside out, postulating consumer preferences as exogenous parameters of the economic system, quite to the detriment of economic understanding.

Smith's precursors described in fairly concrete fashion the actual workings of the endogenous formation of preferences.[9] The ingenuity and industriousness of producers makes things interesting to consumers, and stimulates the desire for luxuries. "[T]he ingenuity of workmen begets a taste in the rich,"[10] wrote Steuart. The multiplication of wants also spreads to the nonrich as they succumb to the allure of luxurious goods. "[A]s the ingenuity of workmen begets a taste in the rich, so the allurement of riches kindles an ambition, and encourages works of ingenuity in the poor,"[11] Steuart explains.

In addition to the quality of multiplicity, consumer preferences em-

5. Steuart in Meek 1973, p. 152; original emphasis removed.
6. Steuart 1966, p. 724.
7. Ibid., p. 279. Rousseau also saw this: "Superfluity awakens cupidity. The more one has, the more one wants" (Rousseau as cited by Durkheim 1975, p. 81).
8. Steuart 1966, p. 42.
9. The "preclassical economists" include Cantillon, Hutcheson, Hume, Turgot, Mirabeau, Quesnay, Steuart, and Tucker. For a good introduction to their work, see Meek 1973. Though not all of them recognized endogenous formation of preferences, the remarkable fact is that some of them did. See also Hutcheson in Meek 1973, p. 31.
10. Ibid. 11. Steuart in Meek 1973, p. 155.

body a standard of taste with some social objectivity, rather than wholly arbitrary, subjective desires, according to preclassical economic analysis. Preferences with a standard of taste are endogenously formed, that is, are formed by and within the system of economic relations, in the sense that consumers learn the standard in part from producers, rather than generating it entirely from a subjective origin within themselves. To ingeniously refine objects capable of exciting consumers, producers have to develop a standard of taste in their work. This in turn affects consumers, who try to meet this standard in making their purchases. As Steuart wrote, "In such countries where these [ingenuity and industriousness] are made to flourish, the free hands . . . will be employed in useful manufactures, which, being refined upon by the ingenious, will determine what is called the standard of taste; this taste will increase consumption, which again will multiply workmen, and these will encourage the production of food for their nourishment."[12]

Consider, for instance, the way the standard of taste in stockings came about. Prior to Queen Elizabeth's time, hose were made of common cloth, even those worn by the richest people.[13] The use of knitted stockings did not become widespread until a merchant, Sir Thomas Gresham, gave King Henry VI a pair that caused quite a stir. In 1564, a greatly skilled apprentice on London Bridge, William Rider, prepared a pair of knitted worsted stockings for William, earl of Pembroke.[14] These events suggest that the standard of taste in hose among the English was greatly affected by the "great ingenuity and nice taste" on the production side.[15]

More than a century after Steuart wrote, neoclassical economics introduced an elegant new theory – with a postulate of exogenous pref-

12. Ibid., p. 156. Adam Smith's teacher Francis Hutcheson made a similar point; see Hutcheson in Meek 1973, p. 31.
13. See Adam Smith 1937, pp. 245–46 n213. Smith's authorities on these points are Howell, *History of the World*, vol. 2, p. 222 and Adam Anderson, *Historical and Chronological Deduction of the Origin of Commerce*, 1764, p. 1561. Reference is not given to their publishers. My use of Smith's data to illustrate Hutcheson's point should not be taken to mean that Smith believed in endogenous preferences. Though Smith refined Hutcheson's ideas on social division of labor, he left aside his teacher's ideas on social formation of preferences.
14. Here the more remote origins were Italy and Mantua.
15. Preferences for peanut butter in the 1900s provide a more recent case. The production of peanut butter and peanut oil was not a response to already existing preferences for these goods. Preferences for these goods were stimulated on the production side. George Washington Carver studied the uses of peanuts, and he invented peanut butter, peanut oil, and other goods at the behest of southern planters who needed a new cash crop after the boll weevil threatened the cotton

erences.[16] The theory was, purportedly, empirically and logically superior to preceding theories.[17] But the evidence and arguments of preclassical economics indicate that there was never any empirical basis for the neoclassical view that preferences are wholly exogenously determined.

Sombart gives a wholly different explanation of the formation of luxury tastes, according to which they are largely governed by female courtesans, rather than multiplied by producers. If true, his analysis would undermine the preclassical theory of endogenous formation of preferences. In support of his thesis, Sombart presents some fascinating lists of products bought by the court and its emulators, such as Louis XIV's expenditure of 606,999 livres on his household, 2,274,253 livres on silverware and toiletries, 12,000 on horses, 2,186,748 on petty expenses, 22,000 on lace, and so forth, in 1685.[18] These lists of purchases do not, however, supply proof of the direction of causation in preference formation. One cannot tell who was influencing whom, producers or female courtesans.

Another long-term process – the commodification of wealth – was under way that swamped female courtesans as a factor in the formation of tastes. The commodification of wealth indicates the influence of producers on consumer tastes, and therefore points to the preclassical view of endogenous formation of preferences. Starting in the Middle Ages and then gathering force during the 1600s and 1700s, court tastes changed from desires for long trains of servants, feasts, and large-scale entertainments to desires to possess objects useful for the display of wealth. The change may be characterized as an objectification of luxury tastes. The preferences of female courtesans cannot account for it entirely. Instead, it seems to be a result of the commodification of wealth occurring during that period. "Workmen" were making attractive objects in order to make profits, and in so doing, they were generating objective desires.

In seeking to understand endogenous formation of preferences, we may skip over classical political economy; it does not make a significant contribution in this regard.[19] Smith saw preferences as everything but endogenous to the economy. By turns, he conceived of them as naturally

crops and overplanting of cotton had depleted the soil of nitrogen. See Holt, pp 222–249.

16. See Robbins 1984; Jevons 1871; Edgeworth 1881; Walras 1954; Menger 1950.
17. On the empirical character of neoclassical theory, see Silberberg 1978, Chapter 1.
18. Sombart 1967, pp. 68–69, 79.
19. Classical political economy has an endogenous conception of consumption as productive consumption or reproduction of labor. That view of preferences set

determined "by the narrow capacity of the human stomach" and socially determined by the "custom of the country."[20] The latter determination is not endogenous to the economic system, but rather an exogenous influence upon the economy coming from the surrounding culture.

Following the preclassical period, the next important contribution to the theory of endogenous formation of preferences is made by Hegel. He explained that multiplicity is a defining characteristic of individual needs, as distinct from natural needs. "An animal's needs and its ways and means of satisfying them are," he said, "both alike restricted in scope. . . . [M]an evinces his transcendence of it and his universality, first by the multiplication of needs and means of satisfying them, and secondly by the differentiation and division of concrete need . . ."[21] All economic wants are multiplied wants. Preclassical economics had held that only desires for luxuries are multiplied, not the category of needs for "necessaries." But multiple wants are the general type of economic wants, as Hegel points out. The natural need for the nutrients in wheat, for example, can be differentiated and multiplied, in such a way that this "subsistence" need can take the form of a myriad of needs for different processed foods – bagels, French bread, whole grain bread, and so on.

Endogenous determination is necessary to the account of consumer preferences because alternative explanations of the multiplicity of needs will not suffice. Natural determination cannot account for it, because natural needs are, as Hegel noted, inherently fixed and limited.[22] Subjective preference for more rather than less cannot account for it, because the subjective material of the self does not afford enough stimulation to excite so many interests, as Hegel further reasoned.[23] Endogenous determination can, however, account for the multiplication of wants. Hegel writes: "The multiplicity of objects," created by a system of division of labor united by exchange, "excite[s] interest," yielding a multiplicity of wants.[24] This means that the system of commodity exchange and production is the ultimate determinant of needs, in respect of multiplicity.[25]

back the development of the theory of endogenous preferences, and has little place in an account of *contributions* to such theory. Later in the chapter (pp. 212–217), I address the difficulties in the classical idea of productive consumption, and I suggest an alternative way of formulating endogenous formation of preferences that can overcome these difficulties.

20. Smith 1937, pp. 164, 821, 164.

21. Hegel 1952, para. 190, p. 127. 22. Ibid.

23. Ibid., para. 35, p. 37, para. 39, p. 38.

24. Ibid., para. 197, p. 129. 25. Ibid., para. 196, p. 129.

Preclassical economists showed industrious workmen multiplying the desire for "luxuries" among the nobility, but the subject of endogenous preference formation can be extended to consumers in general. Producers generate wants on the part of a wide spectrum of consumers by multiplying the need for "comforts" on the part of the average consumer. As Hegel pointed out, "What the English call 'comfort' is something inexhaustible and illimitable. [Others can discover to you that what you take to be] comfort at any stage is discomfort, and these discoveries never come to an end. Hence the need for greater comfort does not exactly arise within you directly; it is suggested to you by those who hope to make a profit from its creation."[26] In the development of the theory of endogenous preferences, Hegel's recognition that the need for comfort is suggested to you by producers seeking profits is a milestone, because it implies that the endogenous formation of preferences is an integral part of the process of circulation of capital. Also implied is the idea that consumer goals are brought in accordance with the goal of expansion of capital, rather than being entirely separate, distinct, or alternative to the producer goal of profit maximization. Finally, consumption figures as a sustaining moment in the circulation of capital for Hegel, rather than as the end point draining value from the system, in contrast to the neoclassical portrayal.[27]

While Hegel implicitly understood endogenous preference formation

26. Ibid., add. 122 to para. 191, p. 269. We also see here an historical precursor to the "sour grapes" theory of the genesis of wants proposed by Hirschman and Elster 1983.
27. Hegel's awareness of the endogeneity of needs does not lead him to the conclusion that economic community exists. At most he sees interdependence. It is noteworthy that Hegel does not explicitly consider the relationship between consumer and profit seeker in the context of the circulation of capital. In abstraction from this process, the interests of consumer and profit seeker appear as distinct and different interests: the profit seeker multiplying preferences in the interest of his own capital, and the consumer consuming in the interest of his own needs. Considered in context of the circulation of capital, however, one can see a dimension of community.

    Another reason that Hegel did not posit economic community is inferably that, in his mind, differentiation of needs takes precedence over commonality of needs. Yet individual differences in needs should not disconfirm the existence of community, because the two can exist simultaneously. Since the multiplication of needs is a defining characteristic of modern need, and since endogenous preference formation makes it common to all members of a capital-based market system, individuality does not really take precedence over commonality of needs; the latter stands as a dimension of community running through the whole economy.

as part of the circulation of capital, Marx may have been the first to explicitly posit it as such. Marx pointed out that the determination of the individual by capital helps form a "rich individuality" by providing material conditions for the development of this characteristic. "Capital's ceaseless striving towards the general form of wealth drives labour beyond the limits of its natural paltriness [*Naturbedurftigkeit*], and thus creates the material elements for the development of the rich individuality which is as all-sided in its production as in its consumption . . ."[28] Marx ultimately undercut his potential contribution to the theory of endogenous formation of wants, first by conceiving of wants as primarily naturally and conventionally determined, and second by conceiving of the satisfaction of needs in terms of productive consumption of subsistence, a standpoint that reduces workers to the status of farm *animals,* eradicates choice, and therefore lacks the degree of autonomy requisite to the idea of endogenous formation of *personal* wants.

The endogenous formation of preferences did not cease at the end of the period of artisan labor in the mid eighteenth century, nor at the end of the period of craftsmanship and small-scale manufacturing in the early nineteenth century, but continued into the age of mechanized, heavily capitalized, large-scale factory production later in the nineteenth century. Products were still designed with ingenuity and made by industrious people, though the ingenuity was distributed in different ways among the workforce. The unskilled factory laborer does not possess the sort of ingenuity that stimulates tastes, but many workers in mechanized factories had considerable skill, and their ingenuity created products that stimulated wants. Anyone familiar with nineteenth-century mechanized production, such as the machine tool industry, the carriage-building industry, and the iron and steel industries, will appreciate the ingenuity and skill needed to operate the methods of production.[29] Some of the ingenuity generative of tastes was displaced to the designer, the draftsman, and the expert mechanic. The rest was embodied in the machinery itself. Designers and machinery were, in a sense, functional equivalents of the artisans during the early period of capitalist development. They continued to create wants because they continued to fashion products with taste and ingenuity.[30] Mechanized capitalist factory production wrought more intensive and extensive endogenous formation of preferences than did artisan capitalism. Mass production exposed larger

28. Marx 1973, p. 325.
29. See Depew 1895, vol. II, pp. 347, 520.
30. Weber 1947, p. 193, saw clearly and early that entrepreneurs could shape wants.

numbers of people to low-cost items of greater quality and diversity than most people during the fifteenth century could have dreamed of.[31]

Take the carriage and wagon industry in nineteenth-century America. Fully mechanized factories turned out wagons on a vast scale. One was produced every ten minutes in a single South Bend, Indiana, establishment.[32] Carriages were turned out by the millions. Such repetition of the production of the same product was made possible by mechanized production. Nevertheless, there was considerable ingenuity and taste in the product features, and these had a want-creating effect. The designer, the drafter, and the expert engineer of carriages were often people of ingenuity and taste. As the proprietor of a carriage-building establishment wrote,

> [H]e [the carriage designer] has the . . . faculty of producing new and beautiful forms; . . . keen sense of fair proportions and graceful lines which is the necessary qualification of a designer. Few things fashioned by human skill are more beautiful than a fine carriage; none but a true artist in his line is fit to determine its form, and none but an expert mechanic . . . is fit to supervise its construction.[33]

Carriage designers were "true artists" with a sense of fair proportions and graceful lines. Their designs were not mere adjustments to consumer preferences, but influences upon the standard of taste itself. The inventiveness of the designers was also a multiplier of new needs. "[G]reater novelties will be forthcoming to tempt the lovers of new things" wrote one proprietor.[34]

The transformation from nineteenth-century mechanized factory production to twentieth-century corporate capitalism did not spell the end of the process of endogenous preference formation. This process persisted from the very beginnings of capitalism, through the middle period, and now into the advanced stage of capitalism. This tends to suggest that endogenous formation of preferences is generic to capital-based systems, rather than a transitory phenomenon. John Kenneth Galbraith, an early, astute commentator on twentieth-century endogenous preference formation, remarked upon the "dependence effect" that corporate capitalist producers have on consumer preferences:

31. For an account of the increasing quality and lower cost of goods since the fifteenth century, see Smith 1937, pp. 242–249; Depew 1895.
32. Depew 1895, vol. II, p. 519.
33. Ibid., p. 520.
34. Ibid. In the late nineteenth century Veblen produced an extensive and interesting analysis of endogenous formation of preferences; see Veblen 1998 [1899].

> [W]ants are . . . the fruits of the process by which they are satisfied. [T]he production of goods satisfies the wants that the consumption of these goods creates or that the producers of goods synthesize. Production induces more wants and the need for more production. . . . [O]ur concern for goods does not arise in spontaneous consumer need. Rather the dependence effect means that it grows out of the process of production itself. If production is to increase, the wants must be effectively contrived.[35]

The modern corporation's role as a taste setter is distinguishable quantitatively from that of the ingenious artisans described by preclassical political economy. Larger size confers greater capacity to influence tastes. When a large producing unit, such as General Motors during the 1960s, commands fifty percent market share, "its designs do not reflect the current mode, but are the current mode."[36] The modern corporation's role in taste setting also differs qualitatively from the producer's role in taste setting during the early and middle periods of capitalism. Corporate capitalism brings about a different kind of influence: an *institutionalization* of endogenous formation of preferences, that is, a development of the institutional capacities of the producer for forming preferences. Corporate capitalism adds a set of institutions, bureaucracies, and planning facilities specifically for forming preferences.[37]

It may seem ironic that the modern corporation has to stoop to creating wants in order to sell products. Its power and status far exceed those of the supplicant artisan capitalist during the eighteenth century, who had to lure the nobility in hopes that it might deign to buy something. But it is quite reasonable for a great corporation to humbly seek to encourage consumer wants for its products. It faces essentially the same problem of market vulnerability that led previous producers to create wants, though the new form of market vulnerability differs from previous types. New kinds of uncertainties create a peculiar problematic for the modern corporation that gives rise to the distinctive form of the twentieth-century form that the process of endogenous formation of preferences has taken: to wit, the institutionalization of the social process of forming preferences.[38] The modern corporation uses a method of production that aggravates market uncertainties on both the demand

35. Galbraith 1969, p. 153. See also Lynes 1949, p. 4.
36. Galbraith 1969, p. 30.
37. Hayek argues that Galbraith's "dependence effect" is a non sequitur. See Hayek 1967, pp. 313–317, for a critical analysis of the thesis that corporations create wants.
38. Galbraith 1969 shows this very well, and my discussion of corporate capitalism and endogenous preferences relies heavily on his analysis.

and supply sides, and these hazards in turn create a need to reduce risks. A major means of managing such risks is to intensify the process of want creation.

There is nothing new about demand-side threats to capital investments, but they now threaten larger-scale capital investments than before. Modern production, processing, and packaging of even simple goods requires sophisticated technologies entailing larger commitments of capital. The methods of production involve long lead times before bringing products to market, which heighten demand-side uncertainties. In the intervening months or even years between product design and introduction to the market, there is considerable danger that consumer demand will not materialize. Should this happen, the large capital investment in production technologies exacerbates the consequences of failure.

Such a situation requires that the corporation become a strategic planner, committing its resources far into the future. It has to "to take every step [to insure] that what it decides to produce is wanted by the consumer at the remunerative price."[39] Part of such planning involves anticipating prices, but not only that. The corporation can also reduce uncertainty by taking measures to shape wants favorably, so planning involves the work of market creation. Consequently, the corporate planning agency becomes the institutional locus for the endogenous formation of preferences. As Galbraith writes:[40] "The need to control consumer behavior is a requirement of planning. Planning, in turn, is made necessary by the extensive use of advanced technology and capital and by the related scale and complexity of organization. These produce

39. Galbraith 1971, p. 23.

40. The present account of the corporation's role in want formation follows Galbraith's 1969 and 1971 analyses with a major qualification. Where Galbraith suggests that the corporation's role in want formation is by its very nature an unwarranted interposition in the will of the consumer, I think that corporations could play an essential, nondestructive role in want formation, if certain adjustments were made in the manner in which consumer product information is delivered. There would need to be a new regulatory environment that assures more pluralistic sources of consumer product information. Private interest government is one method of regulating corporate advertising in a way that could restore some balance to the currently one-sided relationship between the great modern corporation and the individual, thereby fashioning a proper place for the corporation in the process of want formation. On private interest government in the advertising industry, see Boddewyn 1985.

For a more recent analysis of the role of the corporation in want formation, see Lindlom's study of circularity in markets, Lindblom 1977.

goods efficiently; the result is a very large volume of production. Most goods serve needs that are discovered to the individual . . ."[41]

Galbraith's "dependence effect" posits a one-way relationship between producers and preferences in which production determines consumption. I argue instead that there is a two-sided process of preference formation encompassing both the system of production and commodity exchange. The demand-side vulnerabilities of the corporation astutely delineated by Galbraith imply reciprocal dependence between it and consumers, not a one-way avenue. Corporations usually cannot entirely dominate their markets, except under conditions of complete monopoly.[42] Their inability to fully control prices and preferences was demonstrated by GM's dramatic loss of market share during the 1980s. The occasional failure to produce the intended desires does not mean, however, that the want creation process does not exist. For the existence of want creation does not hinge on dominance over the consumer or on invariant outcomes. The task of want creation gains prevalence in corporations simply because it can influence wants sometimes and to some extent. Although it plays out imperfectly, want creation is still an integral part of the corporation because of the pressing need to reduce demand-side vulnerabilities. In view of this, want creation is a corporate method of taking into account the conditions of commodity exchange, and shaping them, rather than a method of dominating them.

Reciprocal dependence in want creation also means conditions of commodity exchange affect corporate structure, rather than simply vice versa. The task of creating wants not only alters wants, but also alters the nature of the production process. Out of a need to manage consumer demand, the management of consumer demand gets combined with the planning of production. Production gets reconfigured so that it will have the capacity to create wants. Only when thus affected by commodity exchange can the corporation alter wants. By a dialectical advance, the endogenous formation of preferences turns into a process of determination of production. Preferences are not simply shaped by a causal process within the sphere of production. Endogenous formation of preferences is coextensive with the system of commodity production *and* exchange.

Neoclassical theorists of endogenous preferences often reduce corporate want creation to the practice of advertising. But the planning of consumer wants is not an isolated activity within the corporation or the advertising agency. Various departments of the corporation are involved.

41. Galbraith 1971, p. 201.
42. As Lindblom 1977, pp. 38–39, points out in critique of Galbraith.

It forms an integral part of the hierarchy of committees controlling the corporation, dubbed the "technostructure" by Galbraith.[43] The corporation as a whole, not just the advertising agency or planning department, comprises the bureaucratic center of want creation. The management structure implements a concern with consumer demand every step of the way. Management of product design, in particular, is needed in order to design products that can "insure the needed customer response."[44] FDA investigations have revealed that tobacco companies addicted consumers by manipulating nicotine levels in cigarettes. Lethal manipulation of product content is extreme, but it illustrates a more general point: that adjustment of product design can powerfully affect preferences. As preclassical economists knew, adjusting the composition of the product is very important in want creation.

Advertising plays an important role in want formation, of course. In 1998, $200.8 billion was spent in the United States on advertising alone.[45] Devoting such enormous resources to stimulating desires for goods could give contemporary producers an enormous capacity to create wants. In considering the magnitude of this potential, it is worthwhile to compare advertising expenditures and educational expenditures. The total expenditure for education at all levels in the 1997–1998 school year was $584 billion.[46] Thus, the sum spent on advertising was more than a third of the total expenditures on education by federal, state, local, and other sources in the United States. Considering that advertising seeks to influence a much narrower set of personal aims than education does – preferences over goods versus broad aspects of human development and life experience – the huge amount of resources devoted to advertising could have very potent effects on these preferences.[47]

Though less frequently mentioned than the advertising agency, the management of production also has an important role in the advertising effort, and thus has this indirect mode of influencing wants as well. It assists the advertising and sales promotion efforts. Advertisers rely on the managers of production because the content of a good affects what advertisers can say about a good. This is important, in turn, because awareness of a good provides consumers with some of the incentive to

43. Galbraith 1971.

44. Ibid., pp. 29–30.

45. Caughey 1999, p. 3.

46. U.S. Department of Education, National Center for Education Statistics, *Digest of Education Statistics 1998*, p. 6.

47. For an indication, consider the effects of television on eating habits as described by Erica Goode, "Study Finds TV Alters Fiji Girls' View of Body," *The New York Times*, May 20, 1999, section A, p. 17.

buy it.[48] The marketing staff is involved in production decisions because the product has to be "one around which a sales strategy can be built."[49] Several sets of managers concern themselves with enhancing "selling points." By managing packaging, model design, and product enhancement, they engage in want creation.[50] In these ways, the committees of experts combined in the modern corporation increase the probability that their product will generate interest and desire among consumers.

A wing of neoclassical theory contributes to the formulation of endogenous preferences, despite long neoclassical opposition to such an approach. The standard neoclassical theory of consumer demand was developed by Edgeworth, Antonelli, Pareto, Slutsky, Hicks, and Allen, who posited fixed orderings of preferences.[51] Some neoclassical economists, however, now acknowledge that advertising and other social influences can change preferences. In 1956, Basmann became perhaps the first of these to address in a systematic way advertising's effect on the parameters of the utility function.[52] The utility function (or evaluation of the utility of goods) is denoted $u(x_i, \ldots, x_n; \theta_1, \ldots, \theta_n)$, with x_i standing for the magnitudes of goods and services in current consumption, and θ_i denoting parameters that describe the form of the utility function. The θ_i parameters are dependent upon the variables $\mathbf{a}_j$, the producers' expenditure on advertising the good to the consumer.[53]

Basmann's conception of changes in the utility function due to advertising was empirically well founded. Business research at the time indicated that "consumption behavior . . . is changed . . . systematically by advertising and other forms of sales effort . . ."[54] Later research has con-

48. As El-Safty writes, "Awareness about the content of the good, say, magnitude of mercury, caloric content, percentage of fat, etc. . . . affects θ [the reaction potential of good i] through K [the stimulus-intensity dynamism] and/or V [incentive motivation]" (El-Safty 1976, p. 299). See also El-Safty 1972, Chapter 3.
49. Galbraith 1971, p. 203.
50. Ibid.
51. Edgeworth 1881; Antonelli 1886; Pareto 1927; Slutsky 1915; Hicks and Allen 1934; Hicks 1939.
52. My sense of this accords with Schmalensee's (1972, p. 101) judgment of Basmann's contribution (Schmalensee 1972, p. 101). See also Kaldor 1950; Glaister 1974; Browing and Browning 1986; Else 1968; Comanor and Wilson 1974; Guth 1971; Buxton et al. 1984; Greer 1971; Orr 1974; Paton and Machin 1993; Schmalensee 1978; Smiley 1988; Dixit and Norman 1978.
53. Basmann 1956, p. 49. For a revised statement of the changes in the form parameters of the utility function, see Schmalensee 1972, pp. 101–102.
54. Basmann 1956, p. 48.

tinued to indicate this, and corporations have vastly expanded their advertising efforts.[55]

Two neoclassical schools of thought advance sharply different views of whether advertising generates wants. The "persuasion" school supports the theory of endogenous preferences with evidence and arguments that advertising is formative of wants. The "information" school challenges this theory, arguing that advertising merely helps consumers satisfy preexisting wants by supplying them with information on which utility depends, and does not change tastes or persuade.[56] My analysis of the controversy suggests there are strong bases for the view that advertising creates wants.

The information school's theoretical argument can be reinterpreted in a way that supports the view that advertising creates wants. While the information school is correct that some advertising informs rather than persuades, it does not follow that advertising is not want-creating. Supplying information can be part of the process of want formation. Suppose that someone likes to whistle down the street. This person might be well disposed to a product like a Sony Walkman, yet lack the imagination or time to dream it up. Thankfully, the corporation's product development staff contrives the idea of a compact, portable, encapsulated sound system. One day the woman notices a Sony Walkman advertisement, perhaps not resonating with the adolescents in oversized jeans pictured, but seeing the device's potential for enhancing a stroll down Main Street. The capacities of the machine, compared to whistling, give the consumer a whole new perspective on the possible forms of musical enjoyment on the part of the pedestrian. While the message here may be more informative than persuasive, it leads rather than follows consumers, and it plays a decisive role in creating wants. The new product creates a new want and the advertised idea stimulates a new desire, rather than merely informing the consumer of new means of satisfying old wants. Great success can come to corporations that understand and implement this form of want formation. Akio Morita, cofounder of the Sony Corporation, which introduced the Walkman, eschews market research. "Our plan," he writes, "is to lead the public with new products rather than ask them what . . . they want . . . The public does not know what is possible, but we do."[57]

The information school claims greater empirical validity for the view

55. Stiglitz 1993, p. 510; Bearne 1996, p. 23; Lindblom 1977, p. 214.
56. Becker 1996, p. 38.
57. Morita 1986 quoted by Andrew Pollack, *The New York Times*, October 4, 1999, section B, p. 8.

that advertising in competitive markets is informative rather than persuasive or want-creating. The case that it makes for this view is, however, largely inferential rather than empirical. The information school observes cases in which advertising promotes competition. From this fact, information school analysts infer that the advertising must have been informative rather than creative or persuasive. As Telser writes, "[A]dvertising is frequently a means of competition and a sign of entry. This agrees with the view that advertising is an important source of information."[58] The denial that persuasive advertising creates wants does not proceed from direct examination of its effects on preferences but from the *presumption* that it would not make sense for producers in competitive markets to engage in it, but only for producers to supply price information. Contrary to this view, however, producers in competitive markets – and not just in oligopolistic ones – rarely supply only price information or a simple communication of information, as in a classified ad. More often than not, they find it valuable to embed information in a flattering message about the product. Moreover, the evidence is that it is rational for competitive producers to engage in persuasive advertising, for even if such advertising cannot advance their position relative to other firms in the same industry, it can drive up demand for the products of the industry as a whole relative to other industries.

The information school's position clashes with the everyday experience of business people that advertising can generate sales and profits by increasing consumer desires for their products relative to other products. The school's thesis is that producers are monumentally irrational in spending billions on persuasive advertising. It would be far more rational, they say, to advertise product information at a fraction of the cost of elaborate persuasive statements. But producers are fairly rational people, and their experience tells them that it is worthwhile to purchase costly persuasive advertisements rather than cheap classified ads.

In sum, ordinary experience, theory, and evidence strongly point toward the thesis that commodity production forms part of the process of creation of wants, not merely part of the provision of means to the satisfaction of wants.

58. Telser 1965, p. 31. On the pervasiveness of this mode of reasoning, see Bearne's review of the literature on the economics of advertising (Bearne 1996).

ENDOGENOUS PREFERENCES AND A DIMENSION OF ECONOMIC COMMUNITY

Endogenous formation of preferences helps to demonstrate that community exists, because it helps to form common action between producers and consumers. Multiplying wants helps to assure that consumers purchase commodities from a producer. It thereby helps to make consumption a means by which the producer acquires more money. The acquisition of money is, in turn, the means by which the producer acquires more commodities. In this way the endogenous formation of preferences enables the producer to complete the circuit of his or her capital,

$$\ldots M\text{–}C\text{–}P\text{–}C'\text{–}M' \ldots$$

When consumption proceeds through the purchase of C′, consumption and production form a circuit of capital. Consumer purchases help the producer continue the flow of his capital after production, and they return him to the starting point where he holds money. Thus, the endogenous formation of preferences helps to make the consumer's acquisition of C part of a single connected sequence. By helping to connect production and consumption into a circuit, endogenous formation of preferences helps to form common action. It helps to connect production and consumption into the single connected activity of preserving and expanding capital, which thus constitutes common action. As consumption and production become integral parts of the circulation of capital, they constitute common action. Endogenous formation of preferences therefore produces a dimension of community.

Consumers with socially multiplied wants spend money on commodities and restore money capital to commodity producers, thereby enabling producers to renew the production process and continue the circulation of capital. Endogenously determined consumption becomes a "sustaining moment" of the capital circuit.[59] When capital is preserved and expanded through the unified actions of producers and consumers, it is the result of common action. This indicates a dimension of community in the process of generation of capital.

At different stages of capitalist development, there were different forms of endogenous formation of preferences, but all helped connect consumption and production into a single connected sequence, a circu-

59. This is David Levine's phrase (Levine 1978–1981, vol. 1, p. 248).

lation of capital. Artisan capitalists did so in the 1700s by exciting the interest of the rich in luxury goods. Early nineteenth-century capitalists did so by suggesting new comforts needed by a wide spectrum of consumers. In nineteenth-century heavily capitalized large-scale factory production, the ingenuity of the designer, the drafter, the expert mechanic, and the machine stimulated new tastes and desires, thereby helping to complete the circuit of capital. In twentieth-century corporate capitalism, managers of product design, production, marketing, merchandising, and the advertising agency helped connect production and consumption through the management of demand. By connecting consumption and production into common action, the several forms of endogenous formation of preferences helped create a dimension of community at different stages in the development of capitalism.

The history of endogenous formation of preferences indicates not only a dimension of common action, but also a dimension of common ends among producers and consumers. It supplies empirical evidence for the proposition that the circulation of capital has a principle of self-ordering. Artisan capitalists, mechanized factory producers, and corporate capitalists all multiplied wants so that they might complete the circuit of capital, which indicates that wealth-seeking producers ordered their actions in accordance with the requirements for the circulation of capital. Within three stages of capitalism, wants were evidently ordered by the same principle that ordered the actions of producers. As a result, consumer wants became oriented (whether consciously or not) toward the same end that producers have: the preservation and expansion of capital. In this way, the formation of preferences in accordance with the principle of self-ordering of the capital circuit produced a dimension of community within capitalism at different stages of its development.

One might suppose that the multiplication of consumer wants by a particular producer orients the consumer toward this firm's capital but against the preservation of other firms' capitals. Yet it redounds to the benefit of other capitals. Preclassical economic analysis indicates that infectious desires for luxuries spread to other consumers, thereby aiding all producers. To this degree, endogenous formation of preferences orients consumer wants toward the preservation of the system of circuits of capital in its entirety, and by doing that, establishes a dimension of community throughout the system of producers and consumers.

Empirical analysis of endogenous preferences by neoclassical economists can contribute to showing that consumption forms part of the circulation of capital and, by implication, to proving a dimension of economic community, even though neoclassical economists do not draw these inferences themselves. Neoclassical studies show that endogenously formed preferences increase sales, profits, and market share. Comanor and Wilson report "that heavy advertising leads to increased profits."[60] Schmalensee finds that "[t]he greater the profit rate in an industry, the greater the advertising/sales ratio is likely to be."[61] Evidence is that advertising is so important that it has surpassed relative prices as a determinant of consumer expenditures.[62] Galbraith evidently did not exaggerate when he said that "the modern industrial system . . . could not exist in its present form without it [television]."[63] The neoclassical studies mentioned do not draw the inference that the flow of commodities and money forms a circulation of capital. But the evidence indicates that endogenous formation of preferences helps to make consumption a sustaining moment in the flow of commodities, which, therefore, forms a circulation process. By demonstrating that endogenous formation of preferences increases sales and profits, neoclassical empirical analysis indicates that consumer preferences have become oriented toward the goal of preservation and expansion of capital, which in turn suggests some community of ends among producers and consumers.

Neoclassical analysts would not infer community from this data, because the endogenous formation of preferences can increase one firm's market share at the expense of another firm's share. While that proves that the economy is not fully communal, it does not prove there is no *dimension* of community. Although a firm's advertising can hurt the relative performance of other firms within the same sector, it can evidently drive up demand for all firms within the sector. Such evidence could indicate a dimension of community at the sectoral level. A neoclassical economist could respond that advertising advantages one sector vis-à-vis others, thus ruling out systemwide economic community. Advertising, however, increases interest in goods generally, not just in the sector, which means that consumer preferences are oriented toward the interest of capital in general, and therefore that a dimension of systemwide community exists in the economy. "[A]long with bringing demand under substantial control," Galbraith wrote, "it provides in the aggregate, a relentless propaganda on behalf of goods in general. From early morning . . . people are informed of the services rendered by goods – of their profound indispensability."[64] Moreover, "Goods are what the industrial system supplies. Advertising by making goods seem important makes

60. Comanor and Wilson 1974, pp. 130, 245.
61. Schmalensee as stated by Bearne 1996, p. 31.
62. Comanor and Wilson 1974, pp. 88, 239. See also Cowling, Cable, Kelly, and Guiness 1975; Bearne 1996, pp. 29, 31.
63. Galbraith 1971, p. 209.
64. Ibid., p. 210.

the industrial system seem important."[65] Even if advertising does give the firm or sector a relative advantage over other firms or sectors, there would still be a dimension of systemwide community. While increasing a firm's or a sector's share, advertising does not injure the system of capital-based commodity producers. As part of a firm's or sector's competitive strategy, it contributes to the overall efficiency of capital, and thereby increases the aggregate capital. Thus, the endogenous formation of preferences orients consumer preferences toward the interests of the system of capital-based commodity production in its entirety. It thereby makes for a dimension of community on a systemwide scale.

Dixit and Norman show that advertising levels exceed levels that would be in the interests of consumers and producers, that they are not Pareto-optimal.[66] Clearly, regulation of some sort is needed to bring advertising expenditures down to Pareto-optimal levels. But this does not mean that advertising is inherently antithetical to the interests of producers and consumers. Dixit and Norman acknowledge that moderate levels of advertising are efficient. Endogenous formation of preferences could be consistent with Pareto-optimal community if kept to moderate levels through regulation.

Smithian self-seeking is said to lead to the social interest but not to community. The social interest, in this case, does not mean community because it is not the individual's direct purpose but an unintended consequence of behavior aimed at self-advantage. Contrary to Smithian analysis, however, consciously intending the common interest is not a prerequisite for the existence of community. Community hinges on whether a social end is integral to the individual mind, which could be true even if the individual were not conscious of it. Ever since Freud, psychologists have known that the mind possesses many unconscious elements, which therapy strives to bring to consciousness. The foregoing analysis has shown that consumer behavior has been shaped to tend toward the goal of preservation of capital, and that this end therefore forms some part of the consumer's nature, even though the individual may not know it. The common end – preservation of capital – resides in the nature of the individual, and is a direct result of activity structured toward it, rather than merely an unintended external result of self-oriented behavior. Therefore, community does exist.

The notion of an overarching common end shared by economic agents conflicts with the neoclassical theory of endogenous preferences. The latter theory retains the traditional neoclassical idea of economics

65. Ibid., p. 211.
66. Dixit and Norman 1978.

as the allocation of scarce resources among alternative uses. Even when preference satisfaction is seen as shaped by the advertiser, neoclassical endogenous preference theorists continue to view it as an alternative to producer goals. The rationale is that consumers with shaped preferences still want to buy cheap, while producers want to sell dear. Thus opposed, consumer and producer goals are inconsistent with community. While there is a dimension of truth in this viewpoint, it passes over the fact that consumers have been oriented toward the goal of preservation and expansion of capital through the social multiplication of wants, and therefore that their behavior, perhaps unbeknownst to themselves, aims at the same end that producers consciously strive toward, with the implication of a dimension of common ends. To a significant extent, endogenous determination of consumer and producer interests collapses the distinction between their goals. When consumer wants form in accord with producer goals, and when producer goals are shaped by the requirements of commodity exchange, their goals are interpenetrating, and to this extent a commonality of ends prevails.

ENDOGENOUS PREFERENCES: DOMINATION OR FREE COMMUNITY?

Neoclassical and critical analysts of endogenous preferences find advertising self-serving and even dominating, not generative of community. Comanor and Wilson maintain that the "self-serving character of advertising is . . . its dominant feature."[67] Galbraith regards advertising as a great manipulation destructive to the authenticity of consumer preferences: "One cannot defend production as satisfying wants if that production creates the wants."[68] But between absolute autonomy and social contrivance, there is a form of social self-determination, in which advertising plays an important part. In social self-determination, social influences, rather than vitiating self-determination, are necessary to the constitution of the self.

In a well-ordered system of advertising, the consumer receives vital information about useful products and styles of life that he or she would not otherwise know about. This information is needed in order to form preferences and determine modes of living from the full range of possibilities achievable with available means. This means that the individual needs to draw upon the information, suggestions, and even the enticing persuasions provided by producers. Advertising is, therefore, necessary

67. Comanor and Wilson 1974, p. 13.
68. Galbraith 1969, p. 147.

to the constitution of the self, and is conducive to self-determination rather than a violation of it.

In order for advertising to contribute to want formation rather than contrive wants, however, a significant development of deliberative conscious and critical judgment on the part of consumers is presupposed. To sustain these capacities in the market, there will have to be increased use of government to institute countervailing sources of information and persuasion, particularly from consumer organizations. But once in place, these institutions will help assure that advertising is consistent with consumer freedom and self-determination. When the consumer possesses deliberative consciousness and critical judgment, he assimilates producer suggestions without loss of self-direction. Wants are not simply interposed on the self through the external agency of the producer; the consumer's own mind and will are involved in adopting those wants. Thus, when advertising is coupled with faculties of deliberative and critical consciousness, it helps consumers to form their wants rather than "contriving" their wants. Galbraith's position insists upon absolute autonomy in want formation as a condition for authenticity of wants. But this is not even possible, because absolute autonomy in want formation is inconceivable.[69] Producer-suggested wants can be genuinely the consumer's own when he or she uses her own mind and will in deciding which to assimilate.

If the faculties of conscious deliberation and critical judgment are not well developed among the population, however, the consequence of advertising will be domination by producers. But in this case, advertising is not the ultimate cause of domination. Rather, the domination ultimately stems from the failure of state and society to cultivate the requisite personal capacities.

Advertising will be constitutive, not dominating, if properly structured. The current regime of advertising is often both dominating and self-serving, as critics claim, and it needs restructuring in order to bring it in accord with consumer freedom. But once restructured, there is nothing inherently or necessarily harmful about advertising. John Zaller has proposed a system of nondomination in public opinion formation, and a nondominating system of advertising could be constructed in accord with his guidelines.[70] There have to be different sources of information about consumer products than the immediate producer and his agents. In order to assure adequate pluralism, the state would have to furnish consumer agencies with the financial resources to advertise. The

69. Hobart 1934, pp. 14–15.
70. Zaller 1992, p. 314.

differences in the philosophy of living held by advertisers would have to mirror the philosophies among the general public, so that advertisers would be motivated to examine products from all viewpoints. In cases where the experts disagree, the citizenry would have to be sufficiently well informed and cognitively able to align its preferences with the expert faction that shares its own disposition toward life. With these and other needed conditions in place, the critical understanding of consumer products will be advanced to the betterment of consumers. Advertising will continue to promote the common interest in preserving and expanding capital, but it will do so in a way that is consistent with personal freedom in want formation. With the conditions for nondominant advertising in place, the endogenous formation of a common interest does not violate individual freedom. It contributes to a free union of all.

When the internal and external conditions for nondomination in advertising are in place, the endogenous formation of preferences in accordance with the interests of capital generates a truly common interest. The multiplication of preferences consonant with individual freedom and with the preservation of capital implies the existence of a common end between consumers and producers in the preservation and expansion of capital.

The principle of self-ordering of the capital circuit would not generate a genuine community if it were an operative rule of necessity. If it were effective regardless of individual willing, union would be unfree. The principle of self-ordering of the capital circuit is not, however, like a necessary natural law. It does not operate independent of individual willing. The members of society want to create and acquire wealth, and they willfully carry the principle into practice for this reason. The concept of a willful union does not, however, contradict the other premise of the present argument, the social determination of the individual.

THE COATTAINMENT OF CONSUMER AND PRODUCER ENDS

Rawls has shown that common interest is not sufficient to qualify an association as a community. "Now the shared end of a social union is clearly not merely a common desire for the same thing. Grant and Lee were one in their desire to hold Richmond but this desire did not establish community between them."[71] He conceives of community instead as an association in which members with different capacities pursue different but "complementary" ends in accordance with principles of justice.[72]

71. Rawls 1971, p. 526. 72. Ibid.

Community does not, however, simply consist in complementary action. The latter is a condition of interdependent pursuit of different ends. To confer the added significance of community, the action also has to be common action for a common end. Rawls is right that common ends are not sufficient for community. The members of the association would also have to promote the coattainment of the common end. The existence of community depends, then, on individuals seeking a common end in ways that further its attainment by others.

A Rawlsian might interpret the market relationship between producers and consumers as a condition of complementarity, but as such it would not be a community. The producer seeks his end, profit, in a way that enables the consumer to seek her different end, satisfaction. Their activities are complementary in the sense of interdependent actions for different ends, but there is no community, because of the lack of coattainment of a common end. The Rawlsian interpretation would be correct in claiming a dimension of interdependence for the sake of different ends, but it would leave out another dimension of the market relationship. When consumers buy commodity products, they seek capital in commodity form. They seek it in a manner (paying money) that advances the attainment of the same end, capital (in money form), by producers, who likewise seek this end in a way that advances the attainment of the consumer's end (the acquisition of capital in commodity form). In this sense, producers and consumers engage in activities that further the attainment of the same end (capital) by the other party, which indicates a dimension of community among them. Moreover, endogenous formation of preferences orients consumer self-seeking toward the preservation and expansion of capital. The latter is a common end in the sense that consumers want consumption goods that come out of capital, and in a sense are capital, while producers seek it too. Thus, endogenous formation of producers and consumers promotes the coattainment of the same end by producers and consumers, which underscores a dimension of community.

CLASSICAL AND LEVINIAN ENDOGENOUS CONSUMPTION, AND NEOCLASSICAL OBJECTIONS

While many theories of endogenous preferences have been formulated, few contemporary treatments integrate such a theory with the theory of the circulation of commodities and money. In the present analysis it is important to make that connection because it is crucial for demonstrating economic community. When previous scholars did integrate endogenous preferences with the circulation process, they generally employed a very defective conception of consumption as reproduction of labor or productive consumption. The problem with the classical conceptions, as we may refer to those prior treatments, is that they reduce consumers to the status of farm animals. One could not build an adequate theory of economic community on this basis, because it would imply only a community of feed animals, not of persons. In the proposed method, endogenous consumption continues the circuit of capital without reducing persons to feed animals. For this reason it can provide a basis for an adequate theory of economic community, as a community of persons. It is important, therefore, to distinguish the proposed approach from the classical method.

Endogenous consumption was integrated with circulation in the classical subsistence wage theories (e.g., Malthus), as well as in Marx's economic theory, von Neumann's growth models, and Leontief's input-output models. These theories conceived of endogenous consumption as (1) productive consumption or reproduction of labor rather than relatively autonomous consumption, (2) physiologically, conventionally, or technically fixed consumption precluding consumer choice, or as (3) subsistence consumption rather than luxury consumption. Neoclassical theory argued persuasively, I believe, against the "classical" theory of endogenous consumption. By implication, any theory of endogenous preferences based on the classical approach would succumb to the neoclassical critique, as would any theory of economic community based on the classical theory of endogenous preferences.

The present theory differs from the classical approach, and is based on Levine's theory of endogenous preferences, which is not vulnerable to the neoclassical objections. So my theory of community based on endogenous preferences is not indirectly vulnerable to those objections.

In Marx's theory, labor receives a subsistence wage equal in value to the social labor necessary to produce the subsistence goods that keep the laborer alive and able to work. Consumption of subsistence is endogenous – whether subsistence is defined by physiological requirements or by convention[73] – because it is directed toward reproduction of labor for the capitalist production process, rather than for relatively autonomous personal ends. Endogenous consumption plays an important part in Marx's account of the circulation of capital on an expanding scale.

73. As Meek points out, in the *The Poverty of Philosophy* Marx seems to accept the "subsistence" theory of wages proposed by Ricardo (see Marx 1963, Chapter 1; Meek 1956, p. 144). The later economic works of Marx emphasize the social element in wages. For a discussion of the social concept of needs in Marx's work, see Heller 1976.

When workers are paid a subsistence wage to reproduce their labor, there is no consumption by them out of surplus value, thus assuring "continual reproduction, on an ever enlarging scale, of the capital relation."[74]

The von Neumann model of equilibrium growth similarly conceives of consumption as an input to the production process of labor in the way that coal, say, is consumed in producing steel. This conception reduces labor to the status of a farm animal. "Consumption of goods takes place only through the processes which include the necessaries of life consumed by laborers and employees. In other words we assume that all income in excess of necessaries of life will be reinvested," writes von Neumann.[75] Endogenizing consumption as the production of labor assures the von Neumann model's balanced, maximal growth path. Later, Leontief proposed a "closed system" input-output model in which subsistence goods are used to keep men alive and capable of laboring. Once again, subsistence goods figure as productive inputs into the production of labor. Luxury goods were also included in the original Leontief model. But these too were treated as inputs to the household production of labor. As in the case of Marx's theory and the von Neumann model, consumption as productive consumption plays a crucial role in the Leontief system of fully determinate reproduction that "generate[s] its own future."[76]

The classical theory of endogenous consumption as productive consumption strains the idea of consumption. Many personal purposes in consumption simply cannot be related to the objective of reproducing one's labor, and these goals are simply assumed away by postulating productive consumption. As a class, personal purposes in consumption are among the basic motivations for economic activity, and they are far too important to exclude by fiat. Indeed, neoclassical economics views personal goals as the sole purpose of consumption, a view that takes the point to an unwarranted extreme. "We . . . produce with the sole object of consuming" rather than the other way around, writes Stanley Jevons, a founder of neoclassical economic theory.[77] This has more than a grain of truth, though it also exaggerates the individual's autonomy in consumption. Schumpeter refines the neoclassical objection to productive consumption when he criticizes subsistence-wage theories on the

74. Marx quoted in Heller 1976, p. 24.
75. von Neuman 1945–1946, p. 2.
76. Dorfman, Samuelson, and Solow's description of the Leontief model (Dorfman, Samuelson, and Solow 1958, p. 266).
77. Jevons 1871, p. 47.

grounds that "human purposes are not produced, according to the rules of capitalist rationality, with a view to cost-covering returns."[78] Later Hicks would object to the von Neumann growth model for failing to recognize autonomous consumption: "In the von Neumann system, consumption . . . has disappeared; products have no purpose except to serve as inputs into future production; for maximum growth, growth must be growth, just for its own sake. In economics, production is oriented toward consumption . . ."[79] It simply does not make sense to think of consumption as production of labor, wrote Dorfman, Samuelson, and Solow, with regard to the Leontief model: "the closed [Leontief] system is much harder to understand. In it we . . . speak of the consumption by people (e.g., of food) as really being much like the consumption by machines or horses."[80] Through positing naturally, conventionally, or technically fixed needs, the classical theory of endogenous consumption denies the facts of consumer choice and luxury consumption by labor.[81] While the Leontief model incorporates luxury consumption, it displays a lack of concern with consumer choice by ruling out the technical possibility of input substitutions.

Neoclassical theorists did not respond to deficiencies in the classical concept of productive consumption by formulating a new theory of endogenous consumption, but rather by abandoning the whole category of theory. The modern theory of consumer behavior ushered in worthwhile ideas, such as consumer choice, luxury consumption, and personal aims, but it placed them on a foundation of exogenously given preferences. When the idea of endogeniety was eliminated, the true theoretical foundation for the multiplicity of wants was also lost. Without multiple wants, the breakdown of commodity circulation is immanent. To avert this and other implications, neoclassical theorists resorted to postulation: a nonsatiation assumption that people prefer more to less. Resting on a postulate without theoretical foundation, the circulation of commodities is wholly arbitrary in the neoclassical theory of consumption.

This critique suggests some guidelines for an adequate theory of con-

78. Schumpeter 1954, p. 650.

79. Hicks 1965, p. 22.

80. Dorfman, Samuelson, and Solow 1958, p. 245.

81. Champernowne suggested that productive consumption could involve a role for choice in the form of choice of alternative techniques for producing labor. This may escape the objection to eradicating choice that was advanced by Dorfman, Samuelson, and Solow (1958), but it does not elude Hick's concern with the lack of autonomy of consumption, which remains subordinate to production purposes in the case of the choice of techniques of producing labor.

sumption and circulation. Though classical political economy made some important contributions to the theory of demand, the notion of consumption does not make sense unless we accept some neoclassical innovations in the theory of the consumption side, particularly the ideas of consumer choice, luxury consumption, and the personal aim of preference satisfaction.[82] When these ideas are incorporated into a new theory of consumption, they need, however, to be reconciled with the idea of endogenous consumption, for multiple wants and ongoing commodity circulation are untenable without positing endogenous consumption. When endogenous consumption gets rehabilitated, it needs to be done in a fashion that does not recapitulate classical productive consumption, and this can be accomplished only by reconciling endogenous consumption with relative autonomy in consumption.

David P. Levine's theory of endogenous consumption satisfies requirements for the circulation of capital without reducing consumption to productive consumption. Multiplying wants helps capital to circulate, not by treating consumption as an input requirement to the production of labor, but by generating a market for commodity products. As long as wants are multiplied to provide a market for commodity products they can fulfill production goals while at the same time being directed to

82. In suggesting that the classical theory of value does not adequately integrate consumption-side determinants, it is important to recognize that it does assign some role to demand, but that this role is problematic and limited. Smith believed that "market price" is determined by supply and demand, but also that these forces merely carry out more ultimate production determinants. The market price in his analysis reduces to a natural level set by the cost of productive factors. Demand plays a role in Smith's account of short-run determination of prices, but the main analysis focuses on long-term equilibrium, where demand's role is attenuated. In the short run, scarcity determines price, and scarcity is governed by demand and supply, but in the long run the cost of production is controlling. As Blaug writes, "When it comes to the determination of natural price, demand is supposed to have no influence. Smith did not justify his neglect of demand" (Blaug 1985, p. 40). The value of a good, for him, consists of the normal cost of the productive factors that go into its production. These factors include wages, rents, and profits. If Smith had a theory of wages, rents, profits, or pure interest, the foregoing theory of value could include consumption-side determinants. But Smith did not have a theory of wages and the rest, so the production side dominates by default. It was not until the marginalist revolution in the 1870s that demand began to play an explicit role in the determination of production prices. When Smith accorded demand a role in determining price, utility was not the ultimate factor affecting prices, because he did not see a relationship between demand and utility. Neoclassical economics was the first to show that the theory of value had to take into account individual utility and preferences.

personal aims unrelated to production. In endogenous consumption, as understood by Levine, the social determination of wants in accordance with the requirements of the circulation of capital leaves wants with a relative autonomy vis-à-vis production and circulation. Moreover, endogenous consumption is conceived consistently with the idea of luxury consumption, instead of being reduced to subsistence needs. Endogenous consumption in the form of multiplication of wants creates desires for luxuries rather than for the subsistence requirements for reproducing labor, as distinct from the Marxian and von Neumann versions of endogenous consumption. When we shift from classical endogenous subsistence needs to Levine's endogenous luxury wants, we do not lose the ability to account for ongoing circulation. The multiplication of wants permits the multiplication of commodity products to be connected with consumption in a single interconnected sequence. Whereas Leontief ruled out the technical possibility of input substitutions and thereby negated consumer choice, Levinian endogenous consumption is quite consistent with it, because the multiplication of wants expands rather than contracts the range of choice.

In sum, the Levinian model shows that endogenous consumption can help form a circuit of capital without false presuppositions about consumption. This conclusion has significant implications for the theory of economic community, for such theory rests on the theory of circulation of capital, which in turn hinges on the theory of endogenous consumption. The theory of economic community is bolstered by establishing it upon the basis of the Levine model of endogenous consumption, which is not vulnerable to neoclassical objections to the classical theory of endogenous consumption.

FURTHER IMPLICATIONS FOR ECONOMIC COMMUNITY

Some additional aspects of theories of endogenous formation of preferences bear on the question of whether economic community exists. The preclassical conception of social influences is a conception of endogenous formation of preferences, whereas the neoclassical conception of social influences is a conception of exogenous formation of preferences. That is, preclassical economists understand social influences as influences arising from within the economic system, while neoclassical economists view them as influences from outside it. The preclassical approach is the more advanced of the two, though much older, because it grasps crucial inner tendencies of the capitalist economy that neoclassical theory overlooks. For constructing a theory of economic community, the preclassical conception of social influences as endogenous formation is crucial, because this process forms preferences in accord with the vital purpose of economic association (wealth), thereby contributing to the generation of a community of ends among consumers and producers. Neoclassical economists who take into account only external social determinants of preferences cannot perceive community; they see only individuals inclined toward multiple external ends rather than a common end. Though preclassical economists did not formulate theories of endogenous preferences for the purpose of demonstrating economic community, it is legitimate to use their work for that purpose, where it applies.

The notion of a production determinant of preferences in preclassical economics is a conception of a means determinant of ends.[83] It stands in contrast to the neoclassical conception of production as simply a means to a given end. The preclassical standpoint is necessary for the existence and formulation of economic community, though the preclassical economists did not fully expound this implication. The neoclassical conception of production as a means to an end blinded neoclassical economists to the preclassical data of producer determinants of tastes. Production as a means determinant of ends can help form a common interest and common action among consumers and producers. When the means shape the ends in the interest of the means, and the ends shape the means in the interest of the ends, a common interest emerges between producers and consumers. Consumption and production appear as common action because consumption helps complete the circulation of the producer's capital; and they appear as common interests when consumer needs have been shaped in the interest of capital, and production has become oriented to the satisfaction of multiple wants.

The preclassical understanding of the multiplication of wants limited this process to one category of needs, luxury needs. Hegel, however, showed that all wants are multiplied in a capital-based market system. The expansive concept of multiplied needs is an important step in formulating economic community though Hegel did not use it this way.[84] When all manner of consumer needs are subject to multiplication through endogenous formation, they are all oriented toward the vital purpose of association – the acquisition of wealth. Hence they reflect an overarching community of ends, not just community among a partial

83. This seems to be what Hegel 1952 is saying in para. 192, p. 127, which would make him the first to formulate the point explicitly, though the preclassical economists were implicitly treating production in this way before Hegel.

84. He attempted only to demonstrate subcommunities within civil society, not to show that civil society as a whole was a community; see Hegel 1952, pp. 152–155.

subset of ends. Moreover, such an analysis indicates that the consumer has a very complete dependence on capital. There is no portion of his or her needs that does not require a system of capital-based economic relations. The implication of the preclassical standpoint, that a large category of consumer needs are fixed and limited, means that they are not shaped in accord with the vital purpose of association. Insofar as consumers have a need for fixed and limited subsistence, wealth is not their social purpose. To this degree there is no community of ends, and consumers might not have an interest in capital or a capital-based economic system. However, the fact, demonstrated by Hegel, that all major categories of economic needs are subject to multiplication implies a more complete community of purpose in seeking wealth, and a more complete community of interest in capital. Capital appears as essential to the provision both of subsistence and luxury needs when the former are subject to multiplication. Therefore, its preservation and expansion are a common end of the consumer considered with respect to all categories of need.

Marx's conception of the determination of individuality by capital can also provide a basis for the existence of a dimension of community revolving around capital, though of course Marx did not intend this implication. The general interest of all persons in individuality gives rise to a community of interest in capital, since the latter is a necessary condition for individuality (again, notwithstanding Marx's view of class division). Note that Marx thinks that the generic individual, not just the members of one class, depends on capital for his individuality. Since everyone's individuality depends on capital, all have an interest in the maintenance of capital and in the system of economic relations that preserves and expands it. By providing the material conditions on which a rich individuality depends, capital provides people with the conditions for defining their own ends, so all individuals' economic ends can be subsumed under capital, which stands as an overarching, general end. Moreover, since capital can only be created within the system, not by isolated individuals, individuals also have a general interest in the system of capital-based market relations. This community is comprehensive in the scope of individuals included, but it is not just a community, because its members use products for different personal ends.

11

The Dimension of Community in Capital-Based Market Systems: *Between Capital and Labor*

NEOCLASSICAL THEORY VERSUS THE THEORY OF ECONOMIC COMMUNITY

Neoclassical economists generally ascribe the goal of maximizing profits to "producers" rather than to laborers. Contemporary adherents of classical political economy ascribe the goal of preserving and expanding capital to capital owners and managers, not to laborers. Labor's aim, economists say, is to obtain a wage or to minimize the disutility from work. These formulations distinguish the goals and interests of labor and capital, and counterpose them as competitive categories or opposing classes of economic agents. Neoclassical economics treats labor and capital as having "alternative" ends. That characterization means that their ends are connected in such a way that they are not attained together, but rather one in place of the other. Specifically, producers maximize profit by minimizing wage costs, while laborers increase their wages by reducing profits.

Reviewing the scene, however, the goals of labor and capital lose some of their distinctness, and, with diminished distinctness, some of their character as alternatives fades, though not all of it. In seeking a wage, labor seeks means to the satisfaction of a multiplicity of needs, just as the capital owner does. Labor is not producing with the goal of consuming the immediate product of the productive activity. Nor is capital producing for self-consumption. Like the capital owner, labor does not merely seek subsistence. The laborer pursues a money wage to gain access to the world of commodities. Such an aim involves a desire to gain a share of the wealth or capital of society. In this respect, it is the same end that capital owners and capital managers have when they strive to preserve and expand capital through capital-based commodity production processes.

As labor and capital pursue goals with some commonalities, they find that they can only attain their goals together, not in place of each other, and so they come together in a joint production process. To attain goals with some commonality, it turns out that they must promote the attainment of the other party's goals to some extent, if they want to achieve their own. Promoting each other's goals is the very meaning of common interest. As a seeker of some wealth, labor's interest lies in working in wealth production processes that pay money wages, not in self-subsistent production. Capital owners' pursuit of the preservation and expansion of capital is, therefore, also in labor's interest to an extent. Capital owners have an interest in labor's seeking and getting some wealth, because the sharing of some wealth cements the essential participation of labor in capital's wealth-production processes and expands the market for capital's products.

Economists often note the existence of common interest in the economic system, but the form they see does not lead them to affirm the existence of community. The kind of common interest outlined above has a different structure, however, than a neoclassical or classical common interest, and it is indicative of a dimension of community. From Smith to Arrow, economists have regarded the common interest as an unintended consequence of individuals' seeking different, independent, alternative goals.[1] A Pareto-efficient allocation emerges from this underlying structure. That is, the economy attains a state where no other feasible allocation will make at least one person better off without making someone else worse off. The classical and neoclassical interpretations may be partially true. But the common interest, a system of wealth, also arises from individuals' pursuing goals with significant commonality, that is, the goal of obtaining a portion of wealth through participation in a system of capital-based economic relations. Seeking goals with this commonality leads labor and capital owners into behaviors that promote the social interest, that is, the preservation and expansion of capital. Thus, commonalities in goals have to be part of the account of the common interest, which cannot be explained entirely as an unintended consequence of the independent pursuit of self-gain through exchange relations.

If the common interest resulted purely from individuals' seeking independent and different goals, community would be relatively trivial. But the recognition that it results also from pursuing goals with some com-

1. Arrow 1974.

monalities puts community within the deep structure of economic life.

There are commonalities not only in the object of the activities of laborers and capital owners but also in their nature as subjects. Laborers and capital owners both form their nature and actions in ways that contribute to preserving and expanding capital. Laborers cultivate qualities in order to win employment in capital-based firms. Capital owners (and managers) cultivate abilities that help them to direct production toward the preservation and expansion of capital, such as a keen eye for the kind of labor best suited to their particular trade. The community among productive agents, therefore, runs deeper than a community of ends; it goes to their very nature as subjects in the association.

In traditional economic thought, the common interest results unintentionally from individual activity directed at self-interest. On this view, the common interest is only an indirect interest of economic actors, so mainline economists deny that community exists in the economy. When, however, the laborer molds himself (or herself) in order to get a wage, a common end becomes the direct object of the laboring activity. This is no longer self-subsistent labor, but labor that inherently involves labor for others, including for capital. The cultivation of skills and habits related to the requirements of employment in capital-based firms and the performance of tasks integral to the operation of capital-based production processes, mean the laborer fashions himself or herself in the ways necessary for the preservation and expansion of capital. Laborers are therefore forming themselves in ways that promote a common goal, because all economic actors who want a share of wealth have an interest in the preservation and expansion of capital. The common interest is, then, a more direct object of the activity of labor and capital than mainstream economics appreciates or even than labor and capital consciously know. Preserving and expanding capital is not exclusively the manager's end or labor's end, but an end they hold conjointly. Capital does not get preserved and expanded solely because it provides means to satisfy capital owners' needs, but also because it satisfies labor's needs (otherwise labor would not agree to participate under conditions of voluntary exchange and legal autonomy).

Labor, in constituting itself so that it may qualify for employment in capital-based commodity production, fashions itself for participation in a process with a dual end (joint satisfaction of labor and capital). In other words, laborers are building a common interest – the preservation and expansion of capital – into their nature, activity, and ends. When they act upon their nature, the common interest in preserving capital flows from an end involved in their own tendencies. It makes no matter

– as far as the directness of this interest – whether the laborers intend it or not. It remains the direct object and consequence of their economic activity.

The same can be said of the capital owner or capital manager. His or her activities, such as purchasing labor and combining it with means of production, are oriented toward preserving capital. As such, they are oriented toward an overarching objective that jointly provides means to satisfy the needs of both labor and capital. In that sense, the goal sought by capital is in the interest of labor as well, and it therefore constitutes a common interest. Cultivating abilities to preserve capital is tantamount, then, to building the common interest into the capital owner. The common interest thus forms the direct object of his or her nature and activities, whether intended or not. The directness of the common interest among productive agents suggests a profound community within the economy. Neoclassical economics misses the directness of the common interest in individual behavior because it passes over the intersubjective inner structure of "self-interest."

Two major elements of the economic community identified thus far may be underscored: first, the marked commonalities in the nature, activity, and ends of labor and capital, and second, the directness of the common interest as an object of self-seeking.

Labor's interest in capital gives it a common interest in many actions that capital owners and managers take to preserve and expand capital. These activities all comprise a circulation process, and so labor has a common interest with capital in every phase of this process. Concretely, labor has a common interest with capital owners and managers when the latter (1) acquire labor and means of production, (2) combine them in a production process, (3) direct production toward commodity production, (4) sell commodity products for money, and (5) repurchase productive inputs.

It is in labor's interest that capital owners or managers purchase means of production and labor and that they combine these inputs in a production process. Production is a phase of expansion of value, which is in the interest of labor, for wages are drawn from preserved and expanded value. Isolated from the means of production, labor cannot expand value; it can at most generate subsistence. Labor also has an interest in capital owners and managers selling commodity products for money. The sale of commodities helps to preserve and expand the value from which wages are drawn. Producing and selling commodities can create an increase of value over the cost of the productive inputs. These things can lead to increases in wages down the line. The laborer cannot obtain such an increase by engaging in production for direct consumption. He or she also has an interest in the fact that capital owners and managers continuously repeat this process on an ever-expanding scale. For this can provide a necessary basis for continued and increasing wage payments. There is a limit to how far redistributive policies can advance the interest of labor.

Common interests arise from individual behavior but they do so because of commonalities in the nature and goals of individuals, not just from pursuits on the basis of independent and different goals.

While this discussion is entirely concerned with demonstrating community's existence in the economy, it does not assert the thesis that the economy is fully communal; so it is a qualified view. It only points to a dimension of community within the economic system. The communal dimension is the focus of this study, not because it is the only feature of economic life, but because it is usually neglected, whereas the noncommunal dimensions are already well known.

In the economy, which neoclassical thought divides into sectors of production and consumption, labor is assigned to the consumption sector. The individual supplies labor in her capacity as a consumer, rather than functioning as a producer.[2] She does not have a productive goal, but a consumption goal: to minimize the disutility from labor and to maximize the satisfaction from income obtained by laboring. The goal of profit maximization is ascribed solely to "producers," from which labor is categorically excluded.

Proceeding from sharply different goals, the theory goes, drives labor and capital owners into purely competitive relationships. Producers who seek to maximize profits want to obtain factor services at low prices; while laborers who want to maximize satisfaction (and minimize the disutility of labor) seek high prices for their services. Producers demand more labor services the lower their price; workers supply more services the higher their price (assuming that the "substitution effect" overcomes the "income effect"). As Haveman and Knopf write, "[A] conflict is posed."[3] With businesses competing to purchase factor supplies inexpensively and workers competing to sell labor services dear, the neoclassical factor market is a condition of conflict, not of community.

In neoclassical theory the conflict is resolved at equilibrium. However, the economy has not found a moment of community at this point, because equilibrium is a balance of opposed forces. Workers still want to obtain higher wages, and producers still prefer to pay lower ones, but,

2. Varian 1993, p. 170–171; Debreu 1959, Chapter 4; Haveman and Knopf 1970, pp. 42, 34.
3. Haveman and Knopf 1970, p. 73.

at equilibrium, neither find it in their interest to accept the other's offer. Because they have different and competing goals, a basic common interest cannot emerge even at equilibrium in a neoclassical system.

The neoclassical "story" is not wrong; competition exists, of course, in the factor market. Yet it is incomplete, because it neglects the presence of the theme of common interest. We can infer the common interest by considering the implications of denying that it exists. Suppose, at equilibrium, "producers" were to suffer a lapse of understanding and accede to workers' demands for higher wages for providing factor services. Paying wages above the equilibrium rate reduces or negates profits. Producers' ability to reinvest is diminished. Negative profits set in, leading to a reduction in the scale of production. Producers may go bankrupt. Workers find little or no demand for their services. Producers pay them lower wages or no wages, and so they are less able to have means of obtain goods. The reader can readily imagine a corresponding story for capital owners. If we maximize their profits to the point where labor receives practically nothing from joint activity, the consequences for capital are clear. The injury to labor would prevent it from participating in capital-based production, which would be self-defeating for capital, since the latter cannot make profits without labor's involvement.

As this shows, even if labor could elevate the wage to the diminution of capital, it ought not to try – for its own sake. The fact that driving wages up as high as possible is not to labor's advantage suggests that labor has an interest in the preservation and expansion of capital. In this sense, it shares the goal that producers maximize profits. Labor has an interest in the firm (1) being able to run the production process repeatedly, (2) having enough capital to expand the scale of production, (3) having the capital to replace equipment through new investment and to incorporate advances in productive methods. Continued employment, increasing employment, and increasing wages all hinge on the profitability of the firm. Therefore, certain aspects of profitability are an interest of labor, not just of capital. Labor has an interest in the expansion of the firm's capital because there is a limit to how much labor can increase wages through increasing its relative share of revenue. Beyond a certain degree of equalization of relative shares, further wage increases can only be won by an expansion of capital. Labor and capital thus have a dual relationship: they have alternative ends with respect to relative shares, and simultaneously they have a common interest in the expansion of capital.

All this suggests that neoclassical theory obscures something fundamental about the composition of labor's goals when it attributes profit maximization solely to the goals of producers. It simply does not do justice to labor's profound interest in the expansion of capital. We can only recognize that interest by formally conceptualizing it as part of labor's goal structure or as part of the composition of labor's interests. Moreover, since labor's goals or interests encompass the interest of capital, and do not just compete with it, capital forms a common interest, since capital owners and managers obviously share that interest as well.

Systems of wealth, as usually understood, are entirely divisible into individual productive agents (marginal products of labor and capital), and the social interest is a sum of individual interests in wages, rents, and satisfactions. People can create wealth only through systems or cultures, however, which tells us that economic activity is not entirely reducible to individual activities. A system of action is an irreducible social entity, and it forms an essential condition for economic action. Each individual makes his or her productive contribution through dependence on the system. Because no one can produce except as part of a system, economic action must be a form of common action, to some extent. Capital and labor have an irreducible common interest in a capital-based market system in two respects: (1) as independent agents they are not productive of wealth, so they can only produce wealth through common agency, and (2) they cannot produce more wealth through any alternative system.

THE COMMON INTEREST OF CAPITAL AND LABOR IN WEALTH

The entrepreneur, as portrayed by conventional economics, is a person who hopes to make very considerable returns from a capital investment. He or she is willing to place much at risk for the prospect of great gains. Thus, the entrepreneur, not the laborer, is the wealth seeker in mainstream economics. In neoclassical economics, wealth is pursued in the person of the producer. Producers can make much money through profit maximization. The entrepreneur and the producer provide the resources and the drive that power the economy to generate wealth. Labor in neoclassical economics is not a producer, but an economic agent of an entirely different sort, one who would not sacrifice enough leisure to accumulate significant savings. Being more risk averse, he or she prefers the security of a secure job to the thrill of a risky investment. Laborers, according to neoclassical theory, have relatively less intense desires for goods relative to leisure than do producers. They can be content with a modest level of comfort associated with a moderate expenditure of effort. The differences between labor and capital in modern economic thought really constitute them as different classes of persons with categorically different goals.

Modern economic thought misses the common element in the goals of producers and consumers because it misconceives the goals of labor. Labor also seeks wealth. In seeking a wage, labor does not just seek means to satisfy fixed and limited wants. Having multiple wants, the laborer – like the capital owner and producer – seeks means to the satisfaction of multiple kinds and numbers of wants. The money wage gives labor access to a portion of the world of commodities, not just to a biological subsistence. Wealth may be defined as means to the satisfaction of needs multiplied in kind and number. Seeking this kind of means carries the implication that labor seeks wealth. As such, one cannot flatly distinguish laborers from "producers" in regard to goals. They have in common a desire for wealth, and their common action works toward this community of ends.

ALTERNATIVE SYSTEMS AND COMMON INTERESTS

The existence of common action or cooperation in capital-based markets does not suffice to constitute community. To constitute communities, these systems would also have to be more in the interest of labor and capital than are rival systems, such as natural economy or bureaucratic socialism. For if the participants discovered a better system of provision, they might secede, destabilizing or eroding the "community."

The system of natural economy cannot serve the interests of labor or capital owners better than capital-based markets because it is ill-equipped to keep natural scarcity at bay. In contrast to natural economy, the capital-based market system has a capacity for frequent repetition of production. This gives it a superior ability to reduce the frequency of shortages. Hence it better addresses labor's and capital's common interest in reducing the frequency of shortages. Another commonality in goals is that labor and capital both have resurgent wants and needs, rather than needs that are satisfied once for all time. Capital-based commodity production can engage in a more determinate sequence of productions than does the system of natural economy. So the former can better address the common interest in the reproduction of the surplus.

Still another commonality in the goal structure of laborers and capital owners is that they are not content with a fixed level of wealth. They seek higher and higher levels of comfort, which "is something inexhaustible and illimitable," as Hegel observed.[4] A capital-based market system outclasses nature in its ability for expanded reproduction of the surplus. So it better serves the common interests of labor and capital in expanding means of satisfaction.

For a long time, many Marxists touted the productive capacity of bureaucratic socialist systems, proclaiming them to be in the interest of labor. The USSR's GDP proved that bureaucratic socialist systems could produce wealth in the sense of an immense accumulation of commodities. Yet the term "wealth" should be used advisedly in connection with bureaucratic socialism, for it is not really wealth in the proper sense of the term. From the beginning of modern economic thought in the seventeenth and eighteenth centuries, wealth has meant a capacity to satisfy wants and needs.[5] Bureaucratic socialist systems do not achieve wealth in that sense. Instead of letting consumers discover and reveal their needs in the market, government planners hypostatize needs. A mismatch between production goals and felt needs results from the state's usurpation of the functions of individual self-determination in defining preferences. Because the productive apparatus is combined with excessive misconsumption, bureaucratic socialism fails the minimum requirements for a system of wealth, and it cannot rival the ability of capital-based markets to serve the interests of labor.[6]

A DIMENSION OF COATTAINMENT OF ENDS

Merely pursuing the same goal (or tending toward the same end) would not establish community unless each party pursued it (or tended toward it) in ways that promoted coattainment of this goal (or end) by the others.[7] The point applies to laborers and capital owners or capital managers as well.

Labor promotes the coattainment of wealth by capital owners and managers when it participates in the process of circulation of capital, sells services to capital owners and managers, works in a production process in combination with capital, and coproduces commodity products and commodity capital. Capital owners and managers, correspondingly, promote the coattainment of a share of wealth by laborers. They

4. Hegel 1952, add. to para. 191, p. 269.
5. Smith 1937, p. 22.
6. On the limits of synoptic decision making one cannot do better than to consult Lindblom 1977.
7. Indicated by Rawls 1971 to be a condition for community.

do so when they undertake a course of circulation of capital by purchasing labor and means of production, combining them in a production process, directing production toward commodity production, selling commodity products for money, and repurchasing productive inputs.

In the wage bargain, however, capital owners and managers do not promote the coattainment of wealth by labor in capitalist systems, which precludes capitalism from being a community in the view of many theorists. Such a conclusion stems from dichotomous reasoning that does not, however, fit the complex reality in which the parties promote coattainment at some points and constrain it at others. The fact that all productive agents engage in some actions that promote a necessary condition for coattainment of ends implies that a dimension of community exists within the system. Economic community is neither comprehensive nor absent, but dimensional. Perhaps capital and labor just play along with each other, intending all the while to thwart the other's interests at the critical juncture? This interpretation overemphasizes subjective intentions as indicators of the nature of the process. The objective nature of the process is the way the participants do the things that are necessary for both to acquire wealth.

THE DIMENSION OF COMMON ACTION

The content of laboring and of managing shows that they are not entirely separate categories of activities. It shows that they partially consist in one single action – the production of wealth, though they may expend different quantities and sorts of effort. Producing wealth involves making multiple products, because wealth is something virtually illimitable. Labor makes them by separating itself from the product in the following way. The laborer generally has to forgo the endeavor to concretely determine specific features of the product as an expression of his or her own personality.[8] This marks a major distinction between labor in commodity production and artisan labor in precapitalist production. The artisan experience involves an intimate connection to the product. His specially cultivated skills, tastes, movements, and implements go into the makeup of the specific features of the product. This profound connection may yield great art, but it can interfere with the task of multiplying the product, and the laborer in commodity production must relinquish this connection. Products are multiplied by embodying the idea of the product in the machinery. Machinery designed and built in accordance

8. Levine 1978–1981, vol. 1, p. 163.

with the idea of the product can stamp out multiple copies of it. So the idea of the product must be at least partially removed from the laborer.[9] Insofar as the idea of the product is embodied in the machinery, the major product features are concretely determined by the machinery rather than by the labor. Given the importance of machinery in commodity production, labor consists in large part in adapting to the means of production (rather than in adapting the machinery to itself). The adaptation of laboring to the means of production merges laboring with the management of capital, thus constituting one single action: the production of wealth. The latter is, therefore, common action.

Labor's role as a productive agent is to activate, operate, and use the means of production to produce wealth. The capital owner's role is to supply means of production that contain the productive potential of society. Neither of these roles is productive in itself; labor and capital cannot produce wealth when placed apart from one another. The means of production would be idled without labor; they cannot activate, use, or operate themselves. Likewise, labor separated from the instruments of production could produce subsistence or poverty, but not a vast accumulation of commodities. The creation of wealth involves the cooperation of the activating principle of wealth represented by labor and the productive potential of society embodied in the means of production.[10] It is, therefore, irreducibly joint or common action.

While capital-based commodity production combines labor and capital, it cannot be understood simply as an admixture, half labor and half capital, as though they were equally important principles of economic organization. Labor produces as an element of capital. It is itself part of productive capital, resulting from the conversion of money into productive inputs. Labor is purchased by capital, entered into a process of circulation of capital, and oriented toward the preservation and expansion of capital. Thus, the coactivity of labor and capital is best understood as a capital-based and capital-oriented production process. As David P. Levine writes,

> With the purchase of labor-power . . . , the two principles [the activating principle and the money] are united into capital as two elements of its process: on the one side there is the wealth existing as capital, on the other side there is labor-power, as the activating force within production, also existing as capital . . .

9. See also Winfield 1990, p. 136. In advanced capitalism, the forms of labor exhibit more flexibility, the so-called flexible process production (Reich 1984, pp. 130–139, 235–237). But this is not a flexibility in terms of latitude for personal idiosyncrasy. Greater flexibility in the labor process is needed by the developing requirements of advanced capital-based commodity production.
10. For the term "activating principle," see Levine 1978–1981, vol. 1, p. 159.

Labor-power can only produce commodities when it does so as an element of capital. Labor-power only becomes active, becomes labor, when it has first become capital. In this sense, it is capital alone which is able to produce commodities and which is alone capable of accounting for the value of the product . . .[11]

The fact that labor produces as part of a capital-based and capital-oriented process seemingly undermines the claim of common action between labor and capital, because it subordinates labor to capital. But labor actually has an interest in the preservation and expansion of capital, and it therefore has an interest in capital-based commodity production. Since labor's own interest lies in incorporation into this process, the resulting action has the character of action taken in common.

The unity of labor and capital goes beyond their union within the firm. The individual laborer does not just shape her activity so that a particular production process can be carried out. Her activity is also, indirectly, shaped so that other production processes can go forward, and indeed so that the system of production can proceed. Labor works on means of production differentiated within a system of production processes. As she adjusts to the means of production within the firm, the laborer is also, indirectly, adjusting to the system of production processes. The interdependence of production processes molds labor in accordance with the operation of the system of production processes. Marx explains,

Simultaneously, with the differentiation of the instruments of labour, the industries that produce these instruments, become more and more differentiated. If the manufacturing system seize upon an industry, which, previously, was carried on in connexion with others, either as a chief or as a subordinate industry, and by one producer, these industries immediately separate their connexion, and become independent. If it seize upon a particular stage in the production of a commodity, the other stages of its production become converted into so many independent industries. . . . In order to carry out more perfectly the division of labour in manufacture, a single branch of production is . . . split up into numerous, and to some extent, entirely new manufactures.[12]

The interdependence of production processes is effected through exchange relations. The division of labor and means of production within the firm does not cut off labor from the rest of the system of production processes. For the differentiated production process is unified through exchange. Marx grasped this: "Exchange brings what are already different into relation, and thus converts them into more or less

11. Ibid., p. 160.
12. Marx 1967a, p. 353.

inter-dependent branches of the collective production of an enlarged society."[13]

The character of the immediate production process of a particular firm reflects the interdependence of production processes. Productive inputs are obtained from other firms, and productive outputs are made for other firms. The shoemaker, for example, transforms leather into shoes. But he or she obtained the leather from the tanner, who produced it by transforming into leather the hides purchased from a cattle owner. The shoemaker preserves and expands the value of the leather by transforming it into shoes. The tanner preserves and expands the value of the hides through productive consumption of the hides. Thus the system of production processes interpenetrates the immediate production process.

As this happens, a specific act of labor is an adaptation not only to the means of production within the firm but also to the capital of society as a whole. The specific means of production within a steel factory, automotive plant, or semiconductor manufacturer that a laborer works with are themselves a function of the division of productive processes in society. "In order to carry out more perfectly the division of labor in manufacture," Marx writes, "a single branch of production is split up into numerous, and to some extent, entirely new manufactures."[14] When labor is united with the means of production in a particular firm, whose productive process has itself been differentiated and united with a system of production processes, labor is united with the system of capital-based production processes. This makes individual labor a form of common activity with all capital owners and laborers.

The production of almost any item requires intersectoral linkages. The transformation of inputs into a particular final good is split up into a great number of steps within a particular firm and between many different firms and sectors of the economy. As Lowe writes, "Each step is entrusted to a different member of the economic society in question. Therefore the productive success – the attainment of the intended output – depends on a sequence of technologically adequate decisions capable of interlocking the actions of many individuals at every stage and between successive stages."[15] Through intersectoral linkages, the labor of the attendant at the bakery counter becomes a single connected sequence with the actions of the miller, the farmer, the producer of ovens, of trucks and trains, of millstones and grinders, and the actions of all the other laborers who operate this equipment. Such a sequence can only be called common action.

13. Ibid., p. 352. 14. Ibid., p. 353.
15. Lowe 1965, pp. 19–20.

The novelist Elizabeth Gaskell was particularly clearsighted with respect to this aspect of economic life. In her 1855 account of early industrial relations, *North and South*, she wrote: "I see two classes dependent on each other in every possible way yet each evidently regarding the interest of the other as opposed to their own; I have never lived in a place before where there were two sets of people always running each other down."[16]

THE PRINCIPLE OF SELF-ORDERING AND A DIMENSION OF COMMON ENDS

In attempting to understand why labor fashions itself as it does, we have to shift, to an extent, from the logic of subjective preference to the laws of creation of wealth. Is there a preference for adjusting labor to the means of production rather than the other way around? Does labor really *want* to surrender the idea of the product to the machine rather than reserve some creative rights? Instead, labor finds itself in the following condition. Given a desire for a share of wealth, labor develops attributes helpful in getting a wage, not necessarily because of the inherent desirability of the attributes to labor. The attributes are tailored to the requirements for earning a wage, which derive from the requirements for commodity production, more than from the capital owners' preferences about how to produce. These requisites stem, in turn, from the requirements of capital. The fact that the production of wealth is based on capital is indicated, for example, by the fact that production is based on machinery. Suggesting that labor adjusts to the machinery is just another way of saying that it fashions itself in accordance with the requirements of capital. The reader can easily elaborate a parallel story with respect to capital owners; in short, given a desire for wealth, the capital owner acts in accordance with the requirements of capital-based commodity production, and does things that bear little resemblance to subjective preferences about how to produce. The molding of labor and management in line with the requirements of capital reveals that these activities are shaped by the principle of self-ordering of capital-based production, and that they cannot be entirely comprehended by the unfolding logic of subjective preference, individual activity, or subjective intention.

The principle of self-ordering of capital governs not only the individual firm, but also its relationship to the system of firms. This is especially significant for the existence of systemwide community, not merely of

16. Gaskell 1951 [1855], p. 131.

community within the firm. While the principle of self-ordering yields commonalities between the ends of labor and capital within the firm, its ordering of the system produces commonalities between their ends on a systemwide scale.

The division of productive processes in society (including the division and content of the laboring performed on the means of production) is governed by the principle of self-ordering of the system of capital-based commodity exchange and production. When a capital owner splits up an existing branch of production, and to this extent establishes a new manufacture, he functions within a given division of productive processes in society that he cannot determine by himself, and that is determinate for him. The interdependent nature of the process is such that, to advance his or her own interest, he or she will have to differentiate his or her production process in a way that furthers the interests of other producers and furthers the interests of the system of differentiated producers. If a producer did not do so, he or she would find neither appropriate inputs for the firm nor customers among producers for its output. Ordered in accordance with the principle of self-ordering of the system of capital-based production, the firm's production process is differentiated in a way that advances the interest of the capital of the system of producers.

Labor is also shaped in accordance with the principle of self-ordering operating at the level of the system of commodity producers. When the laborer adapts to means of production, which have been differentiated systemically, his or her labor is indirectly shaped by the requirements of the system of commodity producers and laborers. Thus determined, individual labor is shaped to sustain and expand not only the capital of the firm, but also that of the system of producers in its entirety.

With the activities of labor and capital ordered by the same principle (the self-organization of the system of commodity production and exchange), they are oriented toward a common end: the preservation and expansion of the capital *of the system* of capital-based producers and exchangers. Thus oriented, there is a veritable community of ends on a systemwide scale, underlying their different pursuits and purposes.

The principle of self-ordering is crucial to the account of a dimension of community. If economic agents were simply guided by their subjective intentions, there would be as many different ends in the system as there are laborers and capital owners. If the social determinations affecting the identity and ends of the laborer and the capital owner were expressions of different principles of social organization, no community would obtain among them. It is because the constitutive influences in a capital-based system proceed in accordance with a single organizing principle –

the preservation and expansion of capital – that such a system has a community of ends.

Although Marx emphasized the element of class division and exploitation, it should be underscored that he acknowledged the existence of a dimension of community within capitalist economies. Marx thought production proceeds through common action within the firm (a system of "co-operation"),[17] that this unity is just a subordinate part of a systemwide common action based on the "invisible bond uniting the various branches of trade,"[18] and therefore that even capitalism is a system of "collective production."[19] Thus, the work of the most forceful and brilliant advocate of the theory of class division and exploitation strongly supports the thesis that a dimension of community exists in capital-based market systems, including capitalist ones.

Marx's analysis of the need for regulation shows his presumption of some community within capitalism. For when he called for regulation due to the system's disorganization, he did so not because he thought community was absent from it, but because the unity of producers was capriciously and contingently arranged. "[I]n . . . society . . . , chance and caprice have full play in distributing the producers and their means of production among the various branches of industry."[20] His advocacy of regulation was founded on the belief that interdependence exists, but imperfectly so. Consequently, when he criticized capitalists' opposition to regulation, he did so on the ground that they neglected to see the systemwide interdependence that would justify social intervention, not because he believed that no community existed in the capitalist economy: "The same bourgeois mind which praises division of labour in the workshop, life-long annexation of the labourer to a partial operation, and his complete subjection to capital, as being an organization of labour that increases productiveness – that same bourgeois mind denounces with equal vigor every conscious attempt to socially control and regulate the process of production . . ."[21]

THE DIMENSION OF CONSTITUTIVE COMMUNITY

To be a community, an association must be constitutive of the members of the association, to some significant extent. Common attributes, actions, and ends signifying community exist insofar as they are constituted by and within the association. Qualities general to a system of

17. Marx 1967a, Chapter 13.
18. Ibid., p. 356. 19. Ibid., p. 352.
20. Ibid., p. 355. 21. Ibid., p. 356.

individuals can be explained only upon the basis of pervasive common causes. Sandel adds another reason for regarding constitutiveness as a criterion of community. Sharing common ends is not enough to constitute a community, he says. To form a community, the subject herself – and not just the object of her feelings – must be constituted by the association to which she belongs.[22] For, if the subject were unformed by community, then she would be antecedently individuated prior to community, and would owe her identity more to herself than to the community. The existence of community would be capricious and indeterminate because contingent on the coincidence of a multitude of subjective preferences.

Labor's association with capital owners is constitutive to an extent, thereby forming a dimension of constitutive community among them. The qualities of labor requisite for commodity production are formed, as we saw in the preceding section, by and within the system of capital-based commodity production and exchange. The qualities of capital owners and managers are formed by and within the same process. Reynolds and Gregory's study of workers in Puerto Rico identifies qualities acquired in the transition from a traditional agricultural economy to a capital-based market system.[23]

> 1. The discipline imposed by the time requirements of the factory and by the necessity of prompt and regular attendance, particularly in multiple-shift operations.
> 2. The discipline imposed by the task, particularly in assembly line or other machine-paced work, which leaves the worker little latitude to adjust the tempo to his own preferences.
> 3. The discipline imposed by quantity and quality requirements: the need to meet certain output standards within narrow margins of tolerance.
> 4. A residual area which involves acceptance of a system of authority structured along impersonal lines and a web of rules administered without respect for the identity of a particular individual.
> 5. [Familiarity] with wages, employment . . . and the market mechanism.
> 6. [Breakdown of . . . personal relations that bind workers to employers]; conversion of the . . . employment relation to an impersonal cash basis.

22. Sandel 1982, pp. 150, 148-149.
23. The following are excerpted from Reynolds and Gregory 1965, pp. 261, 253, 252, 259, 261.

> 7. Receptivity to factory employment . . . ;[expectation] to like [factory employment; belief that wages are higher because of it, belief that] working conditions [are] more pleasant; [belief that higher status is associated with it than with the alternatives].
> 8. Like to work . . . , like particular job, pride in seeing the work get done [rather than traditional attitude to work] as "the worst punishment in this life."
> 9. [Acceptance of] the "culture" of the factory: [and particularly] the impersonality of human relations . . .
> 10. [Acceptance of] the exacting nature of factory tasks [and of] the level of . . . nervous effort required.

These qualities of labor are not cultivated as a matter of subjective preference. The labor that produces value for a mass market, as distinct from use-value for self-consumption, has been shaped by the laborer herself and by the system, so that it meets a necessary requirement for the preservation and expansion of capital. Labor and capital could well echo the words of Sandel's generic individual: "I am indebted in a complex variety of ways for the constitution of my identity" to the community,[24] but with two differences. The community to which they belong is the economy, whereas Sandel does not identify the economy as a community.[25] And economic society only has a dimension of community, it does not constitute a thoroughgoing community.

An association cannot be a constitutive community if the constituting influences vitiate the freedom of the participants. That would be a holistic community of "radically situated subjects"[26] who are merely receptacles for social influences and social attributes. Labor and capital in a capital-based economic community are not radically situated subjects. Capital acquires labor services through exchanges in which the laborer's personhood and his property in his own labor are recognized. Moreover, both the laborer and the capital owner have legal autonomy. The social influences that contribute to the constitution of labor in a capital-based economy do not constitute external impositions upon labor. The laborer uses his own mind and will to cultivate the qualities necessary in order for him or her to sell labor to capital owners. He is developing himself in ways that will enable him to acquire means to the satisfaction of a multiplicity of kinds and numbers of needs. The requirements for the labor process, though sometimes onerous, are willingly

24. Sandel 1982, p. 143.
25. Ibid.
26. The term "radically situated subject" is due to Sandel (1982).

met. Shares of wealth do not come easily. Since the social formation of labor and capital do not violate their freedom, but help constitute it, their association has a dimension of constitutive community rather than forming a holistic community.

THE SIGNIFICANCE OF THE REVISED THEORY OF ECONOMIC COMMUNITY

One would expect the surge of communitarianism to have restored the element of community to its proper place in the conception of economic life. But for various reasons, it has not. Communitarians who identify community solely in the "family, city, tribe, class, nation, culture" ascribe community only to noneconomic spheres, passing over economic community entirely.[27] In this way, communitarianism has a tendency to treat community as something external to the economy. Communitarians, of course, deal with things economic, but many of their forays into economics do not particularly search for economic community. In his book *Democracy's Discontent*, Sandel deals extensively with political economy, but he is searching for the economic preconditions for political community, not for economic community. Moreover, the preconditions that he identifies, such as individual self-proprietorship,[28] are by no means inherently communal, but instead suggest Lockean individualism.

Since communitarian concerns are often directed away from economic community, one cannot readily grasp economic community's meaning from communitarian analysis. It is, therefore, worth pointing out what economic community is and what it is not.

Proposition 1. Economic community does not so much consist in the economic preconditions of an extrinsic political community as it does in the common actions, attributes, and ends that intrinsically constitute the economy as a community within itself, to some significant extent. That is, a dimension of community obtains, not only to the surrounding political cocoon, but also inheres in capital-based markets as an essential facet.

The conception of economic community is sometimes attenuated

27. Ibid., p. 143.
28. Sandel affirms the Jeffersonian view that economic independence is required for republican citizenship (Sandel 1996, pp. 125, 143).

when communitarians think of its scope as limited to subsystems within the economy. They identify it with the firm, the factory, the large-scale economic enterprise, the industrial sector, some department of the economy (e.g., the sphere of consumption), or any of the other "various We-nesses," as Etzioni puts it,[29] but not with the systemwide level in the economy. The revised theory of economic community supports a different view:

Proposition 2. A dimension of economic community extends systemwide in the economy. It is a community embracing all members of the system of commodity exchange and production, not just a subset of economic actors. As a union of actors on a systemwide scale, economic community cannot be reduced to a number of distinct, disunified subcommunities.

Etzioni's recent communitarian formulation of "supracommunities"[30] seemingly has an affinity with the proposed notion of systemwide economic community; but Etzioni ultimately rejects the notion of community in the economic system, instead ascribing supracommunity to the city, the nation, or the surrounding social capsule,[31] but not to the economy.[32]

The communitarian analysis associated with the "socioeconomics" school treats community as something exterior to the economy in the sense that the economy derives whatever unity it has from external agencies, such as the social system or the government.[33] "The scope of the transactions organized by the market is largely determined by the social capsule."[34] The revised theory of economic community, as having internal forces of cohesion, does not deny that markets are not wholly self-regulating. It calls, however, for a characterization of the economy that recognizes internal forces of cohesion without asserting purely self-regulating markets:

Proposition 3. Although the market system is not entirely self-regulating, many causes that help to unify and sustain it lie within the economic system. So it has its own internal forces of cohesion. The great preponderance of the bases for the unity of the economic system lie

29. Etzioni 1988, p. 244.
30. Etzioni 1993, p. 147.
31. Etzioni 1988, pp. 212, 199–216.
32. Etzioni 1993, p. 147.
33. Etzioni 1988, pp. 199–216.
34. Ibid., p. 256.

within the economic system. While not purely self-regulating, the economy has a principle of self-organization that accounts for a great deal of its unity.

COMMUNITY OR CLASS DIVISION AND EXPLOITATION?

Marx considered the capitalist economy to be a system of class division. It is, in his view, an exploitative one that permits capitalists to deprive laborers of their just deserts. His theory of exploitation, based on the labor theory of value, is an attempt to demonstrate this idea scientifically. Although Marx drew his conclusion from analyzing the economy as a whole, it is primarily on the basis of the phase of distribution that he concluded the system was essentially class-divided.[35] Marx perceived a union of production and consumption in the circulation of capital, a union of capital owners and labors in production, and a union of exchangers.[36] But he judged the system to be utterly class-divided, without any dimension of community, primarily upon the basis of inequalities in the phase of distribution. Marx's understanding of the structure of the economy is represented in Table 11.1.

The capitalist economy should not, however, be judged to be devoid of community simply on the basis of social divisions within one phase of the process, distribution. If we take into account the other phases of the

35. The number and nature of the conflicts Marx sees between labor and capital are matters of controversy. Some scholars maintain that Marx thinks that distribution of income is the main point of conflict between capital and labor, while others think the control of surplus value forms an additional conflict between labor and capital. There are some good reasons for both of these interpretations, and one cannot fully resolve the controversy because of ambiguities in Marx's analysis. In light of this controversy, I would like to clarify my position that there is a sense in which distribution is the main conflict seen by Marx.

    Nancy Holmstrom argues that Marx's primary concern was that "inside the factory, workers work under the despotism of capital" and that they "do not control" the product (Holmstrom 1977, p. 358). There is textual evidence to support her interpretation that Marx sees a conflict of interest between labor and capital with respect to control within the factory and control of the product. Such an interpretation opposes the interpretation that distribution is the main point of conflict for Marx. But Holmstrom's argument does not take account of other places where Marx holds that "the general character of the labor process is evidently not changed by the fact that the worker works for the capitalist instead of for himself" (Marx 1977, p. 291). Insofar as labor would operate the labor process in the same way capital does, the conflict in a capitalist society centers on distribution, and there is much less conflict about control.
36. These unities are discussed at length in Marx's *Grundrisse* (Marx 1977).

Table 11.1. *Structure of the economy in Marx's theory*

Phases of economic activity	Relationship: union or division
Consumption	Union of production and consumption
Production	Union of capital owners and laborers
Exchange	Union of exchangers
Distribution	Class division and exploitation

process, then most of the economic phases are seen to display some significant degree of community. Part III shows that production and consumption display a dimension of community, that labor and capital exhibit a dimension of unity in the firm and on a systemwide basis, and that the process of circulation of individual capital involves a dimension of common action between labor and capital for the common end of the firm. The system of interrelated circuits of capital, moreover, exhibits a dimension of systemwide community between labor and capital. Taking all phases into account, there is as least as much reason to think the capitalist system has a dimension of community than to consider it class-divided or stratified.

One can easily appreciate why Marx believed that distribution was the nub of the issue, however. Common action in production and consumption amounts to little if the wage bargain distributes a meager share to labor. Class division in distribution could easily lead one to conclude that division is the essence of the system, notwithstanding the guise of common action for common ends. But I think we should resist this conclusion. The objective nature of the process is that most phases involve common action for a common end. The fact that capitalists seize bounty does not erase this fact.

There is even more reason to attribute a dimension of community to the capitalist system when one considers the sources of divisions and unities within it. The division in distribution is largely a function of the laws of property and contract, which permit extreme inequalities in returns to labor and capital. That is to say, the division in distribution has a source extrinsic to the economy, whereas the unities in production and consumption have an intrinsic source in the principle of self-ordering of the capital circuit (see Table 11.2).

The fact that the major division in the economy between capital and labor in the phase of division has an external source, while the dimensions of community in production, consumption, and exchange have an

Table 11.2. *Origin of the structure of Marx's economic phases*

Phases of Economic Activity	Union or Division	Source
Consumption	Union of production and consumption	Intrinsic
Production	Union of capital owners and laborers	Intrinsic
Exchange	Union of exchangers	Intrinsic
Distribution	Class division and exploitation	Extrinsic

internal source, is all the more reason why the dimensions of community should be included in the characterization of the economy.

Marx knew that class differences in remuneration for productive contributions could be implemented only through the laws of property and contracts, and that, to this extent, distributional inequalities had an external legal source. But the conceptual framework of base and superstructure – with legal relations epiphenomenal of economic relations – minimized this fact. Marx exaggerated divisions in the market when he suggested that they mainly emanate from within the economy itself. In actuality, class divisions in a capitalist economy can have more to do with the laws of property and contracts than with the intrinsic nature of the economy, which displays significant elements of community in phases other than distribution.

Throughout *Capital* Marx elaborates the view that class division is mainly intrinsic to the capitalist economy, arguing that class opposition is a function of the fact that in a capitalist economy the creation of surplus value is performed as a function of capital. "Industrial capital is," he writes, "the only mode of existence of capital in which not only the appropriation of surplus-value, or surplus product, but simultaneously its creation is a function of capital. Therefore with it the capitalist character of production is a necessity. Its existence implies the class antagonisms between capitalists and wage-labourers."[37] In saying that class opposition arises when surplus value is created as a function of capital, Marx means that antagonism arises when commodity production takes place under the auspices of capital owners and at their direction.

But is this really how opposition develops? Consider the case of the capital owner who pays his laborers relatively little while reaping a huge capital return. The ability of the capitalist to do this actually stems from

37. Marx 1967b, p. 55.

legal authorization to pay labor whatever he can get labor to agree to, not because capitalist commodity production inherently generates inequalities. Exchange between labor and capital cannot proceed *in abstracto* from the laws of property and the legal rules of distribution. Any value transferred from one person to another in an exchange relation has to be a contract or property relation, which legally regulates the terms of remuneration that can be struck by labor and capital. The terms of the wage bargain, high inequality or low, are almost entirely a matter of what the law permits.[38] Legal rules of distribution could be placed upon capital owners that would restrict their right to distribute income unequally, while leaving private ownership of capital in place. This would in turn alleviate serious class divisions on the issue of income distribution. Thus, the creation of surplus value under the auspices of capital need not generate class divisions. Such antagonism will only occur if the law implements a regime of inequality, for it does not necessarily spring from the capitalist economy. When one recognizes that income inequalities between capital and labor in a capitalist economy stem from the law of property, one can appreciate that the capital-based economy really has an intrinsic element of community.

Although Marx understood the unities in a capitalist economy better than "bourgeois" economists of his day or ours, he may have played down this knowledge because it could undermine his moral criticism of capitalist injustice. He saw class division and exploitation as the crucial fault of capitalism, and the adduction of community might diminish the force of such criticism. For much the same reason, neo-Marxists have not utilized his insights into capitalist unity.[39] As Samuelson writes, "Marx did do original work in analyzing patterns of circular interdependency among industries. Such work gains few converts and is not very helpful in promoting revolution . . ."[40] Well, such may have been the presumption, but Samuelson, like the neo-Marxists, failed to perceive that circular interdependency implies some community and that community can have egalitarian moral implications.

The demonstration that community exists in capitalist economies could invoke an egalitarian ethics of community that revives the moral criticism of capitalist injustice. Community can provide a moral foundation for a principle of equal distribution of some income, because membership in a community intuitively warrants sharing. Most theo-

38. It should be recognized that both inequality and equality are the effect of heavy legal interventions in the economy.
39. One exception to this is Gould 1978.
40. Samuelson 1957, p. 911.

rists, like Kant, who think a principle of equal distribution is morally entailed by community nevertheless reject equal distribution *of income*. They oppose it because they reject the premise that economic community exists, while acknowledging that community has egalitarian entailments if it does exist. By demonstrating the existence of a dimension of community within the economy, my analysis provides grounds for invoking a principle of equalization of some income.

While Marx was the preeminent theorist of class division, he also contributed enormously to the theory of the unity of the capitalist economy. Although he would have rejected an ethics of economic community for capital-based market systems, his work provides much of the necessary logical foundation for it. One of the lesser known facts about Marx is that he contributed greatly to the foundations of the theory of the unity of the capitalist economy.[41] Marx first conceptualized capitalist production as the unity of capital and labor: "For production to go on at all," he wrote, "they must unite."[42] It is he who first recognized that labor is a form of capital, and that labor produces commodity products as an element of capital, hence that they are engaged in common action.[43] Marx's theory of circulation posited the unity of all individual capitals through connecting links between the circuits of all individual capitals.[44] Laborers who become part of a particular commodity production implicitly form part of the wider social unity, through the firm's relation to the whole system of producers. When we couple this conception of the (partial) unity of the capitalist economy with another proposition, that membership in a community morally entails equal distribution, his thought provides the ethics of community with a necessary premise for the justification of some significant egalitarian redistribution.

CONCLUSION

This study calls into question the modern or neoclassical view that labor and capital are entirely distinct and competitive categories of economic actors. They share a deep commonality as members of a system of capital-based economic relations, and so their alternative purposes are just one dimension of the character of their ends. Analysis shows that there is neither a complete lack of community, nor a full community, but

41. On this see Gould 1978; 1988.
42. Marx 1967b, p. 34.
43. Ibid., p. 35.
44. Marx 1956, vol. II, pp. 353–354.

rather a dimension of community in these systems. Although far from fully communal, the economy has a greater degree and kind of community than even contemporary communitarians suggest. Beyond the subcommunities within the firm that communitarians see between capital owners and laborers, there is a dimension of community on a systemic scale in the economy. In contrast to the neoclassical view of an indirect and unintended common interest, this study shows that a common end – the preservation and expansion of capital – is the direct object of both labor and capital, whether intended or not, as a result of the social structuring of productive activity in accordance with this end. The interrelationship between capital owners and laborers in a system of interrelated circuits of capital is found to constitute a dimension of system-wide common action, because their actions would be utterly noneconomic upon abstraction from the system. The forms of common action and common ends between capital and labor indicate a dimension of systemwide community in the deep structure of capital-based market systems.

12

The Right to an Equal Share of Part of National Income

LIBERAL PROPERTY OR RIGHT TO AN EQUAL SHARE OF PART OF NATIONAL INCOME?

The dimension of community running through economic society has ramifications for the just way of distributing property. When incorporated into moral reasoning, it entails a rule of distribution quite different from the one found in liberal theories. Its distributive implications can be seen by substituting it in Kant's reasoning about property and distribution.

"Men" in their original condition (a state of nature), Kant reflects, are faced with the dilemma that they benefit from living together but that their unregulated interactions can also do them harm.[1] The problem can be solved, they discover, by uniting for the purpose of living under conditions of right. The union thus formed is the condition known as civil society – not to be confused with an economic community, whose existence Kant denies. The civil union's purpose is to legislate a set of laws that constitute "public right."[2]

The conditions of right in Kant's theory are conditions of freedom that meet criteria of ethical freedom. By implication, the community of right is a union for the sake of living under conditions of ethically valid freedoms. It may also be characterized as a union for the joint goal of living under conditions where each person can define and pursue his or her own ends, for that is what Kant means by freedom. The moral foundation for the equal entitlement to rights stems from membership with-

1. Kant 1991, pp. 121–122.
2. Ibid., p. 311; Kant 1887, p. 165.

in this sort of union. "In all social contracts," he writes, "we find a union of many individuals for some common end which they all share . . . [A] union as an end in itself in which all *ought to share* . . . is . . . found in a civil state."[3] And, "The members of a Civil Society . . . united for the purpose of legislation . . . are entitled to demand to be treated by all other Citizens with natural Freedom and Equality."[4] This entitlement from community subsumes an equal right of property, because property is a matter of right, since it protects the freedom of will in relation to and over things. When people build stocks of things by freely using them, unequal distribution of property results from their choices. Unequal distribution flows from people's capacity to define their own ends, so it is in line with the very reason that people unite in civil society, and so it is rightful; and thus, from Kant's perspective, it is authorized by the civil union.

Unequal distribution also receives moral support from the nature of the desire for the good and of the pursuit of the good in civil society. Civil society consists, according to Kant, not only of conditions of right, but also of people seeking means to their happiness and to the realization of particular aims and ends. We may refer to the latter activity as the sphere of the good (though Kant does no use this term), as distinct from the conditions of right. Whereas people in the sphere of right legislate the general conditions protective of choice-making capacities, the same people in the sphere of the good define more specific ends, which they seek at their own initiative, within the general framework of rules provided by the sphere of right.

Since the unity that grounds equal entitlements to rights within the sphere of right does not obtain in the sphere of the good, unequal amounts of property are logically and morally consistent with the disunity reigning there. The common will in the former sphere, that everyone should be able to choose his or her own ends, does not carry over to what they will in the sphere of the good. As regards the content and ends of their willing, people differ, rather than agree. "Men have different views of the empirical ends of happiness," Kant writes, "so that so far as happiness is concerned, their will cannot be brought under any common principle."[5]

Kantian civil society includes, then, radically different associations: a community of right that is a union about the general conditions needed

3. Kant 1970, p. 73.
4. Kant 1887, pp. 167–168.
5. Kant 1970, pp. 73–74.

for free choice of ends, and a disunified multitude with regard to the good, involving independent conditions for achieving disparate ends.[6] Disparate ends pursued independently render community alien to the sphere of the good, because it does not contain common ends.

Just as community's presence in the sphere of right entitles members to an equal right to property, its absence from the Kantian sphere of the good nullifies any supposed right to equal amounts of property. Disparate ends and independent pursuits dissipate the necessary communal prerequisites for equalizing means to individuals' ends. For this reason, Kant says the "uniform equality of human beings as subjects of the state is perfectly consistent with the utmost inequality of the mass in the degree of its possessions."[7] People with different goals need different amounts of property to achieve them, so the diversity of goals precludes general agreement about how property should be distributed, and no general rule can be constructed. The upshot of the Kantian combination of a community of right and a disunion regarding goods is classical liberal distributive justice: an equal right to highly unequal amounts of property.

But this view of distributive justice may be called in question, because its underlying presupposition, a disunified economic society, is inaccurate. Since economic society cannot be reduced to a multitude, the Kantian principle of highly unequal distribution, derived from the premise of disunity, is exceedingly vulnerable. While Kant claims that citizens agree only on the procedural conditions of free choice, they actually also agree on a substantive end – creating and acquiring wealth – that is fundamental to economic life. Agreement on this goal indicates agreement with respect to some content of the will, not only with respect to the procedural point that people should define their own ends. That the members of a capital-based market system share the goal of acquiring and creating wealth is indicated by the fact that they do not seek mere biological subsistence afforded by nature. Few, if any, subsist on a biological cocktail of nutrients. Even members of the lower strata of a capitalist economy reveal preferences among many different types of bread and other processed foods, for example, that could only be produced by a system of wealth. The fact that people develop a very wide

6. For a good discussion of the liberal distinction between the right and the good, see Sandel 1982. Kantian civil society may also be characterized as (1) a procedural formal community, since people agree that everyone should have decision rights (over things), and as (2) devoid of substantive community, since people disagree on the ends of decision.
7. Kant 1970, p. 75.

range of needs and interests, far from implying that they have only different ends of happiness, suggests that they have in common needs that are not satisfiable without particles of social wealth. They want televisions, radios, a telephone, McDonald's hamburgers, records, tapes, expensive sneakers and other fashionable garb, among many other things. As evidence of their desire for a portion of social wealth, they not only produce useful items for self-subsistence but also seek a money wage, something that affords them command over a part of the world of commodities, that is, over social wealth. Since the seeking of wealth commonly occurs among the members, including the lower strata, a community of ends forms a dimension of their economic ends.

Against the claimed existence of economic community, one might argue that people pursue a great variety of different ends, not just the end of wealth. You use your wealth to buy a house because you like suburban living, I rent an apartment because I prefer urban living. But the goal of seeking wealth permeates every other goal of economic agents, whatever else they seek. Both an apartment and a house are forms of social wealth, bought and built with particles of social wealth; so they are not merely forms of natural shelter. The common goal of wealth, permeating different particular ends, substantiates a claim that a dimension of community pervades the economy.

The unity of civil society obtains not only with respect to an overarching goal, but also with respect to the underlying structure of action. At one level people seem to be engaged in independent careers, vocations, jobs, and tasks of all sorts. Beneath this level, different activities are interwoven in a single sequence of actions comprising a structure of common action. To acquire a share of wealth, economic actors have to take part in an integrated process of circulation of commodities and money, which consists in an interconnected sequence of actions. The particles of wealth sought by all are only obtainable with some cooperation, for the task of generating wealth requires some common action on a systemic scale. Civil society is therefore a complex reality where the multitude is interlaced by a thread of community when everyone seeks an overarching common end through some common action on a systemic scale.

The dimension of economic community indicated by commonalities in economic ends and actions supplies a communal basis for demanding equal distribution of part of national income. It does not, however, morally warrant equalization of all national income, because the economy is not entirely communal.

If union with regard to conditions for choosing one's own ends equally entitles members to the right of property, then union for the pursuit and acquisition of wealth must entitle them to equal distribution of part of national income, proportionate to the extent of community. Conversely, if the communal dimension of the system of wealth does not give everyone a right to equal distribution of part of national income, then the union regarding the conditions of choice does not entitle members equally to the right of property. Though they are often viewed as contradictory ideals, there cannot be equal entitlement to property unless there is an entitlement to an equalized portion of part of national income, for these rights' moral legitimation flows from the same source: community, albeit of different sorts. They stand or fall together.

The idea of a right to an equalized portion of national income may be put in question by the apparent fact that some people do not seek wealth, which undermines the claimed community of economic ends requisite for this right. Many people are content with a comfortable or decent living, rather than manifesting a supposedly general craving for wealth; in fact they may reject the seeking of wealth as excessive, garish, or materialistic. This counterargument, however, misunderstands wealth's nature, and it leads to a false denial of the generality of the pursuit of wealth, on which the community of ends hinges. Although some in capital-based market economies are purportedly uninterested in wealth, they are not content with mere subsistence. They want a sort of abundance, perhaps not that associated with being "wealthy," but something very much more than mere subsistence, even if a limousine and a penthouse are not their way. The seemingly modest requirements for "comfort" – like an automobile, refrigerator, toaster oven, television, stereo equipment, processed foods of manifold varieties, microwave oven, clothes of considerable variety, furniture of various sorts, vacations, restaurants, computers, books, leisure for study or recreation, college education, movies, graduate school education, internet connections, highly advanced medical treatment – result from a prodigious system of wealth generation, whose products are parcels of wealth. That an immense accumulation of commodities is needed to satisfy quantitatively and qualitatively multiplied wants shows how little the term "comfort" conveys about the average person's objectives in economic society. Wealth is, quite clearly, the only appropriate term to designate the amount and diversity of stuff under consideration.[8] Since everyone in a capital-based market system seeks wealth in the sense just described,

8. There is strong precedent for the proposed definition of wealth in a neglected usage of the term by classical political economists and by Marx, for whom wealth meant a vast accumulation of commodities. Wealth in this sense is not just the abundance that goes to the rich, and it is not limited to a particular category of goods, such as luxuries, consumed by the rich, but is a general cate-

a community of economic ends exists within the economic system. The communal basis for a right of equalization of a part of national income is thus also in evidence.

Kant correctly observes that people have different ends of happiness, but this observation does not necessarily warrant his conclusion that there cannot be a community of ends of happiness. One may, therefore, doubt his further assertion that difference reduces economic society to disunity. In conception, different ends of happiness can coexist with a common end of happiness, just as particular species can be subsumed under a genus. The common end of wealth may be thought of as an overarching end that subsumes different ends of happiness. In economic reality, the desire for a car, television, or fiberglass sailboat are all particular cases of the general goal of seeking particles of social wealth, not just subsistence. Different preferences for goods are variations on a theme about happiness as involving wealth. The common theme of happiness as involving wealth – that is, the theme of wanting much more than means of subsistence – implies that the ends of happiness are unified at a higher level of abstraction, with different preferences being subsumed under a common perspective on the dominant end of economic life.

If Kant is correct that a union for the sake of living under conditions

gory referring to the wealth of the nation. As the multiplication of the kinds and numbers of goods of all sorts, wealth is the means to the satisfaction of a multiplication of kinds and numbers of needs. When Smith said that the accommodation of an industrious peasant is not significantly less than that of a European prince, he was thinking of wealth as a broad category of goods sought by all members of "civilized" society – his term for a system of wealth; Smith 1937, p. 12. He thought it was meaningful to speak of a system of wealth, not merely of a wealthy class, because the working class share in the general advance, despite inequalities. (The evidence supports Smith on this point; see Phelps Brown 1988, p. 324.) Though the desire to be "wealthy" has come to mean an aspiration to join the upper class in consuming luxuries, professional economists should not, in my view, restrict the term to this limited category of goods, because it causes them to lose sight of an essential fact about wealth: that wealth, being an immense accumulation of commodities, is the capacity to satisfy much more than subsistence needs on the part of most or all citizens. The pursuit of wealth, in this sense, has evident universality among the members of civil society. Some people may use wealth for frivolous purposes, but social wealth is vital to self-realization and individuality, which everyone in the system of wealth seeks; so wealth is a common end. With wealth understood as something that satisfies more than subsistence, the system of wealth exhibits a community of ends, and it provides a communal underpinning for the right of egalitarian redistribution.

of freedom warrants equal entitlement to rights, while disunion about the ends of happiness precludes a principle of equal distribution of property, then the common end of happiness, which I have adduced, must justify equal distribution of part of national income. Economic society has the communal composition morally warranting this equalization because (1) wealth is a common end, (2) different ends of happiness are subsumed under this end (as an overarching common end), and (3) different pursuits are variations on a theme of happiness as involving wealth. Economic union must entitle members to some income equalization, if the union to protect conditions of choice equally entitles them to conditions of free will. Another portion of national income should not be equalized. The system of wealth is an overarching community, not a holistic community, and this implies a limit on the extent of community within it, in turn limiting the legitimate degree of income equalization.

Civil society is not a Kantian combination of a union regarding the conditions of free choice and a disunion for the pursuit of different ends of happiness. So property cannot be an equal right to unequal amounts of property. Rather, civil society is (1) a union with regard to the conditions of freedom of choice, (2) an overarching union for the pursuit of wealth, and (3) a concrete multitude seeking different particular aims and ends. Civil society's trichotomous structure implies that property is an equal right to an equal portion of one part of total social income and a right to an unequal portion of another part of this income.

The process of circulation of capital indicates further communal basis for equalizing a portion of national income. In contrast to the Kantian image of a disunified multitude, economic agents are unified in the process of ongoing circulation of capital, as preceding chapters have shown. Producers and consumers, laborers and capital owners/managers create and acquire wealth through an interconnected sequence of actions with the goal of preserving and expanding capital. If a unity of individuals for the sake of living under conditions of right and a disunity with respect to goods justify an equal right to unequal amounts of property, then the union of economic agents within the process of circulation of capital and the common goal of preservation and expansion of capital justify an equal right to an equalization of a portion of national income.[9] Since the

9. Against this theory of property it could be argued that many members of capital-based market systems engage in production for direct use by the immediate producer, rather than production for sale, so they are not entirely engaged in the process of circulation of capital, nor directed toward the preservation of capital as an end. As a result, there is no systemwide common action for a common end

nature of the circulation process indicates that economic agents are united, not only with respect to being able to choose their own ends, but also with respect to an element of what they will (the preservation and expansion of capital), there should be a corresponding equalization of the distribution of property. However, accross-the-board equalization of income is not warranted, because individuals seek different economic ends in relatively independent ways through the overarching economic unity. Kant's proposition that men differ in the empirical ends of happiness failed to consider the process by which they seek their ends. The process of capital circulation orders seemingly independent pursuits of different ends of happiness in accordance with a single principle, preservation and expansion of capital. There is no other basic principle of economic life, such as preference satisfaction or natural subsistence, that takes precedence in their economic lives. Interpolating this into the Kantian formula of entitlement yields the conclusion that individuals, united within a process of circulation of capital for the purpose of preservation and expansion of capital, are entitled to demand an equalization of a portion of national income.

This analysis shows that conclusions about the just distribution of property can be altered by changing only one component of liberal property theory. Most of Kant's reasoning from premises has been retained, particularly his view that membership in a community confers equal entitlement to rights and that a disunifed multitude does not. In view of this, a Kantian is logically bound to accept the new conclusion after the original premise has been refuted and replaced.

that could morally ground a right of equalization of some income. But I do not think that we should define a capital-based market system as one that consists partly of production for direct use and partly of production for sale. Countries such as India and Pakistan, where production for direct use accounts for a major part of productive activity, are only partially developed capitalist systems. Their reliance on production for use makes them systems of poverty, not of wealth. It would be unwise to define the capital-based market system in terms of its undeveloped and failed forms. In a fully developed capital-based market system, production for sale provides the essential dynamic of wealth creation, accounting for the vast bulk of wealth created. Since most productive activities in this system consist of production for sale, they are interwoven as part of a process of circulation of capital, forming a kind of common action that morally supports redistributive rules. Whereas if they were equally composed of production for direct use, economic activity would devolve to the standpoint of the self-subsistent producer, making redistributive justice irrelevant.

WELFARE OR EQUAL SHARES OF PART OF NATIONAL INCOME?

Many twentieth-century liberals believe the classical liberal system of rights falls short of economic justice. Beyond traditional rights of property and freedom of contracts, economic justice also requires entitlements such as welfare and antipoverty programs, unemployment insurance, social security, and forms of national health insurance. To spread the cost of governmental operations more fairly, modern liberals also advocate inheritance taxes and progressive income taxes.

Some analysts view the welfare state as an egalitarian response to the inequities of unregulated capitalist markets. They see egalitarianism in the provision of a safety net that protects the welfare of the worst off and prevents them from falling into the depths of poverty. Welfare policies may be motivated by genuine humanitarian sentiments, but they do not, in my view, have a particularly egalitarian purpose or consequence. They may offset the affront to human dignity that poverty presents, but they do not necessarily increase the degree of economic equality and, when they do, they may not increase it by very much.

Welfare is an income transfer to the poor that raises money incomes or consumption to the "poverty line" or marginally above it. But just as laying a floor does not govern the height of a room, setting a minimum income does not limit the height of the income hierarchy. When the government sets a minimally decent standard of living it does not define or achieve an acceptable level of income inequality.[10] Without altering per capita benefits, income inequality can rise, fall, or stay the same within a given welfare state, depending on changes in many variables.[11] During the 1980s in the United States, the top one percent of families increased their share of the growth of national income to sixty percent after taxes despite hundreds of billions of dollars spent on a variety of social welfare programs.[12] Since the raison d'être of welfare policy is poverty reduction, not the achievement of an acceptable level of income inequality, it should be designated humanitarian rather than egalitarian.

The right to equal distribution of part of national income differs from welfare entitlements in the sense that it seeks to define not just a minimum, but an ethically valid degree of income equality; so this right is

10. Danziger, Sandefur, and Weinberg 1994, pp. 27, 55.
11. The degree of income inequality will vary depending on the status of other variables, such as the rate of economic growth (Danziger, Sandefur, and Weinberg 1994, p. 52).
12. Danziger, Sandefur, and Weinberg 1994, p. 9; Burtless 1994, p. 52.

egalitarian in purpose. It requires a reduction in market-generated inequalities of income that would be implemented through governmental or societal adjustment of market incomes on an ongoing basis. Though redistribution would not be carried to the point of equalizing all of national income, the right of partial equalization is truly egalitarian, rather than just a poverty-reducing measure, because it reduces the gap between all strata: between the lower strata and the middle and upper strata, and between the middle and the upper strata, not just between the lower strata and the others.

With the transformation from classical liberalism to the welfare state, modern liberals believed that Western political economies had established a basic structure that was as just as any attainable in the real world. But the classical system was blighted, not only by poverty, but also by extreme inequalities of income that the welfare state did not end, as we have seen. If such inequality is unjust, then the welfare state has not fully overcome the distributive injustice of the classical system. Then the question is, does economic justice require only a set of welfare entitlements, or does it also entail an egalitarian approach that levels the distribution of part of national income?

Some modern liberals argue for the welfare state on the basis of an enhanced recognition of community, among other grounds for it. They hold that classical liberals did not sufficiently appreciate community within the political economy and that a proper regard for community in civil society obligates the state to protect indigent members of society through a set of entitlements to welfare, not just to property rights. But while it may be more communitarian than classical liberalism, modern liberalism may not grasp the full extent of community in the economy, which can have implications for the adequacy of welfare state entitlements.

The adequacy of the entitlements provided by the welfare state hinges partly on the nature and extent of community in the economy. Entitlements should be commensurate with the character of the community they are morally derived from. Are the entitlements provided by the welfare state proportionate to the extent of community in the economy? If the economic community is of different kind and greater extent than modern liberals realize, as the preceding chapters have suggested, then it has to be considered that the welfare state needs to be supplemented or replaced by egalitarian rules more appropriate to this community.

It is difficult to define the liberal "paradigm" regarding community and its implications for distribution, since modern liberal theories vary in their exposition of these matters. The thought of John Maynard Keynes can, however, provide a good example of one important approach to community and its moral implications for distributive rules.[13] He works out the conception of community more concretely than Rawls does, and he then gives it a greater role in deducing rules of distributive justice.

Keynes opposes some of the inequalities within the classical system. "The outstanding faults of the economic society in which we live," he writes, "are its failure to provide for full employment and its arbitrary and inequitable distribution of wealth and incomes." These intolerable inequalities stem, in his view, from the philosophy and practice of capitalistic individualism.[14] "The world will not much longer tolerate," he declares, "the unemployment which . . . is inevitably associated with capitalistic individualism."[15] Keynes clearly rejects the elements of capitalistic individualism that give rise to objectionable forms of inequality, particularly the inequality between employed and unemployed. This implies that Keynes thinks that there are communal grounds in political economy that can justify a reduction in this inequality. He goes on to discuss several different kinds or facets of community within capital-based market systems that morally and practically warrant some equalities in distribution.[16]

One form of community seen by Keynes is a union for the sake of employment. This term does not appear in his text, but one can infer

13. Rawls's theory of justice would be the more obvious choice because of its great influence in contemporary thought. But, as Sandel points out, Rawls's analysis of community suffers from abstraction, internal inconsistency, and from the fact that it is often "couched in metaphor," mixed metaphor, and "uncertain imagery" (Sandel 1982, p. 151). Keynes's treatment of community has the advantage of being written with greater precision of meaning and internal consistency.
14. Keynes 1964, p. 381.
15. Ibid.
16. Sandel maintains that Keynes justifies regulation "in the name of the voluntarist conception of freedom" (Sandel 1996, p. 271). I believe that such an interpretation overstates individualistic justifications of regulation in Keynes. And it neglects the fact that Keynes justifies regulation on the bases of the communal nature of the macroeconomy; the role of the communal agency of the state in correcting aggregate variables; and the communal agencies in the macroeconomy (such as "the community's propensity to consume") responsible for the growth of the capital wealth of the nation. The community basis of redistributive governmental policies varies in explicitness at different points of Keynes's discussion, but it is there to be discerned, whether through inference or direct textual evidence.

that he subscribes to such a conception because he rejects the inequality between employed and unemployed arising from capitalistic individualism. Classical liberal political theory does not support the idea of a community for the sake of employment. Kant's view that individuals differ with respect to the ends of happiness implies that they differ about whether or not to work, with some choosing not to work out of laziness or moral turpitude. But Keynes showed that unemployment is structural rather than voluntary. If the unemployed are cast out of work by macroeconomic processes, then the condition of unemployment does not represent a preference for idleness, but rather disappointment about not having a job, which indicates that there may be a community for the sake of employment. This community of ends then provides modern liberals with a moral basis for reducing the inequality between the employed and unemployed, which could be effected through full-employment policies.[17]

There is another facet of community implicit in many modern liberal analyses. They call for welfare when full-employment policies fail and people fall below a minimally decent level of consumption. Although modern economists hold that people's preferences differ, a fact which precludes economic community, they also acknowledge a common denominator underlying people's ends when they support welfare policies on the ground that everyone wants at least a minimally decent level of consumption. So a form of implicit community underlies the liberal justification for welfare. Before the Reagan era and the 104th Congress, even free marketeers like Milton Friedman supported welfare in the form of a negative income tax.[18]

The economic community perceived by modern liberal theory is, however, sharply limited in kind and extent, and very limited entitlements are entailed by it. The thinness of the modern liberal conception of community in the economy is such that it is morally compatible with the extreme inequalities of income permitted by the communityless classical liberal economy. Although modern liberals acknowledge a community for the sake of employment and of a minimally decent standard of living, they continue to subscribe to the bulk of the classical liberal view that people have different ends of happiness. They believe that people have different views of the ends of employment and different views of the ends of consumption above a social minimum, which implies that community does not obtain with respect to the particular ends of

17 Keynes 1964, Chapter 24.

18. Friedman 1962, pp. 190–202. Friedman says he "accepts . . . governmental action to alleviate poverty." The only question is "how much and how" (p. 191).

employment or to the ends of consumption above subsistence. Since modern liberals do not see any community in these regards, they do not believe that the will of employed persons can be brought under a common principle regarding how income should be distributed among them. It also follows that the wills of consumers cannot be brought under a common principle regarding how to distribute income among persons consuming above subsistence. The only common principles concerning relative distribution that modern liberal theory admits are those regarding some redistribution of income between the employed and the unemployed and regarding the distribution of a minimally decent consumption. The predominant feature of the modern liberal conception of the economy, disunity, provides a philosophical justification for unlimited inequalities of income between individuals who are consuming above subsistence.[19]

The theory of community offered in previous chapters clearly has a bearing on the validity of the liberal welfare state conception of community and the principles of distribution based upon it. Contrary to theories of the welfare state, Chapters 8–11 have shown that economic actors are united not just for the sake of employment or a minimally decent income. They are united also with respect to a larger share of the economic resources of society. They are united for the sake of the preservation and expansion of the capital of the firm and of the system in its entirety. Given the interdependence of individual pursuits of wealth, there is a unity among them with respect to all of the capital wealth of the nation that is used for consumption. Labor has an interest, not only in a wage, but in all of the capital wealth of the firm and of the nation. Consumers seek not only to satisfy preferences but also to satisfy a multiplication of kinds and numbers of preferences, so they have a common desire for wealth. Analysis of their wants revealed that they have not only a common denominator in wanting at least a minimally decent level of consumption, but also a common denominator with respect to the rest of consumption. This common denominator consists in the quantitative and qualitative multiplication of all consumers' wants, which implies that they have a common desire for wealth. The community of ends is, therefore, much broader than theorists of the welfare state recognize. The consumers' goal of seeking wealth cannot be achieved without their participation in a system of commodity exchange and production based on capital, which has a dimension of common action, since individual circuits of capital are interconnected. Individual action in pursuit of wealth therefore exhibits a dimension of common action. The

19. Keynes 1964, p. 379.

multiplication of wants unites consumers with producers in the circulation process, because this process continues and expands the circulation of capital.

Since economic agents are united with respect to many more economic resources than modern liberal theory realizes, they must, correspondingly, have an equal entitlement to a larger part of economic resources than such theory posits. The unity of capital owners, laborers, and consumers for the sake of the creation and acquisition of capital gives every member an equal entitlement to an equal share of part of the national income devoted to purposes of consumption. They are not just entitled to employment or subsistence, since their unity is not limited to the common pursuit of employment or subsistence. Given the interdependence between individual pursuits of wealth, there is a unity between them with respect to all of the capital wealth of the nation used for consumption. Claims based on membership in this sort of union extend to all of the capital wealth of the nation that is directed toward consumption and that is created by community. This membership does not, however, justify a strict equalization of income, because the overarching unity of economic actors includes a lot of relatively independent action for somewhat separate ends.

There is another major element of economic community in the modern liberal theory of political economy. It consists, according to Keynes, in the fact that communal rather than individual agencies are responsible for much of the growth of the capital wealth of the nation. On the basis of this form of community, Keynes sees a rationale and justification for reducing the inequalities of wealth due to inheritance.

Keynes's analysis challenges the classical view that individualistic factors largely account for the growth of the capital wealth of the nation. The rich were formerly thought to have a greater motivation to save than the poor did, so growth was seen as largely a function of the rich, and it was thought that reductions in inequality would impede growth. Countering this view, Keynes argues that growth is due, not mainly to "the motivations toward individual saving" among the wealthy, but also significantly to the "community's propensity to consume," which is an aggregate variable, not an individual agency.[20] Moreover, this variable is not simply an aggregate of individual propensities, but has deeper communal significance because it is formed through the causal influence of other communal agencies, such as the state (a communal agency, in Keynes's mind). The state can increase the community's propensity to consume by legislating redistributory taxes, such as "death taxes," that

20. Ibid., pp. 372–373.

is, inheritance taxes. These taxes are tantamount to an income transfer to the lower strata; they permit the government to fund its operations while reducing taxes on the lower strata. Inheritance taxes put more money into the hands of those who are apt to spend it rather than save it, and they thereby increase the community's propensity to consume. There is then an expansion of business activity in response to increased demand (itself communally generated in part), which leads to the augmentation of the capital wealth of the nation. Thus Keynes gives a liberal communal account of economic growth.

By refuting the view that economic growth depends primarily on wealthy individuals' motivations to save, Keynes claimed to have removed "one of the chief . . . justifications of great inequality of wealth."[21] The role of communal causes in economic growth gives the state both moral and rational grounds for redistributive policies, particularly inheritance taxes, and for the reductions in inequality of wealth between economic strata that these policies entail.

Although Keynes supports a reduction in inequalities of wealth due to inheritance, he opposes redistributory policies that would reduce the inequality of income *among the employed*. In this respect, the liberal theory of the welfare state condones the extreme inequality previously accepted in classical theories of relatively unregulated capitalist markets. The different ways in which Keynes treats inequalities of wealth and income spring from the different kinds of causal agency he sees as producing wealth and income, one communal, the other individualistic. Since the growth of the nation's capital wealth stems from communal agencies in the macroeconomy, there should be redistribution of wealth, according to Keynes; whereas unequal incomes arise from individualistic factors in the microeconomy, so they should not be subject to redistribution. In Keynes's view, the individualistic causes of unequal income provide rationale and justification for differential reward.

Keynesian principles of distributive justice emerge from a dual view of the economy. The macroeconomy, consisting in a community, supplies moral and rational justification for redistributing some wealth: the wealth arising within the macroeconomy. The microeconomy is not a community, and there is, therefore, no moral or rational basis for redistributing incomes earned in the microeconomy. Keynes's attempt to restrict redistributory policy to the matter of wealth and to leave inequalities of income relatively unfettered hinges on his contention that the microeconomy is a disunified multitude that lacks the communal

21. Ibid., p. 373.

characteristics of the macroeconomy. If the microeconomy displayed a dimension of community, it would justify redistributory and egalitarian income policies, just as community in the macroeconomy justifies inheritance taxes. The question of just distributive principles then comes down to the question of whether Keynes is right about the microeconomy's noncommunal character. If he is not, the lack of egalitarian income distribution in the welfare state may be wrongful.

As viewed by Keynes, the economy is a certain admixture of community and individualism, consisting in a shell of community containing a subsphere of individualism. It is, more specifically, a macroeconomic community and a microeconomic multitude. The communal shell consists in the general environment of business. Individual enterprises and consumers operate within the general environment set by aggregate variables, such as the "community's propensity to consume" and the aggregate volume of output. As the language of the "community's propensity to consume" suggests, Keynes thinks of these aggregate variables as communal agencies within the economy. The communal shell is also comprised of the adjustment of the aggregate variables by the communal agency of the state. Within this shell lies a large subsphere of private action for self-interest involving microeconomic decisions about what to produce and what to consume, and how much of each. "If we suppose the volume of output to be given, i.e. to be determined by forces outside the classical scheme of thought," Keynes writes, "then there is no objection to be raised against the classical analysis of the manner in which private self-interest will determine what in particular is produced, in what proportions the factors of production will be combined to produce it, and how the value of the final product will be distributed between them . . ."[22]

Though some redistribution can be justified because of macroeconomic community, it should be kept limited, in Keynes's view, because community has a secondary place in the economy. "[M]ost of the economic life of the community" is not subject to state allocation and redistribution, because private action for self-interest is the greater part of the economy.[23] Personal choice" and "personal initiative" contribute to the efficient growth of capital by keeping productive factors well employed. They are also to be prized because they contribute to the goal of human diversity. So "there is no more reason to socialize economic life than there was before," Keynes argues.[24] The significant scope of individual-

22. Ibid., p. 379.
23. Ibid., p. 378.
24. Ibid., p. 379.

ism within the economy justifies a significant amount of inequality, in his view. "For my own part," Keynes holds, "there is social . . . justification for significant inequalities of income and wealth."[25] In other words, the outcomes of microeconomic decisions should not be subject to redistribution, because community does not penetrate the microeconomy.

Putting in doubt the Keynesian view of the economy and its redistributory implications, Chapters 8–11 have shown a dimension of economic community extending across the microeconomy, not just across the macroeconomy. Individual choices about what to produce, in what proportions the factors of production should be combined, and what to consume are not unlimited. They are decided in accordance with the requirements for the preservation and expansion of capital. Therefore, a common end infuses decisions in the microeconomy. Behaviors activated by these decisions are not entirely independent or separate, but constitute a connected sequence of actions composing a circulation of capital. A dimension of common action, therefore, pervades the microeconomy.

Since the microeconomy is permeated by a dimension of common action for a common end, its members are entitled to an equalization of some of the income generated by microeconomic decisions. If the economy consisted of a macroeconomic community and a microeconomic multitude, then Keynes would be correct that income inequalities due to microeconomic decisions should not be reduced. But the finding that community penetrates to the level of the microeconomy calls for a deeper equalization. If one accepts, as Keynes does, that community in the macroeconomy justifies a reduction in inequalities, then one is logically bound to accept an equalization of additional inequalities if a dimension of community exists in the microeconomy. The equalization should be proportionate to the degree of community in the microeconomy. Strict equalization of all income is not called for, however, since people vary in the particular ways that they contribute to the dominant end of economic life.

Consider the microeconomic decisions of the consumer in the choice of a consumption bundle. Which goods he or she buys can be affected by the endogenous formation of preferences. The ingenuity and good taste of the producer or the alluring advertisements prepared by the advertising agency can increase the marginal utility to the consumer of one firm's goods relative to another firm's goods. This can injure particular firms while increasing the efficiency of capital in general, thereby

25. Ibid., p. 374.

advancing the interests of capital as a whole. The multiplication of wants through endogenous processes can increase the quantity of goods that the consumer will buy. This can increase the demand not only for the products of a particular firm, but also for the sector or for the industrial system generally. As a result of these determinations, consumer decisions in the microeconomy reflect – and are oriented toward – the same end that producers have: the preservation and expansion of the capital of the firm and of the system of firms. In this respect, there is a community of ends in the microeconomic decisions of consumers and producers.

As a result of the multiplication of consumer wants, consumer behavior becomes a sustaining moment in the process of circulation of capital. When the consumer with multiplied preferences decides to buy the products of a particular firm, she becomes an integral part of the circulation of capital of that firm. And, due to the interlocking of individual circuits of capital, she also becomes an integral part of the process of circulation of capital in its entirety. The actions of consumers and producers interconnect into a sequence of actions, producing a dimension of common action between producers and consumers *in the microeconomy.*

In deciding the proportions in which factors of production should be combined, the capital owner aims at the preservation and expansion of capital, which initially appears to be solely in his own self-interest. But the growth of a firm's capital has many qualities of a joint goal shared by laborers, managers, and capital owners. For one, wages, salaries, and profits all come out of firm capital, and they are limited by the extent of that capital. Labor has an interest in the maintenance of the firm's capital because the magnitude of the wage is a function of the firm's capital, so labor has an interest in the maximization of the firm's revenue. The capitalist's profits come out of revenue, and he has an interest in maximizing the revenue of the firm. The immediate interest of the capitalist in revenue maximization may be to increase his own profits, but the capital owner cannot keep all of the revenue to himself because he cannot produce the product by himself, so the goal of revenue maximization has elements of a common goal.

The manner in which income shares are distributed in a capitalist economy is often unfair, because in this economy ownership confers control, including the right to distribute shares unfairly. But the fact that the interests of labor are often harmed to some degree in a capitalist economy does not mean that the preservation and expansion of the firm's capital is not a joint goal of labor and capital. Rather, the jointness of the production process and the jointness of the interest in the expansion of capital is being prevented from full realization. The proper conclusion to be drawn is not that the process lacks any communal dimension but that its communal character should be taken into account when it comes to distribution, so that distribution will better reflect the truly communal dimension of the process.

A dimension of common ends and common actions within the microeconomic decisions and actions of the capital owner extend beyond the members of the firm to the system of capitals and the laborers within those firms. Since "the circuits of individual capitals . . . presuppose one another," as Marx put it, the microeconomic decisions of the capital owner carry out system requisites. In deciding what to make and how to make it, the capital owner has to take into account the production needs of other firms (if she wants to sell them commodity products), and the capital owner can only produce what they need if she takes into account what other firms can provide in the way of means of production. So the microeconomic decisions of the capital owner promote those individuals' capital and, therefore, the laborers in those firms. Although the capital owner intends self-gain, the circumstances of decision are conditioned so that she can only preserve and expand firm capital in ways that promote the circuits of other capitals and the laborers in those firms who get a wage out of capital. Microeconomic decisions within a system of interdependent generation of capital are socially conditioned by and within the system of commodity exchangers and producers so that they help to preserve and expand the capital of the system in its entirety.

Marx evidently recognized a dimension of community between labor and capital in their microeconomic decisions when he maintained that workers would not operate the labor process any differently than capitalists if they owned the means of production. His contention suggests that there is some community of purpose between labor and capital, otherwise labor would run things differently upon assuming control. Marx writes,

> Let us now return to our would-be capitalist. We left him just after he had purchased, in the open market, all the necessary factors of the labour process; its objective factors, the means of production, as well as its personal factor, labour-power. With the keen eyes of an expert, he has selected the means of production and the kind of labour-power best adapted to his particular trade . . . He then proceeds to consume the commodity, the labour-power he has just bought, . . . , to consume the means of production by his labour. The general character of the labour process is evidently not changed by the fact that the worker works for the capitalist instead of for himself.[26]

26. Marx 1977, p. 291.

In stating that workers would not run the production process differently, Marx is in effect saying that capitalists carry out firm requisites and system requisites for preserving and expanding capital. In this respect capitalists are, therefore, carrying out communal purposes that labor shares. Marx would deny that this constitutes community on the ground that sharp economic inequalities hurt labor and disproportionately advantage capital. But rather than precluding a dimension of economic community, these sharp inequalities reflect the fact that legal institutions outside the economy authorize capital owners to take more than their fair share from a common troth. The economic process has a communal dimension even though the legal process lets capitalists seize more bounty than the nature of the economic process morally warrants.

From the foregoing, it follows that community permeates individual decisions in the microeconomy. Community does not exist just in the Keynesian macroeconomy. There should, then, be an equalization of some of the income generated in the microeconomy. Common action for common ends contributes to the creation of income in the microeconomy, not just in the macroeconomy. Reducing inequalities due to inheritance is justified by community in the macroeconomy, but the latter does not exhaust the form of community in the economy. The dimension of community in the microeconomy morally entails a right to equal distribution of part of national income devoted to consumption.

Part IV

Democracy and Economic Justice

13

Democractic Distributive Justice

> Which Axiom, though received by most, is yet certainly false.
>
> Hobbes

When the majority, through the democratic process, commits a systematic injustice, such as a distributive injustice, is it being undemocratic or simply unjust? If it is undemocratic for a political system to be unjust, then a democracy must be morally committed to substantive justice, as part of what it means to be a democracy. But if it is not undemocratic to violate substantive rights, then a country need be committed only to preserving the electoral procedure in order to be a democracy. Thus, the nature of democracy's relation to justice underlies the central distinction between substantive and procedural democracy.

The essential characteristics of democracy, I argue, include the conditions necessary for attaining not merely political equality and popular consent, but also the primary economic rights of citizens. The concept of substantive democracy is, of course, not unprecedented. Its venerable tradition goes back to Locke's theory, in which the preservation of property is the chief end of democratic government. But while the objections raised to theories of substantive democracy are not insurmountable, procedural approaches have predominated the period from which we are emerging, and democracy's links to substantive rights have become obscure and uncertain. We therefore need to examine these links systematically.

Because there would be little value in introducing a vague and general notion of distributive justice into democratic ideals, I propose instead to synthesize democracy with a specific rule of distributive justice. In particular, I argue that the citizens of a democracy have the right to share equally in a portion of total income and wealth. It follows, then, that the list of defining characteristics of democracy should include the redistributory property right along with the procedural rights. This proposition, too, is not without precedent. In a major liberal theory, Dworkin views democracy as substantive in the sense that it is morally obligated to enforce a principle of equal treatment, and more specifically, a principle of equality of resources.[1] While nominally similar to my proposal, Dworkin's principle subsumes a wide category of unequal distribution that, I believe, is too broad.[2] The redistributory property right rules out a large part of the economic inequality sanctioned by Dworkin's principle of equality of resources, though it does not rule out all income inequality. I question, then, whether his liberal theory fulfills the claim of equal treatment. His theory does not recognize certain equalities in the social nature of persons that morally entail a more egalitarian distribution of income and wealth than is called for by the liberal theory of substantive democracy. My formulation, in contrast, is a "social theory" of substantive democracy, because the "concrete equalities" underlying egalitarian democratic distributive justice have a social origin. By "concrete equalities" I mean equalities in the content of persons' capacities, faculties, and ends, as distinct from the merely abstract equality of persons in having such attributes.

THE STATE OF THE ART

After a procedurally oriented period, mainstream democratic theory is now beginning to recognize substantive aspects of democracy. Polyarchal theory, in its 1980 version, acknowledges substantive rights that the democratic process should not violate. The 1989 version of polyarchal theory notes that procedural rights distribute matters of substance, namely, political resources: "Integral to the democratic process are substantive rights . . . that are often mistakenly thought to be threatened by it."[3] Rawls's new liberal theory of democracy similarly advances

1. Dworkin 1985, p. 196.
2. Another difference between Dworkin's analysis and mine concerns the meaning of the phrase "equality of resources." According to Dworkin 1981, market inequalities that occur after an initial equal distribution of resources are consistent with a principle of equality of resources. Thus "equality of resources" can mean "inequality of resources." In the social theory I propose, "equalization of a portion of income" simply means equalization of a portion of income.
3. Dahl 1989, p. 174.

a substantive view of democracy in the sense that the basic liberties are "not merely formal."[4]

Despite these trends, the procedural emphasis remains dominant in current democratic theory. Polyarchal theory's recognition that the democratic process should not violate fundamental rights is ambivalent because it excludes social and economic rights from the defining characteristics of democracy.[5] Moreover, polyarchal theory (in its 1989 version) does not specify any economic or social rights within the definition of democracy. Rawls's theory of democracy includes basic liberties within the constitutional essentials of a democratic republic, "such as the right to vote and to participate in politics, liberty of conscience, freedom of thought and of association, as well as the protections of law," but not "the principles regulating matters of distributive justice, such as . . . social and economic inequalities."[6]

As procedural theorists become more substantive in analyzing democracy, and theorists of justice become more procedural in doing so, democratic theory remains much the same, for neither orientation is sufficiently substantive to create a substantive theory of democracy. Both address many important questions, but their treatment of the relation between democracy and distributive justice has sometimes been superficial.[7] Construing procedural rights as matters of substance does not add

4. Rawls 1993, pp. 324–327.
5. Dahl 1980, p. 28.
6. Rawls 1993, pp. 324–327. The difference principle remains in the general theory of justice but not necessarily in political liberalism, which allows for variations from general justice; see Rawls 1993, p. 7 n6.
7. Recent studies of the relation between democracy and social justice examine democracy's relationship to the politics of recognition, identity politics, and the politics of difference; see Benhabib 1996. My analysis deals, rather, with democracy's relationship to distributive justice.

   Other works integrate democracy with considerations of distributive justice. Among them are Gould 1988; Simon 1995; Lummis 1996; Warren 1995; and Shapiro 1996. I discuss some of these works in course. Gould's analysis is largely concerned with justifying the extension of democracy to the governance of the economy and economic enterprise. I focus to a greater extent on rules of relative distribution rather than on extending majority rule to other spheres of society. Then I integrate democracy with the rules of distributive justice. In Gould's analysis, there is a distributive rule; she employs a principle of equal positive freedom in guiding moral reasoning about distribution. In this analysis I examine a different principle of distribution – the principle of rewards for economic contributions. For an attempt to unify the social justice and distributive justice paradigms, see Fraser 1997.

a single right to the earlier list of democratic rights. Formulating a genuine theory of substantive democracy requires something more than recasting procedural rights in substantive terms or recognizing the possibility of substantive rights. One way of doing so would be to incorporate into democratic theory additional substantive rights derived from the theory of distributive justice.

As they do in mainstream theory, substantive rights have a somewhat marginal place in the social theory of democracy recently formulated by Habermas. Although his treatment is not congruent with the theories of Rawls and Dahl, it resembles them in including only the procedural aspects (a set of civil rights) in the general definition of democracy, and not including social and economic rights.[8] He justifies different social and economic rights for different republics with different socioeconomic contexts, rendering substantive democracy a relative concept rather than a general one.[9] In my view, however, rule in accord with the redistributory property right is a defining characteristic of all political systems with capital-based market systems that deserve the name democracies. This sort of right is not simply a characteristic of republics with special socioeconomic contexts.

THE INTERNAL RELATIONSHIP BETWEEN DEMOCRACY AND JUSTICE

Some theories of procedural democracy do recognize that justice is part of democracy, but only in the sense that the procedures of political equality form a just distribution of political control over the policy-making process.[10] In theories of substantive democracy, however, justice plays a larger part, and in the social theory of substantive democracy, its internal relation to democracy is especially extensive. At the same time, this theory also maintains that justice is extrinsic to democracy in some ways.

In the pluralistic theory of justice, each sphere of society, such as the family, the market, and the state, constitutes its own sphere of justice.[11] Justice is external to democracy in the sense that each sphere has an independent nature with its own "distributive principles," such as free exchange, desert, need, and equal rights. In another view of democracy, as a "subordinate foundational good," justice is more intrinsic to

8. Habermas 1996, pp. 122–123.
9. Ibid., pp. 389, 391, 403.
10. Dahl 1989, p. 164.
11. Walzer 1983.

democracy, because the ethical rules of each social domain develop within evolving "democratic constraints."[12] Justice is nevertheless external to this democracy because it has only one foundational moral commitment, to itself; all other basic elements of justice fall outside its province. In maintaining that economic and social rights, while integral to justice, are not necessary to the democratic process, recent polyarchal theory reinforces this contemporary tendency to externalize justice.[13] I argue, however, that substantive economic and social rights do play a role within the democratic process, not just in its ends or outcomes (see Chapter 14, pp. 297-298).

In the social theory I propose, democratic rule consists in the maintenance of both substantive rights and procedural rights. This concept derives, first, from the abstract ideal of democracy as a government for the people (not just by the people); for it makes no sense to call a country democratic that rules against its own people. The second underlying principle is that rights have supreme ethical worth,[14] so that their preservation becomes a quintessential element of rule for the people. When democracy consists of rule in accord with rights, substantive rights are part of democracy itself, not merely part of justice broadly considered. Hence more of distributive justice is intrinsic to the social theory of substantive democracy, vis-à-vis the other theories discussed. Procedural democracy only includes justice that deals with the distribution of power. Substantive social democracy also includes the form dealing with income and wealth.

The rationale for substantive democracy is that it is necessary for the realization of justice. Though morally supreme, justice has no authority without democracy. Since its rules are not self-enforcing, justice must come under democracy's dominion in order to be actualized. The social theory of substantive democracy internalizes the purpose of justice when it posits rule in accord with substantive rights. Theories of procedural democracy, which require only the just distribution of power, do not recognize that the purpose of that distribution is to preserve other forms of justice, such as a just distribution of income.

As democracy internalizes justice, and becomes obligated to maintain justice, it acquires many foundational moral commitments from the breadth and depth of justice itself. It no longer has only one basic commitment, to the democratic process itself, as it does in the theory of

12. Shapiro 1994, p. 138.
13. Dahl 1989, p. 167.
14. On the supreme ethical worth of rights, see Winfield 1991, Chapter 9; Winfield 1989, Chapter 9.

democracy as a "subordinate foundational good." Democracy's basic moral commitments, which define its ruling tasks, extend to the many basic freedoms inherent in substantive rights – for example, property rights, which are necessary conditions for freedom of will in relation to things. It has a further obligation to equalize a portion of individual income and personal wealth – an obligation enjoined by two branches of justice, the ethics of dueness for economic contributions and the ethics of economic community.

In one sense, however, justice is external to democracy. It is an expansive notion involving many categories of ethically valid forms of freedom. Considered narrowly, democracy is simply political freedom. So one cannot deduce the content of each substantive right from the concept of democracy alone. Rather, it must be deduced from a theory of freedom specific to the social domain in which this freedom subsists. The theory of property rights, for example, derives less from the requirements of political freedom than from the requirements of freedom of property owners and exchangers in civil society.

SUBSTANTIVE SOCIAL DEMOCRACY AND WELFARE DEMOCRACY

In the social theory of substantive democracy, redistribution goes beyond the welfare state's commitment to meeting basic needs. Instead of simply entitling citizens to welfare, this form of democracy upholds a "redistributory property right," that is, each citizen's right to an equalized portion of income and personal wealth. The substantive social democracy puts this right into effect through redistributory laws and legislation, using the tax system to apportion part of total individual income equally among all citizens after each market period. Unlike a welfare state, this form of government can alleviate poverty without exhausting its redistributory responsibilities. Only when this type of democracy equalizes a substantial portion of individual income does it fulfill its redistributory charge. In this sense, the substantive social democracy strives toward a partially egalitarian economic order, not merely a welfare system; but it need not institute a strictly egalitarian order. With respect to the portion of individual income not subject to redistributory ethics, market-generated inequalities prevail.

In a welfare democracy, the guarantee of means to meet basic needs involves the redistribution of subsistence. The substantive social democracy, however, redistributes wealth in relation to general needs. Some of these needs may not be basic, but they are important to the people concerned, who seek to satisfy multiple needs, not just fixed natural needs.[15] In equalizing a portion of income through laws, legislation, and procedures, redistributive democracy reduces differentials, effectively checking extreme disparities. While the least advantaged will be the major beneficiaries, redistribution will also have an equalizing effect on the relative positions of the lower class and the middle class, the middle class and the upper class, and the lower class and the upper class.

Redistribution is the major means of equalizing some individual income, but it is not the only one. In substantive social democracy, the economy would be organized to produce wealth using partially egalitarian methods. The market would be preserved, but the incentives relied on to increase productivity would be modified. As Keynes insightfully suggests, "There are valuable human activities which require the motive of money-making and the environment of private wealth-ownership for their full fruition. . . . But it is not necessary for the stimulation of these activities . . . that the game should be played for such high stakes. . . . Much lower stakes will serve the purpose equally well, as soon as the players are accustomed to them."[16] Contemporary Japanese capitalism affords a powerful example of the productive potential of moderate differentials. In Japanese society, a top professor of economics at the University of Tokyo makes little more than an elementary schoolteacher, and a executive makes only about three times more, yet the workforce is wonderfully industrious and talented.[17]

While a reduction of differentials (at least over some individual income) may diminish the motivational force of rewards, the substantive social democracy cannot depend on sharp differentials to generate wealth. Its principles of just equalization mandate other ways of stimu-

15. On the notion of needy individuals as seekers of means to the satisfaction of a multiplication of needs, and therefore as seekers of wealth, see Levine 1977, Chapter 1, "The Science of Wealth."

16. Keynes 1964, p. 374.

17. The official income, that is, the income before benefits and deductions, of a top Japanese professor at the leading university in that country was 523,828 yen monthly in 1994. That of an elementary schoolteacher in 1998 was 465,088 yen monthly. In Japan, teachers and professors are paid according to age. The figures presented from 1998 and 1994 approximately equate the ages of these two men, as the professor is three years older than the schoolteacher. At the start of his career, an elementary schoolteacher actually makes greater income than a university professor. By the end of their careers the situation is reversed. But the lifetime earnings of the university professor may not exceed those of the schoolteacher because of the former's extra years in graduate school.

An executive's salary is supplemented by a chauffeured car and a substantial expense account, which do, however, involve the expenditure of the executive's own time.

lating productive activity, and disallow Rawls's assumption that extreme inequalities are just because they improve the welfare of the worst off. "Moral incentives" may lessen the impact of lowered rewards on productive effort.[18] The Japanese case also shows that egalitarian distribution can strongly motivate a workforce.[19]

The main features of substantive social democracy emerge when it is compared to the welfare democracy that Rawls advocates. His political economy is based on two principles: (1) equal basic liberties coupled with the stipulation that political liberties must have equal worth for all citizens, and (2) an arrangement of social and economic inequalities intended to raise the absolute position of the worst off (the "difference principle").[20] These provisions, Rawls maintains "express an egalitarian form of liberalism."[21]

Citizens cannot exercise their basic liberties equally if their basic needs are unsatisfied, so Rawls's first principle presupposes the redistribution of a minimum of income and wealth. This sort of redistribution need not involve reducing the disparity in means among economic strata. Guaranteeing the fair value of the political liberties is not a redistributory measure at all, much less an egalitarian one. Rather, the policies it entails, such as the public financing of elections, work by insulating political parties from large corporations.[22] A Rawlsian democracy addresses economic inequality by carrying out the difference principle. It improves the absolute position of the least advantaged, but not necessarily through redistribution, and indications are that it would not do so through egalitarian redistribution. It fact, it sets forth conditions that justify widening disparities. A social democracy, by contrast, administers an egalitarian redistribution of a portion of individual income.

THEORY OF SUBSTANTIVE DEMOCRACY

Democracy and Rule for the People

As conventionally defined, democracy includes the following rights:

1. the right to free speech
2. the right to vote
3. the right to freedom of inquiry and expression

18. See Carens 1981, pp. 94-95.
19. Reich 1984, pp. 20, 16; Oppenheim 1992, pp. 28, 200–201; Vogel 1987, p. 165.
20. Rawls 1993, p. 6. 21. Ibid. 22. Ibid., p. 328.

4. the right to alternative sources of information
5. the right to seek public office
6. the right to free and fair elections
7. the right to form and join secondary associations
8. the right to a government responsive to the preferences of the demos.

Note that there are no economic rights on this list. This exclusion reflects a deep-seated conviction that democracy consists in political equality and popular sovereignty, without regard to economic justice.[23]

According to the social theory of substantive democracy, however, a political system does not qualify as a democracy unless it brings about a just economic order as well.[24] By implication, the standard list of democratic rights is incomplete because it lacks the conditions of economic justice.

This conclusion derives from the essential notion of democracy as rule of, by, and for the people.[25] A political order cannot realize rule for the people unless it maintains conditions of economic justice. A government that supports an unjust economic order is wronging the people rather than ruling for them. Therefore, the defining characteristics of democracy must include economic rights along with the primary political rights.

Since property rights are a large part of economic justice, and therefore also of rule for the people, a democracy must preserve them. They are crucial because they make possible individual freedom of will in relation to and over things. Although they lack the redistributory provisions necessary for a just economic order, even such an order requires property rights, without which people could not exercise control over redistributed resources, free from interdiction by others.

A democracy has no obligation to maintain unethical forms of property, however. States that permit unequal forms of property, such as the ownership of other persons, violate economic justice and warp "rule for the people." The obligation to rule in accord with rights requires a democracy only to maintain ethically valid forms of property. The ethically valid form of this right consists partly in a right to an equalization

23. Dahl 1979; 1980; 1989; 1976, p. 45; Lindblom 1977, p. 133. Certain economic conditions are mentioned as external, empirical, facilitating preconditions for democracy, but not as parts of the defining characteristics of democracy.
24. As far as may be possible, that is.
25. On the relation between democracy and rule for the people, see Zucker 1990, vol. I, Chapter 10; Simon 1995.

of some individual income, as I have argued in Parts II and III. The redistributory property right also seems to be consistent with the ethics of economic freedom.[26] From the three foregoing propositions – that democracy consists in rule for the people, that rule for the people involves maintenance of economic justice, and that the redistributory property right is ethically valid – it follows that the redistributory property right is a defining characteristic of democracy. No procedurally democratic system that fails to recognize and protect it qualifies fully as a democracy.

Substantive rights are not simply empirical preconditions of democracy, as they are in polyarchal theory, where dispersed inequalities of income and wealth are regarded as "favorable" to the development of democracy but not essential to the meaning of democracy.[27] In the social theory, substantive rights are constitutive of democracy, not merely conducive to it. And thus they are more central to democratic ideas than polyarchal theory supposes.

Democracy and Redistributive Property Rights

Theories of substantive democracy have often been effectively empty because they do not specify the rights that democracy should maintain. Madisonian theory, for example, defines a nontyrannical republic as one that involves no severe deprivation of a natural right, and Dahl has criticized that theory for failing to specify the natural rights to be preserved.[28] Polyarchal democratic theory in its recent, more substantive versions (e.g. Dahl 1980) has become vulnerable to similar objections.[29] By excluding primary social and economic rights, it too becomes effectively empty (see Chapter 14, pp. 287-291). Difficulties in specifying substantive rights lead some theorists to conclude that substantive democracy inevitably lacks operational meaning.[30]

There are, however, two ways by which one could arrive at a con-

26. Zucker (1990) examines the relationship between the redistributory property right and the concept of freedom. The present work does not explore in any detail the deduction of the redistributory property right in accordance with the concept of freedom. That sort of justificatory argument is distinct from the ethics of contributions and the ethics of community. The freedom-based deduction of redistributory property forms one of the major areas for subsequent research into the ethical validity of this right and of substantive democracy.
27. Dahl 1989, p. 252; Dahl 1971, Chapters 5 and 6.
28. Dahl 1956, pp. 7, 23–24.
29. Dahl 1980.
30. Dahl 1956, Chapters 1 and 3.

cretely meaningful theory of substantive democracy. One is to formulate a "decision rule" through which citizens could define their rights.[31] The second method, which has certain advantages, is to deduce a right through a course of reasoning.[32] One can specify a redistributory property right, for example, through the following thought process:

1. "Dueness" is an element of economic justice that provides an ethical basis for conferring title to property. A person can justly claim title to things that are "due" him or her.
2. The activities for which a person is "due" a benefit are economic contributions, with the degree of dueness corresponding to the amount of those contributions.
3. Economic contributions consist in acts that help create economic value (exchange value) rather than in acts of production alone.
4. Consumer attributes, such as wants and needs, contribute to the creation of economic value (as detailed in Chapter 6), and so consumer activities should be categorized as economic contributions and consumers should receive entitlements under the ethics of dueness.
5. But one cannot understand consumer contributions solely in terms of the neoclassical economic theory of individuals maximizing subjective preferences. Consumer contributions stem from socially self-determined attributes of their wants and needs. Consumers adopt their own attributes, but relations between consumers and other commodity exchangers and producers are also formative of their value-creating attributes. Since the formative influences of others on the consumer are indirect sources of value, they also count as economic contributions.
6. Responsibility for these indirect contributions spreads to all members of the economic system, because all of them, not just a subset of individuals within a subsystem, influence the consumer. The social influence on the consumer is systemic. It comes from all individuals in their capacity as system members.
7. The spread of responsibility socially, to all members, brings

31. Ibid., p. 24.
32. Even if the decision rule for selecting rights could be specified, one would still have to provide a theoretical deduction of the right in order to be sure that the rights selected had ethical validity. Selection of the rights through the decision rule could provide democratic legitimacy, but it would not prove that the rights selected were ethically valid forms of freedom. Only a theory could establish that.

about a vast social dispersion of dueness, which morally entails a corresponding equalization of a portion of income.

8. Equalization of a portion of income is justified because individuals have a roughly equal amount of formative influence on one another's economic contributions. In several ways, individuals are the same with respect to the qualities that affect the formation of other consumers' economically creative consumer attributes, as I will detail in the following section. Since individuals make some equal indirect social contributions to value, they are due proportionate benefits.

9. While consumers differ in the intensity of their preferences and thus make differential contributions to relative prices, they also share some characteristics, such as a profound infinitude of wants. This common characteristic is as important to the creation and determination of economic value as are subjective preferences. In this respect, consumers make relatively equal contributions to value.

10. These steps imply the right of all members of economic society to an equalized portion of individual income.

The same right has also been specified through the ethics of economic community (see Chapter 12). Thus, if democracy is defined as rule in accord with rights (Chapter 13, pp. 272–274 and 276–278), it consists in part in rule that preserves redistributory property rights.[33] With redistributive property specified as a defining characteristic, the social theory of substantive democracy acquires operational meaning. It is not vulnerable to the charge of emptiness. The social theory uses a nonarbitrary way of formulating the content of democracy. Since its redistributory right is not merely postulated or stipulated, inevitable disagreements and

33. Gould's integration of democracy with distributive justice requires democracy to preserve "equal rights to those goods and services that are minimal conditions for any human actions whatever" (Gould 1988, p. 153). But beyond the guarantee of a minimum, this democracy authorizes differential distribution on grounds of desert or social value (p. 154). The principle of differential distribution is based on "the rights of agents to control the products of their activity" (p. 154). To prove that differential distribution deprives people of the products of their activities one needs a theory of the economic process that sorts out contributions. But Gould does not take into account the fact that much economically creative activity takes place on the consumption side. My analysis of the social origins of economically creative contributions suggests that equalizing a portion of income would not deprive people of control of their productive contributions, but would restore value to those who had lost control of it during the course of tangled market interactions.

differences in interpretation cannot reduce the theory merely to one person's opinion versus another's. The theoretical deduction of the social theory gives it a validity that can be contested only by disputing the underlying reasoning and premises.

Democracy and Concrete Equalities

In the "social theory," democracy's redistributive obligations derive from a premise of socially formed, concrete equalities in the nature of persons. When the theory of substantive democracy takes this premise into account, it leads to more egalitarian rules of distribution than are required by a liberal theory of substantive democracy. Dworkin bases his theory on a principle of equal consideration, which seems equivalent to the social theory's principle of concrete equality. However, liberal theories pass over the concrete equalities in the nature of persons. As a result, liberal democracy in these formulations limits the extent of equal treatment that it accords people. Substantive social democracy is a social theory because the concrete equalities originate in formative relations between individuals within the economy, in ways that I will specify.

From democracy's obligation to maintain substantive rights and economic justice, the theory of substantive democracy acquires an intrinsic relationship to two ethical systems associated with justice: the ethics of dueness for economic contributions and the ethics of economic community. It is within these systems that the concrete equalities in the nature of persons are identified (see Parts II and III).

As a first concrete equality, members of the economic system make an equal contribution to the creation of economic value in the sense that they all contribute to forming the economically creative attributes and capacities of other persons, such as wants, needs, and orientation toward the economic process.[34] In some ways, economic agents exert an equal influence on one another's contributions. Goods derive much of their value, or price, from the willingness of consumers to pay for them. Such value could not exist without the division of labor that leads consumers to seek satisfaction of their wants from others. Prices would not emerge if goods were produced only for self-consumption. In a sense, all economic agents bear equal responsibility for the division of labor and, therefore, for the value generated on this basis. Although a great organizer of workers, like Henry Ford, is in some ways more responsible for the division of labor than are those he employs, the major factor under-

34. As discussed at length in the ethics of economic contributions (Part II, this volume).

lying the division of labor is the willingness of workers to engage in production for others and to perform specialized labor. Since the members of the exchange system share this willingness, they are equally responsible for the value generated on the basis of division of labor.

Second, members of the exchange system are concretely equal in the sense that, in some regards, they make equal contributions to the formation of one another's dual will to contract, which is an important value-generating relationship. I am taking contract in the sense of an economic relationship rather than a juridical relationship. As an exchange of equivalent values, it is an integral part of the value creation process, not merely a legal relationship of reciprocal recognition of right. The dual will to contract is simultaneously a will to acquire value and to surrender value, as distinct from a will to directly appropriate value, seize it, or otherwise acquire it through unilateral means. This dual will to contract is crucial to the preservation of economic value because without it there cannot be an ongoing circulation of commodities. How the dual will to contract forms – and the character of people's influence upon the formation of one another's dual will to contract – is therefore critical in the calculation of dueness for value created. If a person who wanted something from another person simply seized it, without surrendering property in exchange, the second person would lose not only some economic value, but some ability to take part in the exchange system. If generalized, this sort of experience would lead many people to drop out of the exchange system, causing it to break down. In the exchange system, nobody, neither the rich nor the poor, will hand over goods without valuable consideration. This condition exerts a profound influence on the formation of the dual will to contract. Anyone who wants what another has must surrender something of equivalent value. To this degree, every person makes an equal contribution to the formation of other persons' dual will to contract. In an ethics of dueness, this form of equal contribution to value generates an equal indirect entitlement to a portion of the value created by the dual will of others.

Persons share some additional concrete equalities in the exchange system. In the division of labor, one has to contribute means to the satisfaction of the needs of others in order to gain means to the satisfaction of one's own needs. To provide others with such means, one has to constitute oneself accordingly – one has to become the kind of person who can contribute means to the satisfaction of their needs. There is thus a concrete equality in the nature of all labor in a system of division of labor. The willingness of workers to produce products for others is of course a necessary condition for the existence of economic value, and in this sense they all share a concrete equality and an equal responsibility for the existence of value. Although some people work harder or better than others, and in this sense deserve different amounts of remuneration for their differential contributions, a portion of income should be distributed equally because other contributions are made on an equal basis. Individuals differ in the amount of effort that they expend, but their labor displays an equality in the sense that these activities are all contributions to the satisfaction of the needs of others.

To attain satisfaction from commodities produced by others, a person must want them. To want them, a person must constitute herself and her needs in such a manner that she can be satisfied by what other persons can provide. This commonality establishes a final concrete equality among persons. Clearly, people's shaping of their desires to accord with what the market offers is a necessary condition for the existence of economic value. Commodities cannot have economic value, or price, unless they attract consumers. Thus, those who shape their wants so that they can find satisfaction in other persons' products are, in this respect, equally responsible for the existence of value and entitled to an equal portion of the value created on this basis. Some people may have more intense wants, and may therefore contribute more to the creation of economic value, but their shared preference for the goods of others establishes a dimension of equality among them.

A substantive social democracy takes these concrete equalities into account. When equalities in economically creative attributes are incorporated into the ethics of economic contributions, they morally entail a right to an equalization of a portion of individual income. The social theory of substantive democracy proceeds in accord with such an ethics, since substantive democracy and distributive justice are intrinsically related. On this basis, substantive social democracy implements an equalization of income in proportion to the degree and kind of equalities of contribution. It also allows inequalities in income and wealth that arise from differential productive capacities. To implement an egalitarian ethics of economic contributions, the substantive social democracy engages in ongoing redistribution of market inequalities. The equalities in economic contributions mentioned earlier are not commodified and therefore do not receive payment through unregulated market processes. To give them their due, a democracy must continuously reduce market inequalities by means of a redistributory apparatus.

As compared with the substantive social democracy, Dworkin's liberal substantive democracy does not require this kind or degree of egalitarian redistribution, despite its being advanced as an egalitarian democracy.[35] It "enforces the right of each person to respect and concern as an individual."[36] A general rule of equal consideration, however, is only as egalitarian as the particular equalities it recognizes in the nature of persons who are so recognized. Differences get differential treatment under a regime of equal consideration!

The liberal theory of substantive democracy uses an ethics of reward for economic contributions that does not note any equalities among the non-natural attributes and capacities of persons in their economic activities. Income and wealth are seen as arising from differences in life choices, such as differences in choices of vocation, in choices between labor and leisure, and so forth. Inequalities of income and wealth that result from these differences receive moral approbation under a principle of equal consideration. So liberal substantive democracy is prohibited from engaging in egalitarian redistribution of these inequalities. Inequalities in income and wealth arising from differences in natural talents are recognized as incompatible with the principle of equal consideration. This category of inequalities is subject to egalitarian redistribution by the liberal substantive democracy because it arises "though no choice of their own."[37] This element of the liberal substantive social democracy does indeed have some egalitarian force; and it must also be observed by the substantive social democracy.

It should be emphasized, however, that the liberal theory of substantive democracy does not mention any concrete equalities in persons' non-natural economic capacities, attributes, or contributions. With regard to this category of capacities, it perceives only differences among persons. "If one person chooses work that contributes less to other people's lives than different work he might have chosen, then, although this might well have been the right choice for him, given his personal goals, he has nevertheless added less to the resources available for others, and this must be taken into account in the egalitarian calculation."[38] Since the liberal theory sees only differences in persons' non-natural economic contributions, it does not implement an egalitarian redistribution of any portion of income derived from non-natural attributes.

Though Dworkin's theory proposes a principle of equal consideration, there is a gap in its egalitarianism with respect to the ethics of economic contributions, which is carried into the theory of substantive

35. Dworkin 1985, p. 196.
36. Ibid., p. 196.
37. Ibid., p. 207.
38. Ibid., p. 206.

democracy. His theory fails to recognize the concrete equalities that exist in the nature of persons' economically creative attributes, capacities, and contributions. In this respect, the egalitarian liberal theory is indistinguishable from an inegalitarian theory. What this suggests is that the principle of equal consideration is in liberal hands really an abstract principle of equal consideration. And the abstract principle turns out to be an inadequate criterion for an egalitarian theory. What really distinguishes an egalitarian democratic theory from an inegalitarian one is whether it takes into account the concrete equalities in the nature of persons. The liberal theory of substantive democracy does not give adequately equal treatment because it does not take into account the concrete equalities in the nature of persons' (non-natural) economic attributes, qualities that would mandate greater equality in distribution.

The social theory of substantive democracy uses a more concrete form of the principle of equal consideration, a rule of distribution based on a premise of concrete equalities in the nature of persons. This is the crucial distinction between egalitarian and inegalitarian democratic theories. The social theory holds that the portion of income derived from concrete equalities in persons' economically creative capacities should also be distributed equally. More important, though, than the issue of which theory is more egalitarian is the question of which theory has greater ethical validity. The social theory has more ethical validity, because it takes into account a category of economic contributions overlooked by the liberal theory, which makes an inaccurate assessment of appropriate distribution.

GENERAL OR RELATIVE SUBSTANTIVE DEMOCRACY?

The redistributory property right is a defining characteristic of democracy in general, at the level of the state and in relation to all capital-based market systems.[39] Not justified merely with respect to some democracies and not others, it is also justified by conditions that inhere in all capital-based market systems. In contrast to this view, Habermas formulates a theory of democracy in which the substance of democracy has no general defining characteristic and is relative to particular socio-economic contexts. Only the procedural civil rights "are absolutely justi-

39. The rule is fully general for countries that have reached a minimal level of economic development, but it may be qualified for systems so undeveloped that transfer costs would significantly worsen poverty.

fied categories."[40] "[T]he category of social and ecological rights [which includes economic and welfare rights] . . . can only be justified in relative terms."[41]

To determine the relativity or generality of substantive democracy, one must consider whether the concrete equalities underlying redistributory property right have universality. First, there is the equal responsibility of system members for the division of labor and the value created upon this basis. This concrete equality is common to all capital-based market systems, because all require a capital-based division of labor. Second, there is the equal responsibility for the formation of each persons' dual will to contract and for the economic value arising upon that basis. No capital-based market system can sustain an ongoing circulation of value without a dual will to contract. So this form of concrete equality is also common to all capital-based market systems. Third, each person contributes equally to the creation of economic value in the sense that each person shapes his wants so that he can be satisfied by what others can provide. This quality is necessary for uniting production and consumption into an interconnected sequence of actions, without which the circulation of commodities would break down. Since the concrete equalities justifying the redistributory property right are common to all capital-based market systems, substantive democracies with this right are generally justified with respect to such systems, rather than justified only in special socioeconomic contexts.

40. Habermas 1996, p. 123.
41. Ibid.

14

Democracy and Economic Rights

INCLUDING CONTROVERSIAL ECONOMIC RIGHTS

Dahl's revised theory of polyarchy (Dahl 1980) includes primary political rights in the definition of democracy but excludes economic rights as too controversial: "claims to primary social rights tend to be more debatable and uncertain in democratic theory and practice than claims to primary political rights."[1] Rawls's liberal conception of political justice uses much the same reasoning to exclude distributive justice from the constitutional essentials of democracy (Rawls 1993).[2] Although agreement between Rawls and Dahl on this point lends great weight to their argument, I believe that the controversiality of economic rights does not disqualify them from being among the defining characteristics of democracy.

The worldwide increase in the number of polyarchal democracies in recent years, from twenty-nine in 1969 to ninety in 1990, seemingly confirms that there is an emerging consensus on primary political rights.[3] However, when polyarchies were in the minority and their rights were more debatable globally, American political scientists nevertheless included these rights in the definition of democracy. Now that economic rights are relatively more controversial than political rights, these scholars exclude economic rights as more debatable. There is an apparent inconsistency in their treatment of the implications of the controversiality of different categories of rights. If political rights could be included in 1969, when they were more controversial than at present, then eco-

1. Dahl 1980, p. 14.
2. Rawls 1993, p. 229.
3. Dahl 1971, p. 248; Fukuyama 1992, pp. 49–50.

nomic rights should be includable despite their being more controversial than political rights. Although primary political rights may now be relatively less controversial than economic rights, they are still highly controversial.

The considerable range and depth of theoretical controversies about primary political rights can be indicated by the debates between elitist democratic methods (Schumpeter) and classical democratic ideas (Rousseau and Mill); between elitist and polyarchal approaches; between strong democracy (Barber; Berry, Portnoy, and Thompson) and polyarchal democracy and liberal democracy (Dahl); between corporatist democrats and polyarchal democrats; between collectivist democrats and proceduralist democrats; between communitarian democrats (Sandel) and liberal democrats; between polyarchal democrats and Madisonian and Jeffersonian democrats; between Machiavellian republicans (Mansfield) and constitutional democrats; between substantive democrats (Simon) and procedural democrats; and between deliberative democracy (Fishkin, Habermas) and depoliticized procedural democracy.

Polyarchal democratic procedures have been repeatedly and intensively contested from several standpoints, often involving different views of primary political rights. Berry, Portnoy, and Thompson advance a set of "strong democratic procedures," which entail more popular participation within the policy-making process than does polyarchy.

Polyarchal Democracy	Participatory Democracy
Polyarchal condition 3. Every member . . . performs the acts we assume to constitute an expression of preference among these scheduled alternatives, e.g., voting.	Participation condition 3. Every citizen performs the acts we assume to constitute an expression of preference among the scheduled alternatives, for example, takes part in the participation process.
Polyarchal condition 6. Alternatives (leaders or policies) with the greatest number of votes displace any alternatives (leaders or policies) with fewer votes.	Participation condition 6. Alternative policies that receive the greatest support in the participation process displace any alternatives with lesser support.[4]

Barber supports a different alternative to polyarchal and liberal views of democratic procedure. His proposal for strong democratic procedures

4. The participatory conditions are from Berry, Portnoy, and Thompson 1993, p. 54; the polyarchal conditions are from Dahl 1956, p. 84.

includes neighborhood assemblies, civic communications, civic videotex service, a civic educational postal act, decriminalization and informal lay justice, initiative and referendum processes, electronic balloting, election by lottery, an internal voucher system, universal citizen service, local volunteer programs, and architecture of civic and public space.[5] Actualizing these strong democratic conditions would entail promulgating several primary political rights not listed among the polyarchal rights.

Thus, primary political rights are beset by multiple, intense, and profound controversies in democratic theory and practice. It is not just primary economic rights that are subject to serious controversy. But while controversy has led to the exclusion of primary economic rights, it has not prevented mainstream democratic theorists from including political rights. If primary political rights can be included despite a high level of controversy, it does not make sense to exclude primary economic rights simply for being relatively more controversial.

Another issue to consider in deciding whether primary economic rights should be included among the defining characteristics of democracy is the extent of disagreement that could break out over whether a given society has attained them. The liberal theory of political justice argues that principles of distributive justice should not be included in the constitutional essentials of a democratic republic because there is bound to be wide disagreement about whether they have been attained in particular circumstances, which might cause political instability. Rawls writes, "[W]hether the aims of the principles covering social and economic inequalities are realized is far more difficult to ascertain. These matters are nearly always open to wide differences of reasonable opinion; they rest on complicated inferences and intuitive judgments that require us to assess complex social and economic information about topics poorly understood."[6] Since the attainment of basic liberties is easier to assess, "we can expect more agreement about whether the principles of the basic rights and liberties are realized than about whether the principles of social and economic justice are realized."[7]

The problem of assessing the attainment of rights is not, however, peculiar to the principles of distributive justice. The question of whether the aims of distributive justice have been met will not be subject to more disagreement than the same question regarding basic liberties. Consider the attainment of equal political liberties regarding the control of the

5. Barber 1984, p. 307.
6. Rawls 1993, p. 229.
7. Ibid., pp. 229–230.

policy-making process. According to one expert, measuring their attainment is "far beyond the scope of these essays and perhaps beyond the scope of political science at the present time."[8] It presumes that we know the necessary and sufficient conditions for their existence in the real world. Another complication is the possibility of ideological hegemony,[9] which could diminish the integrity of the process and the amount of political participation despite legal promulgation and protection of rights. Alternatively, a low level of participation might result from political apathy or antipathy. In such cases, determining whether political liberties have been attained or suppressed can be extremely difficult.[10]

All the assessment problems relating to distributive justice – "complex social . . . information about topics poorly understood" that rest on "complicated inferences and intuitive judgments"[11] – apply with equal or greater force to the assessment of the basic liberties. It should not be more difficult, therefore, to get agreement that distributive justice has been attained than to get agreement that political rights have been attained. If the basic liberties can be included in the constitutional essentials of a democratic republic, despite all the prospective disagreement to which they are subject, then there seems no reason not to include the principles of distributive justice as well.

It may indeed be easier to assess whether the aims of a principle of distributive justice have been met than to determine whether a basic liberty has been attained. The attainment of the proposed redistributory right, for example, is relatively easy to measure. Analysts readily express income in terms of a nation's currency. Assessing the attainment of a basic political liberty is more difficult, because it cannot be gauged merely by the distribution of votes. The relative ease of assessing the attainment of the redistributory right should facilitate reaching agreement about whether it has been attained.

Even if it were difficult to identify the conditions marking the attainment of distributive justice, there would be no insuperable barrier to including these principles within the constitutional essentials of a democracy. Constitutions almost never specify the particular facts that define the final attainment of a right or liberty. U.S. history shows that such specification is usually left up to the high court and legislative enactments to establish over a long period. In 1868, the Fourteenth Amendment was adopted, providing guarantees against state depriva-

8. Dahl 1956, p. 75.
9. Poulantzas 1973; Lukes 1974; Lindblom 1977; Gaventa 1980.
10. Polsby 1963.
11. Rawls 1993, pp. 229–230.

tions of "life, liberty or property, without due process of law." It took almost a hundred years and many major Supreme Court decisions – *Gitlow v. New York* (1925), *Near v. Minnesota* (1931), *Wolf v. Colorado* (1949), *Mapp v. Ohio* (1961), *Gideon v. Wainwright* (1963) – to determine that the aims of the Fourteenth Amendment would be realized by "incorporating" all of the Bill of Rights into its provisions. Similarly, it would also have been impossible to specify at the nation's founding the particular conditions that would mark the attainment of the aims of the First Amendment, but this limitation did not exclude the amendment from the U.S. Constitution. In view of the nature of constitution making, principles of distributive justice should not be excluded simply because it is difficult to assess the attainment of their aims.

DISTRIBUTIVE JUSTICE AS FIRST-ORDER DEMOCRATIC PRINCIPLES

Democratic theorists tend to include only first-order moral principles among the defining characteristics of democracy, while excluding second-order principles. Distributive justice is frequently considered to be a set of second-order moral principles. It is better, the reasoning goes, to leave it out because it is controversial, than to jeopardize first principles with unnecessary political instability. Rawls classifies principles of distributive justice as second-order rules because they deal with economic inequalities and inequalities of goods rather than with basic freedoms, which he takes as lexically prior in moral order.[12] Economic inequalities, he acknowledges, can affect "the worth of liberty, that is, the usefulness of . . . liberties," but they are not direct conditions of liberty.[13] Rendering distributive justice morally secondary eases the removal of its principles from the constitutional essentials of a democratic republic.[14]

Principles of distributive justice do not, however, deal only with economic inequalities or with inequalities of goods or with the worth of liberty as distinct from liberty itself. They also regulate basic freedoms, so one cannot readily eliminate them from the constitutional essentials of a democratic republic. Consider the right of property. Property is a right of basic freedom, the person's fundamental freedom of will in relation to

12. Ibid., p. 326; Rawls 1971, pp. 61, 151.
13. Rawls 1993, pp. 229–230. It may be noted, however, that Rawls retains the principles of distributive justice in the liberal conception of political justice (Rawls 1993, pp. 4–7), which he does not seem to regard as a realizable form of substantive democracy.
14. Rawls 1993, p. 228.

and over things. Without property, "freedom would," Kant wrote, "so far be depriving itself of the use of its voluntary activity, in thus putting *usable* objects out of all possible *use*."[15] The proposed redistributory property right redistributes conditions of freedom of will in relation to and over things in an ethically valid way. So it also regulates a basic freedom. As a condition of basic freedom, the redistributory property right accrues the supreme ethical worth possessed by other rights of basic freedom. Having supreme ethical worth, the redistributory property right is indispensable to the core of a democracy that internalizes justice. As such, it belongs among the constitutional essentials of a republic and cannot be removed without diminishing the democratic character of the republic.

DEFINABILITY AND INCLUSION OF ECONOMIC RIGHTS

To be included among democracy's defining conditions, a right has to be reasonably well defined and theoretically definite. At present, the redistributory property right does not fully meet these requirements, because it is not yet completely developed, but I believe that further study can provide the requisite specification. According to mainline democratic theory, however, social and economic rights are theoretically uncertain and cannot be well defined. Because they are too vague to be enforced, the argument goes, it is pointless to include them among democracy's defining characteristics. Dahl (1980, p. 14), for example, characterizes the right to an education as a "vague aspiration."

This general view of economic rights can be called into question by the fact that property, which is an economic right, can be reasonably well defined. The advent of the right of property has entailed changes in the field of economic relations as definite as any caused in political relations by the right of self-government in political relations. The equal right to property dramatically increased individual freedom by contributing to the eradication of feudalism and master-servant relations in many countries. Though in their liberal form property rights have not provided adequate conditions for freedom, they are still sufficiently precise and meaningful to base economic relations on wage labor. Property rights show that economic rights are not too vague to be enforceable, for they have been enforced around the world. Consequently, they can clearly be included in substantive democracy. And, if the case of the right of property is any guide, other economic rights can be well defined and theoretically definite, and so can be included within a list of democratic

15. Kant 1887 [1796], p. 62.

rights. By extension, the redistributory property right may not be inherently vague but may simply await further theoretical development.

The redistributory property right provides important bounds and guidelines for democracy. It demands more income equality than does the difference principle, which aims only at improving the absolute position of the worst-off members of society, not at increasing relative equality among all strata. The principle of egalitarian redistribution of a portion of income would significantly equalize the relative standing of all strata, but would not flatten out the income hierarchy. A democratic country abiding by the redistributory property right would reduce extremely differential incentives. The redistributory property right requires that whatever portion of individual income is morally susceptible to redistribution should be distributed equally. The concrete equalities in persons' economic attributes are as important – to the creation of economic value – as the concrete differences between their attributes. So, in a substantive social democracy a substantial portion of income will be subject to egalitarian distribution and a substantial portion will be open to market-generated inequalities.

Some vagueness does not necessarily deprive the right to an equalized portion of income from having strong influence. A great deal of vagueness in the classical liberal right of property has not prevented it from having massive influence. What the right of property did was to bring the entitlement to value into closer correspondence with the creator of value, so that proprietorship would have more to do with the making of value.[16] Hitherto, groups controlled economic resources simply on the basis of royal and feudal privileges, and there was very little relationship between economic contributions and entitlement.[17] Property law increased the relationship between production and entitlement because it gave producers, who formerly had not owned their own labor, a right to the things they produced and a right to bring them to market. The change was great enough to institutionalize the position of the middle class in society. The fact that property did not perfectly define the nature of economic contributions did not prevent it from making this important contribution to the progress of society. Parts II and III have demon-

16. The liberal right of property does not effect a complete congruence between economic contributions and proprietorship, but it brings them into much closer correspondence than did ownership determined on the basis of feudal privileges, which bore little if any relation to economic contributions. Liberal property right therefore represents a revolutionary increase in the correspondence between economic contributions and proprietorship, despite leaving wide gaps between them.

17. Schlatter 1951, pp. 155–156.

strated that liberal property law takes insufficient account of certain forms of equality in the nature of persons' contributions, some indirect economic contributions, common economic actions, and common economic purposes. The redistributory property right could tighten the relationship between contributions and entitlements because it takes into account these additional forms of economic contributions and gives them their due. By analogy to experience with classical liberal property, it could improve the relationship between contributions and entitlements even if there were some residual vagueness in its underlying assumptions about the nature of contributions. By legally recognizing concrete equalities among economic agents' economic contributions, it could improve the relationship between entitlement and economic creation that Locke's theory originally meant to establish, but only partially realized.

THEORETICAL OR HYPOTHETICAL SUBSTANTIVE DEMOCRACY?

There are several concerns about using a theoretical methodology, as this study does, to define rights and democracy. On the one hand, it is based on reasoning, not on the actual choices of individuals.[18] On the other hand, this approach may be necessary because citizens often make choices without adequately understanding their own interests. Dahl proposes a method that would keep individual choice at the forefront of analysis, would not make recourse to theory, and would bring the fullest attainable information to bear on the determination of rights. In his hypothetical-choice procedure, "a person's interest or good is whatever that person would choose with fullest attainable understanding of the experience resulting from that choice and its most relevant alternatives."[19] Defining fundamental moral interests by means of a hypothetical choice procedure can lead to a formulation of substantive democracy as a system that preserves fundamental moral interests. It does not, however, yield a theory of substantive democracy, since it does not employ a theory of rights. I argue that theoretical deduction is a more satisfactory method of defining rights.

The hypothetical choice procedure does not really secure actual individual choice. A third party, who represents the individual, but who has the fullest attainable understanding, makes the choice. The method implies choice but really goes around it. So it does not offer a coherent

18. This is Dahl's concern (Dahl 1989, pp. 66–67, 180–181).
19. Dahl 1989, p. 182.

strategy. Let us suppose, though, that the hypothetical choice procedure is indeed a coherent strategy. Can it yield adequate knowledge for defining rights? It cannot, in my judgment.

Experiencing a supposed right does not necessarily provide the knowledge needed to determine its rightness, no matter how well the experience is understood. In the formulation of rights of property and distribution, much of the requisite knowledge is not based on experience. To formulate rights, one needs the fullest attainable knowledge deriving from theoretical conceptions. Understanding based upon experience may not have much validity beyond what one gathers from experience.[20] Take, for example, a person considering the choice between the liberal right and the redistributory property right. Let us assume that she has fullest attainable understanding of the experience resulting from the choice and the alternative.

Suppose that she experiences herself as an independent actor in her economically creative activities, as many people do. She has at her command full knowledge of advanced neoclassical economic theory, an individualistic theory that deduces the system of relative prices from individual preference orderings, among other postulates. And she fully understands Marxist theory and the theory I have proposed, which argue – in different ways – that individuals' economically creative capacities are formatively related to the other members of the system of commodity producers and exchangers. Our hypothetical choice agent brings these theories to bear on her own economic experience. Since she experiences herself as an independent agent, only neoclassical theory really relates to, and explains, this experience. Marxist theory and the theory I propose do not square with it.

But fullest attainable understanding of one's experience may not be terribly relevant for theorizing rights. Adam Smith noted many years ago that labor is "an abstract notion," by which he meant that one encounters it in thought – in particular, in theoretical reflection – but not in life.[21] The work of a workhouse, he said, is but a part of the work that goes into a manufacture. In the theoretical concept of labor, each individual is not labor; rather, labor consists of a system of individual laborers in a societywide division of labor united by exchange relations.[22] The individual may not grasp this, however, because, as Smith points out, the system is not a matter of experience.

20. Hegel 1975, p. 61.
21. Smith 1937, p. 32.
22. One may experience the division of labor within the firm, as in the pin factory example; but Smith also develops a concept of the division of labor between a system of firms, and says that one will not experience this sort of division.

> In those great manufactures, on the contrary, which are destined to supply the great wants of the great body of the people, every different branch of the work employs so great a number of workmen, that it is impossible to collect them all into the same workhouse. We can seldom see more, at any one time, than those employed in one single branch. Though in such manufactures, therefore, the work may really be divided into a much greater number of parts, . . . the division is not near so obvious, and has accordingly been much less observed.[23]

On the basis of experience, and the feeling of independence, the individual may choose the familiar liberal right of property, authorizing final ownership of all that comes to him or her through market activities. But this produces an incomplete right, because it leaves out the implications of the social formation of individuals' economically creative capacities. The systemic formation of these capacities morally entails an equalization of part of the income of each individual. Since the knowledge of systemic interrelatedness comes from theory, theoretical reasoning is the more appropriate method of formulating the substantive right of property.

Can theory better serve? In responding to this question we need to keep in mind the subject of the theory of rights – namely, the conditions of freedom of will.[24] Moreover, one of the formal conditions of justice is universalizability. In other words, a certain state of affairs can be right for person A only if it is also right for person B. The principle of universalizability is inherent in the idea that murder is wrong, that it is something no one should do, not just something Charles Manson, for example, should not do.[25] The question, therefore, is whether theory can formulate universalizable principles of freedom. If a theory can show that a condition, such as property, is logically necessary for freedom of will, then the condition will meet the criterion of universalizability. Logical analysis can demonstrate that a condition is logically necessary for the existence of an entity. Witness the remarkable success in identifying necessary conditions for the logical possibility of general equilibrium in economics.[26] When a condition has been shown to be logically

23. Smith 1937, p. 4.
24. As Hegel writes, "[F]reedom is both the substance of right and its goal" (Hegel 1952, para. 4, p. 20).
25. Fried 1978, p. 9. The point cannot be refuted by adducing the admissibility of killing in self-defense. The latter is not murder. The meanings of the terms in a universal principle give it boundaries that save the principle from excessive absolutism without compromising universality. For a valuable discussion of why judgements of right take the form of categorical norms, see Fried 1978. On universalizability, see J. C. Smith 1976 and Singer 1961. See also Rawls 1971, p. 131.
26. See Quirk and Saposnik 1968.

necessary to the concept of freedom of will, then such freedom is inconceivable without that condition. All individuals depend on that condition for their freedom of will. Since theory can grasp the conditions necessary for freedom of will, it can formulate fully universalizable rights. Thus it is an appropriate method for defining the rights to be included in the definition of substantive democracy.

SUBSTANTIVE DEMOCRATIC PROCESS

Mainstream democratic theory tends to identify democracy with the democratic process (i.e., means), rather than with a set of democratic ends (i.e., substance). A recent treatise states, "Democracy means, literally, rule by the people."[27] Thus, the democratic process is often understood as a "way of ruling" or a "political method."[28] It consists in effective participation, voting equality at the decisive stage, enlightened understanding, final control of the agenda, and inclusiveness, but not in substantive rights.[29]

In the contrasting substantive theory, as usually understood, a political system has to achieve a set of ends or outcomes to be considered democratic.[30] But a substantive democracy is not only "outcome-centered" but also "rule-centered." It is constituted so that social and economic rights are integral parts of the democratic process.

The democratic process is fraught with substantive rights in the sense that substantive rights promulgated in the constitution shape citizens' basic values. These in turn shape their political preferences, which can affect everything that follows in the policy-making process. "A constitutional law," according to Kelson, "is part of every norm created on its basis."[31] A citizen's norms with regard to basic substantive rights condition their preferences over political alternatives. As the neo-Hegelian Denton Snider wrote in his early work *The State*:[32] "[T]he constitution is to be seized not only as the constituted, but likewise as the constituting . . . [T]he constitution of the Self is the Self of the constitution."[33]

27. Dahl 1989, p. 106.
28. Ibid.; Schumpeter 1943, p. 242.
29. Dahl 1989, Chapters 8 and 9. The procedural rights are said to have substantive aspects in the sense that they distribute political power. But no substantive rights in the sense of economic or social rights are included in the specification of the democratic process.
30. Shapiro 1994, p. 135.
31. Kelson's view (Kelson 1961) as stated by Raz 1970, p. 71.
32. Snider 1902, p. 383.
33. Ibid., p. 399. See also p. 383.

Bills of rights, by educating the public, can have an enormous influence on political ethics and in turn on the democratic process.[34] They can encourage an emphasis on rights in the political and judicial systems that leads to more rights claiming. The increased salience of rights, due to such influences on the public mind, can increase the likelihood that rights will get the attention and protection they deserve. The majority will generally adopt policies that fall within the limits of the consensus composed of the basic values of the active electorate.[35] To win election, moreover, candidates must select policies that are consistent with majority values shaped by constitutional rules and norms. Substantive rights are therefore heavily involved in majority rule and in any other equivalent democratic process aimed at securing political equality. They are no less a part of the democratic process than procedural rights are.[36]

REGIME CLASSIFICATION AND DEMOCRATIC LEGITIMACY

When a democratic theory regards substantive rights as external to democracy, it will classify policies as democratic even when they violate substantive rights, so long as these policies are adopted by the democratic process. Since the theories of procedural democracy, of spheres of justice, of democracy as a "subordinate foundational good," and of polyarchy (Dahl 1989) all view justice as largely extrinsic to democracy, they classify violations of substantive rights as democratic even though unjust. By providing democratic legitimation for such violations, they can jeopardize the security of social and economic rights. For example, the equation of democracy with majority rule underlies Bork's argument regarding *Griswold v. Connecticut* (1965) that majority preferences sup-

34. Epp 1996, p. 776.
35. Macedo 1991, pp. 54, 179–185.
36. From Hamilton to Dahl, American democratic theorists have expressed concerns about including substantive rights in the democratic process. Their inclusion "would even be dangerous," Hamilton argued, because they "would contain . . . exceptions to the powers" of the people (Hamilton in Lewis 1967, p. 404). While substantive rights provide an exception to the powers of the people, they do so, however, only on a *provisional* basis. Yet it is, paradoxically, the very capacity of substantive rights to provide a provisional exception to the power of the people that makes them an inherent part of the democratic process. They are a part of it because one of the people's most important powers is the ability to limit its own powers, on a provisional basis, in ways necessary for the freedoms involved in justice. I say provisionally because the demos retain the power to amend any provision of the Constitution by virtue of the right of self-government.

porting a Connecticut statute against contraception should hold sway over the right of privacy.[37]

The theory of substantive democracy has very different standards. It does not classify regimes as democratic simply because they hold valid elections. To qualify they must also maintain justice by enforcing substantive rights, because this theory views justice as intrinsic to democratic obligations.

SUBSTANTIVE DEMOCRACY OR "SUBORDINATE FOUNDATIONAL GOOD"?

One of the recent, partially substantive formulations of democracy holds that only the democratic process in practice can define the substance of democracy, because there is no way, "independent of what democratic procedures generate, to determine what outcomes are democratic."[38] In this view there cannot be a *theory* of substantive democracy because there cannot be a theory of rights. Theory cannot define ethical rules because (1) "our knowledge of the world of politics seems so meager,"[39] (2) the subject matter of politics does not lend itself to theoretical analysis,[40] and (3) theories of rights cannot be ethically validated, because they inevitably advantage some at the expense of others, despite claims that they further general interests.[41]

In this formulation of democracy as a "subordinate foundational good," democracy would be partially substantive in the sense that the democratic process would partially decide the ethical rules of multiple social domains.[42] At the same time it would not be substantive, because these derivative ethical rules are not foundational moral commitments. In opposition to this view, I support the proposition that there can be a theory of substantive democracy, because rights theory can define rights.

Significant advances in political thought show that our knowledge of politics is not "meager." Kant's theory of property illustrates the development of genuine political knowledge through theoretical means. Kant justifies property by holding that to deny that anything could be rightfully one's own contradicts the principle of right, that is, the principle of ethically valid freedom. Denial of property would contradict the principle of right, he further reasons, because such denial would be incom-

37. Bork 1971, p. 9.
38. Shapiro 1994, p. 136.
39. Ibid., p. 140.
40. Ibid. 41. Ibid., p. 141.
42. Ibid., p 135.

patible with freedom of will. To support this proposition, he first assumes the negation of property. Then he compellingly reasons that "freedom would . . . be depriving itself of the use of its voluntary activity, in thus putting *usable* objects out of all possible *use*."[43] Moreover, he shows that property must have a private dimension. Unless the will of others were interdicted, one could not use one's will in relation to things, and could not have external freedom.[44] In this way, Kant provides a theoretical justification for property.

Though Kant thinks that property can be willed as a categorical imperative,[45] some doubt that he achieves ethical validation for property, because property does not promote general interests. Critics of liberal property theories persuasively argue that property laws can be devised to create a legal framework for exploitation. Such critiques often fail, however, to take into account that property is morally necessary even in a just redistributory order because redistributed resources would be useless to the less fortunate unless they received proprietary rights over them. While the lack of just redistributory principles prevents Kant's theory from achieving sufficient conditions for a just economy, it nonetheless provides real knowledge of a general ethical condition and a significant part of the justification for a necessary part of economic justice.

The theory of externalities calls into question the notion that property can provide a theoretical resolution of social conflict by showing that voluntary exchange relationships among property owners can have unwanted third-party effects.[46] Yet the theory of externalities does not call for the abolition of property rights, but only for coupling them with a market for externalities.[47] So the classical liberal theory of property stands as a contribution to the resolution of social conflict, and as a way station in the eventual theoretical resolution of further dimensions of economic conflict.

While our knowledge of ethics is still problematic, footholds already gained suggest that we can eventually provide theoretical specification for substantive democracy, and that democracy is not faced with impending devolution into a "subordinate foundational good" without any substantive rights. Since a property right has been proved theoretically, and a redistributory right has been deduced theoretically, a theory of substantive democracy with determinate egalitarian provisions seems quite possible.

43. Kant 1887 [1796], p. 62. 44. Ibid., p. 69.
45. Kant 1965 [1797], p. 60.
46. Mishan 1971. 47. Wellisz 1964, p. 347.

References

American Law Institute. 1936. *Restatement of the Law of Property*. St. Paul, MN: American Law Institute.

Antonelli, G. B. 1886. *Sulla Teoria Matematica Della Economia Pura*. Pisa: Folchetto. Reprinted in *Giorale degli Economisti*, n.s., vol. 10, 1951, pp. 233–263.

Arrow, Kenneth J. 1971. *General Competitive Analysis*. San Francisco: Holden-Day.

1974. "General Economic Equilibrium: Purpose, Analytic Techniques, Collective Choice." *The American Economic Review*, vol. 64, no. 3, pp. 253–273.

Ashcraft, Richard. 1987. *Locke's Two Treatises of Government*. London: Unwin Hyman.

Atkinson, Anthony B., Timothy M. Smeeding, and Lee Rainwater. 1995. *Income Distribution in OECD Countries*. Paris: Organization for Economic Cooperation and Development.

Auerbach, P. 1988. *Competition*. Oxford: Basil Blackwell.

Austin, John. 1869. *Lectures On Jurisprudence*, 2 vols. 3rd edn., ed. Robert Campbell. London: John Murray.

Barber, Benjamin. 1984. *Strong Democracy*. Berkeley: University of California Press.

Barry, B. 1973. *The Liberal Theory of Justice*. Oxford: Oxford University Press.

1989. *Theories of Justice*. Berkeley: University of California Press.

Basmann, R. L. 1956. "A Theory of Demand with Variable Consumer Preferences." *Econometrica*, vol. 24 (January), pp. 47–58.

Bearne, Andy. 1996. "The Economics of Advertising: A Reappraisal." *Economic Issues*, vol. 1, part 1 (March), pp. 23–38.

Becker, Gary S. 1996. *Accounting for Tastes*. Cambridge, MA: Harvard University Press.

Becker, Lawrence. 1977. *Property Rights: Philosophical Foundations*. London: Routledge and Kegan Paul.

Benhabib, Seyla. 1977. "Natural Right and Hegel: An Essay in Modern Political Philosophy." Ph.D. Thesis, Yale University.

1984. "Obligation, Contract, and Exchange: On the Significance of Hegel's

Abstract Right." In *The State and Civil Society*, ed. Z. A. Pelczynski. Cambridge: Cambridge University Press.

ed. 1996. *Democracy and Difference*. Princeton: Princeton University Press.

Bentham, Jeremy. 1871 [1802]. *Theory of Legislation,* trans. R. Hildreth. London: Trubner.

1970 [1789]. *An Introduction to the Principles of Morals and Legislation*, ed. J. H. Burns and H. L. A. Hart. In *The Collected Works of Jeremy Bentham*, ed. J. H. Burns. London: Athlone Press.

Berolzheimer, Fritz. 1968. *The World's Legal Philosophers*. New York: Augustus M. Kelley.

Berry, Christopher. 1980. "Property and Possession: Two Replies to Locke–Hume and Hegel." In *NOMOS XXII: Property*, ed. J. Roland Pennock and John W. Chapman. New York: New York University Press.

Berry, Jeffrey M., Kent E. Portnoy, and Ken Thomson. 1993. *The Rebirth of Urban Democracy*. Washington, D.C.: The Brookings Institution.

Bertalanffy, Ludwig von. 1968. *General System Theory*. New York: George Braziller.

Blackstone, William. 1979 [1766]. *Commentaries on the Laws of England*, 4 vols. Chicago: University of Chicago Press.

Blaug, Mark. 1985. *Economic Theory in Retrospect*. 4th edn. Cambridge: Cambridge University Press.

Boddewyn, J. J. 1985. "Advertising Self-Regulation: Organization Structures in Belgium, Canada, France and the United Kingdom." Chapter 4 of *Private Interest Government*, ed. Wolfgang Streeck and Philippe C. Schmitter. London: Sage Publications.

Bonin, Richard. 1997. "How We Won the War." *60 Minutes*, vol. 29, no. 36 (May 25), CBS News.

Bork, Robert H. 1971. "Neutral Principles and Some First Amendment Problems." *Indiana Law Journal,* vol. 47, pp. 1–35

Boswell, Jonathan. 1990. *Community and the Economy.* London: Routledge.

Bowles, Samuel, and Herbert Gintis. 1976. *Schooling in Capitalist America.* New York: Basic Books.

Bradsher, Keith. 1995. "Widest Gap in Incomes? Research Points to the U.S." *The New York Times,* October 27, section D, p. 2.

Brown, R. S. 1978. "Estimating Advantages to Large Scale Advertising." *Review of Economics and Statistics,* vol. 60, pp. 428–437.

Browning, E. K., and J. M. Browning. 1986. *Microeconomic Theory and Applications.* 2nd edn. New York: Little Brown and Co.

Buchanan, James M., and William Craig Stubblebine. 1969. "Externality." In *Readings in Welfare Economics*, ed. Kenneth Arrow and Tibor Scitovsky. Homewood, IL: Richard D. Irwin.

Bureau of Labor Statistics. 1999. *Employment and Earnings*, vol. 46, no. 8 (Summer), pp. 45-47.

Burtless, Gary. 1994. "Public Spending on the Poor." In *Confronting Poverty*, ed. Sheldon H. Danziger, Gary D. Sandefur, and Daniel H. Weinberg. Cambridge, MA: Harvard University Press.

Buxton, A. J., S. W. Davies, and B. R. Lyons. 1984. "Concentration and Advertising in Consumer and Producer Markets." *Journal of Industrial Economics,* vol. 32, no. 4 (June), pp. 451–464.

Carens, Joseph H. 1981. *Equality, Moral Incentives, and the Market*. Chicago: University of Chicago Press.

Caron, Paul, Grayson M. P. McCouch, and Karen C. Burke. 1998. *Federal Wealth Transfer Tax Anthology*. Cincinnati: Anderson Publishing Co.

Carver, George Washington. 1931. Letter to the Editor, *The Peanut Journal*, December 15.

Caughey, Andrew. 1999. "Reviewing the Nineties." *The Pulse of Capitalism*, issue 99-3 (October), pp. 1–10. Web publication by The Commonwealth Institute: www.comw.org/poc/9910.html.

Champernowne, D. G. 1945. "A Note on J. V. Neuman's Article on 'A Model of Economic Equilibrium'." *Review of Economic Studies*, vol. 13, pp. 10-18.

Clark, J. B. 1902. *The Distribution of Wealth*. New York: Macmillan.

Coase, R. 1960. "The Problem of Social Cost." *Journal of Law and Economics*, vol. 3 (October), pp. 1–44.

Cobban, A. 1964. *Rousseau and the Modern State*. London: Allen and Unwin.

Cohen, Felix. 1954. "Dialogue on Private Property." *Rutgers Law Review*, vol. 9, no. 2 (Winter), pp. 357–387.

Cohen, Felix, and Morris R. Cohen. 1951. *Readings in Jurisprudence and Legal Philosophy*. New York: Prentice-Hall.

Cohen, G. A. 1993. "Equality of What? On Welfare, Goods, and Capabilities." In *The Quality of Life*, ed. M. Nussbaum and A. Sen. Oxford: Clarendon Press.

Coleman, Jules L. 1982. "The Economic Analysis of Law." In *NOMOS XXIV: Ethics, Economics and the Law*, ed. J. Roland Pennock and John W. Chapman. New York: New York University Press.

Collins, Susan M. 1991. "Savings Behavior in Ten Developing Countries." In *National Savings and Economic Performance*, ed. B. Douglas Bernheim and John B. Shoven. Chicago: University of Chicago Press.

Comanor, William S., and Thomas A. Wilson. 1974. *Advertising and Market Power*. Cambridge, MA: Harvard University Press.

Connolly, William E. 1972. "On 'Interests' in Politics." *Politics and Society*, vol. 2, pp. 459–477.

Cowling, K., J. Cable, M. Kelly, and T. McGuiness. 1975. *Advertising and Economic Behaviour*. London: Macmillan.

Dahl, Robert A. 1956. *A Preface to Democratic Theory*. Chicago: University of Chicago Press.

1971. *Polyarchy: Participation and Opposition*. New Haven: Yale University Press.

1973. *Size and Democracy*. Stanford: Stanford University Press.

1976. *Democracy in the United States*. Chicago: Rand McNally.

1980. "The Moscow Discourse: Fundamental Rights in a Democratic Order." *Government and Opposition*, vol. 15, no. 1, pp. 3–30.

1982. *Dilemmas of Pluralist Democracy*. New Haven: Yale University Press.

1985. *A Preface to Economic Democracy*. Berkeley: University of California Press.

1989. *Democracy and Its Critics*. New Haven: Yale University Press.

Dahl, Robert A., and Charles E. Lindblom. 1976. *Politics, Economics and Welfare*. Chicago: University of Chicago Press.

Dalton, H. 1920. "The Measurement of Equality of Incomes." *Economic Journal*, vol. 30, pp. 348–361.
Danziger, Sheldon H., Gary D. Sandefur, and Daniel H. Weinberg. 1994. *Confronting Poverty: Prescriptions for Change*. Cambridge, MA: Harvard University Press.
Debreu, Gerard. 1959. *Theory of Value: An Axiomatic Analysis of Economic Equilibrium*. New Haven: Yale University Press.
Demsetz, H. 1967. "Toward a Theory of Property Rights." *American Economic Review*, vol. 51, pp. 346–360.
Depew, Chauncey M. 1895. *One Hundred Years of Commerce: 1795-1895*. New York: D. O. Haynes.
Derber, C. 1993. "Coming Glued: Communitarianism to the Rescue." *Tikkun*, vol. 8, no. 4, pp. 53–78.
DiQuattro, A. 1983. "Rawls and Left Criticism." *Political Theory*, vol. 11, no. 11, pp. 53–78.
Dixit, Avinash, and Victor Norman. 1978. "Advertising and Welfare." *Bell Journal of Economics*, vol. 9, no. 1, pp. 1–18.
Dobb, Maurice. 1973. *Theories of Value and Distribution since Adam Smith*. Cambridge: Cambridge University Press.
Donahue, Charles, Jr. 1980. "The Future of the Concept of Property Predicted from Its Past." In *NOMOS XXII: Property*, ed. J. Roland Pennock and John W. Chapman. New York: New York University Press.
Donahue, Charles, Jr., Thomas E. Kauper, and Peter W. Martin. 1974. *Cases and Materials on Property: An Introduction to the Concept and Institution*. St. Paul, MN: West Publishing.
Dorfman, Robert, Paul A. Samuelson, and Robert M. Solow. 1958. *Linear Programming and Economic Analysis*. New York: McGraw-Hill
Dunn, John. 1969. *The Political Thought of John Locke*. Cambridge: Cambridge University Press.
Durkheim, Emile. 1957. *Professional Ethics and Civic Morals*, trans. Cornelia Brookfield. London: Routledge and Kegan Paul.
1975. Montesquieu and Rousseau. Ann Arbor: University of Michigan Press.
Dworkin, Ronald. 1981. "What Is Equality: Part 2: Equality of Resources." *Philosophy and Public Affairs*, vol. 10, no. 4, pp. 283–337.
1985. *A Matter of Principle*. Cambridge, MA: Harvard University Press.
1997. "The Roots of Justice." Unpublished manuscript, Program for the Study of Law, Philosophy, and Social Theory, New York University.
Edgeworth, Francis Y. 1881. *Mathematical Psychics*. London: Kegan Paul.
Eisenstein, Louis. 1956. "The Rise and Decline of the Estate Tax." *Tax Law Review*, vol. 11, pp. 223–259. Excerpted in *Federal Wealth Transfer Tax Anthology*, ed. Paul Caron, Grayson M. P. McCouch, and Karen C. Burke. Cincinnati, Ohio: Anderson Publishing, 1998.
El-Safty, Ahmad E. 1972. "Adaptive Behavior and the Pure Theory of Consumer Demand." Ph.D. thesis, Massachusetts Institute of Technology.
1976. "Adaptive Behavior, Demand and Preferences." *Journal of Economic Theory*, vol. 13 (June), pp. 298–318.
Else, P. K. 1968. "The Incidence of Advertising in Manufacturing Industries," *Oxford Economic Papers*, vol. 23, pp. 799–810.
Elster, Jon. 1983. *Sour Grapes*. Cambridge: Cambridge University Press.

Ely, James W., Jr. 1998. *The Guardian of Every Other Right*. New York: Oxford University Press.
Epp, Charles R. 1996. "Do Bills of Rights Matter? The Canadian Charter of Rights." *American Political Science Review*, vol. 90, no. 4 (December), pp. 765–779.
Erikson, Robert, and John H. Goldthorpe. 1993. *The Constant Flux: A Study of Class Mobility in Industrial Societies*. Oxford: Clarendon Press.
Etzioni, Amitai. 1988. *The Moral Dimension*. New York: The Free Press.
1993. *The Spirit of Community*. New York: Crown Publishers.
Ewald, William C. 1988. "Unger's Philosophy: A Critical Study." *Yale Law Journal*, vol. 97, no. 5, pp. 665–756.
Ferguson, C. E. 1972. *Microeconomic Theory*. 3rd edn. Homewood, IL: Richard D. Irwin. (First edition published in 1966.)
Fishkin, James S. 1991. *Democracy and Deliberation*. New Haven: Yale University Press.
Flathman, Richard E. 1987. *The Philosophy and Politics of Freedom*. Chicago: University of Chicago Press.
Frank, Robert. 1999. *Luxury Fever*. New York: The Free Press.
Fraser, Nancy. 1997. "Social Justice in the Age of Identity Politics: Redistribution, Recognition, and Participation." Paper presented at the Conference for the Study of Political Thought, Columbia University, April 4–6.
Fried, Charles. 1978. *Right and Wrong*. Cambridge, MA: Harvard University Press.
Friedman, Milton. 1962. *Capitalism and Freedom*. Chicago: University of Chicago Press.
Fukuyama, Francis. 1992. *The End of History*. New York: The Free Press.
Galbraith, James Kenneth. 1998. *Created Unequal: The Crisis in American Pay*. New York: The Free Press.
Galbraith, John Kenneth. 1969. *The Affluent Society*. 2nd edn., rev. Boston: Houghton Mifflin.
1971. *The New Industrial State*. Boston: Houghton Mifflin.
Gaskell, Elizabeth. 1951 [1855]. *North and South*. London: John Lehmann.
Gauthier, David. 1986. *Morals by Agreement*. Oxford: Clarendon Press.
Gaventa, John. 1980. *Power and Powerlessness: Quiescence and Rebellion in an Appalachian Valley*. Urbana: University of Illinois Press.
Gintis, Herbert. 1972. "An Analysis of Welfare Economics and Individual Development." *Quarterly Journal of Economics*, vol. 86, no. 4 (November), pp. 572–599.
1974. "Welfare Criteria with Endogenous Preferences: The Economics of Education." *International Economic Review*, vol. 15, no. 2 (June), pp. 415–430.
Glaister, S. 1974. "Advertising Policy and Returns to Scale in Markets where Information Is Passed between Individuals." *Economica*, vol. 14, pp. 139–156.
Goode, Erica. 1999. "Study Finds TV Alters Fiji Girls' View of Body." *The New York Times*, May 20, section A, p. 17.
1999. "For Good Health, It Helps to Be Rich and Important." *The New York Times*, June 1, section F, pp. 1, 9.
Gould, Carol C. 1978. *Marx's Social Ontology: Individuality and Community in Marx's Theory of Social Reality*. Cambridge, MA: MIT Press.
1988. *Rethinking Democracy*. Cambridge: Cambridge University Press.

1995. "Social Justice and the Limitation of Democracy." In *Morality and Social Justice: Point/Counterpoint*, ed. James P. Sterba, Tibor R. Machan, Alison M. Jaggar, William A. Galston, Carol C. Gould, Milton Fisk, and Robert C. Solomon. Lanham, MA: Rowman and Littlefield.

Green, T. H. 1967. *Lectures on the Principles of Political Obligation*. Ann Arbor: University of Michigan Press.

1969. *Prolegomena to Ethics*. New York: Thomas Y. Crowell.

Greer, D. F. 1971. "Advertising and Market Concentration." *Southern Economic Journal*, vol. 38, pp. 10–32.

Gregor, Mary. 1963. *Laws of Freedom*. Oxford: Blackwell.

Guth, L. A. 1971. "Advertising and Market Structure Revisited." *Journal of Industrial Economics*, vol. 19, pp. 179–198.

Gutman, Amy. 1985. "Communitarian Critics of Liberalism." In *Philosophy and Public Affairs*, vol. 14, no. 3, pp. 308–322.

Habermas, Jurgen. 1996. *Between Facts and Norms*. Trans. William Regh. Cambridge, MA: MIT Press.

Hacker, Andrew. 1997. *Money*. New York: Scribner's.

Hammond, Peter J. 1976. "Endogenous Tastes and Stable Long-Run Choice." *Journal of Economic Theory*, vol. 13, pp. 329–340.

Hart, Vivien. 1994. *Bound by Our Constitution: Women, Workers, and the Minimum Wage*. Princeton, NJ: Princeton University Press.

Haveman, Robert H., and Kenyon Knopf. 1970. *The Market System*. 2nd edn. New York: Wiley.

Hayek, F. A. 1960. *The Constitution of Liberty*. Chicago: Henry Regnery.

1967. *Studies in Philosophy, Politics and Economics*. New York: Simon and Schuster.

1976. *Law, Legislation and Liberty. II: The Mirage of Social Justice*. Chicago: University of Chicago Press.

Hegel. G. W. F. 1870a. "The Science of Rights, Morals, And Religion." *The Journal of Speculative Philosophy*, vol. 4 (translated from the *Philosophische Propaedeutik,* 1808, by T. Wm. Harris), pp. 38–62.

1870b. "Outlines of the Science of Rights, Morals, and Religion." *The Journal of Speculative Philosophy*, vol. 4 (translated from the *Philosophische Propaedeutik,* 1808, by T. Wm. Harris), pp. 155–191.

1952. *Philosophy of Right,* trans. T. M. Knox. London: Oxford University Press.

1975a. *Logic,* trans. by William Wallace. Oxford: Clarendon Press.

1975b. *Natural Law,* trans. T. M. Knox. Philadelphia: University of Pennsylvania Press.

Heilbroner, Robert, and William Milberg. 1995. *The Crisis of Vision in Modern Economic Thought*. New York: Cambridge University Press.

Heller, Agnes. 1976. *The Theory of Needs in Marx*. New York: St. Martin's.

Henderson, James M., and Richard E. Quandt. 1971. *Microeconomic Theory: A Mathematical Approach*. 2nd edn. New York: McGraw-Hill.

Hicks, John. 1939. *Value and Capital*. 1st edn. Oxford: Clarendon Press.

1946. *Value and Capital*. 2nd edn. Oxford: Clarendon Press.

1963 [1932]. *The Theory of Wages*. London: Macmillan.

1965. *Capital and Growth*. New York: Oxford University Press.

Hicks, J. R., and R. G. D. Allen. 1934. "A Reconsideration of the Theory of Value," parts I and II. *Economica*, vol. 1, pp. 52–73, 196–219.

Hilts, P. J. 1993. "Doctors' Pay Resented, and It's Underestimated." *The New York Times,* March 31, section A, p. 9.

Hobart, R. E. 1934. "Free Will as Involving Determination and Inconceivable without It." *Mind*, vol. 43, no. 169 (January), pp. 1–27.

Hobbes, Thomas. 1958 [1651]. *Leviathan*, ed. Herbert W. Schneider. Indianapolis: Bobbs-Merrill.

Hohfeld, Wesley N. 1923. *Fundamental Legal Conceptions.* New Haven: Yale University Press.

Holland, Thomas Erskine. 1924. *Elements of Jurisprudence.* 13th edn. Oxford: Clarendon.

Holmstrom, Nancy. 1977. "Exploitation." *Canadian Journal of Philosophy*, vol. 7, no. 2 (June), pp. 353–369.

Holt, Rachham. 1946. *George Washington Carver: An American Biography.* Garden City, NY: Doubleday.

Humboldt, W. von. 1969 [1852]. *The Limits of State Action*, trans. J. W. Burrow. Cambridge: Cambridge University Press.

Iwai, Katsuhito. 1981. *Disequilibrium Dynamics.* New Haven: Yale University Press.

Jappelli, Tullio, and Marco Pagano. 1994. "Personal Saving in Italy." In *International Comparisons of Household Saving*, ed. James M. Poterba. Chicago: University of Chicago Press.

Jevons, W. S. 1871. *The Theory of Political Economy.* London: Macmillan.

Johnston, David. 1995. "Equality and Moral Pluralism." Unpublished paper, Department of Political Science, Columbia University.

Johnston, David Cay. 1999. "Gap between Rich and Poor Found Substantially Wider." *The New York Times*, September 5, p. 16.

Kaldor, Nicholas. 1950. "The Economic Aspects of Advertising." *Review of Economic Studies*, vol. 18, pp. 1–27.

Kant, Immanuel. 1887 [1797]. *The Philosophy of Law: An Exposition of the Fundamental Principles of Jurisprudence as the Science of Right*, trans. W. Hastie. Edinburgh: T. and T. Clark.

1896. *Critique of Pure Reason.* trans. F. Max Muller. New York: Macmillan.

1964. *Groundwork of the Metaphysics of Morals*, trans. H. J. Paton. New York: Harper.

1965 [1797]. *The Metaphysical Elements of Justice*, trans. John Ladd. Indianapolis, IN: Bobbs-Merrill.

1970. *Kant's Political Writings*, ed. Hans Reiss. New York: Cambridge University Press.

1991 [1797]. *The Metaphysics of Morals*, trans. Mary Gregor. New York: Cambridge University Press.

Kaufman, Alexander. 1999. *Welfare in the Kantian State.* New York: Oxford University Press.

Kelson, Hans. 1961. *General Theory of Law and State.* New York: Russell and Russell.

Keynes, J. M. 1964. *The General Theory of Employment, Interest, and Money.* New York: Harcourt, Brace and World.

Klinkenborg, Verlyn. 1999. "The Man at Microsoft; or How High the Moon." *The New York Times,* Sept. 4, section A, p. 12.

Koopmans, T. C. 1957. *Three Essays on the State of Economic Science.* New York: McGraw-Hill.

Kremer, Gary R. 1987. *George Washington Carver in His Own Words.* Columbia: University of Missouri Press.

Kronman, Anthony. 1976–1977. Book Review. *Minnesota Law Review*, vol. 61, pp. 167–203.

Kymlicka, Will. 1989. *Liberalism, Community, and Culture.* Oxford: Clarendon Press.

Lakoff, Sanford. 1964. *Equality in Political Philosophy.* Cambridge, MA: Harvard University Press.

Larmore, Charles. 1987. *Moral Complexity.* Cambridge: Cambridge University Press.

Laursen, John Christian. 1989. "Skepticism and Intellectual Freedom: The Philosophical Foundations of Kant's Politics of Publicity." History of Political *Thought*, vol. 10, no. 3 (Autumn), pp. 439–455.

Lerner, Ralph. 1963. *Parts and Wholes.* New York: The Free Press of Glencoe.

Leuchtenburg, William E. 1988. "Franklin D. Roosevelt: The First Modern President." In *Leadership in the Modern Presidency*, ed. Fred I. Greenstein. Cambridge, MA: Harvard University Press.

Levine, David P. 1977. *Economic Studies: Contributions to the Critique of Economic Theory.* London: Routledge and Kegan Paul.

1978–1981. *Economic Theory*, 2 vols. London: Routledge and Kegan Paul.

1988. *Needs, Rights and the Market.* Boulder, CO: Lynne Reinner.

1991. "Social Justice and the Limits of the Market." Paper presented at the annual meeting of the Society for Systematic Philosophy, symposium on Social Justice and the Limits of the Market, New York City, December 29.

n.d. "The Fortress and the Market." Unpublished ms.

Levy, Frank. 1987. *Dollars and Dreams.* New York: Norton.

Lewis, John D. 1967. *Anti-Federalists versus Federalists.* San Francisco: Chandler Publishing Company.

Lindblom, Charles E. 1977. *Politics and Markets.* New York: Basic Books.

Llewellyn, Karl N. 1962. *Jurisprudence: Realism in Theory and Practice.* Chicago: University of Chicago Press.

Locke, John. 1824. *The Works of Locke*, 9 vols. 12th edn. London: Baldwin.

1958. *Essays on the Law of Nature*, ed. W. Von Leiden. Oxford: Oxford University Press.

1963 [1689/90]. *Two Treatises of Government*, ed. Peter Laslett. New York: New American Library.

1979. *Treatise of Civil Government and A Letter Concerning Toleration*, ed. C. L. Sherman. New York: Irvington.

Lodge, George C. 1987. "Introduction." In *Ideology and National Competitiveness*, ed. George C. Lodge and Ezra F. Vogel. Boston: Harvard Business School Press.

Lodge, George C., and Ezra F. Vogel, eds. 1987. *Ideology and National Competitiveness.* Boston: Harvard Business School Press.

Lowe, Adolph. 1965. *On Economic Knowledge.* New York: Harper and Row.

Lukes, Steven. 1974. *Power: A Radical View.* London: Macmillan.

Lummis, C. Douglas. 1996. *Radical Democracy.* Ithaca: Cornell University Press.

Lynes, Russell. 1949. *The Taste Makers.* New York: Grosset and Dunlap.

Macedo, Stephen. 1991. *Liberal Virtues.* Oxford: Clarendon Press.

Machlup, Fritz. 1963. *Essays on Economic Semantics*. Englewood Cliffs, NJ: Prentice-Hall.

Macpherson, C. B. 1962. *The Political Theory of Possessive Individualism: Hobbes to Locke*. London: Oxford University Press.

1985. *The Rise and Fall of Economic Justice*. Oxford: Oxford University Press.

Mansbridge, Jane J. 1980. *Beyond Adversary Democracy*. New York: Basic Books.

Mansfield, Harvey, Jr. 1989. *Taming the Prince*. Baltimore: Johns Hopkins University Press.

Marx, Karl. 1956 [1885]. *Capital*, vol. 2. Moscow: Progress Publishers.

1956. *Capital*, vol. 2. Moscow: Progress Publishers.

1959. "Critique of the Gotha Program." In *Marx and Engels: Basic Writings on Politics and Philosophy*, ed. L. S. Feuer. Garden City, NY: Doubleday.

1963. *The Poverty of Philosophy*. New York: International Publishers.

1967a [1867]. *Capital*, vol 1. New York: International Publishers.

1967b [1885]. *Capital*, vol. 2. New York: International Publishers.

1967c [1894]. *Capital*, vol. 3. New York: International Publishers.

1973. *Grundrisse*, trans. Martin Nicolaus. New York: Vintage.

1977. *Capital*, vol. 1, trans. Ben Fowkes. New York: Vintage.

McClosky, Herbert, and John Zaller. 1984. *The American Ethos*. Cambridge: Harvard University Press.

McIntyre, Alisdair. 1981. *After Virtue*. Notre Dame, IN: Notre Dame University Press.

McLean, Edward B. 1992. *Law and Civilization: The Legal Thought of Roscoe Pound*. Lanham, MD: University Press of America.

Meek, Ronald L. 1956. *Studies in the Labour Theory of Value*. 2nd edn. New York: Monthly Review Press.

1963. *The Economics of Physiocracy*. Cambridge, MA: Harvard University Press.

1973. *Precursors of Adam Smith*. Totowa, NJ: Rowman and Littlefield.

Menger, Karl. 1950. *Principles of Economics*, trans. J. Dingwell and B. F. Hoselitz. Chicago: The Free Press.

Mill, J. S. 1962. *Utilitarianism. In Utilitarianism, On Liberty, Essay On Bentham*, ed. Mary Warnock. Cleveland: World Publishing.

Miller, Jonathan. 1978. *The Body in Question*. New York: Random House.

Milly, Deborah J. 1999. *Poverty, Equality, and Growth: The Politics of Economic Need in Postwar Japan*. Cambridge, MA: Harvard University East Asia Center.

Miringoff, Marc, and Marque-Luisa Miringoff. 1999. *The Social Health of the Nation: How America Is Really Doing*. New York: Oxford University Press.

Mishan, E. J. 1971. "The Postwar Literature on Externalities: An Interpretive Essay." *Journal of Economic Literature*, vol. 9, no. 1 (March), pp. 1–27.

Moore, Barrington, Jr. 1966. *The Origins of Dictatorship and Democracy*. Boston: Beacon Press.

Morishima, M. 1973. *Marx's Economics*. Cambridge: Cambridge University Press.

Morita, Akio. 1986. *Made in Japan*. New York: E. P. Dutton.

Mower, David C., and Nathan Rosenberg. 1989. *Technology and the Pursuit of Economic Growth*. Cambridge: Cambridge University Press.

Munzer, Stephen R. 1990. *A Theory of Property*. Cambridge: Cambridge University Press.
Nasar, Sylvia 1992 "One Group Saw Relief: The Very Wealthiest 1%." *The New York Times*, Oct. 1, section D, p. 6.
Nekam, Alexander. 1938. *The Personality Conception of the Legal Entity.* Cambridge, MA: Harvard University Press.
Nelson, P. 1975. "The Economic Consequences of Advertising," *Journal of Business,* vol. 48, pp. 213–241.
Neumann, John von. 1945–1946. "A Model of General Economic Equilibrium." *Review of Economic Studies,* vol. 13, pp. 1–9.
Nicholson, Walter. 1985. *Microeconomic Theory*. 3rd edn. Chicago: The Dryden Press.
Nozick, Robert. 1974. *Anarchy, State, and Utopia*. New York: Basic Books.
Okun, Arthur. 1975. *Equality and Efficiency: The Big Tradeoff.* Washington, DC: Brookings Institution.
Ong, Nai Pew. 1979. *Ricardo and Marx: The Development of Homogeneous Physical Capital and the Advance Beyond*. Ph.D. dissertation, Yale University.
Oppenheim, Phillip. 1992. *Japan without Blinders*. Tokyo: Kodansha International.
Orr, D. 1974. "The Determinants of Entry: A study of the Canadian manufacturing industries." *Review of Economics and Statistics*, vol. 64, pp. 376–383.
Palmer, R. R., and Joel Colton. 1995 [1950]. *A History of the Modern World.* New York: McGraw Hill.
Pareto, Vilfredo. 1927. *Manuel d'Economie Politique*. 2nd ed. Paris: Giard.
Pateman, Carole. 1970. *Participation and Democratic Theory.* Cambridge: Cambridge University Press.
Paton, D., and S. Machin. 1993. "Advertising as a Strategic Variable: Survey Evidence from UK Companies." *Occasional Papers in Economics*, no. 93/2, Nottingham Trent University.
Pelczynski, Z. A. 1971. *Hegel's Political Philosophy*. Cambridge: Cambridge University Press.
Pen, Jan. 1971. *Income Distribution: Facts, Theories, Policies*. New York: Praeger.
Phelps Brown, H. 1988. *Egalitarianism and the Generation of Inequality.* Oxford: Oxford University Press.
Pollack, Andrew. 1999. "Akio Morita, Co-Founder of Sony and Japanese Business Leader, Dies at 78." *The New York Times,* October 4, section B, p. 8.
Pollak, Robert A. 1976. "Interdependent Preferences." *American Economic Review,* vol. 66, no. 3 (June), pp. 309–320.
Polsby, Nelson. 1963. *Community and Political Theory.* New Haven: Yale University Press.
Popper, Karl. 1963. *The Open Society and Its Enemies: The High Tide of Prophecy*. Princeton: Princeton University Press.
Posner, Richard. 1972. *Economic Analysis of Law*. Boston: Little, Brown.
1981. *The Economics of Justice*. Cambridge: Cambridge University Press.
Pound, Roscoe. 1957. *The Development of Constitutional Guarantees of Liberty*. New Haven: Yale University Press.
1959. *Jurisprudence,* 5 vols. St. Paul, MN: West Publishing.

Poulantzas, Nicos. 1973. *Political Power and Social Classes*. London: Verso Editions.

Prestowitz, Clyde V., Jr. 1989. *Trading Places*. New York: Basic Books.

Quinn, M. 1991. *Justice and Egalitarianism*. New York: Garland.

Quirk, James, and Rubin Saposnik. 1968. *Introduction to General Equilibrium Theory and Welfare Economics*. New York: McGraw-Hill.

Radin, Margaret Jane. 1982. "Property and Personhood." *Stanford Law Review*,. vol. 34, pp. 957–1015.

Rae, Douglas. W. 1975. "Maximum Justice and an Alternative Principle of General Advantage." *American Political Science Review*, vol. 69, no. 2.

1981. *Equalities*. Cambridge, MA: Harvard University Press.

Raz, Joseph. 1970. *The Concept of a Legal System*. Oxford: Clarendon Press.

Rawls, John. 1971. *A Theory of Justice*. Cambridge, MA: Harvard University Press.

1993. *Political Liberalism*. New York: Columbia University Press.

Reading, Brian. 1992. *Japan: The Coming Collapse*. New York: HarperCollins.

Reich, Robert. 1984. *The Next Frontier*. New York: Penguin.

Reingold, Jennifer. 1997. "Executive Pay." *Business Week*, April 11, pp. 56–68.

Reynolds, Lloyd G., and Peter Gregory. 1965. *Wages, Productivity, and Industrialization in Puerto Rico*. Homewood, IL: Richard D. Irwin.

Riley, P. 1982. *Will and Political Legitimacy: A Critical Exposition of Social Contract Theory in Hobbes, Locke, Rousseau, Kant, and Hegel*. Cambridge, MA: Harvard University Press.

Ritchie, David G. 1894. *Natural Rights*. London: George Allen and Unwin.

Robbins, Lord. 1984 [1932]. *An Essay on the Nature and Significance of Economic Science*. New York: New York University Press.

Roemer, J. 1988. *Free to Lose*. Cambridge, MA: Harvard University Press.

Rousseau, Jean-Jacques. 1967. *The Social Contract and Discourse on the Origin of Inequality*, ed. Lester Crocker. New York: Washington Square Press.

Ryan, Alan. 1965. "Locke and the Dictatorship of the Bourgeoisie." *Political Studies*, vol. 13, no. 2, pp. 219–230.

1993. "The Liberal Community." In *NOMOS XXXV: Democratic Community*, ed. John W. Chapman and Ian Shapiro. New York: New York University Press.

Samuelson, Paul Anthony. 1948. *Foundations of Economic Analysis*. Cambridge, MA: Harvard University Press.

1957. "Wages and Interest: A Modern Dissection of Marxian Economic Models." *American Economic Review*, vol. 47, no. 6, pp. 884–912.

1971. "Understanding the Marxian Notion of Exploitation: A Summary of the So-Called Transformation Problem between Marxian Values and Competitive Prices." *Journal of Economic Literature*, vol. 9, pp. 399–431.

Sandel, Michael J. 1982. *Liberalism and the Limits of Justice*. Cambridge: Cambridge University Press.

1996. *Democracy's Discontent*. Cambridge, MA: Harvard University Press.

Schaar, J. H. 1980. "Equality of Opportunity and the Just Society." In *John Rawls' Theory of Social Justice*, ed. H. G. Blocker and E. H. Smith. Athens: Ohio University Press.

Sawyer, Malcolm. 1976. "Income Distribution in OECD Countries." *OECD Economic Outlook Occasional Studies*, July.

Schlatter, Richard. 1951. *Private Property: The History of an Idea*. New York: Russell and Russell.

Schmalensee, Richard. 1972. *The Economics of Advertising*. Amsterdam: North Holland.

1978. "Entry Deterrence in the Ready-to-Eat Breakfast Cereals Market." *Bell Journal of Economics,* vol. 9, pp. 305–327.

Schumpeter, Joseph A. 1943. *Capitalism, Socialism, and Democracy*. London: George Allen and Unwin.

1951. *The Theory of Economic Development*. Cambridge, MA: Harvard University Press.

1954. *History of Economic Analysis*. New York: Oxford University Press.

Schwartz, Tony. 1999. "Is This Any Way to Run a Meritocracy?" *The New York Times Magazine,* January 10, section 6, pp. 30–51.

Scitovsky, Tibor. 1952. *Welfare and Competition*. London: George Allen and Unwin.

1954. "Two Concepts of External Economies." *Journal of Political Economy,* vol. 17, pp. 143–151.

Sen, A. 1979. "Personal Utilities and Public Judgments: Or What's Wrong with Welfare Economics." *The Economic Journal*, vol. 89, pp. 537–558.

1992. *Inequality Reexamined*. Cambridge, MA: Harvard University Press.

Shapiro, Ian. 1986. *The Evolution of Rights in Liberal Theory*. Cambridge: Cambridge University Press.

1991. "Resources, Capacities, and Ownership: The Workmanship Ideal and Distributive Justice." *Political Theory*, vol. 19, no. 1, pp. 47–72.

1994. "Three Ways to Be a Democrat." *Political Theory*, vol. 22, no. 1 (February), pp. 124–151.

1996. *Democracy's Place*. Ithaca: Cornell University Press.

Sher, G. 1987. *Desert*. Princeton: Princeton University Press.

Shweder, Richard A. 1997. "It's Called Poor Health for a Reason." *The New York Times,* March 9, section 4, p. 5.

Silberberg, Eugene. 1978. *The Structure of Economics*. New York: McGraw-Hill.

Simon, Thomas W. 1995. *Democracy and Social Injustice*. Lanham, MD: Rowman and Littlefield.

Simons, A. John. 1992. *The Lockean Theory of Rights*. Princeton: Princeton University Press.

Singer, Joseph William. 1997. *Property Law: Rules, Policies, and Practices*. 2nd edn. New York: Aspen Law and Business.

Singer, M. G. 1961. *Generalization in Ethics*. New York: Alfred A. Knopf.

Skowronek, Stephen. 1993. *The Politics Presidents Make*. Cambridge, MA: Harvard University Press.

Slutsky, E. 1915. "Sulla teoria del bilancio del consumatore." *Giornale degli Economisti,* vol. 51, pp. 1–26.

Smart, Carol. 1989. *Feminism and the Power of Law*. London: Routledge.

Smiley, R. 1988. "Empirical Evidence on Strategic Entry Deterrence." *Journal of Industrial Organization*, vol. 6, pp. 167–180.

Smith, Adam. 1937. *The Wealth of Nations,* ed. Edwin Cannan. New York: Modern Library.

Smith, J. C. 1976. *Legal Obligation*. London: Athlone Press.

Snider, Denton J. 1902. *The State*. St. Louis: Sigma.

Sombart, Werner. 1967. *Luxury and Capitalism*. Ann Arbor: University of Michigan Press.

Sraffa, Pierro. 1960. *Production of Commodities by Means of Commodities*. Cambridge: Cambridge University Press.

Steuart, Sir James. 1966 [1767]. *An Inquiry into the Principles of Political Economy*, 2 vols., ed. Andrew S. Skinner. Edinburgh: Oliver and Boyd.

Stiglitz, Joseph. 1993. *Economics*. New York: W. W. Norton.

Stillman, Peter. 1980. "Property, Freedom, and Individuality in Political Thought." In *NOMOS XXII: Property*, ed. J. Rolland Pennock and John Chapman. New York: New York University Press.

Strauss, Leo. 1950. *Natural Right and History*. Chicago: University of Chicago Press.

Sunstein, Cass. 1993. "Endogenous Preferences, Environmental Law." *The Journal of Legal Studies*, vol. 22, no. 2 (June), pp. 217-255.

Tachi, Ryuichiro. 1993. *The Contemporary Japanese Economy: An Overview*, trans. Richard Walker. Tokyo: University of Tokyo Press.

Taylor, Charles. 1979. *Hegel and Modern Society*. Cambridge: Cambridge University Press.

1985. *Philosophy and the Human Sciences*. Vol. 2. Cambridge: Cambridge University Press.

Telser, L. G. 1965. *Advertising and Competition*. New York: Steller Press.

Thatcher, Margaret. 1993. *The Downing Street Years*. London: HarperCollins.

Tierney, John. 1998. "Rich and Poor, Consumed by Consuming." *The New York Times*, November 30, section B, p. 1.

Tocqueville, Alexis de. 1945. *Democracy in America*, 2 vols. New York: Vintage Books.

Tully, J. 1980. *A Discourse on Property: John Locke and His Adversaries*. Cambridge: Cambridge University Press.

Tushnet, Mark. 1984. "An Essay on Rights." *Texas Law Review*, vol. 62 (May), pp. 1363–1403.

Unger, Roberto Mangabeira. 1975. *Knowledge and Politics*. New York: The Free Press.

United for a Fair Economy. 1999a. "CEO Pay in '98: Insanity Marches On." *Too Much: A Quarterly Commentary on Capping Excessive Income and Wealth*, vol 5,. no. 1 (Summer), p. 3.

1999b. "The Trillion-Dollar Gang," *Too Much*, vol. 5, no. 2 (Fall), p. 1.

U.S. Bureau of the Census. 1998. *March Current Population Survey*. Washington, DC: U.S. Government Printing Office.

U.S. Department of Education. National Center for Education Statistics. 1999. *Digest of Education Statistics, 1998*. NCES 1999-036, by Thomas D. Snyder. Washington, DC.

Urban, G., S. Gaskin, T. Carter, and Z. Mucha. 1984. "Market Share Reward to Pioneering Brands." *Management Sciences*, vol. 32, pp. 645–659.

Varian, Hal. 1993. *Intermediate Microeconomics*. 3rd edn. New York: W. W. Norton.

Veblen, Thorstein. 1998. *The Theory of the Leisure Class*. Amherst, NY: Prometheus Books.

Vogel, Ezra F. 1987. "Japan: Adaptive Communitarianism." In his *Ideology and National Competitiveness*. Boston: Harvard Business School Press.

Waldron, Jeremy. 1988. *The Right to Private Property*. Oxford: Clarendon Press.

1999. *Law and Disagreement*. Oxford: Oxford University Press.

Wallach, John R. 1987. "Liberals, Communitarians, and the Tasks of Political Theory." *Political Theory,* vol. 15, pp. 581–611.

Walras, L. 1954. *Elements of Pure Economics*. Homewood, IL: Richard D. Irwin.

Walzer, Michael. 1983. *Spheres of Justice*. New York: Basic Books.

Warren, Mark E. 1995. "Rights and Radical Democracy." Paper delivered at the annual meeting of the American Political Science Association, Chicago.

Weber, Max. 1947. *The Theory of Social and Economic Organization*, trans. A. M. Henderson and Talcott Parsons, ed. Talcott Parsons. New York: The Free Press.

Weiss, Roger. 1969. *The Economic System*. New York: Random House.

Weizsacker, Carl Christian von. 1971. "Notes on Endogenous Change of Taste." *Journal of Economic Theory*, vol. 13, pp. 345–372.

Wellisz, Stanislaw. 1964. "On External Diseconomies and the Government-Assisted Invisible Hand." *Economica*, vol. 21, no. 124 (November), pp. 345–362.

Westergaard, J. H., and H. Resler. 1975. *Class in a Capitalist Society: A Study of Contemporary Britain*. New York: Basic Books.

Whitehead, Alfred North. 1960. *Process and Reality*. New York: Harper.

Wildavsky, Aaron. 1991. *The Rise of Radical Egalitarianism*. Washington, DC: American University Press.

Williamson, J. G., and P. H. Lindert. 1980. *American Inequality, a Macroeconomic History*. New York: Academic Press..

Wilner, Richard. 1997. "The Bucks $top Here." *The New York Post,* April 11, p. 7

Winfield, Richard D. 1977. *The Social Determination of Production*. Ph.D. dissertation, Yale University.

1982. "Freedom as Interaction: Hegel's Resolution of the Dilemma of Liberal Theory." In *Hegel's Theory of Action*, ed. Lawrence S. Stepelevich and David Lamb. New York: Humanities Press.

1984. "Hegel's Challenge to the Modern Economy." In *History and System: Hegel's Philosophy of History*, ed. R. L. Perkins. Albany: State University of New York Press.

1988. *Reason and Justice*. Albany: State University of New York Press.

1989. *Overcoming Foundations*. New York: Columbia University Press.

1990. *The Just Economy.* New York: Routledge.

1991. *Freedom and Modernity*. Albany: State University of New York Press.

Wolf, Edward N. 1995. *Top Heavy*. New York: The New Press.

Wolgast, Elizabeth H. 1987. *The Grammar of Justice*. Ithaca: Cornell University Press.

WuDunn, Sheryl. 1999. "To Revive a Sick Economy, Japan Hands Out Coupons." *The New York Times*, March 3, p. 6.

Yaari, Menahem E. 1976. "Endogenous Changes in Tastes: A Philosophical Discussion." In *Decision Theory and Social Ethics*, ed. Hans W. Gottinger and Werner Leinfellner. Boston: Reidel.

Zaller, John R. 1992. *The Nature and Origins of Mass Opinion*. Cambridge: Cambridge University Press.

Zamagni, Stefano. 1987. *Microeconomic Theory.* Oxford: Basil Blackwell.

Zucker, Ross. 1990. "Social Elements of the Theory of Property Rights." Ph.D. thesis, Yale University, 2 vols.

1991. "'Social Self-determination and Equality in Property Right." Paper presented at the annual meeting of the American Political Science Association, Washington, DC.

1993. "Two Visions of Property: Social and Liberal." Paper presented at the conference of the Society for the Advancement of Socio-Economics, New York City, March 260–28.

1995. "Preface to a Social Theory of Property." *Ratio Juris*, vol. 8, no. 2 (July), pp. 195–207.

Index

abstract equality, 8, 15, 46, 270; *see also* concrete equality, equality
agency, 3, 44, 60, 63, 86, 199–201, 206, 210, 226, 256, 259, 260-62
Allen, R. G. D., 202
American model, *see* United States
Americans, 11, 22, 23, 24, 144
Antonelli, G. B., 202
Arrow, Kenneth J., 181, 182, 221
Ashcraft, Richard, 34, 35, 38, 40–1, 47–9
Atkinson, Anthony B., 20, 144
attributes: of the self, 29; common attributes, 182, 235, 238; concrete differences in, 293; concrete equalities in, 284; of consumer, 86, 99, 110-11, 115, 279; consumptive, 85, 99, 104, 111, 125-26; contributions by, 90; economic, 55, 90, 114, 125, 285, 293; economy's influence on, 126; economically creative 14, 125, 279-81, 283, 285, 301; equal, 2; given, 61; internal causes of, 7; productive, 126; shared, 170; social, 76, 127, 237, 284; socially self-determined, 87, 103, 111, 114-15, 140, 279; subjective, 80, 120; universal, 168
Austin, John: theory of property, 65-66; and subjective individuality, 65; unequal accumulation, 66
Australia, 20, 144
Austria, 144

Barber, Benjamin, 288, 289
Barry, B., 27, 91, 96
Basmann, R. L., 202
Becker, Gary S., 203 n56
Becker, Lawrence, 29, 39 n24, 75 n71, 91 n9, 92 n11, 96, 98, 101
Benhabib, Seyla, 10, 28, 90, 127, 271
Bentham, Jeremy: apparent social determination of property, 63; denial of social interests, 65; fictious community, 64; individual utility, 63; meaning of "social," 63; reduction to subjective utilities, 65; social determination as restriction, 63; social principle of general utility, 63-4; subjective interests, 65; theory of property, 27, 29-32, 63-66, 71
Berolzheimer, Fritz, 33 n3
Berry, Christopher, 33 n3
Berry, Jeffrey, 288
Bertalanffy, Ludwig von, 19
Blackstone, William, 54, 66, 73, 74
Blaug, Mark, 216

Boddewyn, J. J., 199
Bohm-Bawerk, Eugen von, 12
Bork, Robert H., 298, 299
Boswell, Jonathan, 17
Bowles, Samuel, 135
Bradsher, Keith, 20–1
Browning, E. K., 202
Buchanan, James M., 103
Burtless, Gary, 132, 254
Buxton, A. J., 202

Canada, 144
capacities, 43, 55, 93, 111, 113, 125–26, 198, 203, 210–11, 247, 270, 281, 284–85, 295, 296, 301; productive capacities, 2, 46, 73, 79; socially produced, 43; socially self-determined capacities, 114
capital, 169–87, 188–219, 220–45, 264–65, 272, 285–86, 301; all elements of the circuit are, 172; capital gains tax, 133, 147; as common end, 63, 176–79, 188, 259; as common substance, 172; commodity capital, 171–72, 177–79, 230; definition of, 172; determination of individuality by, 196; as goal, 3; income from, 129; and Keynesian state, 131; money capital, 172, 205; movement of total capital, 180; preservation and expansion of, 3, 19, 172, 176–78, 183–85, 188, 205–09, 211–12, 219, 220–22, 225, 230–31, 234, 235, 237, 245, 252–53, 258, 262–65; principle of shapes individual ends, 253; productive capital, 171–72, 178, 230; unity of economic process, 169; and wealth, 184
capital managers, 153, 220, 228
capital owners, 153, 171–72 185, 220–38, 240–45, 252, 263–65; microeconomic decisions of, 264–65
capital-based market systems, 3, 17, 74, 90, 96, 117, 128, 153, 154, 161, 169, 188, 244, 252, 256, 272, 285, 286, 301; application of communally derived rules to, 18; community within, 3, 17, 19, 63, 238, 255; dimension of community in, 6, 12, 18; multiplied needs in, 137; *see also* system
capitalism, 18–20, 131, 133, 178, 189, 196, 198, 206, 229, 230, 235, 243, 248, 275; artisan form of, 206; and class division, 19; communal cum competitive, 4, 12, 17–20, 103, 153, 154, 158, 160, 170, 174, 175, 207, 224, 238, 245, 248–52, 256, 259, 260, 261, 264–65; corporate capitalism, 197–8, 206; free market, 20; individualistic, 4; mechanized capitalist factory production, 196; a society of mixed metaphors, 4; *see also* system, capital-based market system
capitalist systems, *see* capitalism, circulation of capital
capitalists: conceived as socially constituted, 12; *see also* capital owners
Carens, Joseph H., 276
Caron, Paul, 133
Carver, George Washington, 188, 192
Caughey, Andrew, 201
Champernowne, D. G., 215
China, 12
choice, 10, 29, 50, 60, 62, 76, 79, 86, 105, 117–18, 156, 196, 213, 215, 216–17, 247–48, 250, 252, 256, 261–62, 284, 294-95; priority of, 7, 53, 127
circuit of capital, *see* circulation of capital
circulation of capital, 171, 173, 195, 217, 228, 230, 252, 258, 262, 263; and community, 179–80;

consumption as part of, 176; generated by endogenous formation of preferences, 205–06; goal of preserving and expanding capital, 171, 253; interest of circuit as a whole, 189; interrelated circuits, 179–80; and neoclassical exchange, 175–76; not a wholly self-determining system, 185; self-organized, 183–84, 253; as series of metamorphoses, 172; single connected sequence, 172; societal acceptance of, 173; sustained by common action, 3
circulation of commodities and money, 110, 112, 122–24, 128, 184, 190, 212, 249
Clark, J. B., 101, 162–63
classical political economy, 3, 14, 100, 193, 216, 220
coattainment of ends, *see* ethics of economic community
Cobban, Alfred, 27, 51
Cohen, Felix: liberal assumptions of, 73; not a social theory, 73–75; property as social relations, 27, 32, 66, 72–75; subjective individualism, 73; and theory of value, 74
Cohen, G. A., 92 n13, 155 n3
Collins, Susan, 145 n9, 146
Comanor, William, 202, 207, 209
commodity exchangers, 8, 121, 264, 279
common activity, *see* ethics of economic community
common end, *see* ethics of economic community
common goal, *see* ethics of economic community
common interest: as direct object of economic agents, 222; as indirect interest, 179, 222
commonalities, 8–10, 19, 154, 221–24, 234, 249
communist economies, 155
Communitarianism, 16, 17, 166; dispossession of the individual, 16; noneconomic community, 238; and property rights, 4; radically situated subjects, 16; supracommunity, 17, 239; and theory of economic community, 238-40; wider subject of possession, 16; *see also* Etzioni, Sandel, ethics of economic community, ethics of community
community (*see also* ethics of economic community), 1–8, 19–20, 30, 35-6, 46–7, 78–9, 134, 153–55, 163–66, 169–71, 175, 178–88, 190, 195, 205–19, 221–24, 227–29, 233–45, 246–65, 274, 278, 280–81, 301–02; abstract, 8; as basis for deriving principle of equality, 153, 156–61, 165–66, 167, 168, 255; and Bentham, 64; deep structure of economic life, 222; dichotomous thinking about, 17; and entitlement logic, 11; extent of community, 20, 252, 255; Hegelian, 52, 67, 69, 90, 297; and justice, 11; and Kant, 60; and neoclassical economics, 18; noneconomic, 17, 126, 238, 245; and Rawls, 76; and self-determination, 16; and sharing, 47, 157, 243; small-scale, 3, 17, 196; systemwide dimension of, 12, 18; unity of purpose, 46, 157;
concrete equality, 8–10, 15–16, 34, 46, 55, 68–9, 270, 281, 282–86, 293–94, 301; socially generated, 9; universality of, 10
concrete unity, 9
consumer, 2–4, 14, 19, 86–7, 90, 99–106, 108–120, 122, 124, 138, 140, 153, 170–71, 173–219, 224, 227–28, 252, 258-59, 261–63, 279–81, 301; common action of

consumer (*cont.*)
unrecognized, 174; defective formulation of, 102
contemporary social theories, 89; insufficiently egalitarian, 89
contributions, *see* ethics of dueness for economic contributions, economically creative attributes
cooperation, 3, 18, 93, 110, 161–64, 174, 227, 230, 249; cannot be resolved into separately identifiable actions, 18; irreducible, 93, 110, 163, 226
Cowling, 207
Cuba, 12

Dahl, Robert A., on contributions, 125; defining moral interests, 294, democracy and primary political rights, 287; democracy as political equality, 297; on democracy and substantive rights 192, 270–71, 278–79; democracy and social and economic rights, 271, 277, 287, 292; equality in free-farmer America, 21 n32; justice extrinsic to democracy, 273 n13, 298; on large-scale democracy, 133; meaninglessness of Madisonian theory, 278; measuring political equality, 290 n8; procedural democracy, 270–72; rights and decision rules, 279; selective centralization of income distribution, 5 n5; theory of polyarchy, 270–71, 287–88; vagueness of social rights, 292
Dalton, H., 105
Danziger, Sheldon H., 132, 254
Debreu, Gerard, 100, 181, 182, 224
"democratic" capitalist systems, 20
democracies, 5–6, 272, 285, 286, 287; nominal and true, 5
democracy, 1, 4–6, 20-1, 53, 95, 133, 134, 139, 238, 267, 269, 272, 274, 275, 280, 285, 286, 297–98; actual world of, 5; and concrete equalities, 281–84; defining characteristics of, 5, 269–70, 271, 277, 287, 289, 291, 302; and distributive justice 1, 291-92, 301; and economic rights, 287–91, 292–94; highest court of moral appeal, 6; and inequality, 20–21; and justice, 1; participatory, 288; and political equality, 1, 269; polyarchy, 270–71, 273 278, 287–89, 288 n4, 298; and primary political rights, 287–90; procedural, 1, 269, 273; and process, 297-98; and redistributive property rights, 4–7, 278–280, 302; rule for the people, 4, 6, 273, 276-78, 301; strong, 288–89; as subordinate foundational good, 299–300; *see also* substantive democracy
democratic distributive justice, 270
Demsetz, H., 32, 75–6
Depew, Chawncey M., 196–97
Derber, C., 90
derived from membership, 159
desert, 32, 88, 91, 93, 272, 280
developing economies, 21
difference principle, 76–9, 93, 131–32, 276, 276 n6, 293; basis in subjective personality, 77; inegalitarian, 78; and inequality, 78t; and political liberalism, 271 n6; and Rawlsian democracy, 276; *see also* Rawls
differential pay, 11
dimension of community, *see* ethics of economic community
DiQuattro, Arthur, 78
distribution of income, 1–22, 28, 30–4, 37-8, 42, 45–8, 59–62, 64–70, 72–3, 75–8, 80–1, 85–96, 101, 103, 108, 114, 120–21, 129, 132, 134–40, 141–49, 153–61, 164–68, 169, 240–49, 252–56, 258, 264–65, 270–73, 290, 295, 301; egalitarian, 4, 6, 7, 9, 11–16, 28, 30, 32–34, 38, 41–2, 44–47,

51, 53–55, 62, 67, 76–77, 85–86, 88–90, 105–06, 112, 114, 119, 131, 137–38, 140–46, 148, 155, 164–66, 243–44, 250, 254–55, 261, 270, 274–76, 281, 283–85, 293, 300, 302
distributive justice: 1, 4, 7, 10, 17–18, 20–21, 42, 45, 47, 60, 68, 68 n 46, 75–6, 95, 101, 128, 129, 134 n44, 139, 139 n 57, 169 n3, 248, 252 n9, 256, 260, 269, 283, 287, 289–91, 301, 302; general rules of, 10, 17
division of labor, 116, 163, 232, 281–82, 286, 295; absence from Cohen's theory of property, 73; not crystallized by Locke, 43; unified by a system of exchange, 163
Dixit, Avinash, 202, 208
Donahue, Charles, Jr., 33, 37, 58, 67
Dorfman, Robert, 214, 215
dueness, notion of: *see* ethics of dueness for economic contributions
Dunn, John, 35, 38, 41, 44, 48
Durkheim, Emile, 51, 191
Dworkin, Ronald, 32, 76, 281, 283-84; equality of resources, 270 n2

Eastern Europe, 12, 21
economic agents, 2, 3, 10, 13–14, 17, 125, 168, 170, 208, 220, 234, 249, 252–53, 259, 281, 294
economic community, *see* ethics of economic community
economic justice, 1, 2, 4, 6, 21, 86, 136–37, 169, 254–55, 267, 277–79, 281, 289, 300
economic relations, 10, 13, 63, 74, 87, 90, 128, 163, 169, 180, 188, 192, 219, 221, 242, 244, 292
economic rights: *see also* rights
economic society, 2, 16, 140, 156, 232, 237, 246, 248, 250–51, 256, 280
economic theory, 2–3, 32, 98–9, 102, 109, 115, 125, 137, 170, 181, 213–14, 279, 295, 301
economically creative activities, 89, 92, 110, 295; consumer activities are, 102; social composition of, 14; *see also* ethics of dueness for economic contributions
economics, 2, 3, 5, 14, 18, 75, 86, 99–100, 102, 109–10, 115, 130, 142, 162–63, 171, 179, 181, 188, 192–94, 204, 208, 214–18, 220, 222–23, 226, 238, 275, 296; conventional, 2, 12, 35, 48, 110, 125, 131, 142–4, 148, 154, 226
economy: as self-ordering, 18
Edgeworth, Francis Y., 12, 181, 193, 202
egalitarianism, 4 n4, 11 n19, 15 n23, 27 n1, 33 n1, 41 n33, 76, 76 n74, 89, 101, 105 n54, 143 n2, 148, 164 n30, 166, 250 n8, 254, 284
Eisenstein, Louis, 133
El-Safty, Ahmad E., 202
Else, P. K., 202
endogenous consumption: Leontief's input-output models, 213; von Neumann's growth models, 213; *see also* endogenous formation of preferences
endogenous formation of preferences: 15, 130, 183, 188–219; in artisan capitalism, 190–91; coextensive with process of commodity production and exchange, 190; compatible with freedom, 211; in corporate capitalism, 197–99; and economic community, 288–90, 205-19; enables completion of circuit of capital, 205; forms common end, 211–12; Hegel on, 194–95; information school, 203; institutionalization of, 198; and interests of capital, 211; Levinian, 212, 217; Marx on, 196; in mechanized capitalism, 196–97; neoclassical version connected to theory of exogenously determined systems, 18, 183; persuasion

engogenous formation of preferences (*cont.*)
school, 203; preclassical, 191–94, 195, 198, 201, 206, 217–19; and preservation and expansion of capital, 211–12; Sombart on, 193; Steuart on, 191–93; and theory of self-ordering systems, 18–19; toward a vital purpose of association, 188; within the process circulation of capital, 195; within the theory of self-determined systems, 183
endogenous preference formation, *see* endogenous formation of preferences
entitlement, 4–5, 11–14, 16, 28–31, 39–40, 43–44, 54, 57–59, 62, 67–68, 71, 75, 79–80, 86, 88–89, 91–92, 94, 96–99, 101–06, 108–14, 118–19, 121, 124–25, 128, 131-32, 138, 158–59, 246–47, 250, 252–53, 254–55, 257, 259, 279, 282, 293–94; coherent pattern of, 125; equalizing, 112–19, 119–21, 121–24; systematic level of analysis of, 125; *see also* rights
entitlement to equal shares, 123; *see also* right to an equalized portion of income
Epp, Charles R., 298
equal attributes, 2
equality, 1, 11, 15, 67, 92, 134, 153, 165, 167, 247; and economic growth, 142; equality of what?, 155; high rates of productivity, 147; principle of derived from community, 153, 156, 158; and savings, 142–49, 226; weak commitment to, 155; why equality?, 155; *see also* abstract equality, concrete equality
Erikson, Robert, 23
ethical community, 16, 17; *see also* ethics of economic community
ethics of community (*see also* ethics of economic community), 154, 156, 168, 243, 244, 301; and economic egalitarianism, 12; right to equal fulfillment of ends, 12, 157, 160
ethics of dueness for economic contributions, 3, 6, 12–15, 18, 32, 85–90, 93–94, 96–119, 121–24, 129–30, 134, 137, 140–41, 153, 161–64, 171, 175, 177, 179, 181–85, 191–93, 95, 202–03, 206–09, 213–18, 221, 224–26, 242–45, 274, 271, 274, 279–82, 293–95, 301; applicability to capital-based market systems, 18; as basis for egalitarianism, 11; consumer contributions, 85, 86, 87, 99-100, 104–06, 108, 110–111, 115, 125, 216, 279; contrasted to reward for contributions, 12, 14, 88; and contributions by socially formed consumer attributes, 85-87, 90, 103; current contributions, 128; differential contributions, 115, 162, 280, 283; differential reward, 91, 159, 161-63; dispersion of accountability, 114; dispersion of contributions, 87, 114, 141, 280; economically creative attributes, 14, 55, 86; equal attributes, 2; and equal distribution, 18, 249–53, 259–60, 262–65; forms of equal contributions, 2, 14, 87, 92, 108, 114, 118–19, 128, 280, 282; forms of equal dueness, 87, 108, 117, 124, 141 280; inegalitarian form of, 10; inseparable contributions, 164; and neoclassical economics, 3; pattern of dueness, 86, 95; productive contributions, 2, 46, 73, 79, 86–87, 96, 99, 108, 111, 125–26, 192, 216, 283, 301; separable contributions, 164; social contributions, 110; social

formation of economically creative attributes justifies equal shares, 113–14, 121, 124; and social theory of the consumer, 103; and social theory of remuneration, 12; unequal contributions, 2 n1, 115, 119; *see also* economically creative activities, indirect entitlement

ethics of economic community, 1, 3–6, 12, 16, 18–19, 153–68, 178, 183, 186, 213, 237–39, 244–65, 265, 274, 281, 301; coattainment of ends, 212, 228–29; common action, 3, 14, 18, 20, 46, 52–53, 63, 66, 75, 157, 160–65, 168, 170–180, 183–84, 205–06, 212, 218, 222–32, 235, 241, 244–45, 249, 252, 258, 262–63; common attributes, 182, 235, 238; common ends, 3, 9, 18, 20, 62, 75, 157, 167, 181–83, 187, 206, 209, 212, 236, 241, 245, 248, 265; common interest, 176, 179, 208, 211, 218, 221–23, 225–27, 245; common purposes, 14, 19, 160; community as dimension of capital-based market systems, 6, 17–18, 153–56, 161, 164, 169–70, 174, 178–80, 185, 187–88, 195, 205–09, 212, 219–21, 224, 228–29, 233–39, 241–42, 244–46, 249, 262, 265, 301; community between consumers and producers, 170, 173–78, 179–81, 183–86, 190, 205–09, 211–12, 217–19; community between labor and capital, 170, 184 n34, 241, 243, 220–23, 225–33, 263–64; community of ends, 190, 218, 222, 250, 257–58; compatible with property, 16; constitutive community, 10, 70, 110, 127, 210, 234–38, 278; community for the pursuit of capital, 259; community generated by endogenous determination, 181, 188–90, 205–09, 211–12, 217–19; community within subsystems of the economy, 17; economic community contrasted to supracommunity, 17, 239; economic community depends on principle of self-organization of the economy, 180–185; economic community and a right to an equalization of some income, 18, 154, 249–53, 259, 262–65; generated by endogenous formation of preferences, 183–85, 190, 205–09, 212–17, 217–19; generated by self-determining system, 183–84; and Hegel, 16; and the individual, 17; justifies redistribution, 17; Keynesian form of, 256–58, 260–62; macroeconomic community, 261–262; Marx's view of, 19, 240–44; Marx and Levine on unity, 178; microeconomic community, 261–65; overarching particular ends, 187; and principle of equality, 12, 20, 46; for the pursuit of wealth, 249-50, 258; and state ownership, 17; and systems theory, 18; theory of economic community and distribution, 17; systemwide economic community, 12, 17–18, 153, 170, 175, 178, 179–80, 182, 187, 207–08, 233–35, 239, 241, 245, 252 n9, 301; unintended common end, 173; *see also* community

ethics of reward for economic contributions, 1, 88, 98, 99, 100, 284; as basis for egalitarianism, 11; Marx's approach, 14; neglect of consumer attributes and contributions, 99

ethics of the marginal productivity distribution, 92, 100–01, 106 n56, 161–64

Etzioni, Amitai, 239

Ewald, William C., 28, 30, 34, 40, 53

exchange system, 10, 97, 112, 282
exclusive individual dominion, 27, 35–37, 40–41, 43, 54, 57–58

Ferguson, C. E., 163
Finland, 144
Flathman, Richard, 76
France, 144, 190
Frank, Robert, 24, 148
Fraser, Nancy, 271
Fried, Charles, 140, 296
Friedman, Milton, 257
Fukuyama, Francis, 287

Galbraith, James K., 21 n31
Galbraith, John Kenneth, 197–02, 207, 209–10
Gaskell, Elizabeth, 233
Gauthier, David, 92, 125
Gaventa, John, 290
Germany, 144
Gini coefficient, 143–44
Gintis, Herbert, 135
Glaister, S., 202
Goode, 21, 201
Gould, Carol C., 13, 28, 89, 156, 160–61, 243, 244, 271, 280
Green, T. H., 23, 30, 72, 127
Greer, D. F., 202
Guth, L. A., 202
Gutman, Amy, 76

Habermas, Jurgen, 272, 285, 286, 288
Hacker, Andrew, 129
Haveman, Robert, 170, 177, 224
Hayek, F. A., 59, 91, 93–94, 96, 101, 103–06, 198
Hegel, G. W. F.: abstract personality and property, 67; and concrete equality, 9, 12, 68, 68 n46, 168; corporate subcommunities, 17; on derivation of equality from community, 168; and distributive justice, 68; dyadic view of property, 73; and economic community, 195 n27; economic understanding, 12; and endogenous formation of preferences, 194–96; and ethical community, 16; and experience, 295; and freedom, 296; and individualism, 66–69; individualistic cum social theoretical inegalitarianism, 69; insufficiently developed equalities, 10; and higher classes of rights, 67–68; and liberal theories of property, 27; on liberalism, 28 n3; moral implications of social formation, 13; on multiplication of needs, 115 n8, 218–19; and mutual dependence, 10, 112 n6; and property, 13, 16, 66–69; and redistribution, 17, 68; sees interdependence not community, 195 n27; social determination, self-determination and individuality, 10, 90 n5, 127 n23; social theory of rights, 10; and socialized ownership, 13; and social theory, 66–69; society reinforces inequality, 68; subjective inegalitarian, 66, 69; systemic social influence, 9; and unequal distribution, 168; and unequal property, 67–69
Heilbroner, Robert, 110
Heller, Agnes, 213–14
Hicks, John, 101, 109, 202, 215
Hilts, P. J., 130
Hobart, R. E., 210
Hobbes, Thomas, 27, 32, 51–54, 67, 81, 269; and liberal theory, 53; and social theory of property, 52
Hohfeld, Wesley: theory of property, 71–72
Holland, Thomas Erskine: theory of property, 29, 69–70
Holmstrom, Nancy, 240
Holt, Rachham, 192
Hong Kong, 145
Humboldt, W. von, 30, 59

incentives, 4, 78–79, 131, 275–93
income: principle of equalizing a portion of, 4
income distribution, 2, 20, 22, 142–46, 166, 243, 261; annual wages, 23, 24; chief executives, 23; comparative analysis of, 145; in developing countries, 145, 146; income gap, 21; in OECD countries, 144–45; selective centralization, 5; in United States and Japan, 143
income equality and growth, 146
indirect entitlement, 40, 58, 111; due to indirect contributions 121; equal social influence generates equal, 114, 124, 282; indirect responsibility gives rise to, 118; *see also* ethics of dueness for economic contributions, contributions
individual, *see* subjective individual, persons
individualism, 3, 28, 30–63, 67–69, 71–77, 238, 256–57, 261; individualistic inegalitarianism, 42, 69, 71–72, 160
individuality, 7, 13, 65, 68, 80, 127, 195, 196, 219, 250;
Indonesia, 145, 146
inegalitarianism, 15 n23, 27, 30, 34 n7, 37–38, 42, 45, 47, 52, 54–55, 59–60, 69, 71–72, 76, 78, 88–89, 101, 106, 138, 142, 160, 285
inequality, 15, 17, 20–23, 30, 33, 37, 41, 44, 47, 55, 59, 67–68, 74–79, 89, 105–06, 119, 131–32, 135–37, 140–47, 154, 159, 243, 248, 254–57, 259–60, 262, 270, 276; Gini coefficient of, 144; ongoing and preexisting sources of, 128–30
interdependence, 49, 85, 112, 114, 116, 160, 180, 195, 212, 231, 232, 235, 258, 259; instrumental, 90, 92, 112
intersubjectivity: and distribution, 88; and dueness, 88; and entitlement, 58; and income redistribution, 88; as inner structure of personality, 29, 31, 57, 80; in Kant's theory, 60, 62; and liberal distribution, 81; and liberal property, 70, 80–81; and needs, 90; and principle of equality, 1; as structure of self-seeking, 175, 223; and wants, 113
Ireland, 144
Italy, 144, 192
Iwai, Katsuhito, 19

Japan, 20, 143–45, 147, 166, 275; cultural traditions, 144; tax policy, 147
Jappelli, Tullio, 144
Jevons, W. S., 12, 100, 181, 193, 214
Johnston, David, 15, 22
joint activity, 4, 158, 160, 225
jurisprudence, 32, 56, 65, 69, 71, 72, 80, 91
justice: as dueness, 88, 91-94, 138; *see also* distributive justice, ethics of dueness for economic contributions, ethics of economic community, economic justice

Kaldor, Nicholas, 202
Kant, Immanuel: theory of property, 8, 29–32, 56–3, 69, 157, 160, 167, 168, 244, 257, 292, 299–300; claimed to be intersubjectivist, 59; differences between individuals' ends, 167, 247, 251–52; disunion regarding the good, 246–253; and intersubjective judgment, 60; individualistic premises, 62; and social theory, 62; and social constitution of person, 57; subjective individualist, 57; and unequal distribution, 62; union for freedom and rights, 246–53; and welfare state, 59
Keynes, J. M., 27, 32, 131, 257, 258, 259; adequacy of moderate

Keynes, J. M. *(cont.)*
incentives, 275; communal agencies and growth, 256, 259–60; communal character of consumption justifies death taxes, 103; communal macroeconomy and microeconomic disunity, 256 n16, 260–61; community and individualism in, 261; on community and redistribution, 260, 262; critique of individualism, 256; limited redistribution, 260, 262; multiplier mechanism, 102; precedent for consumer contributions to wealth, 102 n46; reassertion of individualism, 261
Keynesian economic ethics, 32, 131

labor, 3, 10, 12, 14, 18–19, 29, 32, 34, 37–38, 67, 71, 73, 79, 89–101, 106, 110, 112, 116–17, 122–245, 258, 263–65, 281–84, 286, 292–93, 295; interest in the preservation and expansion of capital, 222; negative utility, 137; socially constituted, 12, 235–38
labor and capital, 184, 220, 222, 223, 227, 230, 231, 240, 241, 243, 263, 264; dimension of common action between, 229; goals with commonality, 221
Levine, David P., 51, 54, 90, 96, 112, 122, 127, 190, 213, 229; alternative to utility theory, 101; and circulation of capital, 171–73, 178; consumption and the capital circuit, 205; Levinian endogenous consumption, 212–13, 216–17; on capital, 169; on self-organizing systems, 183–84; on sequence of consumptions, 176; social needs, 101, 275; social theory of the economy, 101; unity of labor and capital, 230
Levy, Frank, 129
Lewis, John D., 298
liberal theories, 9, 27, 65; dual premise of, 8; pervasive inegalitarianism in, 89
liberal theories of property: fundamental logical structure, 30; independent individual in, 29; lack social concept of the person, 51; place of social factors in, 30; types of, 31, 135, 137, 142, 198, 248; *see also* property
liberalism, 6, 8, 27, 32–33, 51, 58, 69, 75, 158–59, 255, 271, 276; classical, 3, 6, 8, 10, 14, 33, 40, 51, 52, 54, 99–100, 111, 193, 206, 213-17, 220–21, 248, 250, 254–57, 259–61, 288, 293–94, 300; and democracy, 270; Rawlsian, 8, 27, 126, 127, 212, 276
Lindblom, Charles E., 199–200, 203, 228, 290; democracy as political equality, 277 n 23; rights in democracy, 276–77
Llewellyn, Karl N., 71, 72
Locke, John: and community, 46–47, 157–58; and differential rationality thesis, 34, 45; and egalitarianism, 34, 41, 44, 45–47; ensemble of premises, 30, 35, 37, 45, 54–55; entitlement and economic creation, 294; and independent labor, 40–41, 44, 47, 48; independent person, 37; individualism and unequal property, 36–37, 40, 42–45, 46, 49; and individualism, 34, 37, 39–41, 42, 43–5, 47–51, 55; and inegalitarianism, 34, 42, 38, 44, 45–47; and natural law ; 35, 37, 40–42, 44, 47–50, 55; primary premise, 37; revisionist Locke scholarship, 34, 42, 45; and social determination, 49; and subjective labor, 40, 42; theological argument, 35, 38–39,

41, 44, 47–51; and theory of substantive democracy, 269; and unequal property, 37–38, 41–45
Lodge, George C., 142, 166
Lowe, Adolph, 174–75, 186; final common end, 186; formation of compatible behavior, 185; interlocking pieces, 232
Lukes, Steven, 290
Lummis, C. Douglas, 271
Luxembourg, 144
Lynes, Russell, 189, 198

Macedo, Stephen, 298
Machlup, Fritz, 161
Macpherson, C. B., 27-8, 33-5, 37, 44, 45
Malaysia, 145
Mansbridge, 159
Mansfield, 133, 288
markets, 2, 5, 12, 18, 169, 199-200, 204, 227-28, 238-39, 254, 260, 302; competive, 2, 12, 17-8, 20, 153-54, 177, 179, 204, 208, 220, 224, 244
Marx, Karl, 12–14, 19–20, 89–91, 96, 100, 106, 171, 178–80, 196, 213–14, 219, 231–32, 235, 240–44, 250, 264, 265, 301; ethics, 14; holistic, 13; realization process, 14
McClosky, Herbert, 2, 11
McLean, Edward B., 71
Meek, Ronald L., 191–92, 213
Menger, 12, 181, 193
microeconomic theory, 86
Milberg, William 110
Mill, J. S., 30, 91, 288
Miller, Jonathan, 183
Milly, Deborah J., 166
Miringoff, Marc, 20–21
Mishan, E. J., 300
modern economics: and choice, 2; on consumer, 99; on equality and saving, 142; neglects equal contributions, 14; on theory of value, 100; *see also* neoclassical economic theory
Morishima, M., 100
Morita, Akio, 203
Munzer, Stephen, 33, 39, 65, 89, 91-92, 96, 98, 101, 105, 125
mutual dependence, 10, 13, 110, 112–13, 116–18, 122; system of mutual dependence, 113

Nasar, Sylvia, 23, 132
needs, 3, 5, 16, 35–38, 53, 61, 66, 85–6, 89–91, 96, 97–99, 101, 103, 105, 106, 112–13, 115–22, 134–35, 142–43, 148–49, 156, 163, 173–74, 176–77, 179, 182–83, 189, 191, 194–97, 200, 209–10, 213, 215–20, 222–23, 227–28, 237, 249–50, 255, 264, 274–76, 279–83, 295; interdependent formation of, 112, 113; multiplication, 10, 115, 116–17, 137, 191, 194–95, 206, 209, 211, 217–19, 250, 258–59, 263, 275; needs-based theories of justice, 137–39
neoclassical economic theory, 7, 100, 218, 220, 226; and the consumer, 3; cooperation not a factor of production, 162; and economic community, 18, 175, 181–83; economics as adjustment mechanism, 18, 181; economics as allocation between alternative ends, 171; general economic equilibrium, 18, 126; neglects social attributes of consumers, 99; no interpersonal comparisons of utility, 13; as theory of property, 109-10; *see also* modern economics, utility
neoliberal, 9
Netherlands, 144
New Economic Analysis of Law: and property 27, 29, 32, 75–76

New Zealand, 144
Nicholson, Walter, 182
Norman, 202, 208
North Korea, 12
North Vietnam, 12
Norway, 144
Nozick, Robert, 8–9, 27, 39, 62; rights as side constraints, 9; on separate existence, 9

Okun, Arthur, 92, 93–94, 97, 101, 125, 158–59, 161; on tax policy, 147
Ong, Nai Pew, 80
Oppenheim, Phillip, 166, 276
Orr, D., 202
ownership, 12–13, 16–17, 29, 31, 35–36, 42–43, 46–47, 53, 57–58, 60–61, 70, 80, 128–29, 158, 243, 263, 275, 277, 293, 296; Marx's theory of 14; socialized, 14

Palmer, R. R., 35
Pareto, Vilfredo, 202, 208, 221
Paton, D., 202
Pelczynski, Z. A., 10
Pen, Jan, 22; parade, 22
person, *see* persons
persons: abstract person, 66, 67, 68; abstract equality of, 8, 46; autonomous, 57–66; and basic humanity, 92; concrete differences among, 88; concrete equality of, 34, 46, 69, 281–85, 293; differences between, 31, 32, 46, 284; entitlement of, 27–28, 29, 30, 134; and equal income, 29; equality of, 34; and equality of persons, 30–31, 34, 45, 55, 67; as feed animals in classical theory of endogenous consumption, 213; and freedom, 92, 127; independence of, 37; individualistic concept of, 7, 37; and inequality, 31; intersubjective inner structure of, 29–31, 57–58, 60–62, 70, 80–81, 88, 90, 113, 122, 223; in liberal theory, 28, 30, 75, 126; as natural, 90; and property, 29–30, 40, 41; purposes of, 214, 219; and redistribution, 88; in relations, 9; and relative distribution of property, 88, 89; and rules of distribution, 30; self-determined, 56; social constitution of, 12, 63, 65–66, 70, 89; social concept of, 1, 7, 51, 56, 76, 90, 126–27; socially formed, 13, 16; socially self-determined, 73, 89, 90; subjective form of, 13, 28–30, 53, 57–59, 66, 69–70, 72–73, 76–77, 79–81, 88–9, 126; supreme ethical worth of, 16; and unequal property, 30–32, 58, 74, 81
personality, *see* persons, intersubjectivity
Phelps Brown, 11, 21–22, 37–38, 129, 130, 132, 250
Philippines, 145
policies: promoting growth in an egalitarian order, 147–48, 224, 254, 256–57, 260, 261, 276, 288, 298
political equality, 1, 269, 272, 277, 298
Pollack, Andrew, 203
Polsby, Nelson, 290
Popper, Karl, 10
Posner, Richard, 29, 75
Poulantzas, Nicos, 290
Pound, Roscoe: individualistic inegalitarianism, 71; methodological individualism, 71; and sociological jurisprudence, 70–71; subjectivism, 71; theory of property, 27, 29, 32, 70–71; unequal property, 71
precapitalist society, 127
preferences, 8, 14–15, 18–19, 29, 65, 87, 99 n31, 100, 103–06, 109–10, 114–15, 118, 122, 126, 130, 137, 140, 175, 182–85, 188, 189–90,

191–93, 215–16, 217–218, 228, 233, 236, 248, 251, 257–58, 262–63, 277, 279–80, 297, 298
premises, 7, 11, 31, 35, 40, 55–56, 59–62, 66, 71–72, 75, 88, 105, 158, 160, 253, 281; social theoretical, 7, 51, 69
Prestowitz, Clyde V., Jr., 147
principle of equalization, 8, 87, 155, 244
producers, 3, 4, 8, 14, 18, 101, 103–04, 120, 140, 153, 161, 170, 173–87, 189–220, 224–27, 234–35, 244, 259, 263–64, 279, 293, 295
production, 3, 12–14, 18–24, 42, 44, 53–54, 73, 78, 85–86, 88, 90, 93–4, 96–104, 110–11, 119–20, 129–30, 139, 15–59, 162–64, 169–87, 189–220, 221–44, 252, 258, 261–65, 279, 282, 286, 293
production values, 100
productive capacities, 111, 125–26, 283; *see also* capacities,
productive activities, 86, 89, 97, 101, 104, 118, 158, 161, 164, 168, 175, 220, 276; *see also* ethics of dueness for economic contributions
productive factors, 88, 90, 102, 164; in classical theory of value, 99; cooperation and, 162; Marx's emphasis on, 14, 100, 106
property: and democracy, 6, 269–70, 277–78, 278–80, 285–86, 291–92, 292–94, 299–300, 301–02; in contemporary liberal theory of justice, 76–79; direct appropriation, 116, 118; distributive rules and, 3; in ethics of dueness for economic contributions, 3, 11, 85–107, 108–41; in ethics of economic community, 3, 11, 154, 246–65; forms of, 2–4, 8–9, 11, 14, 28, 33, 34, 71, 85, 90, 106, 119, 128, 133, 135, 139, 172, 177, 189, 202, 203, 205–06, 230, 245, 249, 254, 256, 273–74, 277, 279, 294, 301; Hegel's theory of, 4, 17, 66–69; in Hohfeld's jurisprudence, 71–72; individual's right, 5; Kant's theory of, 56–63, 299–300; laws of, 243; liberal theory of, 8, 27–32, 33–55, 56–81, 153; Locke's theory of, 33–55; in neoclassical economic theory, 8; in New Economic Analysis of Law, 75–76; possibility of a deductive theory of, 299–300; premises of theories of, 7; problems of unregulated, 16; production theories of property, 96; property as dueness, 91; in Rawls's theory, 8; as redistributive rule, 4, 95–96; relational theory of, 72–75; social theory of, 11; socialization of, 13, 14; in sociological jurisprudence, 70–71; in utilitarian jurisprudence, 32; value theories of, 96; *see also* liberal theories of property

Quinn, M., 27, 76

Rae, Douglas W., 15, 27, 78, 133, 135, 155
Rainwater, 20, 144
Rawls, John, 4, 7, 8, 27, 30, 32, 56, 78, 81, 91, 108, 129, 131–32, 155, 270–72, 276, 287, 289–91, 296; argument from subjective personality, 77; conception of community, 8, 18, 157, 228 n7, 256, 257, 258; on contributions, 92-93; and democracy, 270–71, 276; distributive justice, 76; and economic community, 211–12; egalitarianism, 76; and ethical relativism, 127; freedom, 127; and income inequality, 77, 79, 131, 276; individualism, 76, 77; inegalitarianism, 76, 78; and liberalism, 8, 270; on plurality of distinct persons, 8;

Rawls, John (*cont.*)
and procedural democracy, 270–71; rejects identification with others, 77; and relative distribution, 132; and self-interest, 77; and social theory, 76–77; and substantive democracy, 271; worst off, 132; *see also* difference principle
Raz, Joseph, 297
Reading, Brian, 143-44, 147
redistribution, 4, 14, 17, 43–44, 62, 68, 95, 131–33, 138, 142, 244, 250, 255, 258, 260–61, 262, 274–76, 283–84, 293; capital gains taxes, 133; economic growth, 142, 147, 166, 254, 260
redistributory property right, 5, 6, 136, 153, 270, 278, 286, 292, 301–02; tightens relation between contributions and entitlements, 293–94
Reich, Robert, 159, 166, 230, 276
Reingold, Jennifer, 23–24
relativism, 127
remuneration, 2, 12, 14, 79, 88, 92–94, 104, 106, 109, 118, 129, 161–63, 176, 242–43, 283
reproduction, 19, 115, 119, 173, 193, 213-14, 227–28
Reynolds, Lloyd G., 236
righst: economic rights, 13, 269, 271–72, 277–78, 288–89, 292, 297–98, 302; liberal theory of property, 22, 300; primary political rights, 277, 287–88, 289, 302; property, 3–17, 24–55, 56–81, 85–106, 153–58, 178, 237, 241–43, 246–55, 269–70, 274, 277–280, 286, 291–302; redistributory property, 5–6, 16, 119, 136, 143, 153, 270, 272, 274, 278–80, 285–96, 292–95, 301–02; social theory of, 10, 13
Ritchie, David G., 43
Robbins, Lord, 105, 126, 182, 193
Roemer, John, 128–29
Rousseau, Jean Jacques, theory of property, 27, 32, 51–54, 133, 191, 288; lacks social production, 54; not social egalitarian, 54; seen as social liberal, 53.
Ryan, Alan, 30, 76

Samuelson, Paul, 100–01, 181, 214, 215, 243
Sandel, Michael, 16, 28, 76, 154, 158–59, 237–38, 248, 256, 288; on constitutive community, 236; derives sharing from community, 159; dispossession of the individual, 16; radically situated subjects, 16, 237; wider subject of possession, 16
Sawyer, Malcolm, 143
Schaar, J. H., 27
Schlatter, Richard, 33, 41, 293
Schmalensee, Richard, 202, 207
Schumpeter, Joseph A., 126, 214–15, 288, 297
Schwartz, Tony, 136
Scitovsky, Tibor, 103, 179
self, 29, 38, 70, 76, 210
self-determination, 10, 13–14, 38–39, 50, 59, 61, 90, 110–12, 114, 116–19, 121, 123, 127, 156, 209–10, 228
self-determining system, 183–84
self-ordering system, 19, 183, 185; compatible with freedom, 212; generates commonalities, 19
self-organizing economy, *see* self-ordering system
self-renewing economy, 110, 119, 121
self-seeking, 10, 81, 85, 113, 116–19, 122, 124, 175, 185–86, 208, 212, 223
Sen, Amartya, 15, 101, 105, 134, 135–37, 155; capabilities, 130, 133–40

Shapiro, Ian, 27–28, 37, 39, 48, 76, 91, 94–95, 111, 125–26, 139, 271, 273, 297; deemphasizes property, 94; democracy as subordinate foundational good, 272, 274, 298, 299–300; and economically creative activity, 98; on indecipherable contributions, 124; on labor theory of value, 97; liberalism and single-unit themes, 30; Locke's egalitarianism, 34, 45; Locke's theology of property, 48; production theory of property, 96; subjective basis of entitlement, 97–98, 104; workmanship ideal, 92, 96–8

Sher, G., 91

Shweder, Richard A., 21

Silberberg, Eugene, 182, 193

Simmons, A. John, 33

Simon, Thomas W., 271, 277, 288

Singer, Joseph William, 33, 296

Slutsky, E., 202

Smeeding, 20, 144

Smith, Adam, 97, 98, 100, 104, 123, 126–27, 191–94, 197, 216, 221, 228, 250, 295, 296; toil and trouble, 97, 104

Snider, Denton, J., 297

social concept: of economic agents, 13

social constitution: of individual, 3, 14, 51, 63, 65, 74

social determination, 8, 10, 13, 90, 106, 111, 127, 190; conflicts with self-determination in liberal theory, 10; constitutive of free will 127; economic form of, 90; expands range of choice, 10; generates community of ends, 190; Hegel's view of, 10; in holistic social theory, 13; Marx's version of, 13, 13 n21; neoclassical version of, 106 n56; reconciled with self-determination, 10, 90; restriction on the individual in Bentham, 63; systemic form of, 111; not violative of freedom in Rawls's view, 127; unsystematic account of, 8; *see also* needs, wants, attributes, social formation

social formation, 86; of concrete equality, 9; of consumer attributes, 85–86, 125; of consumer contributions, 140–41; of consumption-side activities, 85; of economic actors, 8, 101; of the individual, 7; of labor, 238; and moral entailment of different forms of property, 13; neglected by liberal theories of property, 7; neglected by neoclassical theory, 106, 106 n56; of wants, 118; omitted by Hohfeld, 72; of preferences, 192 n13; of productive capacities, 125; *see also* endogenous formation of preferences, social determination

social influences, 2, 10, 15, 19, 65, 76, 81, 87, 106, 127, 202, 209, 217, 237; flow from system requisites, 15; fundamental, 10; generate commonalities, 19; generate equal contributions, 13–14; part of self-ordering system, 19; systemic form of, 9

social labor, 12; and indirect entitlements, 40; and Marx's theory of value, 14

social mobility, 23

social needs, 115

social organism, 13

social premises, 1, 7, 13, 66, 89, 90; unsystematic, 7, 8

social qualities: of persons, 12

social self-determination, 90, 110, 111, 112, 116, 117, 118, 119, 121, 123, 127, 209

social theory, 2, 13, 30, 51, 63, 66, 67, 72, 75, 90, 101, 105, 270, 273, 280, 281, 283, 285; basis for

social theory (*cont.*)
deductive theory of egalitarian distribution, 15; of capital circulation, 18, 253; of dueness, 12; of economic rights, 13; of the ethics of remuneration, 12; identifies concrete equalities, 15; of property rights, 11; of rights, 10, 12
social theory of property, *see* ethics of dueness for economic contributions, ethics of economic community
socially conditioned, 10; *see also* socially determined, socially formed
socially constituted, 12
socially self-determined wants, 87, 101, 110–15, 117, 121
Sombart, Werner, 193
Soviet Union, 12, 21
Sraffa, Pierro, 119-20, 183
Strauss, Leo, 35
subjective individual, 7, 12, 15, 28–32, 40–42, 48, 50, 53, 56–59, 64–66, 69–81, 82, 86–90, 93–94, 96–105, 109, 112–18, 120, 122–23, 126–28, 130, 140, 158, 181–82, 192, 194, 229, 233–34, 236–37, 279–80
subjective personality: *see* subjective individual
subsistence, 40, 42, 47, 86, 115, 117, 122, 124, 137, 139, 148, 194, 196, 213–14, 217, 219–20, 223, 227, 230, 248–51, 253, 258–59, 274
substantive democracy, 1, 269, 274, 276–86, 291 n13, 292, 294, 297, 299–300; compared to democracy as a subordinate foundational good, 299–300; definability of, 292–94; defining characteristics of, 280; and democratic process, 297–99; and economic justice, 1-6, 277; and economic rights, 287–92, 292–94; egalitarian, 270; and ethics of economic contributions, 283; and ethics of economic community, 280; general theory of 294–97; inclusion of distributive justice, 1, 273, 283; and justice, 269, 272; liberal theory of, 270; Locke's theory of, 269; measuring attainment of, 289–91; and polyarchy, 270–71, 273, 278, 287–89, 288 n4, 298; possibility of theorizing, 294–97; and principle of concrete equality, 285; and problem of controversiality, 287–91; and procedural democracy, 1, 269, 272–73; and procedural rights, 273; and redistributive property rights, 4–7, 278–80, 302; and right to an equalized portion of income, 280; and rule for the people, 276–78; and the right to an equalized portion of income, 278–80; social theory of, 270, 272–74, 277, 283, 285; and substantive rights, 273; and welfare democracy, 274–75; *see also* democracy
supreme ethical worth: of individual, 4, 10, 13, 14, 16, 50, 273, 292
Sweden, 144
Switzerland, 144
system: of capital-based commodity production and exchange, 6, 116, 121, 123, 163, 188, 189, 200, 208, 219, 221, 234, 239, 244, 245, 258, 264, 295; of interconnected circuits of capital, 179, 206, 236, 241, 245; mutual dependence, 10, 13, 112–13, 118
systems theory, 18, 19

Tachi, Ryuichiro, 144
Taylor, Charles, 154, 156–61
Telser, L. G., 204
Thailand, 145
Thatcher, Margaret, 9
theory of dueness, *see* ethics of dueness for economic contributions

Tocqueville, Alexis de, 133, 134
Tully, J., 35, 41, 48, 91, 97
Turkey, 145

U.S. Bureau of the Census, 22
U.S. Department of Education, 201
Unger, Roberto Mangabeira, 28, 33-4, 40, 53, 89; ascribes individualism to liberal theory, 53
United for a Fair Economy, 23
United States, 6, 129, 130, 133–34, 136, 201, 254; economy, 143; free farmer society of, 21; income inequality, 20–24, 143–45; savings in, 142–44
utilitarianism, 135; *see also* Bentham, Austin
utility, 3, 14, 15, 29, 31, 63–65, 75–6, 79, 100–06, 109–10, 113, 122, 135, 137, 177, 182, 202–03, 216, 262; intertemporal, 122; unique and nonquantitative, 101; utility maximization, 122

value: causes of, 7, 21, 99, 126, 135, 260; consumer in Marx's theory of, 90; contributions to, 2, 33, 53, 86, 87, 88, 94, 96, 102–05, 108, 109–11, 118–19, 124, 134, 162–63, 193, 216, 280, 282, 283, 301; created by equalities in person's wants, 113, 117, 118; created by producers, 2, 3, 86, 90, 104, 140; created by socially self-determined attributes and wants, 87, 101, 110–15, 117, 121; creation of value as an economic contribution, 86; determinants of, 2, 86, 87, 90, 100, 101, 112, 115, 124, 218; determined by consumers, 85, 86, 99, 104–05, 108, 109, 111, 140; determined by wants and needs, 85, 87; developments in theories of, 99; and ethics of reward for economic contributions, 100, 109; expandable, 116; entitlement and extra-production sources of, 98-107; expansion of, 171, 223; as goal of capital circuit, 171; indirect sources of, 87; labor theory of, 100; Marx's theory of, 12, 106; and Marx's theory of exploitation, 106; and use-value, 237; metaphysical idea of, 178; multipliable substance, 116; neoclassical theory of, 14, 109, 115; production theory of, 102; property and theory of value, 91, 96–98; should accrue to whom it is due, 102; social labor as source of, 12; theory of value and dueness theory of property, 98, 102; ultimate determinant of, 100, 194; unpaid factors of creation of, 2; and use-value, 117; value theory of property, 91, 102, 100, 113
Varian, Hal, 224
Vogel, Ezra F., 166, 276

Waldron, Jeremy: on community and equality, 154, 164–65; on Locke, 33, 36, 39; on moral origin of inequality, 38
Wallach, John R., 28, 76
Walras, Leon, 12, 100, 181, 193
Walzer, Michael, 129, 272
wants, 2, 4, 8, 10, 47, 50, 56, 73, 79, 85, 87, 94, 97, 99, 103, 106, 109–19, 121, 132, 175–77, 183–86, 189–91, 194–98, 227–28, 250, 257, 258–59, 263–264, 279–83, 286, 296; concrete differences in, 8, 9, 46, 68, 293; social determination of, 10, 49, 65, 66, 106, 118, 120, 211, 217; social self-determination of, 116–17
Warren, Mark E., 271
wealth, 1, 3–4, 6, 8, 12, 14, 20, 23, 27, 29–30, 33, 42–4, 46, 48–9, 52–53, 55, 63, 75, 85–86, 89, 92, 96-7, 102–03, 111–12, 114–15, 125–26, 128–29, 131, 133–39,

wealth (*cont.*)
142, 144, 155–56, 159–61, 163, 168–69, 172, 176, 181, 183–84, 189–91, 193, 196, 206, 211, 218–22, 226–30, 233, 238, 251–52, 256, 259–60, 262, 270, 273–78, 283–84; as common end, 248, 250, 251; disinterest in wealth, 250; distinguished from subsistence, 250; goal of seeking wealth, 248; union for pursuit of, 249-50;
Weber, Max, 196
Weiss, Roger, 161
welfare state, 22, 32, 59, 60, 131, 132–33, 154, 158–59, 254, 255, 258, 260, 261, 274; liberal, 4, 6–10, 12, 27–33, 50, 53–56, 63, 66, 69, 72–76, 79–81, 88–89, 131–32, 153, 159, 246, 248, 253–55, 257–60, 270, 281, 283–85, 287–89, 291–96, 300
Wellisz, Stanislaw, 300
Westergaard, J. H., 129
Whitehead, Alfred North, 19
Wildavsky, Aaron, 11
Williamson, J. G., 21
Wilner, Richard, 23, 24
Winfield, Richard Dien, 28, 50, 54, 90, 127, 230, 273
Wolf, Edward N., 22, 291
worst off, 4, 77, 79, 93, 131-32, 254, 276
WuDunn, Sheryl, 103

Zaller, John, 2, 11, 210
Zamagni, Stefano, 161, 162

By exploring the integral relationship between democracy and economic justice, *Democratic Distributive Justice* seeks to explain how democratic countries with market systems should deal with the problem of high levels of income inequality. The book acts as a guide for dealing with this issue by providing an interdisciplinary approach that combines political, economic, and legal theory. The book also analyzes the nature of economic society and puts forth a new understanding of the agents and considerations bearing upon the ethics of relative pay, such as the nature of individual contributions and the extent of community in capital-based market systems. Economic justice is then integrated with democratic theory, yielding what Ross Zucker calls "democratic distributive justice." While prevailing theory defines democracy in terms of the electoral mechanism, the author holds that the principles of distribution form part of the very definition of democracy, which makes just distribution a requirement of democratic government.